IMAGINING
MONSTERS

IMAGINING MONSTERS

MISCREATIONS OF THE SELF IN
EIGHTEENTH-CENTURY ENGLAND

DENNIS TODD

THE UNIVERSITY OF CHICAGO PRESS
CHICAGO AND LONDON

DENNIS TODD is associate professor of English at Georgetown University.

The University of Chicago Press, Chicago 60637
The University of Chicago Press, Ltd., London
© 1995 by The University of Chicago
All rights reserved. Published 1995
Printed in the United States of America

04 03 02 01 00 99 98 97 96 95   5 4 3 2 1

ISBN (cloth): 0-226-80555-7
ISBN (paper): 0-226-80556-5

LIBRARY OF CONGRESS CATALOGING-IN-PUBLICATION DATA

Todd, Dennis
    Imagining monsters : miscreations of the self in eighteenth-
century England / Dennis Todd.
        p.   cm.
    Includes index.
    ISBN 0-226-80555-7 (cloth). — ISBN 0-226-80556-5 (pbk.)
    1. English literature—18th century—History and criticism.
2. Self in literature. 3. Swift, Jonathan, 1667–1745—Knowledge—
Psychology. 4. Pope, Alexander, 1688–1744—Knowledge—Psychology.
5. Imposters and imposture—England—History—18th century.
6. Identity (Psychology) in literature. 7. Toft, Mary, 1703–1763—
Influence. 8. Mother and child in literature. 9. Imagination in
literature. 10. Monsters in literature. I. Title.
PR448.S35T63 1995
820.9'353—dc20   95-4102
                                                              CIP

To Paul, Jeanne, and Dylan, friends

I have been five days turning over old Books to discover the meaning of those monstrous Births you mention. That of the four black Rabbits seems to threaten some dark Court Intrigue, and perhaps some change in the Administration[,] for the Rabbit is an undermining animal that loves to work in the dark. The Blackness denotes the Bishops, whereof some of the last you have made, are persons of such dangerous Parts and profound Abilityes. But Rabbits being cloathed in Furs may perhaps glance at the Judges.

Jonathan Swift to Mrs. Howard, 27 November 1726

CONTENTS

ix

ILLUSTRATIONS

ACKNOWLEDGMENTS

Although this study examines in some detail ideas about the imagination, monstrosity, and personal identity in early eighteenth-century England, in fact it is "about" none of these, and I would mislead the reader if I were to suggest that he or she might find here an exhaustive account or even an especially balanced survey of any one of these topics. What I do focus on is a particular conception of self-identity, one shared by a number of artists and thinkers of the period but articulated most strikingly by the Scriblerians, principally Swift and Pope. This concept of the self is difficult to define, in large part because its nature is belied by definition, for it is a self which is as much a dynamic activity as a state of being and therefore a self which must be enacted in gestures that have no terminus and that must acknowledge—indeed, which derive their legitimacy from their acknowledgment of—their failure to define the self. When formulating this conception of selfhood, these artists and thinkers turned repeatedly to the notion of the imagination and to the figure of the monster, and in this study I attempt to uncover some of the historical determinants and provocations that explain why they did that.

This conception of the self was constructed within the broader culture of eighteenth-century England, of course, and in order to understand it, I have turned to other cultural discourses and practices which expressed in their own idioms central features of this conception, which laid a groundwork of assumptions that enabled such a conception to be formulated, or which provoked anxieties that the conception in part was constructed to resist: traditional assumptions about the psychology of the imagination, for instance, the contemporary philosophical arguments about personal identity and the mind-body relationship, theoretical embryology, teratological debates, the staging of monster exhibitions, and stereotypes about the deformed.

In examining this cultural matrix, I am the beneficiary of the current ferment in cultural and interdisciplinary studies, a ferment which has greatly influenced my thinking, given me fruitful new perspectives, or, in some cases, simply licensed my own interests and intuitions. I have tried to acknowledge these debts in my footnotes, but some I fear I have not acknowledged adequately, for they have permeated my thought in ways that are beyond my power to particularize.

Since much of this book makes use of material that is rare or unique, it could not have been written had not the following institutions opened their collections to me and had not their staffs guided me through them: Guildford Muniment Room, Guildford, Surrey; Niedersächsisches Staatarchiv, Bückeburg; Suffolk Record Office, Bury St. Edmunds; the Public Record Office; the Greater London Record Office; the British Library; the Royal College of Surgeons of England; the Royal Society of Medicine; the Bodleian Library, Oxford; and the Library of the University of Glasgow. In the United States, my four "working" libraries and their fine staffs allowed me to do much of my research without repeated trips abroad: the National Library of Medicine, Bethesda, Maryland; the Folger Shakespeare Library; the Library of Congress; and the Lauinger Library of Georgetown University.

At two crucial moments, I was freed from other obligations and was able to devote myself exclusively to writing, and for this I would like to thank Claude Boccara and Danielle Fournier, both of L'Ecole Supérieure de Physique et de Chimie, who made the stay of my wife and myself in Paris so pleasant and productive; and Georgetown University, which provided me with a grant that allowed me to complete my manuscript.

Almost the entirety of chapter 5 was published as "The Hairy Maid at the Harpsichord: Some Speculations on the Meaning of *Gulliver's Travels,*" *Texas Studies in Language and Literature* 34 (Summer 1992): 239–83. My discussion of Hogarth's *Cunicularii* in chapter 3 appeared, in a rather different form, in "Three Characters in Hogarth's *Cunicularii*—and Some Implications," *Eighteenth-Century Studies* 16 (Fall 1982): 26–46. Here and there I have borrowed phrases, ideas, and occasionally whole paragraphs from two other articles: "The 'Blunted Arms' of Dulness: The Problem of Power in the *Dunciad,*" *Studies in Philology* 79 (Spring 1982): 177–204; and "'One Vast Egg': Leibniz, the New Embryology, and Pope's *Dunciad,*" *English Language Notes* 26

(June 1989): 24–40. I am grateful to the editors of the journals these articles appeared in for allowing me to use them here.

A number of individuals have made this work possible, sometimes by offering substantive contributions, sometimes by questioning my assumptions and procedures, and always by extending their good will and encouragement: Edward Mendelson, David Kirby, LaMaurice Gardner, Terry King, Ralph Nash, Richard Nash, Lucy Maddox, Alex Sens, Lynne Hirschfeld, and Joan Reuss. Ray Reno and Joseph Sitterson read much of this book in an early form and forced me to think through issues more carefully than I had. Leona Fisher heroically read the entire manuscript at a critical moment in its writing and made invaluable suggestions to improve it. My friend Dylan Tan patiently listened to me as I struggled to formulate my ideas one last time and then helped me bring the project to some shapely end. For his erudition, his wisdom, and his extraordinary kindness, I am indebted to, and will always remember, the late Elias Mengel.

My last three debts are the deepest and the most longstanding. First, to Jeanne Flood, who heard my ideas at their inception, urged me to pursue them, read the manuscript repeatedly, argued me toward coherence, and through it all remained my warmest friend.

To J. Paul Hunter, who was first my teacher, then my mentor, and then my friend, and whose scholarly passion, intellectual integrity, and human decency became the models on which I have tried to pattern my own life and work in the hope that I might pass on something of what he has so generously given to me.

And finally, to Lorretta Inglehart, whose patience sustained me through an unconscionably long project.

NOTE

Many of the documents quoted in this study are ephemera; they were written hastily and printed badly. In order not to clutter the text, I have used *sic* sparingly, printing the words as written where the meaning is clear and, where it is not, silently correcting obvious errors. In chapter 5, where I quote extensively from handbills and advertisements, I have regularized some of the wilder typographic diversity. Translations of Latin texts are mine unless otherwise indicated.

References to frequently cited manuscript collections and editions use the following shortened forms:

Corr.	*The Correspondence of Alexander Pope,* ed. George Sherburn, 5 vols. (Oxford: Clarendon Press, 1956)
Douglas Papers	The papers of Dr. James Douglas, Special Collections, the Library of the University of Glasgow
PW	*The Prose Writings of Jonathan Swift,* ed. Herbert Davis et al., 16 vols. (Oxford: Basil Blackwell, 1939–68)
TE	*The Twickenham Edition of the Poems of Alexander Pope,* ed. John Butt et al., 11 vols. (London: Methuen; New Haven: Yale University Press, 1939–69)

1

A NEW WHIM WHAM
FROM GUILDFORD

Sometime in October 1726, Mary Toft, the illiterate wife of a poor journeyman cloth-worker, gave birth, in Godalming, Surrey, to her first rabbit. She went on to deliver sixteen more. Within a month, her story was in London, and within another she herself was too, lodged in a bagnio in Leicester Fields, her room crowded with those eager to witness the miracle. "Every Creature in town both Men & Women have been to see & feel her," Lord Hervey wrote to a friend in the country. "All the eminent physicians, Surgeons, and Men-midwifes in London are there Day & Night to watch her next production."[1] For those who could not get into the bagnio, newspapers reported her condition daily. Rumors grew on rumors. For over a week after her arrival, London awaited the birth of a new rabbit. None was forthcoming. On 7 December, Mary Toft, threatened by several skeptical doctors and a menacing justice of the peace, confessed that it was all a hoax. By the ninth, she was in Bridewell.

The revelation that she was an impostor, however, did little to dampen interest. At Bridewell, *The London Journal* reported, "infinite Crowds of People . . . resort to see her." Indeed, with the fraud uncovered, the public became more fascinated, not only with Mary Toft but also with those eminent physicians, surgeons, and men-midwives who had crowded around her bed for over a month. For these doctors now became involved in a spectacle almost as monstrous as Mary Toft's. Trying to disentangle themselves from the affair, they began to issue explanations, accusations, defenses, and disclaimers. The near success of Mary Toft's outrageous hoax and then these frantic attempts by the doctors to preserve their reputations were much too tempting for the wits and the hacks of Grub Street. London was inundated with diaries, public letters, depositions, factual accounts, facetious accounts that claimed to be factual, satiric poems, street ballads, mock suicide notes, false confessions, true confessions, medical disquisitions, cartoons, engravings, pamphlets, and squibs. John Rich hurriedly created an afterpiece for Drury Lane that recounted the the affair in broad farce. One enterprising businessman who earlier had offered gratis with each purchase of his medical elixir "The true Account how it really happen'd, that the Woman at Godliman near Guildford in Surrey, could have 18 real, true, and living Rabbits within her, and of which she was really and truly Delivered" now offered gratis a true account of "her pretended Deliveries."[2]

How could Mary Toft's claim, so laughable on the face of it, have riveted the attention of all of London for over a month? It is tempting to dismiss this affair as a quaint episode that shows the enormous distance between our own skeptical age and one more gullible. Yet, among those "infinite Crowds" that pressed around Mary Toft were a number of intelligent, educated people, every bit as commonsensical as we, many of them in fact trained in medicine, and they believed the truth of Mary Toft's account or at least were unwilling to set aside her claim without carefully considering it first. Even after it was revealed to be a hoax, when we might expect the affair to be laughed away with a snicker or a guffaw, the incident continued to be taken seriously. Gullibility may explain why some believed Mary Toft, but many of those who did not believe her felt that her story demanded a reasoned response, and they examined the details of her case rigorously and scientifically, testing her assertions against the newest theories of embryology and the established facts of comparative anatomy. Nor can gullibility wholly explain other features of the incident. The sheer fascination she was able to exercise over so many people for such a length of time (she "engross'd all Conversation for six Months"),[3] the crowds that beseiged the bagnio and then Bridewell, and, once the cheat was uncovered, the outpouring of pamphlets and satires, most barely concealing real anger and real fear: these suggest that Mary Toft's story touched some deep reservoir of beliefs, feelings, and anxieties, some core of preoccupations vital to the early eighteenth century.

I

Little is known about Mary Toft. Nathanael St. André, a surgeon from London who met her in November 1726, recorded most of the very few facts we know about her:

> She was born and bred at *Godlyman;* she seem'd to be of a healthy strong Constitution, of a small size, and fair Complexion; of a very stupid and sullen Temper: She can neither write nor read: She has been married about six years to one *Joshua Toft,* Junior, a poor Journey-man Clothier at *Godlyman,* by whom she has had three Children.[4]

Mary Toft was indeed born in Godalming, in 1703, as Mary Denyer. If St. André is correct, she and Joshua were married about 1720, though there appears to be no record of their marriage. The births of only two children were entered in the parish registers: Anne, who was born March 1723, and died July of that year in a smallpox epidemic, and James, born July 1724. But St. André is probably right in saying that there were three children, for there appears to have been an older daughter, perhaps named Mary, whose birth was not recorded.[5]

About Joshua, less is known than about Mary. His father, Joshua Toft, Sr., married Ann Bailey of Godalming at Little Bookham, 29 March 1692, and they raised a large family of at least eight children. Joshua Toft, Jr., was born in 1702.

While little can be learned for certain from such scanty evidence, enough can be inferred from St. André's comment that Joshua was a "poor Journey-man Clothier" to understand why this obscure family from a rural town in Surrey came to fabricate the hoax that would mesmerize all of London. Tofts had resided in Godalming since at least the early 1600s, and for generations most, like Joshua, had been in the woolen trade, many of them prospering. By the mid-seventeenth century, they begin to appear in apprentice records as masters and as clothiers, and the parish registers indicate that a substantial number of Tofts made a good living in the trade until the very early years of the eighteenth century.[6] By the 1720s, however, the family was faring much less well. Although a few Tofts continued to prosper (none of them was closely related to Joshua), on the whole the fortunes of the family were worse, in some cases quite desperate. Increasingly, their names appear in documents that link them to framework-knitting—a sure sign that they were being driven out of cloth manufacturing and were becoming so financially straitened that they had to find work in what was one of the worse pauper trades of the century. The parish registers begin to list Tofts as having died in the workhouse.[7] Joshua Toft himself was not rich, but "poor" as St. André indicates, and although St. André goes on to say that he was a "Clothier," Joshua was actually a cloth-worker, which is an important difference: a clothier was an entrepreneur who bought the raw material, employed artisans to manufacture it, and sold the finished product; a cloth-worker was a very badly paid laborer who was hired to crop and finish the cloth. In other words, Joshua Toft was near the bottom of the woolen trade.[8]

The decline of the Toft family is not mysterious, for the trade that had served so many of the earlier generations so well ultimately undid many of the later generations. The economy of Godalming had been based on the woolen industry since the later Middle Ages, and the business had flourished there through Elizabethan times. But in the seventeenth century, the trade began to falter, and in the eighteenth century it deteriorated badly. Just about the time of the Mary Toft incident, Defoe saw in Godalming only "a small remainder . . . of the clothing trade," and he attributed its decay to a decline in the quality of the cloth. Actually, the causes were much more complicated, and the decline was probably irreversible. The area produced what were generally known as Hampshire kerseys—moderately priced cloth made for export and hence particularly vulnerable to competition. Even as early as 1620, towns producing kerseys were beginning to be affected by foreign competition and increasing tariffs, and by the eighteenth century Surrey wool manufacturing had diminished considerably. Defoe was seeing its vestiges. Soon, it would disappear from the region altogether.[9]

Further, Joshua Toft's position within his trade could not have been particularly gainful. At the time of the incident, he was only twenty-four and, as St. André says, a "Journey-man." At most, he had been out of his apprenticeship for three years—hardly enough time to establish financial stability for himself, his wife, and his two living children. Since the trade was unregulated, it was overstocked with apprentices, making journeymen as a class chronically underemployed or simply unemployable. If Joshua were employed, he probably could not work all year round, even in the best of times, because cloth-work was too dependent on the supply of wool and was too sensitive to the depressions of the market, and 1726 was a year of slack trade. Even if he did find work, he made little money. In a region where, as Defoe noted, "the clothing trade, however small, is very assistant to the poor" because "the lands . . . are but indifferent," to be a poor journeyman cloth-worker was to live in the shadow of disaster.[10] In the summer of 1726, Mary Toft worked in the hop fields, earning a few pennies a day.

The poverty of the Tofts occasioned the scheme of giving birth to rabbits. The hoax was motivated solely by money. It was a way, Mary Toft confessed, "to get so good a living that I should never want as long as I lived."

Now, giving birth to rabbits was an uncommon but not unreasonable way to make money in the eighteenth century. The English fascination with monsters and their willingness to pay to see them were almost proverbial. When Trinculo sees the monstrous Caliban, his first thoughts are of England—and of money: "Were I in England now, . . . and had but this fish painted, not a holiday fool there but would give a piece of silver: there would this monster make a man; any strange beast there makes a man: when they will not give a doit to relieve a lame beggar, they will lay out ten to see a dead Indian." Interest in monstrosities had not waned by the mid-eighteenth century. Goldsmith complained that, "from the highest to the lowest," the English were so "fond of sights and monsters" and so "liberal in rewarding those who shew them," that the exhibitors "all live in luxury." Granted a degree of satiric exaggeration, neither Shakespeare nor Goldsmith is far from the historical truth. If the exhibitors of monsters did not live in actual luxury, they certainly conducted a brisk and profitable trade. Before Mary Toft, the English had flocked to see a wide assortment of human oddities. Earlier the same year as the hoax, Peter the Wild Boy had enjoyed a spectacular success and was, as Swift said, "the subject of half our Talk this fortnight." Before him, Londoners were entertained by giants, midgets, dwarfs, bearded ladies, hermaphrodites, and Siamese twins. These were among the least exotic. There were a boneless girl, only eighteen inches tall, who had had seven sets of teeth; a mermaid; a mother and daughter, both with three breasts each; a man with one head and two bodies, and a woman with one body and two heads; a boy with a live bear growing out of his back; a young man from Suffolk whose body was covered with bristles like a hedgehog's; and a little Dutch boy who was born with the words "Deus meus" inscribed on his right iris, "Elohim" (in Hebrew characters) on his left. Depending on how extraordinary the sight and how high the social standing of the spectator, the exhibitor could charge anywhere between a penny and a half crown. The poor flocked to monster exhibitions, and among the well-to-do, private viewings of monsters were a not unusual pastime. Providing such amusements could be extremely lucrative for the exhibitor. For hundreds of years, not only in England but all over Europe, parents had shown their deformed or monstrous children for a price. With so much money to be made, frauds were common.[11]

It is impossible to know for certain who among the Tofts first thought to make money by pretending to give birth to monsters. In her confession, Mary Toft portrayed herself, not unsurprisingly, as an innocent victim, intimidated into submission by her mother-in-law, Ann Toft, whom she pictured as the instigator and ruthless manager of the entire affair. She insisted that her husband remained completely ignorant of the plot. But her confession is patently self-serving, and the scheme could not have been carried out with such success unless she had devoted herself to it from the beginning. Depositions by those from whom Joshua Toft bought rabbits to keep his wife supplied prove that he knew everything at the outset. No matter whose idea it was originally, Ann, Mary, and Joshua Toft worked very hard to keep the fraud alive. Joshua's older sister, Margaret, played a part, too. She may not have had a hand in devising the hoax, but later, acting as a nurse for Mary, she was the conduit for the rabbits Joshua passed to his wife.[12]

Ironically, the idea for the hoax may have been prompted by an actual monstrous birth by Mary Toft, or at least by what she took to be a monstrous birth.[13] In the summer of 1726, probably late August, she miscarried. It was, she said in her confession, a large, misshapen piece of flesh, "a Substance as big as my arm," "a true monstrous birth." For about a month afterwards, she periodically suffered heavy bleeding. The hoax was conceived somewhere during this time. Originally, it had nothing to do with rabbits. Mary Toft simply was to give birth to a "monster." And so on 27 September, the Tofts cut up a cat, took out its guts and liver, inserted into its intestines the backbone of an eel they had eaten for dinner the previous Sunday, placed the concoction in Mary Toft, and left her alone in the house. She then sent for a neighbor, Mary Gill, complained that she was in great pain, feigned a brief labor, and let her friend hear the monster fall into a pot. Mary Gill fetched Ann Toft, who was a midwife. Other neighbors were called in, and it was decided to send the thing to John Howard of nearby Guildford. Mary Toft's husband took the monster to him.

John Howard was a surgeon who had practiced midwifery in Guildford for nearly thirty years. When Joshua brought him the monster and said that his wife had delivered it, Howard rejected the story out-of-hand, told him he was being imposed upon, and sent him home.[14] And yet, in spite of his reservations, he went to Godalming the next morning to see Mary Toft himself. Ann Toft showed him some pieces of the trunk of the cat that she claimed she had taken away over the night. The neighbors asserted that they thought there had been an actual birth. When Howard examined Mary Toft, however, he found nothing. On cue, she began to go into labor, and Ann, by sleight of hand, pretended to deliver more pieces of the monster. Howard was surprised, but he said that he would not believe the truth of the story until he himself had delivered her. Nevertheless, he was interested enough to stay all that day.

And he was interested enough to come back to Godalming the next day. This time, having secreted more parts of the cat into Mary, the Tofts let Howard deliver her himself. But he still did not fully believe them. This time, he said that he would not be convinced until he had delivered the head of the monster.

Apparently, Howard *was* unconvinced, for he did not return to Godalming for several weeks; and the Tofts did not press the matter with him any further, though they seem to have continued trying to dupe their neighbors. But, after about a fortnight, they made one more attempt to draw Howard into the ruse. By now, with the pieces that had been delivered and with the remaining pieces Ann could say she had delivered in Howard's absence, the Tofts could almost complete the cat. But the head and one foot had been mislaid, and Howard said that he would not believe that it was a true monstrous birth until he had delivered the head. The Tofts decided to use a rabbit. They removed its head and one of its feet.

Ann Toft put the lower jaw of the rabbit in her daughter-in-law. Mary Toft was in such pain after Ann left that she had to call in another local midwife, Betty Richardson, to take it from her. Later that night, Ann put up the rest of the skull. By the time Howard arrived, very early the next morning, she was in excruciating pain and bleeding profusely, but Howard was at last able to deliver her of the head of a rabbit. He brought forth the last foot a few days later. Thus, after almost a month, Mary Toft had delivered the requisite parts that, when put together, as she said, "made a monster."

The Tofts had not planned for the hoax to involve rabbits, but with the delivery of the head, they were committed. Now, it was no longer monsters she was delivering, but rabbits. About this time, they must have agreed upon the story they would use to account for such peculiar births. Mary Toft would claim that in April, when five weeks pregnant, she had been weeding a field and was startled by a rabbit. She and the woman she was working with ran after it but could not catch it. The chase made her long for rabbits. Soon after, another rabbit started up, and that too she failed to catch. "The same Night she dreamt she was in a Field with those two Rabbets in her Lap, and awakened with a sick Fit, which lasted till Morning; from that time, for above three Months, she had a constant and strong desire to eat Rabbets, but being very poor and indigent cou'd not procure any." Four months later, her story went, she delivered something that looked like a large lump of flesh. Three weeks later, it happened again. While she was working in a hop field in early September, milk began to flow from her breasts. On 27 September, she became ill and voided those parts of the monster which were shown to Howard.[15]

With the delivery of the head, Howard became more and more convinced. He had already given Mary some money, and Ann Toft thought there was more to be made from him. And so, as soon as Mary had given birth to her first whole monster, she immediately fell into labor again, and Howard, now apparently completely taken in by the hoax, began to bring forth various parts of rabbits in rapid succession. By early November, she was delivering almost a rabbit a day. Howard, whose practice had suffered because of all the time he was spending in Godalming, moved her to Guildford soon after she had given birth to her ninth rabbit, lodging her with Mrs. Mason, whose house was near his own, and hiring Mary Costen to attend her as a nurse. She was also attended by her sister-in-law, Margaret. By the ninth of November, she was in labor with her twelfth rabbit.

What had converted Howard from a skeptic to an enthusiastic believer in the course of a few weeks? The story of Mary Toft's being frightened by rabbits while weeding in a field, outrageous as it may appear to us, may have satisfied Howard since it was more or less in accordance with respectable medical opinion about the power of pre-natal influence. The eager assurances of the Tofts' neighbors, some of whom delivered parts of her rabbits and were duped themselves, might have carried some weight too. More convincing was the fact that he himself delivered rabbit after rabbit, day after day, without ever once seeing Mary Toft slip them from her pockets into her body. But probably most persuasive was the entire *mise-en-scène* of pregnancy, labor, and birth that Mary Toft staged. Some of the effects were real enough. Her miscarriage had left her with signs of pregnancy. Often she bled, and often her pain was unpretended. What was not real, she could act, and her most impressive performances were enhanced by her ability to set off powerful, pulsating contractions in her abdomen, contractions lasting for hours at a time. Everyone who saw them was astonished and, inevitably, they came to be referred to as "leapings" and "jumpings." Howard later reported "that when she was delivered of one Rabbet, another was immediately felt in her Belly, struggling with such violence, that the Motion thereof cou'd be sensibly felt and seen: That this Motion has sometimes been so strong, as to move the Bed-Clothes, and that it has lasted for twenty and above thirty Hours together." One last piece of stage-business, witnessed by a number of people, gave an appropriately bizarre flourish to the performance. From within her womb came sounds of what were fancied to be rab-bits' bodies being torn asunder: "the Bones of the Animal were sensibly heard to snap, and break by the violent convulsive Motions of the *Uterus*."[16]

There may have been another, less conscious motive behind Howard's conversion. He may have wanted to believe that these monstrous births were real. If her story were true, Mary Toft would become well known, and so too would the surgeon who had assisted her from the beginning. Whether or not some such consideration swayed him, Howard certainly capitalized on the affair quickly enough. He preserved the rabbits in spirits, kept notes of the deliveries, and drew up accounts of the progress of events. With this evidence carefully prepared, he began writing letters to "persons of Distinction" in London, detailing what had happened and offering to present specimens of two rabbits to the Royal Society.[17]

Howard's news spread quickly, and on 22 October a garbled version of the facts was first made known to the London public by a short notice in *The British Journal:*

> They write from Guildford, that three Women working in a Field, saw a Rabbit, which they endeavoured to catch, but they could not, they all being with Child at that Time: One of the Women has since, by the help of a Man Midwife, been delivered of some thing in the Form of a dissected Rabit, with this Difference, that one of the Legs was like unto a Tabby Cat's, and is now kept by the said man Midwife at Guildford.

Such a story was bound to catch the attention of the curious, and it did, in the person of Henry Davenant, a member of the court of George I. Davenant was in Guildford by 4 November. He examined the evidence Howard had collected and returned to London, evidently a believer.

Howard took advantage of his well-placed visitor. He began to write letters to Davenant, keeping him apprised of the progress of Mary Toft's births and promising that any new visitor (provided he had a letter of introduction from Davenant) could inspect the specimens of the rabbits already delivered and "see another leap in her *Uterus,* and shall take it from her if he pleases; which will be a great Satisfaction to the Curious: If she had been with Child, she has but ten Days more to go, so I do not know how many Rabbets may be behind."[18]

II

From one of these letters to Davenant, Nathanael St. André first learned of Mary Toft. In St. André's hands, the case would come to national attention. It would also become a case in which his motives and actions, as much as Mary Toft's, were the subject of intense public speculation, for the role he played in the affair was just as suspect as hers.

Much about St. André, in fact, and not just his conduct in the Mary Toft affair, is suspect—and unresolvable. "Such uncommon men," wrote his only apologist, "must be visited through life with uncommon incidents."[19] Indeed, St. André did have a penchant for finding himself in (or perhaps creating) "uncommon incidents," situations sufficiently suspicious that he seemed guilty and yet ambiguous enough that he just as likely could be innocent. One of his own contemporaries deemed him "a due Composition of Knave & Fool both," and it is often impossible to determine, as John Nichols remarked, whether the "celebrity of this man arose either from fraud or ignorance"—or, as he added, "perhaps from a due mixture of both."[20]

Born in Switzerland about 1680, St. André immigrated to England when he was young, probably as a servant in the household of a wealthy family. Later, he supported himself as a dancing master, and perhaps by teaching fencing, German, and French. He studied under a London surgeon, learned the trade, and schooled himself in anatomy. His name does not appear among the records of the Barber-Surgeons' Company, so he was in the strictest sense an unqualified practitioner. But in the eighteenth century, this signifies little, and it certainly does not mean that he was a charlatan, something implied in many attacks on him. He practiced from his lodgings in Northumberland Court, near Charing Cross, and was the local surgeon at Westminster Infirmary. He translated René-Jacques Garengeot's *Traité des operations de chirurgie* in 1723 and wrote other medical pieces himself. He gave public lectures in anatomy.[21]

How competent he was in his profession is difficult to ascertain. His apologist claimed that he was an avid student of anatomy, that he had made "noble preparations" of anatomical specimens by wax injections, and that the famous William Hunter considered him "the wonder of his time." All of this was disputed by John Nichols, who investigated these claims by talking to St. André's contemporaries. Nichols concluded that his library was worthless, that the "noble preparations" were actually "minutiæ of scarce any value," and that St. André was a mere "frigid dabbler" in anatomy. "Dr. *Hunter,* who has been applied to for intelligence on this occasion, declares that he never described *St. André* as 'the wonder of his time,' but as a man who passed through no regular course of study, and was competent only in the article of injections, a task as happily suited to minute abilities as to those of a larger grasp."[22]

Whatever the degree of his competency, St. André ultimately rose to a position of prestige. In May 1723, he was appointed by George I Surgeon and Anatomist to the Royal Household—more because of his knowledge of German, it was said, than because of his merit as a medical man. St. André boasted of his favor with the king, saying that he had been presented with a sword George himself had worn. There might be some truth in this. Royal favor would explain how such a well-known surgeon could practice in London without ever having been made free of the Barber-Surgeons' Company.[23]

Within a year of his appointment, St. André was visited by the first of his "uncommon incidents." On 6 February 1724/5, a stranger, asking to consult him about a difficult case, led St. André through the maze of dark London streets to a house the surgeon later was not able to locate. He was offered a cordial which tasted so bad he drank only a little. Finally, he was asked to examine a woman for venereal disease. Several hours after he left, he began to experience the effects of poisoning. He was laid up for two weeks, close to death, according to his own account. On the king's orders, he was examined by five of London's most prestigious physicians, and his case was investigated by the Privy Council, which offered £200 for the detection of the alleged offender. But it never was discovered who was responsible or what their motives were. The entire incident is baffling (even St. André's apologist was forced to admit that the story "partakes of the marvellous"). Some of St. André's contemporaries thought he had overdosed himself with mercury in an attempt to cure his own venereal disease; others, according to Nichols, considered the incident "an ostentatious falsehood, invented only to render him an object of attention and commiseration."[24]

After the Mary Toft affair, St. André became involved in another "uncommon incident." When his long-time friend, Samuel Molyneux, M.P. for Exeter, was seized with a fit in the House of Commons, St. André was called on to treat him. Molyneux died within several days. On the night of his friend's death, St. André eloped with Molyneux's wife, Elizabeth. He later married her and came into a sizeable sum of money. Samuel Madden, Molyneux's cousin, openly accused him of having poisoned Molyneux. Eventually, St. André won an action for defamation, but neither he nor his wife was able to live down the scandal. Lady Elizabeth lost her attendance on Queen Caroline, and St. André was publicly humiliated at court. They retired to the country, where they lived for the remainder of their lives.[25]

But the most spectacular "uncommon incident" that befell St. André, the one that created the most perplexity about his motives, was the Mary Toft case. It is not surprising that he would be drawn into this affair or that his conduct would appear so ambiguous that he was accused of being both a fool and a knave. For St. André was anxious to be in the public eye and was willing to use just about any tactic of self-promotion to get and keep himself there. Even his apologist had to admit that "he loved praise," and more than praise he loved attention: "so that people did but talk about him, he seldom seemed to care what they talked against him."[26] A cloud of uncertainty so often surrounded him and his actions, I suspect, not because he actually did anything knavish but because, having come upon or having sought out a promising situation, he exploited it to draw attention to himself, and he exploited it so brazenly that he provoked suspicions about his real motives. In the paper he delivered to the Royal Society, for instance, he managed to turn an account of a burst bowel into a panegyric on his skill as a surgeon and his acumen as an anatomist, thus causing in the minds of his contemporaries doubts concerning both. Questions about the real reason he was made Royal Surgeon and Anatomist and about his qualifications as a surgeon might never have arisen had he not placed advertisements in London newspapers shamelessly trading on his court appointment and touting his skills. The incident of his poisoning in 1724/5 might have passed relatively unnoticed had he not published lengthy accounts in which he gave, in astonishing detail, a day-by-day record of his heroic struggle against death and called attention to how much he was favored by the king and how intimate his relationships were with important members of the court. And so when his friend Samuel Molyneux asked if he would accompany him to Guildford to ferret out the truth of the rumors, St. André must have sensed a situation ripe with possibility.[27] He accepted the invitation eagerly. Molyneux himself was not going out of idle curiosity. Although he was a dedicated scientist who might be expected to have some intellectual interest in the reports about Mary Toft, he was also secretary to the Prince of Wales, and it appears that he was going to Guildford at the prince's command.[28]

St. André and Molyneux arrived in Guildford Tuesday afternoon, 15 November. They sent for Howard, who came to them immediately and told them that Mary Toft was in labor with her fifteenth rabbit. When they entered the room she was lodged in, they saw Mary Toft, dressed in stays, sitting on the side of her bed, surrounded by women attendants. St André quickly examined her, and she complained of new labor pains. Within minutes, St. André delivered her of a trunk of a rabbit, stripped of its skin.

St. André and Molyneux set about investigating this new birth. Their first concern was to discover whether the animal was fetal or not. Luckily, the trunk contained the lungs. "I instantly cut off a piece of them," St. André wrote later, "and tried them in Water; they seemed but just specifically lighter than it, and Mr. *Molyneux* pressing them to the Bottom they rose again very slowly."[29] This seemed to prove that the rabbit had breathed, but the physical appearance of the lungs suggested otherwise: they were smaller and darker than the lungs of rabbits that had breathed for some time.

St. André turned his attention from the rabbit to Mary Toft. There had been no blood or water accompanying her delivery, but he observed that there was milk in one of her breasts. Then, simply by examining her externally, he came to a remarkable conclusion: "in the Course of the *Fallopian Tubes,* there were some Inequalities, but more sensibly on the right side of her Belly; which made me conjecture that the Rabbets were bred in those Tubes, and only came into the *Uterus,* when they gave her those Agitations." ("Sure he is the first Man," scoffed one of his critics weeks later, "that ever felt Inequalities in the *Fallopian Tubes* of a Woman thro' the out side of her Belly.")[30]

St. André, Molyneux, and Howard, confident that nothing new was about to happen, left the room. Two hours later, they were told that Mary Toft was again in labor. By the time they reached her room, the nurse already had delivered her of the lower part of a male rabbit, also stripped of its skin. Once again, St. André examined the animal. "In the *Rectum* . . . we found five or six Pellets, much of the same Colour and Consistence as the common Dung of a Rabbet, little Bodies, like dried Fragments, being matted together with a mucous Matter."[31] But when he inspected the animals Mary Toft had delivered earlier, he found in some only a mucus, like that found in fetal animals. When he opened the intestines of Mary Toft's first "monster," St. André discovered the bones of the eel that had been put there over a month earlier.

The three men left and did not come back to her room until the early evening. Almost immediately Mary Toft fell into labor again, writhing so vigorously "that four or five persons cou'd hardly confine her to an Arm-Chair." What happened next was critical, for it determined the direction of St. André's thinking until the end of the incident. "As soon as the Violence of the first Pain was somewhat abated, I examined her as before, and found the *Vagina* perfectly clear; and the Orifice of the *Uterus* so far closed, as not to admit of the little Finger. I constantly stood before her, nor did any Person whatsoever touch her, during that Time. After three or four very strong Pains, that lasted several Minutes, I delivered her of the Skin of the . . . Rabbet, rolled and squeezed up like a Ball, without the least Moisture of Blood about it; . . . From that Time I did not stir from before her, nor did I withdraw my Hand, but to deliver the Skin to a stander by."[32] Ten minutes later, after a short labor, Mary Toft delivered a head of a rabbit, with part of one ear torn off. This clinched the matter for St. André: having examined her beforehand, having stood before her until he delivered first the ball of fur and then the head, he could only conclude that the rabbit had not been hidden in her vagina but had to have come out of her womb. Later, for his critics, this episode was proof that St. André had to have been a conspirator in the fraud.

In fact, Mary Toft had hidden both the fur and the head in her vagina before the three men had returned to her room. How could St. André possibly have missed them when he examined her? The only explanation is that suggested by Mary Toft in her confession. St. André, she said, made "a very slight examination" of her. Perhaps it was his haste, perhaps his inexperience, or perhaps, as it was for Howard, with whom St. André would draw into a closer and closer alliance, it was simply the fact that he wanted to believe Mary Toft's story, unconsciously seeing in this birth the rudiments of something that could be parlayed into an "uncommon incident" with himself at the center. Whatever the reason, St. André now believed that the woman truly was giving birth to monsters.

Mary Toft had produced an almost complete rabbit in the one day St. André and Molyneux had seen her. The two men gathered together its pieces, inspected once again the rabbits she had delivered earlier, choosing a few to take with them for closer examination, and left Guildford. The next day, in London, they both began a comparative anatomy to learn what kind of creatures Mary Toft had delivered. The evidence was contradictory. The test they had performed on the lungs to see whether the rabbit had ever breathed was, at best, inconclusive. The creatures themselves seemed rather large—perhaps the size of two- to four-month old rabbits. Their hearts and livers, too, were comparatively bulky, though in each heart St. André found the foramen ovale open, a sign that the rabbits were fetuses. Their lungs and intestines were smaller than those of newborn rabbits. The bones appeared to be characteristically fetal. The teeth were not worn. The contents of the intestines gave equivocal testimony, some being pellets like those in rabbits that had lived, others the mucus of a fetus. The eel bones in the intestines of the first "monster" were simply inexplicable, as was the fact that most of its parts resembled those of a cat more than a rabbit.

It was a hopeless hodgepodge of evidence from which nothing sensible could be concluded. But St. André believed the truth of the wonderful births. He patched together the evidence as best he could to support his conviction: "From all these Considerations I was fully convinced, that at the same time that the external Appearance of these

Animals was exactly like such Creatures, as must inevitably undergo the Changes that happen to adult Animals, by Food and Air, they carry'd within them the strongest Marks of *Fœtus's,* even by such parts as cannot exist in an Adult, and without which a *Fœtus* cannot possibly be supposed to live. This, I think, proves in the strongest Terms possible that these Animals were of a particular kind, and not bred in a natural Way." The rabbits were, in short, "Præternatural."[33]

After Mary Toft confessed to the hoax, numerous medical men tried to exonerate their profession by pointing out how inexact St. André's observations were and how faulty his conclusion. But the illogic of his explanation, as well as its manic self-validation, was best captured in a popular squib:

> The Doctors here and Midwives all consult
> If 'tis a fœtus Rabbit or adult
> When up the learned Merry Andrew Starts
> This Animal (quoth he) in all its parts
> Does with a Natural Rabbit well agree
> And therefore it must Præternatural be.[34]

The "explanation" served to confirm those things St. André was sure of, and this was its real value: he himself had delivered a rabbit, the vagina had been clear before he had done so, and therefore there was no fraud involved. And it had an important consequence. It was an explanation that brooked no argument because it subsumed and converted to its own support all contradictory evidence. Anything observed about the rabbits, whether bizarrely anomalous or utterly normal, would now be proof that they were "præternatural." St. André, in spite of mounting evidence to the contrary, held to his belief until Mary Toft herself confessed.

III

After the visit by St. André and Molyneux, interest in Mary Toft was sharpened as rumors of the strange happenings in Guildford spread around London and stories began to appear regularly in the newspapers. One of those most interested was George I. Several days after St. André's return, he dispatched as his representative Cyriacus Ahlers, Surgeon to His Majesty's German Household, to look more deeply into the affair. Ahlers and a friend, Mr. Brand, arrived in Guildford Sunday morning, 20 November.

If St. André had been predisposed to believe Mary Toft, Ahlers was the opposite: he had made up his mind before he arrived in Guildford that the incident was a hoax. Suspicious of everyone, he resolved to play the role of the amiable believer and thus penetrate to the very heart of the plot. "I do not deny," he confessed later, "but that at *Guilford* I behaved my self all along, like one who was perfectly satisfied of the Matter: I had very good Reasons for so doing; and was not ashamed to own it upon my Return."[35]

Shortly after Ahlers and Brand took a room at the White Hart Inn, they sent a message to Howard asking to see him and Mary Toft. The surgeon said that he would see them at his house at once. But when they arrived, they were told that he had gone out on a professional visit to the mayor. They were kept waiting for over an hour. And when Howard finally came to them, he was dressed in a nightgown. Ahlers found this suspicious.

And, after they were conducted to Mary Toft's lodgings, Ahlers found more things to be suspicious about. The nurse told them that Mary Toft had just delivered the skin of a rabbit, but when he examined it, Ahlers could find no evidence, except around the edges, of any blood or water. Nor did Mary Toft appear to be pregnant. She wore stays. Ahlers observed no swelling of her stomach and, when he examined her breasts, he could find no milk. Her pulse was normal. "I observ'd her with some Attention, as she was walking about the Room, and found that she press'd her Knees and Thighs close together, as if she was afraid something might drop down, which she did not care to lose."[36]

Ahlers' suspicions fell on John Howard. Although Howard allowed women attendants and his own brother, Thomas, also a surgeon, to come and go freely, he refused to allow Brand to enter Mary Toft's room—"beyond all doubt," Ahlers thought, "done with some sinister View."[37] Thenceforth, he regarded everything Howard did and said with distrust. And indeed, to someone inclined to suspicion, many of Howard's actions could appear to be those of a guilty man, though all of them can be interpreted quite differently. The fact of the matter is that Ahlers grated on Howard from the outset, and the distrust was mutual. Ahlers' duplicity was so egregious that Howard sensed it early, and he carried himself very circumspectly.

Ahlers did not take this into consideration. When Mary Toft fell into labor soon after he entered her room, he interpreted every circumstance to point irrefutably to Howard's complicity:

> She was now ordered by Mr. *Howard* to sit down again in her Elbow-Chair, upon which he examin'd her, and sat himself down opposite to her upon another Chair, in a Posture which appeared to me very uncommon, and indeed not a little Suspicious: He made her put her Legs between his, and

with his Knees he press'd hers close together. There was a small Charcoal-fire lighted in the Room, and they were both sitting hard by the Chimney, after such a manner, that it was impossible for me to observe distinctly what they were doing, and in particular to mind the Motions of Mr. *Howard*'s right Hand. It was now about a Quarter before Twelve, when the woman fell into fresh Labour-pains, beginning a-new to cry out very strangely. Mr. *Howard* continued all the while to keep her Knees close together; and holding his Head against hers, he took her Hands into his, whilst she stooping with her Head forwards, push'd her Back against the Back of the Chair with such Violence, that I was forc'd to hold the Chair to prevent its going over. She repeated the same afterwards at two or three different Times. Those Pains being gone off, Mr. *Howard* examin'd her again, and then suffer'd me to do the same, which accordingly I did. Upon touching her, I presently perceived some broken Bones, and advancing with my Finger, I discover'd a fleshy Body, which with the bones stood a little way out of the Orifice of the *Vagina*. The *Vagina* was strongly contracted, closely embracing the Body, which presented itself, and which I conjectur'd to be the hind Part of a Rabbit, stripp'd of the Skin. The extreme Dryness of the Parts, the strong Contraction of the *Vagina,* and the Apprehension I was under, lest the Fore-Part should be in the same Condition with that I felt, made me proceed with some Caution, insomuch that I resolved rather to wait the Return of new Labour-pains, than by using any Violence, to tear and to injure the *Vagina*. Having retired for these Reasons, Mr. *Howard* ask'd me, whether I would not extract it; and upon my answering, No, he offer'd to make it easier for me, pretending, that his Fingers were slenderer than mine: Accordingly he examin'd her, and presently desir'd me to touch her again, which I did, and found the Body abovesaid advanced a little way; but when I laid hold of it, the *Vagina* contracted itself so strongly, that it snapp'd back again full the Breadth of a finger. Upon this I would have desisted a second Time; but Mr. *Howard* observing it, urg'd me in strong Terms to proceed. So I took hold again, and to my surprize drew it out with all imaginable Ease.[38]

Ahlers thought this episode to be all sleight-of-hand and theater, but in fact Howard's reasons for acting the way he did were quite above-board. Ahlers, though a surgeon, was no midwife, and when he first attempted to draw out the hind part of the rabbit, he only pushed it in further, and his fumbling hurt Mary Toft badly. "I beg[g]ed Mr How[ar]d to sit down and bring away the rest," Mary Toft said in her confession, "because that gentl[e]man had put me to a great deal of pain." Ahlers did not mention this detail in the account he drew up later, but this was why, when it appeared that she would soon give birth to another part of the rabbit, Howard not only refused to let Ahlers deliver it but would not even let him examine her again. Ahlers protested, and Howard, "with a sudden high Colour in his Face, answer'd me, *By no Means;* alledging, that Mr. *St. André* himself had examin'd her but twice, and that therefore I ought to be satisfied with having extracted part of it my self."[39] Ahlers acquiesced, and shortly thereafter Howard delivered the forepart of the rabbit. To Ahlers, here was one more indication that Howard was implicated in the fraud.

But the deeper his suspicions grew, the more complaisant and believing Ahlers tried to appear. He told Howard "that he was fully satisfied, and convinced of the Truth, and that he could have no Doubts after such Proofs." He feigned compassion for Mary Toft. Howard was encouraged by this and began to petition Ahlers, telling him "what pains he must have been at, and still took, and what the poor Woman had suffered, and that he hoped His Majesty would be so gracious, when all was over, to give them a Pension, there being many that had Pensions, who did not deserve them." Ahlers promised to represent them both to the king in the best manner he could.[40]

With proof of the plot now so obvious, Ahlers was more outraged than ever that Howard had excluded Brand from the room and had thus, as he said later, "depriv'd me of a proper Witness."[41] When Howard once again turned his attention to Mary Toft to see if she was about to deliver the head of the rabbit, Ahlers, on the pretext of arranging for something to eat, sent for Brand and, when he entered the room, told him in High German to observe the peculiar posture both Howard and Mary Toft were in and then, in English, ordered his dinner. He then asked Howard if he could take the parts of the rabbit back to London to show the king. Howard was reluctant but, after Ahlers promised to send them back again, he agreed. Then Ahlers, Brand, and Howard went to the White Hart Inn, where they were joined by Thomas Howard.

There Ahlers continued his dissembling. Even after John Howard left to return to Mary Toft, Ahlers made it known to as many people in the room as possible that he firmly believed that Mary Toft's were really monstrous births. In truth, he was so thoroughly persuaded that it was an imposture that he decided to cut short his intended three-day stay in Guildford and return to London at once. As an excuse, he began to complain of a headache and attacks of giddiness.

After dinner, they all returned to Mary Toft's room so Ahlers could retrieve his specimens and inform Howard that his plans had been altered. When they entered, Howard told them that Mary Toft had been delivered of the head of a rabbit in their absence. But Ahlers was not even tempted to stay longer. He gave Mary Toft a guinea, gathered up the parts of the rabbit she had delivered (except for the intestines and feet: they had gotten lost somewhere on the floor), and quickly examined the other rabbits. In the rectum of one, he noticed pellets of hard excrement; Howard extracted them with a pin and put them in a box for Ahlers to take with him. Howard read to him an account of the case he had drawn up, which Ahlers listened to with little attention or patience. By early evening, Ahlers and Brand had left Guildford.

When Ahlers had more leisure to examine his specimens, he found his suspicions corroborated. The bones and muscles of the rabbit showed clear evidence of having been cut with a sharp instrument. The pellets of excrement contained fragments of hay, straw, and corn. There was no doubt: the births were a hoax, and Mary Toft and John Howard were in collusion. On Monday, 21 November, Ahlers arrived in London and went immediately to Kensington to report his findings to the king.

IV

It was not only the king to whom Ahlers expressed his disbelief; he also spoke to "several Persons of Note and Distinction," showing them the specimens he had brought back from Guildford as evidence that there was a plot afoot to deceive the public.[42] News of Ahlers' claims that the Mary Toft affair was an imposture must have spread quickly, for there is no other way to explain the series of remarkable events that happened the next week.

On 22 November, the day after Ahlers had returned to London, Howard sent him a letter informing him of the delivery of a seventeenth rabbit and requesting him to send back the rabbit he had taken away. And, on the same day, he wrote another letter to a relation in London:

> This Morning I delivered the Poor Woman of Godalmin of the 17th Rabbit, which, I believe, may be the last. On Sunday I had, in his coach, Mr. Ahlers, Surgeon to the King's Household: He came by the King's Order; he took part of the 16th Rabbit from her, and carried it to Kensington. He was to have stayed till all was over; but being taken ill, returned the same Night. Last Tuesday I had Mr. St. Andre, his Majesty's Anatomist, by the King's Order; who took part of one from her, which weighed 22 ounces; and were both satisfied in the Truth of the wonderous Delivery: As was Mr. Molineux, Secretary to the Prince, who was also here. I hear they have made their Report to the King and Prince.[43]

The letter seems innocuous enough but, when viewed within the larger pattern of events of this week, there is little question that it was the first engagement in a battle Howard and St. André were to wage against Ahlers. In the first place, the letter was not really private. It was published in both *St. James Evening Packet* and the *Whitehall Evening*

Post on 26 November. And in it Howard was establishing two points: first, Ahlers had professed that he believed the births to be genuine; secondly, although he had been commanded by the king to stay "till all was over," he left within a few hours of his arrival at Guildford. In the next week, Howard and St. André would use these two facts to publicly challenge Ahlers' veracity.

St. André, too, must have heard of Ahlers' allegations rather quickly, for he hurried back to Guildford, accompanied by his friend, Mr. D'Anteney.[44] They arrived on Wednesday, 23 November. During the few days they were there, Mary Toft delivered twice more—not rabbits now, but membranes that Howard and St. André thought were parts of the chorion.

But St. André was less interested in Mary Toft than in the story Ahlers was spreading in London, and he and Howard spent their time collecting evidence which they thought would so thoroughly compromise Ahlers that his statements would not be taken seriously. The result of their efforts was a bundle of affidavits detailing Ahlers' visit to Guildford.

Howard himself, in a deposition sworn 25 November, recounted how Ahlers had given Mary Toft money, how he had told her that he would procure a pension from the king, and how he had declared that he had no doubts that these were true monstrous births. Both Mary Toft and her nurse, Mary Costen, swore "That Mr. *Ahlers* declared it was wonderful People would not believe a Fact that was so true as this appeared to him,"[45] and Elizabeth Helmes, the proprietess of the White Hart Inn, stated that Ahlers had assured her that when he returned to London he would attempt to convince the unbelievers. Further, Ahlers had said that he had been ordered by the king to stay in Guildford until the affair was concluded—this was attested to by John Howard and Olive Sands, one of the women attendants of Mary Toft.

All these facts were repeated and underscored by John Howard's brother, Thomas. He swore that Ahlers

> told this Deponent he was come to see her the said Woman, and that he was ordered by his Majesty to attend her till 'twas all over. That the said Mr. *Ahlers* himself . . . shewed this Deponent the Loins and inferior Parts of a Rabbet which he told this Deponent HE EXTRACTED HIMSELF OUT OF THE UTERUS. That this Deponent asked him what his Opinion was in this Case, to which he answered, and told this Deponent, HE WAS FULLY CONVINCED AND SATISFIED THAT IT CAME OUT OF THE UTERUS. . . . That after this Deponent was with him at the *White-Hart Inn* in *Guilford,* and there Mr. *Ahlers* repeated part of what he had said before. That this Deponent there pressed him very much to stay all Night, to take away all the rest of the Parts of the aforesaid Rabbet: Upon which he

said he had a Giddiness, and a turning round in his Head, with a pain on his Neck and Shoulders, and a soreness of his throat, which made him very uneasy, and that he was resolved to go back to *London*.[46]

In essence, the depositions accused Ahlers of being a thoroughgoing hypocrite and liar and suggested that, since he could not be believed in Guildford, he should not now be believed in London. They charged him with having carried out such an inadequate and perfunctory investigation that his conclusions were not to be trusted, thus grossly prejudging the case in violation of the king's orders. The affidavits would either pressure him into a recantation or, failing that, completely undermine his credibility.

Of course, none of this rose above mere character assassination. Not a single deposition even touched on the issue of whether or not Mary Toft had actually given birth to rabbits; they were all, Ahlers later complained, "purely levell'd at my Character and Reputation."[47] And it is precisely this turning to personal attack, as well as resorting to the legal formality of affidavits, that marks a real change in the complexion of the affair. From now on, the Mary Toft case would be conducted less and less in a kind of professional seclusion, argued by experts using medical criteria. Increasingly, the investigation would be made public, the arguing would be done publicly, and the rules would not be the rules of medical enquiry. The issues, too, were broader. It was no longer simply a question of the truth of Mary Toft's monstrous births. At stake now were reputations.

As part of the campaign against Ahlers, St. André began writing his *Short Narrative of an Extraordinary Delivery of Rabbits*. In it, he would make public his side of the case and would print the affidavits he and Howard had collected, thus openly challenging Ahlers, who was now, he felt, "strictly obliged, in Justice to the Publick, forthwith to give an Account of what he saw and transacted" while in Guildford.[48]

By 26 November, St. André was back in London. He gave an anatomical demonstration before the king at Kensington proving, contrary to Ahlers' assertions, that Mary Toft truly had given birth to rabbits.

V

Sir Richard Manningham, Fellow of the Royal Society and Licentate of the College of Physicians, was a doctor of some eminence; by 1726 he was becoming a preferred midwife among upper-class society in London. (This is the same Manningham who was too busy with his practice in the city to attend Mrs. Shandy in her delivery.) Late in the evening of the day following the anatomical demonstration before the king, he received a note from St. André asking him to remain at home, where St. André would attend him immediately. Manningham waited up until two o'clock and then sent his servant to ask to be excused. The servant returned with a message that St. André would come presently. Near four o'clock in the morning, St. André at last arrived, accompanied by Mr. Limborch, a German surgeon and man-midwife. St. André apologized to Manningham, explained to him that he had been to Kensington since he had written his first note, and told him that they must all go to Guildford at once—it was his Majesty's pleasure that Manningham examine Mary Toft and deliver to him a full report. And they were to bring the woman back to London.

The entire incident seems a little precipitous: late-night letters, early morning consultations with the king, the rush to Guildford at an inconvenient hour. Howard had sent a note saying Mary Toft was in labor again, but whose sense of urgency—the king's or St. André's— was responsible for all this hurry is impossible to know. Still, the calling in of Manningham is significant. The affair had become too public and too contentious to be left unresolved any longer. And it was to be resolved by someone outside the narrow world of the German court, by someone who was known in London and whose professional opinion would be respected.

The three men arrived in Guildford about noon, 28 November. Howard was not at home, so they went directly to Mary Toft's lodgings. Manningham examined her at once. Unlike St. André or Ahlers, he seems truly to have reserved judgment. He set out to discover the truth or falsity of the monstrous births by deliberate and exhaustive investigation. First, he examined her breasts and found, as he carefully phrased it, a small quantity of "thin *Serous Matter* like *Milk*." He noted that her stomach was soft and that she exhibited no signs of pregnancy. He "diligently search'd the whole *Vagina*" and assured himself that "at that time all was clear from Imposture." The os uteri was closed very tightly. But Manningham remained extremely cautious, for he felt a slight hardness on her right side, around her Fallopian tube, he thought, and he concluded that the uterus seemed "to contain something of Substance in its Cavity."[49]

Manningham had another reason for being cautious. He had heard stories of the "leapings" in the woman's stomach. Mary Toft told him that she had not felt them since one o'clock the previous morning. When he finally joined them later that afternoon, Howard said that perhaps the rabbit was dead. But he added that when hot cloths were applied, sometimes the motions would start again. Manningham decided to try the experiment:

> I immediately ordered Clothes to be made very hot, and apply'd them my self to all her Belly, being very desirous to feel that leaping Motion they so much talk'd of. Upon applying of the first Cloth the Motion began, which they called the leaping up of the Rabbet; it was indeed a Motion like a sudden leaping of something within the right side of her Belly, where I had before felt that particular Hardness.
>
> The Motions were various, sometimes with very strong Throws cross the Belly, especially on the right side, at other times with sudden Jerks and Risings, and tremulous Motions and Pantings, like the strong Pulsations of the Heart; and as I sat on the Bed in Company with five or six Women, it would sometimes shake us all very strongly: The whole appeared to me very different from any convulsive or hysterick Motion I had ever met with before.[50]

In spite of the intensity of these "leapings," Mary Toft delivered nothing. Manningham, St. André, and Limborch left Mary Toft's room and went to the White Hart Inn. In less than an hour, Howard came in and showed them, wrapped in a paper, a piece of membrane which he had just taken from Mary Toft. Manningham was angry. He said that he should have been sent for immediately, that he himself should have delivered it since that was the purpose of his being sent to Guildford. Howard dismissed his complaints by insisting that there was more to come. Manningham's anger turned to suspicion when he examined the membrane. It looked to him like a piece of hog's bladder. It even smelled of urine. Howard insisted that it was part of the chorion and said that he had more at home. He and Manningham went to his house to examine the pieces of rabbit and the membranes that Howard had preserved. Manningham saw nothing that would lessen his suspicions.

At eight o'clock that evening, a messenger came and informed them that Mary Toft was in pain.

> We went immediately, and I found her sitting in a great Chair by the fireside; I ask'd her if she was then in pain, she answer'd, no, but that she had some sharp Pains just before I came in: I then touch'd her, and in the *Vagina* perceiv'd with my Forefinger and Thumb somewhat like a piece of Skin; but being willing to know whether it came out of the *Uterus*, I passed my finger on one side of the said piece of Skin in the *Vagina* to find if there was any part of that Skin or Membrane yet remaining in the *Uterus*; but perceiving the *Os Uteri* close, as before, and in the same Form as I left it last, I presently took out what lay in the *Vagina*, and upon examining it, confess I was much surpriz'd, it appearing to me so like a piece of Hog's bladder, that I was not able to form any other Judgment of it, as I then told Mr. *Howard*, Mr. *St. André*, Mr. *Limborch*, and all that were there present, assuring them that it was my Opinion that Membrane never came out of the *Uterus*.

Manningham asked to see a hog's bladder, and "they presently brought one fresh blown up, which it seems they had in the House: This added to my Jealousy."[51] Manningham compared the bladder to the membrane Mary Toft had delivered and found them so similar that he said he now would not be convinced until he took a membrane out of the uterus itself.

At the suggestion that the affair was a hoax, Mary Toft began to cry. Howard and St. André asked Manningham to have more patience, at which point he lost what little he had left and asked them what the membrane *did* look like if not like a hog's bladder. Both agreed that there was a strong resemblance, and St. André even admitted that had he not taken a rabbit from the uterus itself, he would now concede that he had been imposed upon. Their conversation was interrupted by Mary Toft, who began to have labor pains. They lasted three hours, but nothing came of them.

The men adjourned to the White Hart Inn and resumed their conversation. Manningham told them that "the more I considered the thing, the more strongly I was convinced, that the Membrane I took from the Woman had never been in the *Uterus,* but was really a piece of Hog's Bladder artfully conveyed into the *Vagina.*" Upon this, there arose "very warm Disputes."[52]

St. André reasoned with Manningham. Since the rabbits bore the marks of fetuses as well as of animals that had been born, they were clearly monstrous. And since they were monstrous, they had to have come from the womb of Mary Toft, for if there were any fraud involved, all the rabbits would look only like animals that had eaten and breathed. Therefore, since the rabbits had indeed come out of the uterus, it followed that the membrane had come from the uterus too. Manningham was not persuaded.

St. André and Howard were in a predicament. They had spent the previous week laying the groundwork for a public engagement of the issue with Ahlers; St. André had even finished a draft of his *Short Narrative.* And now, if Manningham's doubts about the membrane became known, their own case would be that much less plausible. They persuaded Manningham to keep silent: "At their joint Desire, I determin'd to make no publick Mention of this Affair till I had seen the Event of the whole Transaction, or had fresh Reason to suspect a Fraud, lest by such an Alarm I should rather obstruct than forward the finding out the Truth."[53] Manningham, of course, knew nothing about the campaign against Ahlers that St. André and Howard had set in motion, and their suggestion, so thoroughly self-serving, seemed to him to be entirely reasonable. He adopted it, and it became his own principle of conduct throughout the entire affair. But there was a further reason why he agreed to keep silent, one which he did not reveal to St. André. In spite of the fact that Mary Toft exhibited few signs of pregnancy and in spite of the palpable suspiciousness of the membrane, Manningham was puzzled by the "leapings" and continued to believe that there was "something of Substance" in her uterus. (Manningham was infuriatingly vague about what he thought this "something of Substance" was. It appears that he thought Mary had found some way of conveying pieces of rabbits into her uterus, but because he never made this clear, later many would accuse him of believing her claims.) Given his doubts, the only responsible thing to do was to await "the Event of the whole Transaction."

All three decided that, the next morning, they would take Mary Toft to London.

VI

On Tuesday, 29 November, Mary Toft finally was brought to London. She was lodged in Mr. Lacy's bagnio in Leicester Fields, very close to St. André's apartments at Northumberland Court, and even closer to those of the Prince of Wales at Leicester House.[54] St. André wrote another late-night letter, as he had to Manningham, this time to Dr. James Douglas, one of the most respected anatomists and man-midwives in London:

> I have brought the woman from Guilford to the Bagnio in Leicester fields. She now has a live rabbit in her and I expect shortly a Delivery: you will infinitely oblige me to deliver her your self. Mr. Amiand is already here.[55]

In fact, she appeared no more ready to deliver than she ever had, and St. André's promise of an impending birth and his offer to let him perform the next delivery were meant to entice Douglas to come as quickly as possible. For, now that he was in London, St. André began to pursue even more energetically his plan of making the incident a public event. Douglas was not the only medical man whom he would invite. Claudius Amyand, Sergeant-Surgeon in Ordinary to George I, already was at the bagnio, and St. André had drawn up a list of other professional men in London to invite. By the time Douglas arrived, he met Amyand, St. André, Howard, Manningham, and "a good Number of Gentlemen more." Four days later, Lord Hervey could write, "All the eminent physicians, Surgeons, and Men-midwifes in London are there Day & Night to watch her next production."[56]

But, even though St. André summoned a crowd of medical men, it was Douglas he valued above the rest, and in the end it was Douglas's good opinion he courted more than any others'. Once, when Douglas refused to have anything further to do with the affair, St. André fell into a panic and "begg'd very earnestly that I would go and attend [Mary Toft] but a little while longer, or promise to come whenever he should send me Word; adding withal, that if he could once satisfy me about the Reality of the Thing, he did not care who else disbeliev'd it."[57]

At first glance, this exceptional reliance might appear odd, for no one could differ more from St. André than Douglas. St. André was excitable, straining to a conclusion on the basis of scanty, contradictory evidence; Douglas was methodical, learned, and skeptical, a man who dismissed the affair as a hoax as quickly as St. André embraced it as true. And yet, it was probably this difference in temperament (and hence in professional reputation and accomplishment) that so attracted St. André to Douglas. For Douglas was everything St. André was not, and much of what he pretended to be. St. André was an anatomist of dubious repute who found himself in a situation that required him to be an obstetrician. Douglas was one of the most respected anatomists in England and one of its best-known midwives. St. André was a member of the court, Anatomist and Surgeon to the Royal Household, but he was appointed, so it was rumored, only because he spoke German. Douglas's connection with the royal family was based on substantial merit. Already he had received a handsome gift from the king for his anatomical research, and within a year he would become Physician Extraordinary to Queen Caroline. Member of the Royal Society, Honorary Fellow of the College of Physicians, friend of Cheselden, Mead, and Sloane, Douglas embodied professional respectability. As a philologist, bibliophile, and expert on Horace, he was also a man of taste and learning.[58] Douglas, in short, was exactly the kind of associate St. André needed: a doctor of stature who, if convinced, could act as a mediator between him and the unbelieving world.

But if St. André had expected Douglas to bolster his position, he was to be severely disappointed, for Douglas believed almost from the beginning that the affair was a fraud, and he had freely declared his opinion in public before Mary Toft was ever brought to London. Since neither reason nor experience, he argued, supported the claim that a woman could give birth to rabbits, and since the structure of the uterus prevented rabbits from being thrust into it, Mary Toft's rabbits had to have been secretly hidden in her vagina: those medical men such as St. André who thought they had come out of the uterus were mistaken.

"These [reasons] I gave openly, as my Sentiments of the Matter, in all Companies where I had Occasion to mention it, while the Woman remain'd at *Guilford,* notwithstanding the repeated Confirmations of it, by new and specious Appearances of Facts, with which the Town was every Day alarm'd."[59]

In spite of his disbelief, Douglas accepted St. André's invitation and went to the bagnio. As soon as he arrived, Manningham told him about the suspicious membrane, and Douglas commented, "Surely this must be a Cheat." When he examined Mary Toft, who was then in labor, he saw nothing to persuade him to change his opinion. He told St. André straight out that "the Motions of her Belly were very different from those caused by a Child, or any other living animal; and therefore were probably Hysterick, or only Convulsive Contractions of the Muscles of the *Abdomen.*" St. André vigorously disagreed, but Douglas, not wishing to enter into a dispute, quickly changed the direction of the conversation.[60]

Douglas's refusal to argue was significant. He had been outspoken and openly incredulous before Mary Toft had been brought to London, but now that he himself was involved in the case, he became more silent, restrained, even evasive. It was a conscious strategy: "from the Time that the Woman was brought to the *Bagnio,* in *Leicester-Fields,* I did not so publickly and frequently talk against the Imposture, as I had before done; nor rail at those who suffer'd themselves to be impos'd on, with all the Ill-Nature and Noise with which some others continu'd to do."[61]

Douglas changed his conduct because he perceived what the stakes now were and how the tenor of the affair had altered. Mary Toft was no longer merely an object of medical curiosity. As the crowd in her room testified, the incident had become a public event, one whose issues were far more pressing than the medical questions it originally raised. The town was, as he said, "alarm'd," and professional reputations were in danger of being destroyed. Like St. André, he was struck with a sense of urgency, a feeling that the affair must be resolved quickly and publicly. But St. André's notion of a resolution was to surround himself with medical men and storm the public, dazzling them with the testimony of the learned. For Douglas, medical opinion had no value, or, even worse, it might be positively detrimental to a proper resolution:

> To be able to determine, to the Satisfaction and Conviction of all sorts of Persons, other Arguments were necessary, than Anatomy, or any other Branch of Physick, could furnish. Of these the greatest Number are not Judges. It was therefore undoubtedly very natural for me to desire that Peo-

ple would suspend any farther Judgment for a little Time, till such Proofs could be brought of the Imposture as they requir'd.

Like Manningham, Douglas felt the only thing to do was to wait for "the Event of the whole Transaction," for the arguments of anatomists and physicians would not settle the issue now that it had become so public. No, "a speedy Discovery of the Imposture" could be made only "by plain, sensible, and undeniable Facts," and the only facts that would be fully comprehended by the public would be those revealed by a confession or by actually catching the fraud being perpetrated.[62]

Thus, Douglas refused to engage in medical arguments with St. André. And he tried to restrain others. When he had first come to the bagnio, he had sent for his friend and fellow physician, William Cheselden. Cheselden, too, was skeptical, but Douglas stopped him from inquiring too closely into the medical aspects of the case: "Mr. *Cheselden* . . . ask'd Mr. *Howard* several Questions, which, however much to the purpose, I took the Liberty to tell him, I thought not at all proper at that Time." Later, when Amyand invited him to view a specimen of a rabbit Mary Toft had delivered earlier, Douglas declined, thinking "such Enquiries were improper at that Time." In public, he lapsed into equivocation. When "several Persons of Great Distinction and Worth did me the honour to ask me what had passed: I told them in general Terms, that no Delivery had as yet happen'd; that Mr. *St. André* and Mr. *Howard* still expected one very suddenly; and that I would not fail to give them Notice upon the first Appearances of any thing that look'd like it."[63]

With Douglas's determination to remain publicly noncommital, the event reached a kind of stasis. St. André needed the weight of Douglas's medical opinion to support his claims. Douglas refused to accept medical opinions as having any weight whatsoever. Both needed Mary Toft to deliver another rabbit—St. André so he could convince Douglas that such a birth actually happened, Douglas so he could detect the fraud in the act. But Mary Toft had last delivered a rabbit over a week previously, and she was not eager to risk a new attempt. The incident had long ago gotten out of her control. She had not wanted to come to London in the first place, and now that she was here and being continually watched, she had neither the opportunity nor the inclination to hazard another birth. Thus, all the main actors were perfectly stalemated.

This is how the affair remained between 30 November and 3 December. And the failure to resolve the question intensified the public's absorption in the event. The "Good Number of Gentlemen" Douglas had seen when he first entered Mary Toft's room presaged the crowds who were to throng into the bagnio during the next few days. Apparently, St. André exhibited her not only to the physicians, surgeons, and men-midwives whom he had invited, but to just about anyone who was curious to see her. "Great Numbers of the Nobility" came, and so did a "great resort" of the less highly connected, "the room being very full" almost continually. By the end of the week, Lord Hervey reported that "Every Creature in town both Men & Women have been to see & feel her."[64] Newspapers flooded London with reports of the activities at the bagnio, and many announced that a new delivery was expected shortly.

Although Mary Toft delivered no more rabbits, she continued to go into labor. She was badly infected by this time and her convulsions were probably involuntary. Once she went into a fit that made her lose consciousness for over two hours (a few days later, when she was at Bridewell, she was reported as being "very dangerously Ill").[65] Throughout these four days and nights, she was constantly attended by Howard, St. André, and Manningham, and often by Douglas. But with no new delivery, each construed the evidence to suit his own theory. For Howard and St. André, the convulsions signaled an impending birth, which they categorically predicted to each visitor to the bagnio. Manningham thought the convulsions were signs that something was still in her uterus. Douglas ascribed them to either hysteria or imposture. Sometimes there were misunderstandings. On Thursday, 1 December, Mary Toft was seized by pains. Manningham examined her and turned to Douglas: "I desired Dr. *Douglass,* who was then present, that *he* would please likewise examine her, and openly declare his Opinion, which he did, and in the hearing of several Persons of Distinction, profess'd that he found the *Vagina* clear, and was of the Opinion the Pains were of the same Nature with Labour-Pains." Douglas remembered the incident differently. He thought the appearance of labor was "very exactly counterfeited" and said "that from any thing in these Pains consider'd in themselves only, I was not able to distinguish them from such."[66]

Such misunderstandings were bound to happen in the atmosphere that had developed in the bagnio. And there were other, more serious conflicts, these caused by Howard and St. André's attempt to manipulate the public perception of the event by inviting people into Mary Toft's room to convince them of the truth of the monstrous births and by excluding those who remained skeptical. For instance, on Thursday, 1 December, the surgeon Thomas Brathwaite was admitted into her room. There, he strongly disagreed with St. André and Howard about the anatomy of the rabbits, and he bested them in the argument. When he came back a few days later, he found himself forbidden entrance.[67]

The conflicts and misunderstandings, the frustration of being caught in a situation that refused to reach an incontrovertible denouement, the sheer chaos caused by the spectators crowded in the bagnio, all began to wear on the emotions. When St. André showed Douglas the proof sheets of his *Short Narrative,* Douglas broke his resolve not to engage in medical squabbles by telling St. André that his pamphlet was "nothing but a collection of Impossibilities"; that it was inconceivable that animals could be brought to birth, as St. André argued, in the Fallopian tubes; that the story of the noise of snapping bones in the womb of Mary Toft was pure romance. The next day, Douglas completely lost his patience. When he went to visit Mary Toft, he was turned away because St. André and Howard were not there. "I told several Gentlemen, then at the Bagnio, that I was afraid some *new Monster* was breeding; and went away with the Resolution to return no more."[68]

St. André was horrified when he heard about the incident later that evening. He sent Douglas a note asking to speak with him; he sent two messengers the following morning, and another letter that noon. Finally, he visited Douglas in person and begged him to return.

It is impossible to know how long the conflicts and confusion would have lasted, but it is certain that, with no other evidence, there could be no satisfactory "Event of the whole Transaction."

VII

When the evidence that would resolve the issue came, it came quickly and from two different directions. While the main participants in London became increasingly immobilized in stalemate, Thomas, second Lord Onslow, Lord Lieutenant of Surrey and Justice of the Peace, set out on his own investigation in Godalming and Guildford. He questioned residents of both places and discovered that, when Mary Toft was in Guildford under the care of Howard, Joshua Toft had been scurrying around the countryside buying up an inordinate number of young rabbits. And, contemptuous of the dupes who had rushed down from London to examine his wife, he had spoken recklessly. He freely had admitted to the sellers that he was taking the rabbits to his wife in Guildford (and, to make the matter worse, Mrs. Mason swore that she had never once dressed a rabbit for Mary Toft while she was under her care there). Once, when he was told that the rabbits he wanted to buy were much too small for eating, Joshua responded that "small or what they wou'd he must have them." Another time, having been informed that the only rabbit for sale had died the night before and had been discarded, he replied, "If you had not thrown it away, it would have done as well for me as a live one." Onslow discovered one further thing: "That *Mary Toft*'s Husband had frequent Conference with his Sister, who attended his Wife." Clearly, Onslow implied, Margaret Toft acted as the intermediary who passed the rabbits from Joshua to Mary Toft.[69] Onslow was able to find six witnesses to all this suspicious behavior. On 4 December, he sent their depositions to London.

Had nothing else been learned, such information would certainly have hastened the end of the hoax. As it turned out, even more compelling evidence was uncovered at the very same time Onslow was taking the depositions. Thomas Howard—not John Howard's older brother, but a porter at Mr. Lacy's bagnio—was caught trying to sneak a rabbit into Mary Toft's room. He had been talked into procuring the smallest rabbit he could find by Margaret Toft.

The porter confessed before Manningham, Douglas, and Lord Albemarle, but they did not immediately act on the information. It was thought, as Douglas said, not "convenient to divulge the Piece of News, till the next Day, that more effectual Measures might be taken to come at the whole Truth."[70] The truth is that Manningham and Douglas no longer considered such evidence adequate, and it is a sign of how grave they thought the affair was that they required something more. Even when they received the depositions Onslow had collected, they did not think them sufficient. Circumstantial evidence, no matter how convincing, was not enough; if the matter was to be cleared up before the public, proof of the fraud must be unequivocal, and the only unequivocal evidence was a confession. And so extracting an admission of guilt from Mary Toft became the goal of Manningham and Douglas, and it was a goal they began to work toward with dogged single-mindedness.

They did not tell Mary Toft what they had discovered but continued to act as before. When she began to have violent contractions in the late afternoon of 4 December, they examined her again. Manningham was astonished to see a swelling above the os pubis and announced that he "apprehended that something would soon issue from the *Uterus*." Douglas, too, was surprised and at first could not explain the cause of the swelling, though later in the day he attributed it to "flatulent Humours." Howard and St. André, of course, were ecstatic. In the teeth of the evidence now accumulated against their patient, they briefly regained their optimism and "very confidently assured" the crowd in the bagnio that the contractions and swelling were "the Forerunners of Labour." But gradually, all signs of an impending birth subsided.[71]

Obviously, the affair would not be resolved unless pressure were put on Mary Toft. On the evening of 4 December, Sir Thomas Clarges, Justice of the Peace, was called to the bagnio. Thomas Howard, the porter, swore a deposition before him. Clarges immediately took Mary Toft into custody and questioned her harshly. She denied everything. Her sister-in-law was then examined and admitted that she had asked the porter to obtain a rabbit clandestinely. Mary Toft was questioned again. She insisted that she had been taken with an overwhelming longing for a rabbit and that her only intention was to eat it. She confessed to nothing beyond that.

Clarges was angry and wanted to put Mary Toft in prison that night. But Manningham, as much as Douglas, wanted to be able to present to the public irrefutable evidence that the affair was a hoax, and with great difficulty he persuaded Clarges to leave her at the bagnio. Indeed, his major preoccupation for the next two days was keeping the Justice of the Peace at bay, and he spent much of his time securing the assistance of "Persons of Distinction" to keep the infuriated Clarges from bringing Mary Toft to swift justice. He called on Molyneux for help. "That our Endeavours fully to detect the Cheat may prove most effectual, and the unnatural Imposture may most clearly appear to the Publick," he wrote to Molyneux,

> I think *Mary Toft* should by no means be sent to Prison, till the Truth comes out; but that she should rather be kept, and most strictly watched in some private House, where all Persons, those of the Faculty especially, may have free and convenient Access to her, which a Prison will not so well afford, till the Matter be as plainly and fully detected as possible.[72]

From the night of the fourth, Mary Toft was beseiged. Although she was not sent to prison, she was confined to the bagnio and continually pressured to confess. Sir Thomas Clarges threatened her. Manningham and Douglas expostulated with her. She was exhorted by the Duke of Montagu and Lord Baltimore. There were promises of leniency. For two days, Mary Toft held out, insisting all the while that she truly had given birth to rabbits. Finally Manningham made a threat that she could not stand up under. He said that, given her uncommon labor and births, she must be differently formed than other women and that he was "resolved to try a very painful Experiment on her" by performing an operation to discover her secret.[73] Mary Toft asked to think the matter over and said that if she did not confess by the next morning, she would allow Manningham to proceed with the operation.

On the morning of 7 December, in the presence of the Dukes of Richmond and Montagu, Manningham, and Douglas, Mary Toft began her confession. "I will not goe on any longer thus[.] I shall sooner hang myself." It is not clear whether her anguish was caused by her guilt or by the extraordinary pressure she had been subjected to in the last few days. Her lament was entered in the fair copy of her confession and then heavily scored through.

In her confession, Mary Toft dwelt on her pain and detailed the events of the first few weeks in Godalming and Guildford. But, as she drew closer to the central issue of the hoax itself, her story became less and less plausible. She said that, soon after her miscarriage, she accidentally met a woman whom she did not know then and could not now identify. The scheme of giving birth to rabbits was the stranger's, and it was performed entirely under her direction.

The next day, unconvinced, Manningham and Douglas pressed her further. She abandoned the story of the mysterious stranger and said that her mother-in-law was responsible for the hoax. She herself was innocent and thought that she had actually given birth to rabbits. She hinted that perhaps Mr. Howard had plotted with Ann Toft.

This story was not entirely credible either. But it was sufficient. It amounted to a confession—or at least to an acknowledgment that the affair was a fraud. And that was all that was needed. Mary Toft was charged with being a Notorious and Vile Cheat and, on 9 December, she was sent to Bridewell. The evidence was unequivocal. The public could now be satisfied.

VIII

The public, as it turned out, was not satisfied. It was not that they believed anymore that Mary Toft gave birth to rabbits—Manningham and Douglas's extraction of a confession succeeded in dispelling any confidence in her claims. No, what proved unsatisfactory was the conduct of the medical men. Now that the details were becoming known, it was felt that the doctors must have had a hand in the hoax or had to have been completely taken in themselves. The doctors brought more suspicion on themselves by rushing into print with their self-vindications.

St. André published *A Short Narrative of an Extraordinary Delivery of Rabbets* on 3 December, the very day the porter of the bagnio was caught trying to sneak a rabbit to Mary Toft. The fact that St. André would allow it to be published at the very moment the hoax was collapsing can be interpreted either as a desperate last attempt to manipulate public opinion or as an extraordinary gesture of blind self-confidence. In his pamphlet, St. André proclaimed that the births were genuine, printed the affadavits he and Howard had gathered to show that Ahlers was not to be trusted, announced that he would "with all convenient speed publish the Anatomy of these Præternatural Rabbets, with their Figures taken from the Life, and compared with the Parts of Rabbets of the same growth, that the differences . . . may be fully understood," and, most astonishing of all, given the fact that Mary Toft had delivered her seventeenth and last rabbit over a week earlier, promised that "the Account of the Delivery of the eighteenth Rabbet, shall be Published by way of a Appendix to this Account."[74] On 8 December, he had to write a retraction:

> Having contributed, in some measure, to the Belief of an Impostor, in a Narrative lately published by me, of an extraordinary Delivery of *Rabbits,* performed by Mr. *Howard,* Surgeon, of *Guildford;* and having been since instrumental in discovering the same; so that I am now thoroughly convinc'd it is a most abominable Fraud: I think myself obliged, in strict regard to the Truth, to acquaint the Publick thereof; and that I intend, in a short time, to publish a full Account of this Discovery, with some Considerations on the Extraordinary Circumstances of this Case, which misled me in my Apprehensions thereof; and which as I hope they will, in some measure, excuse the Mistakes made by myself, and others, who have visited the woman concerned therein, will also be acceptable to the World, in separating the Innocent from those who have been guilty Actors of this Fraud.[75]

St. André never wrote his promised account, but the press was not wanting business. Immediately, other pamphlets began to appear. Ahlers, who considered himself slandered by the innuendoes contained in the depositions St. André had included at the end of *A Short Narrative,* put out *Some Observations Concerning the Woman of Godlyman,* in which he vindicated his own behavior and accused Howard of conspiring with Mary Toft. Manningham, whose actions and opinions seem to have been misunderstood by almost everyone—he was, as one contemporary journal put it, "by some Ill-designing People misrepresented, as favoring Mr. *St. André's* Opinion"[76]—published on 12 December *An Exact Diary of what was observ'd during a Close Attendance Upon Mary Toft* to explain why he acted as he did. Doctors who had played no role in the affair began to respond in print too, concerned that the hoax had damaged the reputation of the profession as a whole. The most popular work of this kind was *The Anatomist Dissected* by "Lemuel Gulliver," which, though sometimes descending to scurrilous personal attacks, especially on St. André, exposed the doctors' mishandling of the case by appealing in the main to reason and medical theory, suitably popularized for a broad audience.

Some of this informed discussion lasted into the next week. One person exhibited an "ANATOMY of HUMAN BODIES in COLOUR'D WAX, . . . in which, by Ocular Demonstration, the Formation of Rabbits in those Parts is entirely confuted; and whereby those worthy Gentlemen who have detected the Falsity, may in their Accounts be thoroughly understood." Thomas Brathwaite published *Remarks on A Short Narrative of an Extraordinary Delivery of Rabbets,* in which he examined the affair with something approaching reason and restraint. But by now everyone was ravenous to know everything about the hoax. Within a week, Brathwaite's *Remarks* went into a second edition, *The Anatomist Dissected* into a third, and Grub Street was willing to further exploit the public's fascination. John Laguerre issued a mezzotint showing Mary Toft seated in a chair with a rabbit in her lap. The documents St. André published over a year earlier describing his poisoning were reprinted as a pamphlet. A broadside purported to print the suicide note of Mary Toft. Much of the new work took what to the doctors was an alarming direction. The comic spectacle of the doctors "flinging their bitter pills at one another, to convince the world that none of them understand anything of the matter," called more for ridicule than reason, and there was an explosion of satiric prose, verse, and prints that mocked all the doctors savagely and indiscriminately. "Shake 'em all in a bag," remarked one satirist, "and the best will come first."[77] Everyone was grist for the satiric mills. Manningham and even Douglas, whose exemplary behavior should have put him beyond attack, found themselves lampooned. Their decision to await "the Event of the whole Transaction," a sensible and responsible policy, in the end undid them, for as soon as they published accounts explaining their actions, their initial silence was interpreted in the worst possible light and their explanations rejected as lies.

There was, in fact, no way for those who had been involved in the affair to salvage their reputations whole. If they protested that they were unjustly accused, they merely confirmed the public's belief that they were hiding their gullibility or, worse, their guilt. The best any of them could hope for was that the incident would fade from the public view. In the interim, it was probably best to suffer the flood of satire in silence. Howard promised "to publish to the World, a particular Account of all that occurred to my Knowledge, relating to *Mary Toft* of *Godalmin,*" but like St. André's promised "full Account" of the cheat, this never saw the light of day. Manningham, after his *Exact Diary* was received with incredulity, wrote and even had printed a further clarification of his behavior, but at the last minute he decided not to distrib-

ute it, presumably because he saw how futile any attempt at self-vindication now would be. Douglas planned to write a medical treatise
proving the impossibility of Mary Toft's giving birth to rabbits. But he,
too, abandoned his project after drafting only a dozen pages of rough
notes.[78]

Gradually, the intense interest in the affair did die out, and London
turned its attention to other diversions, other worries. By mid-January,
John Byrom was writing from London, "Everybody here talks of war,
and Gibraltar, and South Sea, and Ostend, &."[79] The Mary Toft affair
had come to an end.

But, in one sense, there was no event to the whole transaction.
Byrom added a personal aside to his list of the new affairs that were
monopolizing the attention of Londoners: "Everybody here talks of
war, and Gibraltar, and South Sea, and Ostend, &c., while my mind is
running upon . . . Toft." Although the incident disappeared from public view, throughout the century it lay just on the threshold of consciousness, provoking a kind of wonder and disquiet and resurfacing
in new, sometimes oblique forms. Within months, it occasioned the
Turner-Blondel controversy, a significant embryological debate that
continued for decades. In a little more than a year, Pope published the
first version of his great poem, the *Dunciad,* which has at its center a
woman who prolifically gives birth to monsters. Hogarth returned to
the subject over thirty years afterwards in his masterpiece attacking
enthusiastic religion, "Credulity, Superstition, and Fanaticism." References to the affair occur repeatedly throughout the century.

For the major actors, however, the consequences of the incident
were much more immediate. Manningham and Douglas suffered
embarrassment, but it was momentary. The reputations of both men
were secure, and their involvement in the affair ultimately had little
effect on their careers. For St. André, it was different. He lost favor at
court. A year later, the scandal with Molyneux's wife completed his
ruin, and he retired from London for the rest of his life. There is a
story, perhaps apocryphal, that he never allowed rabbits to appear on
his table afterwards.

Howard suffered the most. Having assisted in the monstrous births
from the beginning, he naturally came under a great deal of suspicion.
He was bound over for the first time in early December. He swore his
innocence, but the authorities must have thought they had a good case
against him, for in early January, he "was oblig'd to enter into a fresh
Recognizance of £800 to appear and answer to a Charge of his being
concerned in the Cheat and Conspiracy of Mary Toft, the Rabbit-
Woman; a Constable having made an Affidavit of an odd sort of Con-

versation he heard pass between the said Mr. Howard and Mary Toft, thro' a partition at the Bagnio in Leicester-Fields." But the case against Howard was ultimately dropped, and in the end his good name probably was not damaged. On a survey map of Guildford, 1737, he is listed at the head of the Jury of Baillifs who commissioned the work, and his house is one of the few identified on it. Obviously, he remained respected in Guildford.[80]

The case against Mary Toft was dismissed. Since the evidence for her guilt was certainly strong enough, I can only speculate that those in authority thought either that she had been punished sufficiently by her imprisonment at Bridewell or that further prosecution of her case might embarrass others who had been embarrassed enough.[81]

Mary Toft was rarely heard of again. Charles, second Duke of Richmond, who had a residence in Godalming, occasionally showed her at dinner parties as a curiosity. In 1740, London newspapers reported that she had been charged with receiving stolen goods.[82] Her name appeared once more in the London newspapers in January 1763, when they announced that she had died. The Godalming parish register records her burial for 13 January 1763, after which date is written "Mary Toft, Widow, the Impostress Rabbitt. . . ." The remainder of the epitaph is completely illegible, and even this beginning is barely discernible under the heavy scoring, done by whose hand and for what reason I do not know.

2

DOCTORS IN LABOR

I

 The Mary Toft affair is very puzzling. Not the hoax itself, of course, for the motives behind it and the manner in which it was carried off are understood easily enough. What is puzzling about the Mary Toft affair is the reaction to it.

There is, first and most vexing of all, the question of how such an improbable story could have held sway over so many people for so long. Surely, the credulity of a few doctors like Howard and St. André was not responsible for the success of the hoax. The frenetic excitement engendered by the event could not have seized London unless there had existed some widespread predisposition to believe—or perhaps to fear—that there was something to Mary Toft's story. The crowds who flocked to the bagnio where Mary Toft was lodged, even if they initially were drawn by curiosity or by the ambiance of a social fête that sometimes hovered around the "viewings" of the woman, did not long retain their amused detachment. Many went away believers. London poulters experienced a precipitous drop in the sale of rabbits since few dared to put them on their tables.[1]

How many believed her story? It is impossible to say with any certainty. A few years after the event, James Bramston wrote:

> New Stories always should with Truth agree,
> Or Truth's half-Sister, Probability:
> Scarce could *Toft's* Rabbits and pretended throws
> On half the Honourable House Impose.

There is no evidence that half the members of Parliament believed Mary Toft. But there is evidence that some did. William Whiston recalls that the story was "believed by my old Friends the Speaker [Arthur Onslow], and Mr. *Samuel Collet,* as they told me themselves, and was generally believed by sober Persons in the Neighbourhood [of Guildford]."[2]

"Sober Persons": so, belief in Mary Toft's claims was not confined to the credulous at all. Those who perpetrated the hoax may have been knaves, but those who were taken in by it were not fools. The anonymous writer of *The Anatomist Dissected* felt compelled to write his exposé because "so many Persons of distinguished Sense and Figure" had been "gull'd and deluded by so coarse and palpable a Fraud." Another writer was disconcerted to find that "many not unlearned Persons" had taken her claims seriously. Lord Onslow began his investigation of the affair when he saw that "people of sound judgment" believed Mary Toft. In Oxford, the learned Thomas Hearne eagerly followed the case closely in the newspapers and wrote with obvious excitement that "no doubt is made about the Truth of the Fact." Even the skeptical Lord Hervey seems to have been taken aback: "I know you laugh now, & think I joke, but the fact as reported & attested by St. Andre (who swares he deliver'd her of five) is something that really stagger's one."[3]

There were those who did not believe her—and were willing to say so—even before the affair was revealed to be a hoax. On 3 December, when there still was no solid evidence of a cheat, *The British Journal* briefly reported the event and curtly rejected it:

> The Rabbit-Woman of *Godalmin* near *Guilford*, so much talk'd of, is brought to this City, and lodged at the *Bagnio* in *Leicester Fields*, and is bringing forth more and more Rabbits: A fine Story! *Credat Judæus Appella.*

But what is remarkable about this statement is how anomalous it is. In point of fact, it is difficult to find anyone who was willing to deny the story before the hoax was exposed. Afterwards, of course, everyone denied that he had ever believed her at all:

> No notice has hitherto been taken in this paper of the Woman at Godalmin near Guildford in Surrey, said to have been deliver'd of sixteen or seventeen Rabbits, it being a filthy Story at best, and having withal the Appearance of Imposture. That Matter is now under strict Examination, . . .[4]

Was its being "a filthy Story" the real motive behind their silence? Perhaps.[5] But one contemporary newspaper wondered "why so many learned Surgeons have midwived their jokes into the world after St. André had smelt out the Cheat of the Rabbets and why so few of them laughed at him before." Before it was revealed to be a hoax, Lord Hervey observed that "the whole philosophical World is divided into two partys . . . , & between the downright affirmation on the one hand for the reality of the fact, & the philosophical proofs of the impossibility of it on the other, no body knows which they are to believe, their Eyes or their Ears." Indeed, people appear to have been much more uncertain and hesitant than their later protestations of disbelief would suggest. Some candidly admitted that the real reason they said nothing was because they genuinely were confused about what to believe:

> There have hitherto, been so many various Stories about the Woman of *Godalmin,* in *Surrey,* who is said to have bred several RABBITS, in her UTERUS, that we have thought fit to forbear taking Notice of them; till that Matter was fully clear'd; when we shall give our Readers a full Account of it.[6]

Our ordinary notions of "belief" and "disbelief," in fact, may be too broad and too crude to define precisely the way in which people experienced the Mary Toft incident. Rarely did anyone respond one way or another with real conviction: they tentatively were willing to entertain the possibility that she had given birth to rabbits or they just as tentatively were inclined to doubt her. Occasionally, someone would respond both ways at once. A particularly revealing instance is Samuel Molyneux. Molyneux, after his trip to Guildford with St. André, wrote for his own use an account of his visit. While St. André was writing his *Short Narrative,* he asked Molyneux to draw up a statement on the basis of his account that St. André could print in his own pamphlet. If St. André hoped for some substantial corroboration, he was disappointed, for Molyneux's public demeanor in this situation was a masterpiece of judiciousness, restraint, impartiality—and evasion. He affirmed only the accuracy of St. André narration of events, not the truth of Mary Toft's claims:

> I have carefully read the above Narrative. Whether the Animals mentioned therein were præternaturally produced in this Woman, or that a Fraud is practicable in this Case, I do not take on me to say; Gentlemen who are sufficient Judges will determine that Matter upon proper Evidence; I can only certify, That I did draw up a Relation as is above-mentioned, which, in the most material Circumstances of Fact, agrees with this Narrative; and I can further affirm, that I did not perceive the least Circumstance of Fraud in the Conduct of this Affair while I was at *Guilford.*

But, according to Whiston, this is not how Molyneux behaved in less public circumstances:

> Mr. *Molyneux,* the Prince's Secretary, a very inquisitive Person, and my very worthy Friend, assured me, he had at first so great a Diffidence in the Truth of the Fact, and was so little biassed by the other Believers, even by the King himself, that he would not be satisfied till he was permitted both to see and feel the Rabbet in that very Passage whence we all come into this World out

of our Mother's Womb. Accordingly he told me, he had more Evidence for it, than he had that I had a Nose; whilst he had known that by one of his Senses only, that of seeing, but knew this by two of his Senses, both seeing and feeling.

And Molyneux evidently put enough credit in Mary Toft's story that, when Whiston told him that her monstrous births fulfilled the prophecy of Esdras foretelling the Final Judgment, he became so upset that Whiston was able to calm him down only by reminding him of the "joyful prediction . . . that good Men would be providentially preserved." Molyneux left an equally strong impression on Lord Hervey: "Mr. Mollineux . . . swore to me that he him-self when she was in Labour, took one part of one of the Rabbits out of her Body."[7] Did or did not Molyneux believe Mary Toft's claims? He certainly implied that he did to Whiston, and when he spoke to Hervey, Molyneux even embroidered on events to imply that he had actually delivered Mary Toft of the head of a rabbit, though all the evidence shows that he did no such thing.[8] And yet, to the public, he presented himself so equivocally that, no matter what the upshot, he could never be cornered.

Nor was Molyneux the only one to shift his tone and bearing to suit his audience. Dr. Arbuthnot acted in a very similar way. Arbuthnot was one of those doctors who had flocked to see Mary Toft, and on the evening of Friday, 2 December, he left the bagnio a believer, or at least that was the impression he gave Hervey: "I was last Night to see her with Dr. Arbuthnot," wrote Lord Hervey, "who is convinced of the truth of what St. André relates."[9] But earlier that same day, Douglas was led to believe just the opposite. In an early draft of *An Advertisement,* Douglas recounted his meeting with Dr. Arbuthnot: "Friday nothing remarkable, but that in about noon I was denyd admittance when I wanted to see her, Mr. Howard & Mr. André being both abroad; Sir Rich[ar]d Manningham (which I thought lookd very strange) justifyed the maid in refusing to open the Door. This I told Dr Arbuthnot & others who was by that I was affraid something was hatching who were all of my opinion."[10] At noon, Arbuthnot implied to Douglas that he found the incident suspicious. In the evening of that same day, he gave Lord Hervey the impression that he believed the truth of Mary Toft's story. A few days later, he would write a poem satirizing the whole affair. What, in fact, *did* Arbuthnot believe?

I have, perhaps, made Molyneux and Arbuthnot appear to be greater hypocrites than they were. Surely the significant point in the cases of both men is their willingness to apportion their enthusiasm or doubt to their specific audience and to the color of the moment, giving an impression of assent to a true believer like Whiston or a half-believer like Lord Hervey, sympathetically professing skepticism to an angry Douglas, equivocating when forced to put their thoughts in print, laughing at the folly of the affair when there was no danger of being wrong. It seems almost meaningless to ask whether Molyneux and Arbuthnot "believed" or "disbelieved" Mary Toft's claims; the sheer pliancy of their responses betrays a real unsettledness and lack of certainty.

In dealing with the reactions of many people to the affair, we are often in this hazy psychological realm where distinctions between belief and disbelief are not clear-cut and where degrees of conviction are hard to measure. One *could* be of two minds, and some were willing to say so openly. After the physician Thomas Deacon heard about Mary Toft from his friend John Byrom, he wrote this reply from Manchester:

> As to your rabbits, if there is good evidence I shall certainly believe the FACT, and when you can bring as good proof of a cheat, I will believe that; but at present I neither believe nor disbelieve; because I do not suppose the matter has as yet been thoroughly examined on both sides.[11]

Lord Hervey's observation that the whole incident "really stagger's one" was accurate, for all the evidence indicates that most people were thrown off balance. Hence the enormous desire to *see,* the compulsion to look at the facts, to refrain from judgment until all could be observed more closely. Thus the king brought Mary Toft to London so her claims could be looked into; the crowds thronged to the bagnio to get a view of the woman; the doctors decided to await "the Event of the whole Transaction," to wait to see what would happen. This attitude possessed nearly everyone, including those who were disinclined to believe her. Pope wrote to his friend John Caryll, Sr., who lived near Guildford:

> I want to know what faith you have in the miracle at Guildford; not doubting but as you past thro' that town, you went as a philosopher to investigate, if not as a curious anatomist to inspect, that wonderful phenomenon. All London is now upon this occasion, as it generally is upon all others divided into factions about it.[12]

The bantering tone suggests that Pope did not put much stock in the assertions of Mary Toft. Even so, there is an element of reserve, a pulling back from fully committing himself to a final judgment. The bantering itself, by directing the humor at the anatomists, philosophers, and "factions," allows him to avoid commenting one way or another on Mary Toft's claims and, most importantly, it protects him sufficiently so that he can bring himself to ask the question which, without the banter, he might have been too embarrassed to ask out-right. This is the letter's quite clear purpose: perhaps Caryll was an eyewitness, and the poet wants to know what he has seen. Even Pope, probably unconvinced by Mary Toft's claims, harbored a desire to see.

And what about those who unequivocally dismissed her claims before she confessed to the fraud—someone like Douglas, say, who asserted in *An Advertisement* that "upon the first News I heard of this Affair, I was firmly persuaded the whole was a Trick; so no Part of my Conduct, after the Woman was brought to Town, can have given any just Ground for imagining that I either really did, or was ever inclin'd to change my Opinion"?[13] But Douglas's statement occurs in a passage which has been considerably revised, and in this case we are lucky enough to have evidence of what actually went on behind these protes-tations of disbelief. In an early draft of *An Advertisement,* he spoke with less assurance. Here is what he originally wrote but never published:

> From the very first time I heard the Report of Womans being deliver'd of Rabbits at Guildford, I declar'd in all Companys where I had occasion to talke of it, that I believ'd it false. . . . When the pretended Mother was brought to town, represented still to be big with something, at Mr. St. Andre's request I had the Curiosity to go and see her; and having heard the whole story from his own Mouth and Mr. Howard's with many other Cir-cumstances than he thought proper to be publish'd, and especially being desir'd by them to deliver the woman my self, that thereby the Truth of what they had advanced might be put beyond all possibility of dispute; I then began to think I had gone to farr in openly denying the truth of a fact which tho next to an impossibility, could not be prov'd to be really impossi-ble, and their Conduct appear'd to me in the instance already mention'd so perfectly candid and fair, that I could not help expressing my self so farr in a different manner from what I had done befor, as to desire that the town would suspend any farther Judgment, till I should have an opportunity either of delivering the Woman in case any thing presented, or of discover-ing the trick, and the Authors of it in doing which I was resolv'd to spare no pains nor time. This is all the lenth I ever went, and the substance of all I said upon the Matter, and you are too well acquainted with the Caution that is necessary in examining extraordinary phenomena of Nature either real or pretended, and with regard due to the reputation of all persons who have the least shadow of any to lose, not to be convinced that my conduct was every way suitable both to the dictates of Philosophy, and the Obligations of Society; . . . I need not tell you that all our knowledge of Nature is drawn from experience, that the Laws we deduce from thence are founded on Induction, and consequently can no otherwise be deem'd universall that as no exception to them has been discover'd. Those which Nature observes in the formation of a foetus in particular are as yet but very imperfectly known, and it must certainly be a very great presumption in any man from the small insight he has into them, to venture to binde the effects thereof

any farther than experience directs him, or affirm it Impossible that any
assign'd Phenomenon should ever happen, the existence of which does not
Imply a Contridiction in its Idea. If together with this reflection youll please
to recollect the Instances of Monstrous births already recorded by Pare
Licetus Lamswerde and others, I believe you will own that if these Gentlemen have by good luck been in the right in denying the truth of this particular fact, they have been as certainly mistaken in the foundation on which
they have grounded their Opinion.[14]

In his published account, Douglas gave other reasons why he became
less vocal in his attacks after he saw Mary Toft: he did not want to
alarm the town any further; he wanted all judgment suspended until
he could offer irrefutable proof of the fraud. But, as his early draft
shows, these were neither his principal nor his first reactions. Douglas,
the most articulate debunker, paused for at least one moment, probably
longer, and entertained the possibility that there was some truth to
Mary Toft's story.

The fact of the matter is, almost everyone for whom any record
exists appears to have entertained the possibility that Mary Toft's
claims were true. As late as 1750, William Whiston was arguing in
print that, in spite of her confession that it was all a hoax, she really had
given birth to rabbits.[15]

II

Mary Toft's claims were not dismissed out-of-hand by "sober Persons"
because there were sound intellectual reasons for not dismissing them.
Douglas defended his own suspension of judgment as "suitable . . . to
the dictates of Philosophy," and indeed, he would have been remiss
had he not entertained the possibility that Mary Toft's story was true,
for he was heir to a huge body of writings on monstrosity which had
begun to flood Europe two hundred years earlier and which continued
unabated to his own day, and these put forward hundreds of "Instances
of Monstrous births," as he said, as well as creditable medical explanations that perhaps could account for her rabbits.

The sheer volume of this literature of monsters was immense, span-
ning everything from popular ballads and broadsides to recondite treatises. Some of it was religious, seeking to find in each singular birth a
portent or sign. Much of it was of a more profane character, trading off
an uncritical fascination in the marvelous, often collected in profusely
illustrated, encyclopedic volumes: Pierre Boaistuau's *Histoires prodi-
gieuses,* for instance, which went through at least thirty editions in
French, Dutch, and English; the almost equally popular *Monstrorum*

Historia by Ulisses Aldrovandus; and, in England, the collections of "wonders" by Nathaniel Wanley and William Turner. But much of this literature was learned. Writers like Riolanus and Cardanus (both of whom Douglas consulted for his own treatise, later abandoned, to prove the impossibility of Mary Toft's births) investigated the philosophical and theological implications of monsters. And much of this work, such as Ambroise Paré's *Des monstres et prodigies* and Licetus's *De Monstrorum Caussis, Natura, et Differentiis* (both of which Douglas cited as important sources for cases of monstrous births) submitted these anomalies to the rigors of medical theory and the laws of natural science, a line of examination carried into eighteenth-century England by the numerous reports on monsters in the *Philosophical Transactions.*[16]

All together, this literature presented a multitude of examples of monstrous births, many of them as extraordinary as Mary Toft's, for it was not uncommon for women to give birth to animals (Paré alone cited instances of women bearing frogs, worms, snakes, lizards, strange beasts like harpies, creatures resembling tailless rats, and eels). Many of the cases were apocryphal, many others clearly frauds, but by the time of the Mary Toft affair there had grown such a huge catalogue of "Instances of Monstrous births" that few men of science or learning would deny that there might be some truth to the claims being made by the young woman from Godalming.

Douglas and his contemporaries were heirs, too, to a doctrine that could explain how Mary Toft had given birth to rabbits, the doctrine that the mother's imagination had the power to mark or even shape her fetus. By 1726, this had become the most commonly accepted explanation for monstrous births, and the instances of monstrosity caused by the imagination would alone furnish out a good-sized catalogue. As one contemporary confessed, "It would be endless to recite the strange *Impressions* of *Pregnating Women* on their *Fœtus* in the Womb, by the Force of Imagination."[17] This doctrine of prenatal influence was a staple of midwifery texts:

> And though the child hath its soul, while it is in the womb, it depends upon the soul of the mother, as the fruits partake of the life of the tree while they are upon it, therefore it is probable, that whatsoever moves the faculties of the soul in the mother may move the same in the child: Hence it is that while the forming [faculty?] operateth in the seed and womb of the mother, if any species be sent to the imagination of the mother which she strongly receives, it may make an impression upon the child, yet every imagination cannot make this impression, but that which makes a great admiration and terrour in the mother when the forming faculty is at work, and when she beholds one with six fingers, she brings forth the like, or

when she produces hair where it should not be, or the likeness of a beast in any limb, or when she sees any thing cut or divided with a Cleaver, she brings forth a divided part or Hare-Lip.[18]

It was this belief (along with its corollary, that stimulating the mother's imagination with a beautiful object would produce a beautiful child) that stood behind many of the period's proscriptions regulating the expectant mother's behavior:

> Ye Pregnant Wives, whose Wish it is, and Care,
> To bring your Issue, and to breed it Fair,
> On what you look, on what you think, beware.
>   When in the Womb the Forming Infant Grows,
> And Swelling Beauties shew a Teeming Spouse;
> All Melancholly, Spleen, and anxious Care,
> All Sights Obscene, that shock the Eyes, forbare.
> But a fair Picture, and a beauteous Face,
> By Fancy's mighty Pow'r, refine the Race.
> The Spirits to the Brain the Form convey,
> Which thence the Seed receives, while Nature works her way.
> On ev'ry Part th' Imprinted Image stays,
> And with the *Foetus* grows the borrow'd Grace.
> Strong are the Characters which Fancy makes,
> And good, and bad, the ripe Conception takes.
> As when the Wheaten Mass is work'd to Dough,
> Or swells with Leaven in the Kneading-Trough,
> It takes whatever Marks the Maker gives,
> And from the Baker's hand its Form receives.
> So works the Fancy on the Female Mold,
> And Women shou'd beware what they behold.[19]

Merely looking at or thinking about an object, of course, would not deform the child. The mother's imagination had to be excited in some fashion: by a surprise or sudden fright, an intense or prolonged affection or repugnance, or an unsatisfied longing. But once the fancy was wrought up, it could mark and shape the fetus in a variety of ways:

> But however, to come closer to the IMAGINATION of Pregnant *Women,* who knows not that it affects the INFANT in the *Womb*? Whence is it then that we have so many *deform'd Persons, crooked Bodies, ugly Aspects, distorted Mouths, wry Noses,* and the like, in all Countries; but from the IMAGINATION of the *Mother*; while she either conceives such shapeless *Phantasms* in her *Mind,* or while she frequently and intently fixes her *Eyes* upon such *deform'd Persons* or disagreeable OBJECTS? Wherefore is it very wrong, and highly imprudent in *Women* that have conceived, to please themselves so much in playing with *Dogs, Squirrels, Apes,* &c. carrying them

in their *Laps* or *Bosoms,* and feeding, kissing, or hugging them, as I have both often heard and seen with my own Eyes.

And besides, the same is the case, when the *Natural Faculties* are all at work in *forming,* or ripening the FOETUS; for if the *Woman* be surpriz'd at any sudden Evil, or *frighted* at any unseemly Sight, the *Humours* and *Spirits* presently retire downwards and (as it were) abscond themselves in the *Recess* of the WOMB: From whence immediately a strong IMAGINA-TION of the disagreeable *Thing* (whether *seen* or *heard* only) seizes her *Mind*; and the *Forming Faculty* (going on in the *Interim*) quickly impresses the *Imaginary Idea* of *That* thing heard of, or the *Shape* and *Form* of *That* thing seen, upon the FOETUS. The same is the *Reason,* that if a *Mouse, Rat, Weazel, Cat,* or the like, leaps suddenly upon a woman that has conceived, or if an *Apple, Pear, Cherry,* &c. fall upon any part of her *Body*; the MARK of the thing (be what it will) is instantly *imprinted,* and will manifestly appear on the same *Part,* or *Member* of the CHILD: . . .[20]

The prenatal influence of the imagination was an ancient theory. Undoubtedly predating written records, it had been espoused in one form or another for millennia, and by the time of the Mary Toft hoax it had been, as one commentator wrote, "proved by infinite authorities": Empedocles, Hesiod, Hippocrates, Galen, Plato, Plutarch, Pliny, Cicero, Avicenna, St. Jerome, St. Augustine, St. Thomas Aquinas, Albertus Magnus, Scaliger, and Martin Luther were just some of the more prestigious authorities who argued for the point, or who were thought to have done so.[21] The doctrine even had divine sanction. The story of Jacob making his ewes give birth to the spotted and streaked lambs by placing stippled rods before the rutting sheep was almost unanimously interpreted to be an example of the power of the imagination.

The doctrine was so well established by the early eighteenth century, in fact, that it had overshadowed all other explanations of the causes of monstrous birth, and it was turned to almost automatically to account for a wide variety of anomalies and malformations. This had not always been the case. For example, in 1573, Ambriose Paré had listed over a dozen causes of deformities and monsters: they were formed by God to manifest his glory or his wrath; they resulted from too much or too little semen; from the narrowness or smallness of the uterus; from the bad posture of the mother (such as sitting cross-legged); from a blow to the mother, or a fall; from hereditary or accidental illness; from the bestial practices of sodomites and atheists; from the power of devils and demons; and, of course, from the imagination. A little over a quarter century later, Licetus could cite all these and add over half a dozen more: superfetation, poor nutrition, a defect in the formative faculty, the corruption of the viscosity or natural heat of the male and female semen, or their improper mixture. But already Licetus is beginning to warn that too many people were resorting to the imagination alone to account for monstrous births when other explanations were more reasonable. And by the 1720s, James Blondel, provoked by the Mary Toft affair to publicly attack the notion of the prenatal influence of the imagination, complained that the doctrine had completely usurped all other explanations. In the past, he pointed out, it was believed that there were a great many causes of monstrosity. The power of the imagination had been invoked rarely, and then to account just for small blemishes on the skin:

> This has been the constant Doctrine without any considerable interruption, till within these Hundred and Fifty years: But the Case is now much altered. *Imagination* scorns to be a *petty Pedlar,* and to deal only in foolish Pictures, which were so ill made, that 'twas difficult to distinguish between a *Codling,* a *Trotter,* or a *Potatoe*: She has ingrossed the whole Trade of *Deformities,* and has come to such a Perfection in the Manufacture, that you will find in her *Shop* nothing but *exact* Draughts, and Similitudes of Animals, or their parts, or Vegetables or things inanimate, . . . She can also furnish you with Monsters of all Sorts, at all Times, at a Minutes Warning, without any Delay, or loss of Business.[22]

Blondel was correct: the power of the imagination had become the explanation of first resort within the last century and a half. Its success, in part, came about by default. The attribution of monstrosities to God or the devil had become less convincing as European thought had grown more secularized. Many of the other explanations were based on Aristotelian and Galenic embryological assumptions, and, as these increasingly became discredited, such causes fell out of favor. But a large part of its success had to do with the nature of monsters and deformities and the kind of blunt, commonsensical vigor the doctrine of the imagination brought to explaining them. Blondel himself really suggested the reason for its success when he ridiculed the belief in the imagination's power to make "*exact* Draughts." For monstrosities were not, strictly speaking, formless. To the contrary, they had—or many fancied they had—exact shapes and features: birthmarks looked like fruit, growths resembled small rodents, disfigurements distorted the whole visage or body into the likeness of some beast. Sometimes the resemblance was imagined in astonishing detail: "When I desired the woman . . . to put out her tongue that I might examine it," reported an eighteenth-century doctor,

> I observed something on the tip of it like a plum, of green colour, hard and painful. She told me, that when plums begin to ripen, it grows larger, soft-

er, and less painful; acquires a blue reddish or purple colour: and she feels a hard grisly substance like the stone in the middle; in the winter it shrivels and decreases, and the next season resumes the same appearance. It seems, when her mother was with child of her, she longed for some plums, which she cheapened, but would not buy, because she thought them too dear; however, she had touched the tip of her tongue with one of them, which she afterwards threw down; and by this transient touch the child was affected in the same place.

Almost always, as in this case, these *"exact* Draughts" could be traced back to some concrete details in an event in the past that had preyed on the mother's imagination. A woman who gave birth to a child lacking the top of his skull accounted for the deformity this way:

> Upon the ninth of April, 1747, when she was near two months gone with child, she was grievously frightened with thinking on Lord Lovet, who was that day to be beheaded. Her husband was gone to see the execution amongst the crowd at Tower Hill; and when the news came to her hearing, that the scaffolding was fallen down, by which accident many people were hurt, and some killed on the spot, she immediately feared that her husband might be of that number, and was greatly affected. While she was under this dread and apprehension, an officious idle woman came to her and said, that a friend of hers, for whom she had a great regard, was killed on the spot, and that she saw his brains on the ground; upon this the poor woman put both hands to her head in great agony, and immediately fainted away.[23]

Malformations that so faithfully mimicked real objects and that seemed so exactingly modeled after incidents that occurred during pregnancy were *prima facie* evidence of some relationship between the shape of the child and the mother's experience while carrying it, and such cases undoubtedly influenced the way people perceived other deformities that bore less precise resemblances. And it was only logical to point to the imagination as the cause of such "Draughts," whatever their degree of fancied exactness. For the imagination was that power of mind which trafficked specifically in *images*. Even those who thought that there were other causes of monstrosity agreed that in cases of "determinate errors"—that is, deformities that looked like some specific object, such as a particular kind of fruit or animal—"no other cause can be besides the imagination," for it was the imagination alone that "may impart species [the external appearance or image of an object] sent from the external sense to the forming faculty."[24]

The degree of deformity caused by the imagination varied considerably. The effect could be fairly trifling, the imagination merely impressing, for instance, the image of the thing desired on the skin of the child. Thus, a pregnant woman whose longing for strawberries went unsatisfied might give birth to a child with a "strawberry" birth-mark. Countless similar instances were cited in medical literature. The images of fruits of all sorts—plums, cherries, mulberries—marked children because of the unfulfilled appetites of the mothers, and moth-ers frightened by small animals produced, say, a silhouette of a mouse or a small growth shaped like a lizard on the skins of their children.

But the marks caused by the imagination were by no means restrict-ed to such relatively minor blemishes. The malformations could be more disfiguring, and they could be caused by just about anything. When Ned Ward comments that he saw a man so hideous that a preg-nant "Beggar-Woman, as she ask'd him for a Farthing, turn'd her Head . . . another way, for fear her looking in his Face might cause the Child to be like him," he is perhaps being hyperbolic about the man's ugliness, but he is not exaggerating the fear that lay behind the woman's reaction. Paré reports that a two-headed girl who went beg-ging door-to-door "was at last driven out of the duchy of Braveria because (they said) she could spoil the fruit of pregnant women by the apprehension and ideas which might remain in their imaginative fac-ulty, over the form of this so monstrous a creature. (It is not good that monsters should live among us)."[25] Any sight that was surprising, hor-rifying, or desirable enough to cause a pregnant woman to dwell on it in her imagination might affect her unborn child, and might affect it greatly. There were cases of women frightened in the streets by deformed beggars who gave birth to children with identical deformi-ties or who, after witnessing public tortures or executions, bore chil-dren whose limbs were twisted or broken precisely like the criminals'. Women who contemplated the crucifix or images of martyrs too intently might mark their children with similar wounds. Nor were these marks superficial, mere "symbolic" imprints on the skin of the deformities pictured in the imagination; the children had broken bones, missing limbs, fatal lacerations. One woman who had watched the disembowelment of a calf with fascinated horror gave birth to a child whose viscera hung out from an opening below his navel. Anoth-er, who was standing in the street talking to a friend and was surprised when someone came from behind and playfully knocked her head against her friend's, bore two daughters joined from the forehead to the nose. Another woman was said to have given birth to a boy who was perfectly circumcised at birth: during her pregnancy she had overheard one of her house guests give a detailed description of the Jewish rite.

The effects of the mother's imagination could be even more mas-sively deforming. There were scores of accounts of children born with the heads of cats, dogs, frogs, and apes, all because their mothers were frightened by or overly affectionate to those animals. One child was said to have the facial features, mane, and hooves of a calf. Another, whose mother stared intently at the bear on her family crest, was born shaggy and clawed. One boy, in fact, was born with the neck and ears of a hare. There were numerous reports of wholesale monstrosities, and many of these so grotesque that we can understand why Mary Toft's tale of seventeen rabbits would not appear utterly preposterous to someone in the eighteenth century. Her story was every bit as plausible as the famous case of the sister of Philippus Meurs, apostolical pronotary and canon of St. Peter's, a girl who was

> compleat in the rest of her Body, but without a Head: Instead of which was joyned to her Neck the Likeness of a Shell Fish, having two Valves which shut and open'd; and by which, from a Spoon, she took her Nourishment: And this . . . was occasion'd, for that his Mother [when] with Child of her, had a strong Desire after some Muscles she beheld in the Market, but could not procure at that Instant. This Sister of his lived in this monstrous Condition to be eleven Years old, and dy'd then by Accident; happening angrily and very strongly to bite the Spoon they fed her with, and breaking those testaceous Valves, dy'd quickly after.[26]

When Mary Toft claimed to give birth to rabbits, then, the prenatal influence of the imagination was widely accepted among the medical men ("I am the first," Blondel said when he attacked the doctrine a few years later, "who ever writ on this side of the Question," adding that he feared he would "be mobbed for the Singularity of my Sentiment"). The belief was so current that it was offhandedly used as the basis for innumerable jokes in popular writing, poetry, and drama ("Horrid to view!" wrote one of Alexander Pope's enemies in an attack on the hunch-backed poet, "retire from human Sight, / Nor with thy Figure pregnant Dames affright"), and in novels and romances it had become a conventional mechanism for revealing hidden identities and wrapping up the plot (Joseph Andrews' birthmark was caused by his mother's yearning for strawberries). It was, moreover, the common possession of all levels of society, not only "the Universal Belief and Persuasion . . . with *Philosophers* and *Physicians,*" but also "among the vulgar."[27]

And so, when the illiterate Mary Toft had to account for her miraculous births, it was only natural that she should turn to the most common explanation held by physicians and vulgar alike. Here is the story she told to St. André and which St. André passed on to the public. Significantly, neither one felt that there was a need to "explain" the cause of her monstrous rabbits. To anyone in 1726, this story was self-explanatory:

> The account she . . . gave of herself, was, that on the 23d of *April* last, as she
> was weeding in a Field, she saw a Rabbet spring up near her, after which she
> ran, with another Woman that was at work just by her; this set her longing
> for Rabbets, being then, as she thought, five Weeks gone with Child; the
> other woman perceiving she was uneasy, charged her with longing for the
> Rabbet they cou'd not catch, but she deny'd it: soon after another Rabbet
> sprung up near the same place, which she endeavour'd likewise to catch.
> The same Night she dreamt that she was in a field with those two Rabbets
> in her Lap, and awaked with a sick Fit, which lasted till Morning; from that
> time, for above three Months, she had a constant and strong desire to eat
> Rabbets, but being very poor and indigent cou'd not procure any.[28]

Perhaps the fact that she fashioned her account to include all three
provocations to the imagination—a surprise, an obsessive dwelling on
an object, and an unsatisfied longing—should have made more people
suspect that she was overreaching. And certainly, her giving birth to
complete rabbits (and not, say, to creatures which were identifiably
human but which had some features of rabbits) placed her story at the
very limit of credibility. But such was the faith in the doctrine of the
imagination that her claims were wholly accepted by St. André,
Howard, and "people of sound judgment," and they were just plausible enough to make even the skeptical Douglas pause.[29]

III

One reason why the capacity to misshape the fetus was attributed to
the imagination was because, as I have said, the imagination was conceived to be the image-making faculty, and many monsters were fancied to be the very images of things that had been pictured previously
in the mothers' minds. But there was a second reason why the imagination was singled out. The agent of teratogenesis had to be the imagination because the imagination was the only faculty that could effectu-
ally participate in the kind of psycho-physiological processes that
prenatal influence presupposed. And by understanding these processes
and the role the imagination played in them, I believe, we can begin to
understand why so many people reacted the way they did to the Mary
Toft incident and why they reacted with such intensity.

When Montaigne explained how the mother deformed her child, he
dispatched of the matter in a single sentence: "But all this may be
referred to the narrow Suture of the spirit and the body, enter-communicating their fortunes one unto another."[30] It was precisely because
monsters were thought to replicate in their flesh something in the
mothers' minds that the imagination was thought to be responsible.

For, in the psychological tradition springing from Aristotle and commonplace among the literate at least through the early eighteenth century, the imagination was the faculty that mediated the transactions between the body and the mind, the nexus where mind and body continuously were "enter-communicating," the site of the "Bond or knitting" of the "Rational" and the "corporeal."[31] And so, if something in a mind were to manifest itself in a body, the process would have to take place through the agency of the imagination.

Of course, the transit across that "narrow Suture" of mind and body was no simple affair. Those who sought to explain the imagination's power in more detail than Montaigne did, particularly medical writers, almost always began by saying that the imagination could not *immediately* act on the body. Daniel Turner, for instance, cautioned that "by *Fancy* or *Imagination* doing this or that, we mean not that this Faculty as an immediate Efficient, by a direct Property in it self, or Power of its own, worketh any Effect: But mediately by the Interposition of the Blood and nervous Fluid, set at work by Appetite first excited, which occasions or brings about the same." Another early eighteenth-century doctor, John Maubray, reminded his readers that the imagination "does not want its proper and peculiar *Mediums* by which it may operate." Daniel Sennert attributed startling effects to the imagination, but he was anxious to be understood that these were caused not by the unaided imagination but by the imagination working through a series of intermediaries: "This fact must be made clear right at the outset: those effects do not immediately depend on the imagination, nor does the soul bring about such effects through the imagination immediately; moreover, the imagination in and of itself, directly and by its own individual power, neither produces these effects which are said to arise from it nor acts upon other bodies."[32] The imagination did indeed shape the fetus, but as the first in a chain of causes ("prima vero & remota caussa est imaginatio"). The same point was made most strenuously by Thomas Fienus, who spent over a hundred and fifty pages in his *De Viribus Imaginationis Tractatus* proving by rigorous scholastic logic that the imagination could alter the fetus only through intermediaries.

These men spoke so insistently of mediums and intermediaries because they conceived of human beings as being made up of the double substances of mind and body, and the mind could never affect the body directly because mind and body were substances so different in essence that they could not impinge one upon the other directly. And yet, that having been said, it was clear that mind and body did impinge upon one another in some way. The mother's marking her fetus was merely a remarkable example of the more mundane "enter-communi-cating" between mind and body that was carried on minute-by-minute in everyone's daily life. The physical things of the world are experi-enced by our corporeal senses, and these experiences are converted in some way into incorporeal ideas and concepts in our minds. In our minds, we reach a decision about how we should act on such-and-such a matter, and this decision is translated in some way into movements of the body.

These transits back and forth across the "narrow Suture" of mind and body could occur because a human being, though of a double sub-stance, was not cleaved in a crude duality.[33] It would be more accurate to think of our various bodily members, faculties, fluids, humors, and so on, as being ranged in a continuum running from the material to the immaterial:

> So from the root
> Springs lighter the green stalk, from thence the leaves
> More aery, last the bright, consumate flow'r
> Spirits odorous breathes: flow'rs and thir fruit
> Man's nourishment, by gradual scale sublim'd
> To vital spirits aspire, to animal,
> To intellect, give both life and sense,
> Fancy and understanding, whence the Soul
> Reason receives, and reason is her being.[34]

Milton's specific formulation here may have been too nakedly neo-Pla-tonic for most thinkers (he appears to be saying that body actually con-verts itself into intellect), but his sense of the unity and dynamic conti-nuity of the human psycho-physiological organism was shared by most literate persons, and in the end, they too, no matter what their philo-sophical predispositions, had to explain the interactions between mind and body by recourse to some kind of "neo-Platonic maneuver"[35]— that is, they had to conceive of activities within the whole human econ-omy as translations up and down a "gradual scale" that stretched from the corporeal to the immaterial.

Human beings were composed of numerous powers, faculties, humors, fluids, solids, and spirits, each of which partook of varying degrees of corporeality or immateriality. The body comprised the dense bones, the less dense but still very solid muscles, the thinner flu-ids, the more refined humors, and the highly ethereal spirits. The mind, too, had its "lower" faculties (such as common sense, imagina-tion, memory), which were engaged immediately with the sensual experience of the corporeal world, and its "higher" faculties (variously called understanding, intellect, and reason), whose objects of apperception were incorporeal. All of these, from the bones to the reason, were ranged in a hierarchy that ran with unbroken continuity from the grossly corporeal through the progressively more rarified and subtle, then gradually fading into the spiritual, first in its lower degrees and then moving to the higher reaches of intellect. And all of these stood in instrumental relation to each other, each affecting and being affected by the more corporeal one below it, each affecting and being affected by the more ethereal one above. And so, in the end, the lowest operations of the body might well impinge upon the highest operations of the mind, but never immediately. Mind and body worked on each other up and down this psycho-physiological continuum, through the "proper and peculiar *Mediums*," the complex chains of intermediaries.[36]

Consider, for example, the animal spirits, which illustrate how intermediaries were conceived of in the human economy and how they functioned within the continuum of mind and body. "The blood is itself the matter out of which the animal Spirits are drawn," Willis explained; "and . . . the Vessels containing and carrying it everywhere through the whole compass of the Head, are like distillatory Organs, which by circulating more exactly, and as it were subliming the blood, separate its purer and more active particles from the rest, and subtilize them, and at length insinuate those spiritualized into the Brain." Though corporeal, the animal spirits were extraordinarily tenuous and subtle, sublimed to the last degree of rarity, "the purest and most ætherial particles of all Bodies in the World whatsoever (and so consequently of nearest alliance to Spiritualities)." "Our blood labors to beget," Donne wrote, "Spirits, as like soules as it can."[37] And since they were corporeal and yet "like souls," the animal spirits could act as a medium by which the body pressed upward on the mind, the mind downward on the body. Because they were on the threshold of the material and the immaterial, they had a "two-fold Aspect" that allowed them to perform this double task, "communicat[ing] the bodie and corporeall things with the mind, and spirituall, and intelligible things, after a sort with the bodie."[38] In other words, "it is not possible to passe from one extreme to an other, but by a meane; and no meane is there in the nature of man, but spirit: by this the body affecteth the mind"; and, contrariwise, "This spirit is the chiefe instrument, and immediate, whereby the soule bestoweth the exercise of her faculty in her bodie," acting as a medium to convey the commands of the mind, via other, more corporeal intermediaries, to the proper organs of the body, there to be further translated into bodily movement.[39]

Just as the animal spirits were on the upper threshold of corporeality, so the imagination was on the lower threshold of the mind, and, being liminal like the animal spirits, it had a "two-fold Aspect": it, too, performed the double task of allowing the body to impinge on the higher mental powers and of translating the incorporeal activities of the mind into bodily movements.

From the time of Aristotle, the imagination was an "inward sense" which transmuted the experience of the bodily senses into the stuff of the mind. It was, first and foremost, a means of apprehending the external world, "That Faculty which presents to the Mind's view the Images or Ideas of external sensible Objects, or by which the Mind perceives them." All sense impressions reached the mind only after being processed through the imagination: "whatsoever we understand," Thomas Wright said, repeating the commonplace, "passeth through the gates of our imagination."[40] It was usually understood that the senses conveyed the appearances of things, the *species,* via the animal spirits to the imagination, and the imagination produced from these abstracted mental substitutes (*phantasma* in scholastic terminology, sometimes anglicized as "phantoms," but increasingly called "images" or "ideas"). These images could be handed up to the higher mental powers immediately or stored in memory, to be recalled later.

The imagination was needed as a medium between sense perception and the higher mental powers because the senses were corporeal, but the mind was incorporeal, and the mind could apprehend only things like itself, things essentially incorporeal:

> The understanding abstracts things from their matter, and without consideration of matter, of quantity, with figure, knoweth things, understands things freed from their matter; . . . It performs its functions without all corporal instruments; yet it hath need of the Phantasie as its object to understand, and the Imagination supplies the mind with intelligible matter.[41]

Intellect needed the imagination because it needed an "object to understand," an object which was like itself. And the function of the imagination was precisely to transmute sense images into understandable objects, images "freed from their matter" and made into "intelligible matter" assimilable by the intellect. As the medium between mind and body, in short, the imagination was the faculty that performed the process of conceptual abstraction, converting percept to concept. Since this process was one in which there was a movement from a material world perceived by the senses to an immaterial world conceived in the mind, it was inevitably spoken of, and often thought of, as a refining process in which the corporeal properties of sense images were purged away. The mind turns

> Bodies to spirits by *sublimation* strange;
>   As fire converts to fire, the thinge it burnes,
>   As we our meates into our nature change.
>
> From their grosse *matter* she abstracts the *formes,*
>   And draws a kind of *Quintessence* from things;
>   Which to her proper nature she transformes,
>   To beare them light on her celestiall wings.
>
> This doth she when from things *particular,*
>   She doth abstract the *universall kinds*;
>   Which bodilesse, and immateriall are,
>   And can be lodg'd but onely in our minds.[42]

The imagination sublimed or dematerialized the objects of corporeal sense, "spiritualizing" them so that they became accessible to the mind:

> As the qualities of externall things are the matter subject to the internall senses, so their images conceived by the internall senses, and purged from all bodily matter, are the matter subject to the understanding and spirit. And the spirit labouring about them draweth out certain notions, and knoweth many things from them, which cannot moove the sense and which the senses cannot know. And yet this spirit is first mooved by these images, as the senses are by externall things.[43]

As the medium between sense and thought, the imagination did the work of each. It was the messenger of the senses, creating images that accurately replicated the external world. But the imagination also served the intellect, and like the intellect it was "not tied to the laws of matter": it "may at pleasure make unlawful matches and divorces of things," wrenching the objects of sensation from their original contingencies of spatial placement and temporal succession, and "at pleasure join what nature hath severed and sever that which nature hath joined."[44] Hence, the images of the imagination, since they were the products of sense perception as well as the "intelligible matter" of conceptual thought, seemed to hover between sensation and idea, ambiguous, partaking of something of the characteristics of both. "Images are similar to objects perceived," Aristole said, "except that they are without matter."[45] They were palpable and vivid and fixed, accurately transcribing the external world, but they were also ductile, capable of being shaped, combined, severed, and rejoined. They were solid enough to have form but malleable enough to be transformed. Some thinkers, emphasizing their sensation-like quality, called them "corporeal Phantasms," "material Phantasms," or "Sensible Ideas, Images or Pictures of Outward Objects . . . drawn by the Pencil of that

Inward Limner or Painter which borrows all his Colours from Sense."[46] Others, discerning their kinship to intellectual abstractions, thought of them as sense perceptions "without matter" or "purged from all bodily matter." And still others, perceiving them to be at once both sensible and intelligible, solid and malleable, something like sensations and something like ideas, chose paradox to describe them. For Milton, they were "Aery shapes," and Spenser, in his description of the room of Phantastes in the House of Alma, reached for the same ambiguity:

> His Chambers were dispainted all within
> With sundry colours, in which were writ
> Infinite shapes of things dispersed thin; . . .

But the favored, and most telling, metaphor was clouds or fogs, in part because the metaphor expressed the unreliability of the imagination as an instrument of knowledge, but in part because it captured so economically the paradoxes of form and shapelessness, of substance and incorporeality, of the ambiguous border between the earth of sensual perception and a clear sky of the incorporeal intellect, and especially because it articulated so clearly a process of a substance arising sublimed out of body and transforming itself (but never wholly) into the incorporeal:

> Thoughts must the previous Strokes of Sense attend,
> And huddled Images but slow ascend.
> From earthy Dregs the circling Fogs arise,
> And musty Vapours skim before our Eyes;
> The Soul is forc'd, while pent in darksom Clay,
> To grope in Shades, and guess the doubtful way: . . .[47]

As an instrument of knowledge, then, the imagination translated sense upward to intellect. But the imagination, as I have said, had a "two-fold Aspect." It was also an instrument of action, translating ideas into bodily response and physical movement, transforming mind down to body. When Bacon divided the various faculties of the mind into the judicial (Understanding and Reason) and the ministerial (Will, Appetite, and Affection), he attributed to it this double function, as was traditional:

> It is true indeed that the imagination performs the office of an agent or messenger or proctor in both provinces, both the judicial and the ministerial. For the sense sends all kinds of images over to imagination for reason to judge of; and reason again when it has made its judgment and selection, sends them over to imagination before the decree is put into execution. For

voluntary motion is ever preceded and incited by imagination; so that the imagination is the common instrument of both,—both reason and will; saving that this Janus of imagination has two different faces; for the face toward reason has the print of truth, and the face toward action has the print of goodness.[48]

Those ambiguous images the imagination used to cross the "narrow Suture" from sense to intellect it uses again to recross the boundary from mind to body. If the act of knowledge was a "subliming" process in which the imagination converted sense into intelligible images, the act by which the mind affected the body was the opposite: it was a "corporealizing" process, as it were, in which the imagination concretized the thoughts of the mind into palpable, sense-like images. While the mind conceptualizes in incorporeal ideas, "the Fancy is busy in copying after the Understanding, and transcribing Ideas out of the Intellectual World into the Material" (or, as one more hostile to the imagination put it, when the mind thinks in its "Abstracted Intellections and Contemplations," the imagination is engaged in a kind of parallel "Corporeal Cogitation," "making some kind of Apish Imitations, counterfeit Iconisms, Symbolical Adumbrations and Resemblances of those Intellectual Cogitations of Sensible and Corporeal things").[49] These intellectual cogitations, concretized by the imagination as images, have all the immediacy and cogency of sensually perceived objects, and in this way "voluntary motion is ever preceded and incited by imagination." For the imagination presents to the ministerial faculties these images, which "picture" to them a good toward which to strive—a "print of goodness" that incites them to action. In other words, the imagination, by means of concrete and vivid images, excites the will, the passions, and affections. And these, through *their* intermediaries, ultimately make their effects felt on the body.[50]

Because of its corporealizing power, the imagination was generally believed to have some degree of control over material things. Without question, operating through its proper intermediaries, it could cause physiological changes. The mind willed to walk, and the legs moved. A man remembered a moment of humiliation, he felt shame, his heart beat faster, and his face was suffused with blood. Most thought that the imagination could induce certain diseases and cure others. Indeed, some even believed that, given the presence of the proper intermediaries, the imagination could influence things beyond the confines of the body. Sennert, for example, argued that a menstruating woman could stain a mirror simply by looking at it because the imagination, through the spirits and humors, acted on those "very subtle spirits" which abounded in the eyes, and these in turn acted on the subtle effluvia that backed the mirror. What we might dismiss as credulity on Sennert's part is really a simple extension of that chain of mediation which was felt to bind the corporeal to the psychic; Sennert himself cautioned that such a power could manifest itself only across short distances and could perform only limited effects, rejecting as absurd claims that one could throw a rider from his horse or transplant wheat from one field to another by means of the imagination.[51] Others less cautious *had* argued for just such powers and even more extravagant ones like the imagination's ability to control astral forces, to raise ghosts, even to cause the death of others. By the eighteenth century, of course, much more modest claims were made for the imagination—more modest even than Sennert's—but behind these claims stood the same conception of the imagination and of its power to mediate between body and mind.

And in the eighteenth century, even though the imagination had considerably dwindled in power, the assertion that a mother's imagination could misshape the fetus was modest enough. It seemed, in fact, little more than a logical extrapolation from the commonplace transactions between body and mind that go on in us every minute. A few years before the Mary Toft incident, when he came to explain the power of the mother's imagination over her child, Daniel Turner first mapped out that system of intermediation that undergirds our simplest acts of perception and physical movement. The imagination, he explained, "receives the sensible Species, first only impresst upon the outward Organs, and thence by a most quick Irradiation of the nervous Fluid deliver'd Inwards, and apprehending all the several corporeal things to their external Appearance. . . . The *Fancy* once excited at the Appearance of the Object, presently stirs up the Appetite, and this latter, local Motion." The communication between appetite and local motion itself occurs "mediately," for it is the animal spirits which are "set at Work by Appetite first excited"; and these spirits, working through other intermediaries such as the blood, various fluids, and the heart, progressively translate their effects throughout the body: "So that the Changes and Alterations wrought upon our Bodies, especially the Fluids therein moving, by this Power of Imagination, are almost incredible, which is thought by some of the Learned to have the sufficient Efficacy, as it happens to be set on Work, either to renovate or raise up, or to ruin and destroy the human Structure." And if the imagination could bring about such changes in one's own body, surely it was not illogical to conclude that the mother's imagination could exercise a similar power over her own fetus. For given the "Empire the *Fantasy* of a pregnant Woman has over the Blood and Humours together with the Spirits of her Body," clearly "by their Ministry she is able to give . . . monstrous Shapes and figures to that of the more tender *Fœtus*."[52]

The system of intermediaries was so complex, the manifold concatenations of faculties, potentials, spirits, humors, and so on offered so many possibilities, the interdependency of mind and body was so subtle, that the imagination might work through any number of routes, and the particular route one commentator chose for the imagination to follow often depended on his medical background, his philosophic predisposition, and his theoretical commitments. But, though the precise chain of mediation differed from one commentator to the other, the *fact* of mediation did not.[53] Avicenna argued that the species of things in the imagination were imprinted on the spirits in the brain; these were mixed with the blood which, since it acted as nourishment of the fetus, communicated the image to it. Ficino believed that the imagination communicated with the fetus by means of the sympathetic vibrations of the spirits through the nerves. Licetus thought that the imagination created an image on the animal spirits nearest to it in the brain, and these passed the image along to neighboring spirits, and they to others, until it was directly communicated to the semen and the fetus.[54] Thomas Fienus suggested a more complex chain of intermediaries in which the mother's imagination operated "by the mediating passions and the movement of the humours and spirits."[55] The images in the fancy, intensified and drawn to the heart by the passions, were impressed on the blood and spirits; from there, they were communicated to the uterus and fetus, where they acted as a kind of model or pattern ("exemplar") which directed the shaping faculty of the fetus.[56] Riverius argued for a much less elaborate chain of causes: "extravagancy of desire disturbs imagination, and imprints on the spirits the shape of the thing so desired, which spirits easily brand the tender infant with the mark."[57] Sennert was not sure precisely how the mechanics worked. The imagination he knew, was a cognitive and immaterial faculty and therefore could affect the fetus only by way of intermediaries, either "by the mediating affections of the soul through the motions of the humors and the spirits or by directing the shaping faculties." As a Galenist, he was inclined to the latter.[58]

But what was grist for Galenists was grist for the proponents of other systems. Sir Kenelm Digby saw in the doctrine support for his notion of atomistic sympathy, and he argued that the "Corporeal atoms" of a thing perceived in the mind could be conveyed physically by the imagination and the animal spirits to the genitals, where they

were impressed on the skin of the fetus.[59] The doctrine was malleable
enough to be absorbed whole into the neo-Platonism of Henry More,
for whom it offered proof that the mind of man could manipulate "the
Spirit of Nature," through which medium the mother's imagination
marked the fetus.[60] And the doctrine was retailored once again to serve
the Cartesian-based, occasionalist system of Malebranche, where it
provided evidence of the invariable and intricate correlation between
mind and body:

> Any time there happens any change in that part of the Brain where the
> Nerves meet, there likewise happens some change in the Soul, that is . . . if
> in this part there is any Motion that changes the order of its Fibres, there
> also happens some New perception in the Soul, and it feels or imagines
> some New thing; and the Soul can never perceive or imagine any thing
> anew, except there be some change in the Fibres in this same part of the
> Brain.
>
> So that the faculty of Imagining, or the Imagination, consists only in the
> power that the soul has of forming in it self Images of objects, in producing
> a change in the Fibres of this part of the Brain, which may be called the
> *principal,* since it answers to all the parts of our bodies, and is the place
> where our Soul immediately resides, if we may be permitted to say so.

This correspondence between mind and body was carried out through
the mediation of the animal spirits, which traced the images and
impressed them on the "Fibres of the Brain." The spirits also mediated
between the mother and the fetus: "For the body of an Infant makes
but one with that of the Mothers, the Blood and Spirits are common to
both, and sensations and Passions are the Natural Consequence of the
Motion of the Spirits and Blood, which motions necessarily Communicate themselves from the Mother to the Child." On the basis of this system of mediation, Malebranche would account for the birth of monsters through the power of the mother's imagination. Thus he explains
the monstrosity of "a young Man who was born a Fool, and his body
broken after the same manner as Criminals are broke upon the
Wheel":

> According to the principles that I have established, the Cause of this sad
> Accident was, that his Mother, who heard a Criminal was to be broken,
> went to see him executed; all the blows that this miserable Man received, so
> strongly smote the Imagination of this Mother, and by a kind of Counter-
> blow the tender delicate Brain of her Child. The Fibres of this Womans
> Brain were strongly shaken, and it may be broke in some places by the
> impetuous Course of the Animal Spirits, caused by the sight of so terrible
> an Action, but she was strong enough to hinder their absolute ruine; though
> on the contrary, the Fibres of this child's Brain, being not able to resist the

torrent of these Spirits, were entirely dissipated, and the shock was great
enough to make him wholly lose his Wits; and this was the reason he came
into the world deprived of his Understanding, this was likewise the cause
that the same parts of his body was broken as those of the Criminal, whom
his Mother saw executed.

At the sight of this Execution, which was so capable of frightening a
Woman, the violent course of the Animal Spirits, went impetuously from
her Brain to all the parts of her Body, which answer'd to those of the Criminal, and the same thing passed in the Infant. But because the bones of the
Mother were able to resist the Violence of these Spirits, they received no
hurt; Nay, it may be, she did feel no pain, nor the least trembling in her
Legs, when the Criminal was broken; but the rapid stream of the Spirits
was capable to separate the soft and tender Bones of the Infant. . . .[61]

That the imagination's power to shape the fetus was a commonly
accepted, medically respected belief explains why so many people were
willing to entertain the possibility that Mary Toft truly had given birth
to seventeen rabbits. But other features of this incident cannot be
explained so easily. To fully understand the Mary Toft affair, I believe,
we need to investigate further some of the features of the imagination I
have just sketched. The imagination, precisely because it was an intermediary between the material and immaterial realms, preserved a
comfortable distinction between the body and the mind. But the sheer
variety of ways in which thinkers tried to account for how the imagination regulated this interaction suggests that a sufficiently cogent
explanation was more and more difficult to find. And, historically, this
was increasingly the case. Though the traditional conception of the
nature of the imagination was accepted until well after the Mary Toft
incident, most of the assumptions that had explained its functioning
were destroyed by new philosophical and physiological thinking. Consequently, by bearing witness to a process it could not explain, the
imagination smudged the very line it pretended to draw between the
body and the mind and suggested that the one might easily collapse
into the other.

I shall now explore in more detail some of the responses to the Mary
Toft incident, and I shall argue that many of the anxieties that the incident gave rise to were produced by this historical situation of the imagination.

3

ENTHUSIASM DELINEATED

I

The London Journal for 24 December 1726 reported that "two Persons of Distinction, having had some Words about a Satirical Ballad against a Gentleman concerned in the Rabbet-Affair at Guildford, were to have fought on Wednesday or Thursday at Marybone, but were prevented by being both put under Arrest." Surely there was more at stake here than whether such-and-such a doctor was or was not duped by an illiterate woman from the country. The Mary Toft incident, Pope observed, divided "all London . . . into factions." It provoked anger. Sometimes the anger rose to the surface only briefly in an unguarded remark or in an image whose unexpected violence intimated cruel and retaliatory impulses:

> The cracking of bones gives a mighty surprize
> And the Pricking her Womb causes sorrowfull cryes.
> So people breed birds to peck out their own Eyes.[1]

Sometimes, such impulses were hidden under plausible intentions. Manningham pressed Mary Toft to admit her guilt because he thought it important that she confess, but the way he pressured her—threatening to perform a painful operation to find out if she were formed differently from other women—suggests that he had found at last a way to express his anger by giving it a legitimate pretext. Sometimes, the anger was unalloyed. Sir Thomas Clarges's reaction was wrath pure and simple, and his anger was nearly uncontrollable. He bullied Mary Toft so harshly that even some of his contemporaries were taken aback, and he was so anxious to punish her that Manningham had to use all his skill to keep her out of Bridewell long enough for him and Douglas to get solid evidence of her guilt.[2]

Even some satirists sensed that the anger of the public was disproportionate to the provocation. In *Much Ado About Nothing* (the title
itself indicates the satirist's suspicion about the overwrought reactions
to the incident), "Mary Toft," in her own semi-literate hand, complained, "As for thare barbirus Experiment wich tha intended, of sending *a chimni-sweeper's boy up my fallopin Tubb,* I thank um for thar luff,
but tha shall play no such triks with me: I noes tha wood hang me if tha
cood."[3]

After the affair was exposed as a hoax, when one would suppose
that the anger would dissipate, it was displaced from Mary Toft onto
the doctors and remained just as intense. The incident was so nettling
that many people insisted that there had to be some deeply malignant
purpose behind it. Hence the astonishingly irrational rumor that
sprang up soon after the fraud was exposed: St. André had fabricated
the hoax in order to draw in his rivals among the medical men and to
ruin their reputations and careers.[4] The unrelenting persecution of
John Howard suggests that a scapegoat was needed, and the extraordinary sum of £800 for recognizance can hardly have been motivated by
anything else than the same vindictiveness that drove some to want to
punish Mary Toft. The authors of the pamphlets, poems, and prints
that flooded London after the disclosure of the fraud were angry, too,
and even while insisting that the whole affair had been silly and incon-
sequential, they discharged their anger by figuratively punishing the
doctors with ridicule. Some wished for a more literal punishment:

> Hence let s[ch] Wretches learn if e'er they Aim
> T'establish *Fraud,* their Character's ye Game.
> The Hunt once up, Mankind will cry 'em down
> And make such *Quacks* the Sport of Court & Town.
> The *Eighteen[th]* Birth whenever it appears,
> 'Tis hop'd will bring forth *Pillary* and *Ears.*[5]

One indication of how grave Mary Toft's transgression was felt to be
is "A Full and True Account, Of a most Horrid, Cruel, Barbarous,
Bloody, and Inhumane, Self-Murther," a broadside that purported to
be a genuine account of Mary Toft's suicide in Bridewell and a true
copy of her confession. What is remarkable about this piece is its
assumption that Mary Toft's crime was so heinous, such a "wicked
Action," that she would kill herself because of it, "Cut her own Throat
from Ear to Ear," leaving "the Room all over of a Blood." "Finding my
self in the hands of Justice and could by no means get from it," reads
her confession, "I took this method to rid my self of so great a Torment

which I must have suffered in this World the matter being of my own Contrivance from the very first. . . . So hoping to recover more mercy from God than I deserve I depart this world full of Confusion."

Others, too, thought the incident very grave. Manningham feared the "Ill Consequence" of not exposing the fraud, and Douglas thought that "it was of the utmost Consequence that the whole Truth of this Affair should be detected, because of the bad Effects with which it might otherwise have been attended." "Ill Consequence," "Utmost Consequence," "bad Effects": what we may dismiss as laughable was perceived quite otherwise at the time. London was "every day alarm'd" at each new rumor. The effect of the hoax was to "terrify and abuse" the public. It was a "fatal imposture," an "abominable Contrivance," a "most abominable Fraud," even "diabolical," and Mary Toft herself was a "wicked Woman." "The general allarm that the late imposition of Mary Toft has given," remarked one newspaper, "makes it necessary to spread the Detection of so infamous a Deceit as far as possible." The writer of *The Anatomist Dissected,* sharing this sense that some serious damage had been done to the country, worried about how the understandings of "his Majesty's Loyal Subjects" had been corrupted by the hoax and lamented "the great Detriment like to accrue to our Nation by the Stir which has been made about this foul Imposture."[6]

Such language would be more appropriate for warning about an imminent foreign invasion or the subversion of the commonwealth. And indeed, some seemed to be vaguely apprehensive about such dangers. Even while they turned the incident into humor, they gravitated to images of the collapse of empires and threats to the security of the nation. Here is an account which came out just as the details of the hoax were becoming known:

> I am told that there are depositions actually in the press, which will make it appear to be a viler imposture, than even that of the Warming Pan, and cannot imagine for my Life what consideration should prevail with any Gentleman to support or contenance it. When I just heard the Story, which was told in a company that had been warmly engaged in a chat on Politics, I could not help smiling at this exclamation made by one of the Gentlemen, "I should be glad to know, says he, if these Rabbets are the same kind with those which, Pliny says, destroyed a whole city in Spain; if they are, said he with a thundering Oath, let the Spaniards begin when they will, this very Woman and her breed need only be put upon the Spanish shore, and they'll do more Execution than the Trojan Horse did."

Another satirist was reminded of the fall of Troy, too: "Nor is the Number of little Ones contained within her, at all surprising. . . . We all know that the Story of the *Trojan* Horse was at first look'd on as a Fable." And a third alluded to a different historical crisis, but one with the same associations:

> Hence learn the Ladies have a Place,
> That makes the wisest Man an Ass,
> Nay even Master S[t. Andr]y,
> Surgeon, Anatomist miscarry,
> And puts them to a greater Stand,
> Than Fawkes with all his Slight of Hand: . . .

The Trojan Horse, Guy Fawkes, the rabbits that "undermined" the town in Spain, the Warming Pan conspiracy: all speak of a city on the verge of ruin, an entire nation subverted by deceit.[7]

Not only does the anxiety seem incommensurate to the occasion in these remarks, but because it is impossible to fathom how Mary Toft's hoax could trigger these kinds of national calamities, one senses, too, that the true source of the anxiety was not fully or even accurately articulated. In a piece published in *Mist's Weekly Journal,* 7 January 1727, another writer also envisions impending national collapse:

> But it is said, that if the Force of Imagination in the Female Sex should be able to bring about such strange Effects, who can say how far the Mischief might spread; for at that Rate, a Man of Fortune might be in Danger of having a *Rabbit* for his eldest Son; and how odd wou'd it look in a Family, to see such a diminutive Creature, inherit the Estate, while perhaps his younger Brothers might be Fellows of six Foot high; nay, more, as we know, those Women of Fashion, who live at Ease and take Care of Nothing, are most subject to Spleen, Vapours, &c. and of Consequence more under the Government of Whim and Imagination, (which their Husbands will testify), it is not imp[o]ssible but this way of Breeding might spread upwards, that we might come at last to be govern'd by *Rabbits*.

Although the passage climaxes with an image of national confusion, what is so striking is how inchoate the anxiety itself is, how the writer flits nervously from the collapse of one structure to another (lineage, inheritance of property, psychic stability, gender, family, species, nation) as if he cannot quite spell out the real object of his concern.

The collapse most often referred to in the Mary Toft satires is the collapse of language. The confusion that results when language fails to contain and structure is a topic satirists of the incident returned to again and again. In one poem, for instance, Manningham is portrayed as someone who is confused because he has perplexed himself by misusing language:

> He scorns like vulgar Folk to speak
> He talks in *Latin* and in *Greek*
> For Instance: (which you may rely on)
> He calls a *Cond-m* a *Corion*?
> Then wonders how (O Men's *Supina*)
> Such things should come into *Vagina*.

All the doctors come in for a drubbing for their misuse of language, and in *Much Ado About Nothing,* Mary Toft, in her execrable spelling, writes proudly, "Thof I be ripurzentid as an ignirunt littirat Wuman, as can nethur rite nor rede, yet I thank God I can do both; and thof mayhaps I cant spel as well as sum peple as set up for authurs, yet I can rite trooth, and plane *Inglish,* wich is mor nor ani of um all has dun." In fact, erratic spelling itself is satirized in another piece:

> I heartily wish some of these Glossographists would oblige the World with a Folio Treatise or two, on the word Rabbet: We shall then know whether it is to be spelt with an *e,* or an *i.* For, to the shame of the *English* Tongue and this learned Age, our most eminent Physicians, Surgeons, Anatomists and Men Mid-wives, have all been to seek in this Affair.

> St. *André,*
> *Howard,*   } Spell it { *Douglas*
> *Brathwaite,*   with   and the   } Spell it
> *Ahlers* and   an *e.*   Gentleman   with
> *Manningham,*   who calls himself   an *i.*
> *Gulliver,*

> And some of these great Wits, have such short Memories, that they spell it both Ways in one and the same Page.[8]

Behind this passage, as behind many of the others we have seen, there is a vague anxiety which appears not to know its source, and so it expresses itself in a bizarrely bloated joke in which there is a disjunction between the energy which animates it and the point it seems to make. The objection to the confused spelling of the word "rabbit" seems to spring from sheer discomfort, from the apprehension that some important principle of order has broken down, not language itself exactly, but something which the author cannot definitively name and something which he can reestablish by his shaping his objection itself in this elaborate bracketed and tabular form.

When Lord Peterborough wrote to Swift to compliment him on *Gulliver's Travels,* he made Mary Toft the crowning example of the confusion Swift's work had let loose on the world: "men have lost their Tittles, continents, & islands have gott new names just upon the appearance of a certain Book in the world, women bring forth Rabbetts, and Every man, whose wife has conceived, expects an Heir with

Four leggs."[9] Yet even this final collapse of the distinction between the human and the animal seems not to be the particular anxiety the Mary Toft satires seek to articulate. Giving birth to monsters probably was a real fear for some people, but such a fear is concrete and specific, and the conspicuous feature of the responses we have have seen is that they lack a clear, objective correlative: it is as if what Mary Toft provoked was a generalized feelings of collapsing boundaries and disappearing distinctions, not so much the collapse of this or that structure, but the collapse of structure itself.

This disquietude was given apocalyptic expression by Whiston, who saw Mary Toft fulfilling the prophecy of Esdras and ushering in the dissolution of the world. Whiston was laughed at, but he was giving voice forthrightly to feelings that were harbored in some form by others—undigested apprehensions of an impending but unspecified collapse somehow initiated by Mary Toft, feelings easily dismissed perhaps, after being safely covered over by humor, but strong and troubling enough to rise into consciousness as various images of confusion.

And yet, amidst all this anger and anxiety, there is a puzzling incongruity. With few exceptions, the satires that came out after the affair was exposed as a hoax insisted that Mary Toft was either blameless or the least guilty of the offenders. Some even declared that she was the victim, not the perpetrator, of the hoax. In *Much Ado About Nothing,* to take a single instance, the author appeals to the readers to be certain that "their Resentments fall upon the *true Impostors, or Quacks,* and not on a poor innocent Woman, whose Misfortunes they have made a Cat's Paw of their roguery."[10]

The depiction of Mary Toft as innocent is startling not simply because she was guilty and because her guilt was public knowledge but even more so because it contrasts so strikingly with the anger directed at her before the fraud was uncovered. But, it seems to me that behind the satirists' exculpation of Mary Toft complicated motives were at work, motives that point, once again, to the anxiety the incident provoked and perhaps even to an element of fear. Consider, for instance, these two passages in which Mary Toft is exonerated:

> Poor *Mary Toft* the Tool is only made,
> While her Assistants do perform their Trade.

And,

> The Woman (G-d bless her) a mere simple Tool,
> Was more Fool than Knave, H[owar]d more Knave than Fool.[11]

By clearing Mary Toft of complicity, the satirists not only absolved her of guilt, but they made an implicit imputation: she was innocent by reason of her stupidity and weakness. She was so powerless that her own "Assistants" could make her their tool, and she became a "Tool" because she was "simple" and a "Fool."

It was a point made by almost everyone who had anything to say about Mary Toft. Laguerre, in his popular portrait of Mary Toft (figure 1), chose to depict in her a dumb sluggishness, a dullness so profound she seems almost inert. "St. A-D-E's Miscarriage" used the metaphor of the musician and his violin to reduce her to the utter passivity of an instrument: "As he touch'd his Fiddle the woman did Squeak." Those satirists who did not portray her as completely blameless nevertheless were unable to bring themselves to charge her with any serious guilt. For guilt would imply that she had enough intelligence and industry to have carried out the hoax, and they would grant her neither. And so they simply called her stupid and weak and left as an imponderable puzzle the question of how such a woman could have successfully pulled off such a hoax.

> Poor Mary Toft in Ignorance was bred,
> And n'er betrayed a deep designing head
> Ne'er seem'd cut out for plots: Yet never did wife
> Like her impose so grossly on Man Midwife.
> Who scorning Reason Common Sense and Nature
> Plac'd all their faith in such a stupid Creature.[12]

To pursue so single-mindedly the theme of Mary Toft's weakness and stupidity to the point of contradiction is suspicious. To pursue it in the face of the fact that she had the native shrewdness, energy, and resolution to have almost succeeded in her hoax suggests something more: that Mary Toft's power actively, if unconsciously, was being repudiated. (Even the displacing of her guilt onto the doctors suggests that the satirists not simply refused to recognize her power but sought out scapegoats in order to deny that she had any.) Thus, there may be no real discrepancy between the anger at Mary Toft and the desire to punish her that was so evident before the hoax was exposed and the insistence on her innocence, stupidity, and weakness afterwards. Before the hoax was revealed, the doctors devoted themselves to detecting Mary Toft, forcing her to confess, making her admit that she had no power to do what she claimed she did. After her confession, the satirists directed all their energy into insisting that she did not have the power to commit the very hoax which in fact she did commit. The two were opposite strategies that had a single goal: to deny that she had any power whatsoever.

Figure 1. John Laguerre, *Mary Tofts of Godelman the pretended Rabbit Breeder* (copyright British Museum)

Many years after the affair, the desire to punish Mary Toft, the anxiety about her power, and the need to deny it were expressed less ambiguously. There was a persistent rumor that, upon being released from Bridewell, she returned to the warren where she originally had gotten the rabbits, stumbled on a rabbit hole, and injured herself. The overly neat sense of poetic justice makes it difficult to take this rumor very seriously, and what makes it smack of a vindictive attack on her power is its claim that, when she slipped in the warren, she broke her thigh.[13]

On 10 December 1726, *Mist's Weekly Journal* observed that many people were "not willing that so vile an Imposture, a Blemish on Human Nature, should pass for truth, and as such be inserted into our Histories." That people should wish to expunge from memory the embarrassment of a nearly successful fraud is not too surprising. But the same journal had made a startling observation nearly a month earlier, on 19 November:

> People, after all, differ much in their Opinion about this Matter, some looking upon [the rabbits] as great Curiosities fit to be presented to the Royal Society, &c. others are angry at the Account, and say, that if it be Fact, a Veil should be drawn over it, as an Imperfection in humane Nature.

"If it be a Fact," it must be suppressed! When Mary Toft claimed to have given birth to rabbits, she angered, unsettled, and frightened many people, so much so that the mere possibility that she might have the power to do what she claimed had to be denied.

II

What kind of power could a woman who claimed to have given birth to rabbits possibly have that would give rise to the anxieties she seemed to have provoked? A rudimentary answer to this question is suggested by one of the most brilliant and witty satires of the Mary Toft affair, "The Discovery: or, The Squire turn'd Ferret," a ballad by Alexander Pope and William Pulteney. The target in this poem is Samuel Molyneux, and the occasion is the story, which he helped spread, that he had delivered the head of one of Mary Toft's rabbits when he and St. André had gone to Guildford on 15 November:

> Most true it is, I dare to say,
>   E'er since the Days of *Eve,*
> The weakest Woman sometimes may
>   The wisest Man deceive.
>
> For *D——nt* circumspect, sedate,
>   A *Machiavel* by Trade,
> Arriv'd Express, with News of Weight,
>   And thus, at Court, he said.
>
> At *Godliman,* hard by the *Bull,*
>   A Woman, long thought barren,
> Bears *Rabbits,*—Gad! so plentiful,
>   You'd take her for a Warren.

These eyes, quote He, beheld them clear:
    What, do ye doubt my View?
Behold this Narrative that's here;
    Why, Zounds! and Blood! 'tis true!
. . . .

But *M-l-n-x,* who heard this told,
    (Right wary He and wise)
Cry'd sagely, 'Tis not safe, I hold,
    To trust to *D——nt*'s Eyes.

A Vow to God he then did make
    He would himself go down,
St. A-d-re too, the Scale to take
    Of that *Phœnomenon.*

He order'd then his Coach and Four;
    (The Coach was quickly got 'em)
Resolv'd this *Secret* to explore,
    And search it to the *Bottom.*

At *Godliman* they now arrive,
    For Haste they made exceeding;
As Courtiers should, whene'er they strive
    To be inform'd of Breeding.
. . . .

The Surgeon with the *Rabbit* came,
    And first in Pieces cut it;
Then slyly thrust it up *that same,*
    As far as Man could put it.
. . . .

But hold! says *Molly,* first let's try,
    Now that her Legs are ope,
If ought within we may descry
    By Help of Telescope.

The Instrument himself did make,
    He rais'd and level'd right,
But all about was so opake,
    It could not aid his Sight.

On Tiptoe then the Squire he stood,
    (But first He gave Her Money)
Then reach'd as high as e'er He could,
    And cry'd, I feel a CONY.

Is it alive? *St. A-d-re* cry'd;
    It is; I feel it stir.
Is it full grown? The Squire reply'd,
    It is; see here's the FUR.

And now two Legs *St. A-d-re* got,
　　And then came two Legs more;
Now fell the Head to *Molly*'s Lot,
　　And so the Work was o'er.

The Woman, thus being brought to Bed,
　　Said, to reward your Pains,
St. A-nd-re shall dissect the Head,
　　And thou shalt have the Brains.
. . . .

O! happy would it be, I ween,
　　Could they these *Rabbits* smother;
Molly had ne'er a Midwife been,
　　Nor she a shameful Mother.

Why has the Proverb falsely said
　　Better two Heads than one;
Could *Molly* hide this *Rabbit*'s Head,
　　He still might shew his own.[14]

　　Much of the comedy of this ballad grows out of its central situation, Molyneux's desire to know and the ability of Mary Toft first to tempt him to knowledge and then to frustrate his aim completely (this is one reason, I take it, why she is compared to Eve in the first stanza). The desire for knowledge is figured in terms of sight, an image that pervades the poem. Davenant is described as "circumspect," and his defense of the truth of his story rests on what he has seen: "These eyes, quoth He, beheld them clear: / What, do ye doubt my View?" Even the additional proof written up in his report can be confirmed by the sight: "Behold this Narrative that's here." Molyneux's doubt is expressed as a suspicion of what others have seen ("'Tis not safe, I hold, / To trust to D——*nt*'s Eyes"), a suspicion that can be resolved only if he himself goes to the scene as an eyewitness. Because of his urge to hunt out the truth, to see it for himself, Molyneux is the "Squire turn'd Ferret," an animal whose two proverbial attributes were its tenacious delving into rabbit burrows and its keen eyesight.

　　Sight is important in this poem for several reasons. As I have noted, many people felt compelled to "see" Mary Toft, and the appearance of this compulsion here is an acknowledgment by Pope and Pulteney of the haze of uncertainty that surrounded the incident before it was revealed to be a hoax, a haze that left people muddling between belief and disbelief. This theme becomes increasingly important as the poem goes on, but there is a another, more immediately obvious reason for these allusions to sight. The passion for seeing is particularly appropriate to Molyneux because he was a natural philosopher, born into a family of natural philosophers. His father, William, founder of the Dublin Philosophical Society and one of the pioneers of Irish science, was fascinated with astronomy and optics: he designed instruments, made observations, and wrote two optical treatises. As Samuel himself grew older, he gravitated to the scientific interests of his father. He became a serious astronomer. He wrote on optics, he built his own telescopes (thus the telescope he uses in "The Discovery" to survey Mary Toft: "The Instrument himself did make, / He rais'd and level'd right"), and just a year before the Mary Toft incident, at his home near Kew, he tried, with the help of the astronomer James Bradley, to discover the parallax of the fixed stars. He measured stellar aberrations and calculated, with a fair degree of accuracy, the speed of light.[15]

As a "Right wary . . . and wise" scientist, then, it is proper that Molyneux refuses to take anything on trust, particularly in an affair as indeterminate as Mary Toft's, and demands to be an eyewitness. But there is even another reason why Pope and Pulteney emphasized sight in the poem. Whiston, it will be remembered, reported that Molyneux described to him the delivery of the rabbit's head this way: "Mr. *Molyneux* . . . assured me, he had at first so great a Diffidence in the Truth of the Fact, and was so little biassed by the other Believers, . . . that he would not be satisfied till he was permitted both to see and feel the Rabbet in that very Passage whence we all come into this World out of our Mother's Womb. Accordingly he told me, he had more Evidence of it, than he had that I had a Nose; whilst he had known that by one of his Senses only, that of seeing, but knew this by two of his Senses, both seeing and feeling." Pope and Pulteney obviously knew this story, perhaps from Molyneux himself, who was a friend of Pope's, for they too make seeing inadequate ("all about was so opake, / It could not aid his Sight") and have Molyneux confirm the facts by feeling: "On Tiptoe then the Squire he stood, / (But first He gave her Money) / Then reach'd as high as e'er He could, / And cry'd, I feel a CONY."

In "The Discovery," sight fails utterly. And Pope and Pulteney have emphasized sight in their poem so they could bring it to this failure and thus create a very witty denouement. By placing Molyneux in a situation where suddenly he has lost his ability to see and is forced to identify an object on the basis of touch, they have fashioned a comic variation of one of the most celebrated philosophical problems of the eighteenth century:

> Suppose a man born blind, and now adult, and taught by his touch to distinguish between a cube and a sphere of the same metal, and nighly of the same bigness, so as to tell, when he felt one and the other, which is the cube, which the sphere. Suppose then the cube and sphere placed on a table, and

the blind man to be made to see: *quaere,* whether by his sight, before he touched them, he could now distinguish and tell which is the globe, which the cube?[16]

In the poem, this situation is neatly reversed. Instead of gaining sight, Molyneux loses his; instead of having to identify an object by sight without touching, he must judge by touch without seeing.

There is good reason for this philosophical puzzle to be in "The Discovery." It is called the "Molyneux problem." William Molyneux, Samuel's father, first proposed it to John Locke, who published it under Molyneux's name in *An Essay Concerning Human Understanding.* Both William Molyneux and Locke determined that when the blind man regained sight he would not be able to identify the objects, reasoning that experience and intellectual interpretation modify the fundamental data of the senses, that "the *ideas we receive by sensation are often . . . altered by the judgment.*"[17] In "The Discovery," this wise proposition of the father is proved by the witless son (who, by the way, had been raised in accordance with Lockean educational principles). Samuel Molyneux, ardent for knowledge and determined to establish it on firm empirical footing, allows the evidence of his senses to be altered by his "judgment"—that is to say, by his sexual naiveté and overly eager credulity: "Is it alive? St. *A-d-re* cry'd; / It is; I feel it stir. / Is it full grown? The Squire reply'd, / It is; see here's the FUR."

Molyneux is defeated in his pursuit of knowledge, but this is not the only defeat he suffers at the hands of Mary Toft. There is an additional side of Molyneux that is satirized in this poem. Besides being an astronomer, Molyneux was secretary to the Prince of Wales, and "The Discovery" is just as interested in Mary Toft's duping of Molyneux the courtier as in her duping of Molyneux the scientist.

Pope, in fact, had known Molyneux at court. Ten years before the Mary Toft incident, both had played at being courtiers, Pope self-consciously, never fully believing in the role he had assumed, Molyneux rather more earnestly: it was, after all, to be his career. Molyneux had come to London in 1712 to gain a position in the Harley administration, but he had no success. A year later he applied himself to Harley's enemies, the Duke and Duchess of Marlborough, and by May 1714 he was in Hanover, in effect acting as the Marlboroughs' secret agent, sending back news of the political situation. He now denounced Harley, with whom he had sought an audience two years earlier, as a villainous "sorcerer."[18]

By the time George I came to England as king, Molyneux had become secretary to the Prince of Wales. But his career was neither untroubled nor secure, for much of the time he was enmeshed in the violent quarrels between the king and his son. Throughout, he remained publicly faithful to the prince (as a member of Parliament he consistently supported him, even when he went into opposition).[19] If we can trust that Molyneux's tone was accurately captured by the Earl of Egmont when he recounted the tale many years later, Molyneux was proud that when the final breach between the king and the prince came, he remained loyal to the man he served and that he had never forsaken principle for self-interest:

> My cousin Molineux ... told us ... that upon the order of the late King that whoever remained in the service of one Court should not hold the employments he had in the other, but nevertheless that they were at liberty to make their option, that he had computed what every person concerned lost or gained by the party they chose, and that he found for 20£ advantage the Prince's Court abandoned or stayed with him.

But, in fact, Molyneux was not as detached and principled as he wished to appear, and he was not above a bit of groveling to insure that he not lose out in the shifting fields of power. (Lady Cowper concluded that "it was prudent not to trust Mr. *Molyneux*" after she saw him abase himself before his politcal rivals: he "cried and begged to be forgiven, and has excused himself upon doing Nothing but obey his Master.") Nor did he take the final breach between the king and the prince in 1717 with the equanimity and disengaged amusement he suggested to the Earl of Egmont he had shown. "I must tell you a Story of Molineux," Pope wrote to Mary Wortley Montagu: "The other day at the Princes Levee, he took Mr Edgecomb aside, and asked with an Air of Seriousness, What did the Czar of Muscovy, when he disinherited his Son, do with his Secretary? To which Edgecomb answered, He was sow'd up in a Football, and tost over the water."[20]

There is nothing particularly unusual about Molyneux's political career. Attempting to gain a foothold in one faction and, failing that, going over to its rival, cultivating the appearances of uprightness and loyalty, of being above mean self-interest, even acting on such principles when the cost was not too great, but living in fear of the loss of status, willing now and then to compromise personal integrity in the interests of position and advancement: all of this is what we might expect any young man to go through to get and keep power in the political world of eighteenth-century England. But what must have struck Pope and Pulteney was how Molyneux had played courtier in the Mary Toft affair, too, how his behavior during the incident—his early tacit support for St. André followed by his joining forces with Manningham to expose Mary Toft, his pretending to be an important player at the center of events by suggesting falsely that he delivered the head of the rabbit, his equivocal public statements placing him on safe ground between conflicting claims, his creating different stories suited to different audiences—comically echoed the way he had changed parties, assumed poses, and attempted to remain loyal to the prince and yet excuse himself to the king's party.[21]

And it is Molyneux's very typicality as a courtier—his willingness to enter into games of status, to cultivate appearances, to play roles for place and power—that is satirized in "The Discovery." As the poem continually points out, the Mary Toft affair is an affair of the court, and Molyneux's interest in the case is motivated less by a desire for knowledge than by a desire for status. Indeed, for Molyneux, as for the rest of the court, knowledge has become a mere counter in a larger and more vital game of position and reputation, as the poem makes clear with a pun: "At *Godliman* they now arrive, / For Haste they made exceeding; / As Courtiers should, whene'er they strive / To be inform'd of Breeding." Molyneux's interest in Mary Toft is precipitated by the arrival at court of Davenant, whose news is a challenge to him. To be a courtier is to be in the know, and Molyneux must go see the phenomenon for himself, not only to maintain his reputation as the "wisest Man" but to guard against any machinations by Davenant. "Right wary . . . and wise" describes Molyneux's habits as an empirical scientist, but also his necessary behavior at court, where judicious skepticism and wisdom have been transvalued to mean suspicion and craftiness. To protect his status, Molyneux must be suspicious. Davenant is a "*Machiavel* by Trade." He had something of a reputation for trying to gain court positions by spreading false rumors, and therefore "'Tis not safe" to trust him or his story.[22]

Since at court knowledge has become merely an instrument of position and status, the emphasis in the first part of "The Discovery" on *seeing* is wittily turned at the end of the poem into Molyneux's shame at *being seen*. Similarly, in the last two lines, "Could *Molly* hide this *Rabbit's* Head, / He still might shew his own," "Head" refers to the seat of Molyneux's intelligence but more obviously to his inability to "show his face," and so it makes the same point about how much the desire of knowledge has been subordinated to and subsumed by a concern for reputation. Thus, the brief mention of the Fall in the first stanza is a more meaningful allusion than at first it may appear. Molyneux, like Adam, wants to eat of the Tree of Knowledge, but his motive is pride, for to him knowledge is just a way to move up in status, to become as one of the gods. The first consequence of Molyneux's fall, like Adam's before him, is shame. And Mary Toft, like Eve, conquers by deceit.

"The Discovery" is a witty poem, and I think it is a revealing one. The concerns that lay behind its wit and the patterns that the poem creates out of the event we see again and again in the responses to the Mary Toft incident, and I am going to argue that these patterns and concerns explain why the Mary Toft affair mesmerized London so intently and for so long. Those nebulous apprehensions we saw earlier, those intimations that Mary Toft could initiate some obscurely defined fall into disorder, are given a specific shape in "The Discovery." The collapse figured in this poem is a psychological fall, and it follows a clear trajectory. Mary Toft provokes a moment of fundamental confusion when the senses themselves fail to keep us in touch with the external world because their evidence is used to feed a fantasy constructed by a deluded mind. In the case posed by the "Molyneux Problem," the man who regains his sight sees perfectly yet is perfectly blind. So in the case of Samuel Molyneux of "The Discovery": there is a rupture between what is sensed and what is true; what Molyneux clearly and vividly senses is completely false. And then, this fall into confusion precipitates a second fall, a fall of his reputation and status, a collapse of his identity: Molyneux set out to Godalming to preserve his identity as a wise empiricist and a shrewd courtier, and it is precisely that identity which this moment of confusion causes him to lose.

Other satirists of the Mary Toft affair were equally fascinated with this moment of confusion and loss of identity, and they portrayed it in much the same way as Pope and Pulteney did in "The Discovery." "A Shorter and Truer Advertisement," an anonymous poem whose satiric premise is that Dr. Douglas believed that Mary Toft was going to deliver an eighteenth rabbit, opens with Douglas suffering exactly the same perceptual confusion that Molyneux suffered:

> Have I my Fingers? and have I my Eyes?
> Or are my Senses fled through much Surprise?
> There's *Something* sure? must quickly come
> From out of *Mary Toft* her *Womb*.
>
> See here? Just above the *Pubes*
> Either in Womb, or in the *Tube* is
> *A Huge Swelling,* within her Belly
> Which I'm amaz'd at, let me tell ye?

As in "The Discovery," where the concern with seeing becomes an anxiety about being seen, so in this poem, Douglas's lament about his confusion yields to a plea that he be allowed to confirm what he has seen (again, like Molyneux, by touch) and then that others be allowed to see what he has seen so that he may not lose his reputation:

This is no doubt, a *Curious Case*
Her Pains are Sharp upon her,
   Oh! keep your word, & give me place,
As you're a Man of Honour.

Remember your Promise, break not your Troth,
This Month of December, and Day of the fourth.

Hold, Hold, sweet Sir, do me no Wrong
   Down on my Knees, I implore ye,
Her Labour Pains, are mighty Strong,
   Let's touch't in *Uteri Ore.*
. . . .

There's *Something Curious*! make no doubt,
   E're it be long, I'll pull it out.

A Birth! A Birth! is now at hand
   Come in without delay
Nay, Come Good Sirs, this Moment in
   Or I will run away.

Unless you all come in and see
This *Wondrous Birth,* this *Prodigy*
I never more Belief shall find,
Amongst my Brethern or Womankind
Therefore come in, with one Consent
For I am all *Astonishment.*

Douglas suffers a fall here, like Molyneux, losing his status and his reputation. In fact, the author of "A Shorter and Truer Advertisement" systematically inverts the public identity that Douglas had created for himself in his *Advertisement.* Douglas had said in his pamphlet that he was contemptuous of St. André's opinions and that St. André was so impressed by Douglas's probity that he had brought him into the affair to buttress his own claims. But in "A Shorter and Truer Advertisement," it is Douglas who has become a shameless beggar of favors from St. André ("Hold, Hold, sweet Sir, do me no Wrong / Down on my Knees, I implore ye") asking *him* to confirm his own observations. In *An Advertisement,* Douglas had claimed that on 4 December, when Mary Toft developed a swelling and St. André announced that she was on the verge of delivering her eighteenth rabbit, he reminded St. André that he had promised not to make his speculations public until Douglas himself had examined her to make sure there was no fraud. This, too, is inverted, for when Douglas asks St. André to recall his promise (*"Remember your Promise, break not your Troth / This Month of December, and Day of the fourth"*), the author of "A Shorter and Truer Advertisement" purposely confuses this promise with an earlier promise made by St. André that Douglas would be allowed to deliver the rabbit himself, and so the poem makes it appear that, contrary to what he claimed, Douglas really did believe that she was giving birth to rabbits. Finally, Douglas had chided Manningham because Manningham had believed that "something" was in Mary Toft's uterus, a view which Douglas thought wholly unfounded. In "A Shorter and Truer Advertisement," Manningham's opinion now becomes Douglas's ("There's *Something* sure? must quickly come / From out of *Mary Toft* her *Womb*").

Like Molyneux in "The Discovery," Douglas loses the character he is attempting to retain by attempting to retain it. The comedy of the poem lies in the spectacle of Douglas's trying to steady his public identity as if it were some rickety scaffolding—and making it totter and fall by his very act of trying to steady it. And yet, in exposing this "Truer" character of Douglas, the author, like Pope and Pulteney in "The Discovery," is making no charge of hypocrisy. He is not saying that Douglas had believed Mary Toft initially and then, after the hoax was exposed, pretended that he did not. The author of "A Shorter and Truer Advertisement," like Pope and Pulteney, is interested in the much more complex mental phenomenon of confusion and, more particularly, in how this confusion is caused by a vivid sensory experience which creates a "reality" that is, in fact, not real. Douglas's conviction that Mary Toft is an imposter founders at the sight of her "*Huge Swelling,*" and at this moment, his concrete, sensory experience becomes severed from truth ("Have I my Fingers? and have I my Eyes? / Or are my Senses fled through much Surprise?"). The propulsive rhythms, the turbulent, obsessive rush of ideas, and the extravagant language of this poem wonderfully depict a mind precipitated into disorder and the near-hysterical energy of its attempt to contain the mounting disintegration of its own coherence and identity.

An epistemological collapse like this may seem a bit too catastrophic to have been provoked by a simple hoax like Mary Toft's. Yet the images we have seen before of national calamity, of blurred lines between species, and of failing language had this same perplexing degree of hyperbole, and the epistemological collapse experienced by Molyneux and Douglas is, after all, merely a translation into the psychological realm of the collapse imaged in the realms of language, nature, and the state. And further, something like this dislocation between what was experienced through the senses as a palpable truth and what was known to be true actually did happen. The real Douglas, much like the fictional Douglas presented in "A Shorter and Truer Advertisement," appears to have been so shaken by what he saw and felt in the bagnio on 4 December that he is reported to have said "he c[oul]d scarce believe his own Senses."[23] When Lord Hervey remarked in his letter to Henry Fox that the affair "really stagger's one," he was an accurate witness. People wavered between belief and disbelief because what was sensed as true contradicted what was thought to be true. "Nobody knows which they are to believe, their Eyes or their Ears," Hervey went on to say, because they were caught beween "the reality of the fact, & the philosophical proofs of the impossibility of it." And this same feeling of the uncertainty of the truth of what was experienced through the senses is echoed again in another satire, "Mr P— to Dr. A————t," which summed up the significance of the Mary Toft affair in similar terms:

> Then change the Proverb, teach the Youth,
> Seeings not Faith, nor Feeling Truth.

Given the Mary Toft incident, the single image that most fully expresses this confusion, of course, is monstrosity itself, for in the monstrous, the boundaries which articulate form and identity begin to dissolve toward an unnameable amorphousness. And, in a satiric portrait of Manningham in "Mr. P— to Dr. A————t," monstrosity is used as a figure for his confusion and loss of identity.

> When Conversation grows quite barren,
> We'll talk of *Woman* turn'd to *Warren*.
> Strange Metamorphose! strange and new!
> But what a Knight says must be true,
> He scorns like vulgar Folk to speak
> He talks in *Latin* and in *Greek*
> For Instance: (which you may rely on)
> He calls a *Cond-m* a *Corion*?
> Then wonders how (O Men's *Supina*)
> Such things should come into *Vagina*.
> You know *Vagina* means a Case,
> It is dear Knight a tempting Place,
> Where you have shewn great Inclination
> To bring in Transubstantiation,
> Tho' Doctors have no Faith they say,
> We find that 'Pothecary may;
> O wise, believing, learned Wight!
> Apothecary, Doctor, Knight.

Like "The Discovery" and "A Shorter and Truer Advertisement," "Mr. P— to Dr. A————t" does not bring charges of hypocrisy, focusing instead on what fascinated the authors of the other two poems, mental disarray. And, again like the other two poems, "Mr. P— to Dr. A————t" depicts this confusion as occasioning the dissolution of identity. Indeed, the poem obviously is a response to the self-portrait of Manningham that emerges from his *Exact Diary,* where he appears, despite his intentions, to be profoundly confused. There, Manningham recounted in detail how, when Mary Toft delivered a membrane which Howard and St. André claimed was part of the chorion, he saw that it was a hog's bladder and decided to await "the Event of the whole Transaction" so he could catch Mary Toft in a fraud which was now only too apparent. But Manningham also gave another reason for riding out the events to an end: he thought that her uterus seemed "to contain something of Substance in its Cavity," and even as late as 4 December, after Mr. Lacy's servant confessed that he had been bribed to procure a rabbit for Mary Toft, Manningham persisted in thinking that "something would soon issue from the *Uterus.*"[24] As I suggested earlier, Manningham apparently meant that he thought that she had found some way to convey parts of rabbits into her uterus, but for many of those who read his pamphlet, and even for most of those who dealt with him face-to-face during that last week in the bagnio, it seemed that he truly did believe that Mary Toft was giving birth to rabbits. And as a result, Manningham appeared to many to be both utterly skeptical, detecting Mary Toft's trick with the hog's bladder as soon as he saw it, and utterly credulous, willing to accept the woman's claims in spite of the fact that they had just caught the porter sneaking in a rabbit. He seemed to have seen one thing with penetrating accuracy and then, astonishingly, to have come to a conclusion completely at odds with what he had seen. In short, Manningham has gone through a variation of that moment of perceptual confusion that had stricken Molyneux and Douglas.

What is remarkable about this poem is the way it conceives of this confusion. In both "The Discovery" and "A Shorter and Truer Advertisement," this disorder of a mind ends by subverting personal coherence and identity—hence these poems' emphasis on reversals of opinion, shame, and loss of reputation. "Mr. P— to Dr. A————t" portrays this confusion as a loss of psychic integrity so profound that it results in a dispersion of identity—or, more accurately, in the multiplication of so many centers of personality that the coherent identity of the self disintegrates. Hence the poem moves from the confusion of his language to the confusion of what he "is." Like the doctor he is, he is skeptical, refusing to believe that the membrane Mary Toft delivered was anything but a hog's bladder. Like the apothecary he is, he is credulous, believing that she has given birth to rabbits.[25] Like the knight he is, he is driven by neither belief nor disbelief, but by devotion to his lady (not to put too fine a point on it). Manningham's behavior is so radically incoherent that it is as if he has no single self, as if there were three autonomous people inhabiting the same person. Thus, by the end of the poem, he can be named only by listing the permutations of his identity: "O wise, believing, learned Wight! / Apothecary, Doctor, Knight."

The image of this incoherence is monstrous birth. The poem begins by suggesting that it is going to talk about mysterious changes in Mary Toft's womb or perhaps in Mary Toft herself ("Strange Metamorphose! strange and new!"), but it turns immediately to the strange metamorphosis of Manningham as he flitters through his various, mutually contradictory identities. The truly monstrous product of Mary Toft, so goes the logic of this poem's presiding, though submerged, metaphor, is the shapeless self of Manningham. And in this way, "Mr. P— to Dr. A———t" literalizes the implications of many of the patterns of the responses to the Mary Toft incident. If Mary Toft possessed a power to be feared, that power was her ability to make monsters—that is, her power to dissolve the very identity of the self.

It is not surprising that this anxiety about Mary Toft is played out in primitive sexual images. Consider, for instance, this passage from "The Doctor's in Labour":

> When I (says Moll) five weeks was gone with Child,
> And hard at Work was weeding in the field,
> Up starts a Rabbet—to my grief I view'd it,
> And vainly tho with eagerness pursued it,
> The Effect was strange—Blest is the Womb that's barren
> For that can neer be made a Coney Warren
>
> The Rabbit all day long ran in my Head,
> At Night I dreamt I had him in my Bed;
> Me thought he there a Borrough try'd to make
> His Head I patted and stroak'd his Back.
> My Husband wak'd me and Cry'd Moll for shame
> Let go—what 'twas meant I need not Name.

The joke here is based on the belief that the power of the imagination was particularly efficacious when pregnant woman had a strong longing that could not be satisfied, and "The Doctor's in Labour" makes clear what exactly the object of Mary Toft's desire was. And so do other satires. In fact, almost every one asserted that Mary Toft was sexually profligate, and many used her putative lust as an occasion for baroque fantasizing about her carnal appetites and perversities. A common joke among them was that she was certainly pleased, and perhaps was motivated to stage the hoax in the first place, by having the doctors and the crowds of the curious fumble about her body looking for rabbits. One satirist claimed that she used the rabbit as a dildo and explained her birth of rabbits by quoting the metaphysical ruminations of St. Bernard: "'That by a Constant application of any Part to any particular Thing, we may make that become, as it were, Natural in us which is Unnatural in another.'"[26]

Earlier, I argued that the portrayal of Mary Toft as ignorant, weak, and innocent was a defense against acknowledging her power and the fear her power provoked. So, here, these satires' depiction of Mary Toft uncontrollably yearning for the phallus probably are equally as defensive, springing perhaps from a similar fear. In "The Rabbit-Man-Midwife," Arbuthnot suggests as much, for he attributes Clarges's retaliatory anger to his fear that the phallus has been not merely displaced but dismissed as a necessary object:

> Whip, said Sir Thomas, Whip the Slut,
> It is a Breach of Peace,
> That Woman any thing should put
> But P[in]tles into that Place.[27]

But the most suggestive piece of evidence that this joking about Mary Toft and her rabbit hid an uneasiness about her sexual power and about male incapacity is a long passage from *Much Ado About Nothing* in which "Mary Toft" recounts in her own words the history of the hoax:

> I was alwas dispekid by my naburs, and in pertikulur Mr. —— hoo alwas told me I wos a Wuman as had *grate natturul parts,* and a *large Capassiti,* and kapible of being kunserned in depe *Kuntrivansis;* and as how if I wold be rulid by him, and use *Prickkawshun,* sum think mowt be dun, and as how I luft Rawbits, I shud navar wont: so he tretid me with as fine a Rawbit as effer I tastid in my born days. Now you must noe his Rawbit had an indiffrunt tast from ani I had effer ete, for it wos not byld, nor rostid, nor fricumceed, *but tost up skin and aul with its eres prickt up.* How effer, thank G——, I got it all down, and thote I nevur tastid a dellikittur morsil in my lyf; my husband had giffen me mani and mani a Rawbit before, but no comparrezon. So I neffur aftur vallid his Rawbits, no more then nutthink at all, but alwas honed and honed for my nabur's Rawbit. But he growing wary of suplying me, fobd me off, and sade as how I had too much *Affucktation* for him: so he brought me one *Surjohn,* and another *Surjohn,* but none of these Rawbitts went doun lik his, nor spent hafe so well: and as for takin them at the mouth, I cood not, for evar sense I had tastid his Rawbitt, I tuk them all tuther way, and I humbli kunseve it is the best way, espechally if thay ar not flabby; but if thay are flabby, thay ar not wurth a fart.

Aftur this, *an ugly old Gentilman* in a grate blak wig cam to me, but he
had lost his Rawbit by the way, for I cood see nun he had; and he onli tez'd
me, and tez'd me, but mad nutthink of it; for he fumblid and fumblid; but
to no purpos, for all his grabbin and gropin signefyd as much as nuthink.

Then thay brote a *purblynd Gentilman,* hoo was for *survayin* me with
his *Telluskop;* but it was so dark he cood not see, tho he got upon a gynt-
stool, and had it not bin for anothur Parson, more quick-sited then
himself, he had sartinly lost his *Telluskop.*[28]

Here, too, the rabbit is equated with the phallus and, in the beginning
at least, Mary Toft herself is rather complacently dismissed as a woman
who, because of her lust, is easily governed by the male. She is submissive to her first lover, completely "rulid by him," and he sates her sexual appetite easily: "he tretid me with as fine a Rawbit as effer I tastid in
my born days." But then, amidst all the play with the notion of the
eaten phallus, this fantasy of the dominated woman dissolves and is
replaces by its unsettling opposite. The potential dangers hinted at in
the beginning—her *"grate natturul parts,"* her *"large Capassiti"* and
"depe Kuntrivansis"—shape a new counter-fantasy. Her sexual
appetite no longer satisfied ("I had too much *Affucktation* for him"), she
ceases to be submissive and becomes a voracious, demanding sexual
tyrant, and finally a dangerous one. The passage concludes with a succession of images of male impotence.

From the beginning, we have seen that what was unsettling about
Mary Toft was her power, and so we should not be too surprised to find
these images of impotence here in *Much Ado About Nothing.* They certainly clutter the other satires, sometimes in a generalized way, such as
when Douglas is reduced to a hysterical beggar in "A Shorter and
Truer Advertisement," sometimes more specifically, as in "The Discovery" when Molyneux "rais'd and level'd right" his telescope, inserted it into Mary Toft, and was promptly defeated, or as in "The Rabbit-
Man-Midwife" where the paternity of Mary Toft's rabbits is attributed
to an unnamed lord and their monstrosity to his lack of virility.

> For Lords, as well as other Men,
> Can do but what they can,
> Engend'ring little Monsters when
> They cannot get a Man.

If impotence expresses the fact of Mary Toft's power, the second sexual metaphor in *Much Ado,* the one which precipitates the collapse of
the complacent fantasy of her harmlessness, specifies the nature of her
threat. The conflation of eating and intercourse, the danger that a man
will be swallowed up in her *"large Capassiti,"* suggests that Mary Toft's

frightful power is her power of assimilation. We have seen this before, too, for assimilation expresses in a radical form the fear of the disintegration of structure and the loss of identity which have pervaded the responses to the Mary Toft affair. And it is an anxiety that reveals itself in still one more pattern in the responses to the incident. Consider, for instance, this satire on St. André:

> The Sympathy, good Folks, is wonderous to speak
> As he touch'd his Fiddle the Woman did squeak,
> Which has put our Surgeon in such a sad Pet
> 'Tis fear'd his own guts will to Fiddle strings fret.

The theme, once again, as in so many of these satires, is of power and the loss of power. St. André is under the illusion that he controls Mary Toft, for when "he touch'd his Fiddle the woman did squeak." (St. André, of course, had been a dancing master and, as he once made the cat-gut strings of his fiddle respond to his touch, so now he can make Mary Toft vibrate "sympathetically.") This metaphor, however, merely prepares us for the revelation of St. André's real impotence, for as the next lines show, *he* is the instrument played on, and *his* "guts" vibrate sympathetically to the movements of Mary Toft. And the pun on "guts" spins the metaphor in a new direction: St. André has been transformed not simply into a passive instrument, but into a woman, into another Mary Toft, in fact, and his fretting stomach, like Mary Toft's, has gone into the convulsions of labor (the title of the poem, after all, is "St. A-D-E's Miscarriage").

Impotence and assimilation: the male is denied his potency and then his identity, transformed into an image of the power that controls him. Such a transformation was common notion in the responses to the Mary Toft incident. In "Mr. P— to Dr. A———t," Manningham undergoes his "Strange Metamorphose," a victim of the process of monster-making which goes on in Mary Toft's womb. In "The Discovery," Molyneux falls into the "Labour" of finding out the truth of Mary Toft, and when he is duped by her is henceforth called "Molly." In the pantomime *Harlequin turn'd Imposture,* Joshua Toft, rushing the midwife to his laboring wife, puts her astride the horse while he himself sits side-saddle.[29] And, as the title "The Doctor's in Labour" suggests, the confusion and intellectual contortions of the medical men were often perceived as false or monstrous pregnancies. St. André suffers a "Miscarriage," or else he is "finely brought to Bed." All the doctors, who "by the gravity of their style seemed past childing," have brought forth a "monstrous birth called Afterwit." If they were not another laboring Mary Toft, they were her monstrous births themselves: not

only, as we have seen, does Manningham undergo a "Strange Meta-
morphose," a victim of the process of monster-making that goes on in
Mary Toft's womb, but St. André, too, becomes "this Creature," "this
Animal," this "præternatural Anatomist."[30]

Impotence and assimilation are at the end of a trajectory of a generalized uneasiness that expressed itself under the guise of various dis-
placements, defenses, and images: denials of Mary Toft's power and
then, in covert ways, acknowledgments of it; spectres of a ruined language, blurred species, a subverted nation, all of which eventually yield
to the image of a mind collapsing into confusion and then incoherence;
the loss of status and identity as men are transformed into laboring
women, into versions of Mary Toft herself, into monsters. All of these
are undercurrents, but their persistence suggests that, underneath their
joking and high spirits, many people responded with an edgy apprehension that Mary Toft represented an overwhelming power that, by
sundering what was true from what was experienced as true by the
senses, could precipitate people into confusion so profound that their
identities were destroyed and they were transformed into monstrous
and shapeless things, assimilated into the very power that initiated the
process of their disintegration.

III

Why the power of the imagination would give rise to these particular
anxieties is suggested by William Hogarth's *Cunicularii, or The Wise
Men of Godliman in Consultation,* a satiric print published between 22
and 24 December, at the height of the public furor over Mary Toft.

The print (figure 2) shows many of the principals of the affair gathered around Mary Toft, "The Lady in the straw," who is in the throes
of labor. Howard, "The Guilford Rabbet Man Midwife," stands at the
door and turns away a poulterer offering him a rabbit because "Its too
big" (Hogarth, like most people, assumed that Howard was guilty).
Joshua Toft, his hand hidden suspiciously in the bed curtain, is "The
Rabbet getter." Margaret Toft, seated between Joshua and Mary Toft
and turned around looking at Joshua as if for instructions, is "The
Nurse or Rabbet Dresser."

In addition to these four rogues from Surrey, there are three hood-
winked medical men. The doctor on his knees delivering a rabbit has
generally been identified as Manningham. "The Dancing Master or
Præternatural Anatomist" is, of course, St. André. The third figure,
"The Sooterkin Doctor Astonish'd," shouting "A Sooterkin, a

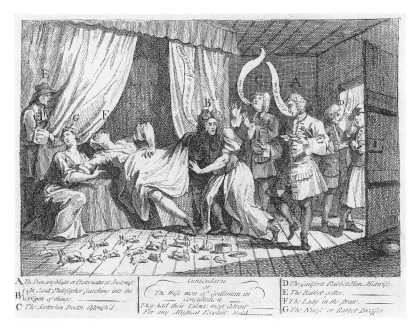

Figure 2. William Hogarth, *Cunicularii, or The Wise Men of Godliman in Consultation* (copyright British Museum)

Sooterkin," is John Maubray. He had earned the title of "The Sooterkin Doctor" because, several years before the Mary Toft incident, he had become notorious in another case of monstrous childbirth when he claimed that he delivered a sooterkin, a mouse-like creature to which, according to folklore, Dutch women gave birth.[31]

Maubray's appearance here identifies the particular moment Hogarth portrays. Maubray attended Mary Toft in the bagnio only once, on 4 December. His visit was duly recorded in Manningham's account of that hectic day in his *Exact Diary,* from which Hogarth seems to have drawn much of the information for this print.[32] On 4 December, it will be remembered, Mary Toft had been in London for five days. She had been in "labor" almost constantly, but she had delivered nothing. The porter of the bagnio had been caught the previous evening. The hoax was about to collapse. But, on the morning of 4 December, Mary Toft suddenly developed a swelling. No one could offer an explanation. Manningham thought the "Swelling [was] in the Cavity of the *Uterus*" and noted that "the *Os Uteri* [was] soft and spread." By late afternoon, she began to have violent contractions. The doctors—St. André,

Howard, Manningham, Douglas, and Maubray—attended assiduous-
ly and, according to Manningham's version, "we agreed, that the
Nature of the Pains were such, and so violent, as we apprehended that
something would soon issue from the *Uterus;* and this we declared in
the hearing of many Persons of Distinction, who were then present:
And I well remember, the Room being very full, I desired if there was
any Person present willing to examine her, that they would do it then
while her Pains were upon her. Accordingly, several Persons did examine her, and declared to the same Purpose: After having received several Pains, they, together with the other Symptoms of Approaching
Labour, vanished on a sudden, as formerly."[33]

Manningham's bland presentation of the facts scarcely suggests the
confusion of that day and the consequent misunderstanding and furor.
To most of those gathered in the bagnio, it appeared that the doctors
were predicting the birth of a new rabbit—and this after the porter
had been caught sneaking a rabbit into the bagnio. The spectators were
flabbergasted. Accusations were made that the doctors were conspiring
to pass the fraud off on the public.

There can be little question that for *Cunicularii* Hogarth had in
mind the events of 4 December, the day when it appeared that St.
André, Maubray, and Manningham, in spite of the evidence to the contrary, predicted the birth of the eighteenth rabbit, betrayed into this
foolishness by their own credulity, an os uteri "soft and spread," and an
unexplained "Swelling." "It Pouts it Swells, it Spreads it Comes," says
figure "B" in *Cunicularii.* Allowing for some satiric exaggeration, this
is pretty much how Manningham reported the events of 4 December in
his *Diary.*

On 4 December, the learned doctors were made to be utter fools,
and this suggests the basic structure of *Cunicularii.* The print is about
fools and knaves, and the characters are carefully chosen and carefully
placed within this framework. The three credulous fools—Maubray,
St. André, and Manningham—literally are surrounded by knaves who
have played on their gullibility: Howard, and Margaret, Joshua, and
Mary Toft. The epigraph, "They held their Talents most Adroit / For
any Mystical Exploit," is adapted from a passage in *Hudibras* which
describes Sidrophel, who has made a career swindling the gullible by
alleging preternatural powers. Sidrophel is a "Procurer to th'Extravagancy, / And crazy Ribaldry of Fancy," exploiting the "*Speculative
Lust*" of those foolish enough to be attracted to his fradulent claims.
Since "he held his *Talent* most Adroyt / For any *Mystical Exploit,*" he
decides to procure a witch who will make him skilled in the art of
transforming shapes. His business flourishes.

> Since which, H'has played a thousand Feats,
> And Practis'd all Mechanick Cheats:
> Transform'd himself, to th'ugly Shapes
> Of *Wolves,* and *Bears, Baboons,* and *Apes*;
> . . . .
> And all with whom H'has had to do,
> Turn'd to as Monstrous Figures too.[34]

The relevance of this passage to *Cunicularii* is obvious: the knaves from Godalming have got a monster-breeding "witch" in Mary Toft and are taking advantage of the "*Speculative Lust*" of the doctors, turning them into monstrous fools.

Or are the doctors fools? The epigraph is placed so that it seems to complete the subtitle, "The Wise Men of Godliman in Consultation," suggesting that somehow the doctors are the knaves. And, indeed, the very fact that Hogarth has placed Maubray in the print considerably complicates any simplistic division between fools and knaves. Maubray may have been made the fool in the Mary Toft incident, but two years earlier he had played the knave when, in his *Female Physician,* he claimed that he had delivered a woman of a sooterkin, one of those "*Monstrous little Animals,*" which had "a *hooked snout, fiery sparkling eyes,* a long *round Neck,* and an acuminated *short Tail,* of an extraordinary *Agility of* FEET. *At first Sight* of the World's Light, it commonly *Yells* and *shrieks* fearfully; and seeking for a *lurking Hole,* runs up and down like a *little Daemon,* which indeed I took it for, the first time I saw it, and *that* for none of the *better Sort.*"[35]

His outrageous claim was not forgotten by other satirists of the Mary Toft affair, and *A Letter From A Male Physician In the Country,* a lengthy pamphlet devoted to a scathing exposé of Maubray, again and again made the point that Maubray was responsible for the Mary Toft incident because his deceitful story about the sooterkin in 1724 had prepared the way for this hoax in 1726. "His book," confesses Mary Toft's mother-in-law, "gave me the first Hint to hatch and contrive Ways and Means to palm an *English* Rabbet on the world for his *Dutch* Sooterkins."

> I thought with my self, That if the Man who had publish'd that he had laid several Women in *Holland* of Sooterkins, and all the other strange things contain'd in that Book, has been encourag'd and esteem'd, . . . [and] if he still goes on to teach and instruct, and find Encouragement, being appointed as I hear, *Physician* to the New Parish call'd St. *George's,* after what he has advanc'd in that Book; will it be any Wonder . . . that if such gross things cou'd pass upon the Great Ones about your Great City, that these, and the like, might not easily be swallowed down in the Country? This very Thought mov'd me to bestir my self how to get a Penny. . . .[36]

And *Cunicularii* not only raises questions about Maubray's past, but it also suggests that the two other doctors are something of charlatans too. The fiddle underneath St. André's arm reminds us of the fact almost every Toft satire underscored: he was once a dancing master, and for his entire career he had been dogged by questions of his competency as a surgeon. And the ludicrous contrast between Manningham's expensive full-bottomed wig and his delivery smock is probably meant to remind us of his rapid and surprising rise from apothecary to physician to knight, something not overlooked by other satires. Who, after these attacks, are the fools, who the knaves, and who is responsibile for the hoax? The Tofts, who easily convinced the foolish doctors of the monstrous births, or the doctors, who knavishly created the climate for this kind of hoax—and who were well rewarded for it? Hogarth's point, I take it, is that all of them—the hoaxers from Godalming and the three doctors—are fools and knaves both, victims and exploiters of themselves, and of each other. In *Hudibras,* Sidrophel "Transform'd himself" into a monster, yet all who dealt with him "Turn'd to as Monstrous Figures too."

It was surely his feeling for a psychological moment dense with ambiguity that drew Hogarth specificially to the events of 4 December. He was attracted, in fact, by precisely the same thing which attracted the writers of "Mr. P— to Dr. A————t" and "A Shorter and Truer Advertisement" to the same day. For what is depicted in *Cunicularii* is that psychological moment which fascinated so many of those who responded to the Mary Toft affair, that moment when something is experienced by the senses as true even though it is known to be false. *Cunicularii* portrays this moment of confusion in a radically enigmatic form: a moment when the knaves become fools, not simply believing as true what is obviously false, but duped by the very fraud they have helped to create.

But, unlike the other satirists, Hogarth lucidly accounts for how this seemingly inexplicable confusion can come about. He does so by placing *Cunicularii* in a genre which provides the context that explains the cause and significance of this confusion.

The genre of *Cunicularii* is suggested by a puzzling detail in the print. When figure "B" says, "It Pouts it Swells, it Spreads it Comes," it is an accurate if slightly exaggerated version of what in fact Manningham did say on 4 December. Hogarth's contemporaries identified "B" as Manningham.[37] And, indeed, I think "B" is meant for Manningham—and for someone else entirely. "B" appears to be Manningham given the evidence within the borders of the picture; but the information outside the borders—the caption and the epigraph—makes such an identification uncertain. The caption reads "B. An Occult Philosopher searching into the Depths of things." The phrase "Occult Philosopher" is part of the fabric of associations established by the epigraph from *Hudibras,* which, as we have just seen, describes Sidrophel, a quack astronomer who exploited the credulous. The phrase "Occult Philosopher" is used in *Hudibras,* too, and it makes the same associations: an "Occult Philosopher" is one who, by cunningly mixing the preternatural claims of astrology with the plausible claims of astronomy, exploits Enthusiasts and at the same time is himself touched by Enthusiastic unreason.[38] The problem with figure "B" in *Cunicularii* is this: nothing in the life of Manningham bears any relationship to the activities of an "Occult Philosopher" or to Sidrophel the astronomer.

It is possible, of course, that Hogarth did not mean this nest of allusions to point to something specific in the real-life career of Manningham. This might be an acceptable explanation if it were not for the fact that the allusions fit so neatly another person we have already met, Samuel Molyneux of "The Discovery":

> But *M-l-n-x,* who heard this told,
>   (Right wary He and wise)
> Cry'd sagely, 'Tis not safe, I hold,
>   To trust to *D———nt*'s Eyes....
>
> He ordered then his Coach and Four;
>   (The Coach was quickly got 'em)
> Resolv'd this *Secret* to explore,
>   And search it to the *Bottom.*

The "wise" Molyneux who "sagely" desires to "search . . . to the *Bottom*" bears an obvious similarity to the "Occult Philosopher searching into the Depths of things," a similarity that might be dismissed as fortuitous were it not for what happens next in the poem.

> But hold! says *Molly,* first let's try,
>   Now that her Legs are ope,
> If ought within we may descry
>   By Help of Telescope.
>
> The Instrument himself did make,
>   He rais'd and level'd right,
> But all about was so opake,
>   It could not aid his Sight.

Molyneux was, to use the language of the anti-Enthusiastic tradition of *Hudibras,* a complete "virtuoso": exactly the kind of scientist Butler attacked in the astronomer Sidrophel in the passage Hogarth quotes as the epigraph to *Cunicularii.* The parallels are too thoroughgoing to be accidental. The "wise" virtuoso-astronomer who is "Resolv'd this *Secret* to explore, / And search it to the *Bottom*"; the "Occult Philosopher"—the very phrase alluding to virtuosi-astronomers—"searching into the Depth of things."

Figure "B," then, is a conflation of Manningham and Molyneux, and Hogarth conflated the two into a single figure, I suspect, because of the genre he was working in. For the astronomer was a stock representative of the Enthusiast, and when Hogarth saw how Molyneux was portrayed in Pope and Pulteney's poem, he probably saw there a way of drawing together the various strands of his own work.[39] By associating Manningham with Molyneux as he was portrayed in "The Discovery," and then by reinforcing that association by alluding in the epigraph to a second virtuoso-astronomer, Sidrophel, Hogarth makes clear that the satiric tradition of *Cunicularii* and the context to which he expects his audience to respond is the genre of the anti-Enthusiastic satire, especially as practiced by Butler and Swift. Hogarth wants us to understand, I think, that the kind of confusion he is portraying in this print, with its inextricable compound of foolishness and knavery, is the confusion typically caused by Enthusiasm. Indeed, this ambiguity of fools and knaves, the impossibility of determining whether they are "deluded or deluding People," is endemic to anti-Enthusiastic satire.[40] In *Hudibras,* Hudibras, Ralpho, and Sidrophel are at once knowing exploiters of others and yet at the same time dupes to their own exploitative rhetoric. In Swift, notoriously, this ambiguity is even more intense and convoluted, his Enthusiastic speakers cycling rapidly from manipulating, self-serving knavery to delusional, even insane foolishness, and back again, endlessly.

Hogarth's conceiving of the confusion caused by Mary Toft as "Enthusiastic" is quite remarkable, for with the exception of Whiston's claiming that Mary Toft fulfilled the prophecy of Esdras, there was no explicit or literal connection between the incident and religious fanaticism.[41] And, yet, the link between monstrous childbirth and Enthusiasm is profound. Both involved extraordinary transactions between the body and the mind, and both shared a common etiology, determined and directed by the same agent, the imagination. Indeed, when Swift defined Enthusiasm as that moment "when a Man's Fancy gets *astride* his Reason, when Imagination is at Cuffs with the Senses, and common Understanding, as well as Common Sense, is kickt out of Doors," and when Henry More, one of the most important theorists of Enthusiastic madness, attributed "the cause of *Enthusiasme*" to "the enormous strength of Imagination,"[42] both had in mind the same dynamics of the imagination that were responsible for monstrous childbirth.

The imagination, as we have seen, was situated between sensation and thought. One of its most important functions was to convey objects of the sense to the higher powers of the mind by way of images. The imagination, of course, had other functions and powers. It could call up images from memory, it could concretize ideas of the mind as images, and it could join or disjoin images of things perceived or things remembered, creating fanciful constructs that corresponded to nothing in the external world. These, too, were presented to the mind as images. And here was the problem. Since sensation, memory, ideas, and the fabrications of the fancy were all reduced to images, the imagination was a great leveller. Because both sense objects as well as the fanciful constructions of the imagination were perceived as images, both could be experienced psychologically as having an identical status: to the eye of the mind, the fictions of the imagination might be seen as possessing the same solidity and reality as things perceived by the senses.

This was the danger of the imagination that Glanvill, for instance, saw. "*Imagination* is inward Sense," he explained. When we conceive of palpable objects, we usually conceive of them as "*material phantasms*": "thus when we would conceive a *Triangle, Man,* or *Horse* or any other sensible; we figure it in our Phancies, and stir up there its Sensible *Idea.*" But if this is true, what is to distinguish conceptions called up in the mind from objects perceived through the senses, for in the act of perception, the imagination sublimates and dematerializes the objects perceived, converting them to images that have exactly the same status as those images of thought. And even worse, how can either of these be distinguished from purest fictional creations of the fancy, for these creations, too, appear as images, sharing this same half-sensible, half-ideational nature. "The apparitions of our frighted *Phancies,*" said Glanvill, "are real *sensibles.*" That is, they appear to the mind as solid and palpable as sensible objects appear to the mind. The insubstantial delusions of our imagination take on the same kind of substantiality as real sense objects.[43]

Of course, it was the function of the higher faculties to protect us against this levelling tendency of the imagination, discriminating among the images of things conceived, images of things in the memory, images constructed by the fancy, and images of objects perceived by the senses. And usually, the distinction betweeen the real and the unreal was made intuitively, sense objects being experienced vividly, while fictive constructions of the imagination were more attenuated and dim. The imagination was, in the memorable phrase of Hobbes, "*decaying sense*." And yet, decaying though it was, the imagination was still sense, and given the power of the imagination to concretize its vagaries in images possessing a sensible presence which had the same psychic feel as the images of things perceived, the imagination could "make impressions as strong and as sensible as those Ideas which come immediately by the senses from external objects soe that the mind takes one for tother[,] its own imaginations for realitys."[44]

Such confusion was almost inevitable under several conditions. Sleep was one. In sleep, the imagination "is far *stronger* then any motion or agitation from without," and so the images of the fancy take precedence over the external world, and "the soul conceits her *dreams,* while she is dreaming, to be no dreams, but real transactions."[45] Madness was a second condition: "Fantasies and Imaginations become as it were substantial unto [madmen], as material things are to those that are in their perfect senses, and under the government of reason."[46] And Enthusiasm was a third. For "it is the enormous strength of *Imagination* (which is yet the Soul's weaknesse or unwieldinesse, whereby she so farre sinks into Phantasmes that she cannot recover her self into the use of her more free Faculties of reason and Understanding) that thus peremptorily engages a man to believe a lie."[47] Enthusiasts are fools to their own knavery, as it were. The "lies" of their imaginations become so palpable and concrete that their higher faculties are "gulled by the vigour or garishnesse of the representation, . . . born down by the weight or strength" of the images produced by the fancy, images which are "*so strong*" that they appear in the mind "in *equall* splendour and vigour with what is represented from *without,*" and thus an Enthusiast cannot "fail to take his *Imagination* for a reall Object of Sense." The images of the fancy, as Swift said, are experienced as realities so palpable that they can "*Dupe* and play the Wag with the Senses."[48]

The confusion we have seen portrayed repeatedly in the responses to the Mary Toft incident is a confusion that arises when something is experienced palpably, apparently through the senses, and yet it is an unreal fantasy. By placing *Cunicularii* within the anti-Enthusiastic tradition, Hogarth is portraying this confusion as a species of Enthusiasm.

The context of Enthusiasm explains a second important thing about *Cunicularii* and, more generally, about the responses to the Mary Toft episode. Since the disorder at the heart of Enthusiasm was the levelling of all things to corporeal images and the experience of each image as "a reall Object of Sense," satirists typically portrayed Enthusiasts (much as those confused by Mary Toft were portrayed) as confusing mind and matter, transforming the insubstantial into the substantial and solid things into spectral notions. Here, for instance, is Butler's portrayal of Hudibras's Enthusiasm:

His Notions fitted things so well,
That which was which he could not tell;
But oftentimes mistook the one
For th'other, as Greek Clerks have done.
He could reduce all things to Acts
And knew their Natures by Abstracts,
Where Entity and Quiddity,
The Ghosts of defunct Bodies, flie;
Where Truth in Person does appear,
Like Words congeal'd in Northern Air.
He knew *what's what,* and that's as high
As Metaphysick wit can flie.[49]

In the mind of Hudibras, the world of things has been so dematerialized that the external world has become a phantasmagoria of "Ghosts of defunct Bodies." Robbed of its solidity, the external world drops away, replaced by the internal world of the fancy, but an internal world now materialized, given a (psychologically) concrete existence: "Truth in Person does appear, / Like words congeal'd in Northern Air." Hudibras's confusion between his own mind and the external world—he "oftentimes mistook the one / For th'other"—ends with the substitution of the one for the other: "His Notions fitted things so well, / That which was which he could not tell." His discovery of "*what's what*" is the consummation of Enthusiasm as a kind of tautological solipsism where the "what" in the mind is concretized as a thing and projected outward to appear as the "what" of the external world. The fanciful notions of the Enthusiast *are* reality, because the things of the world have evaporated, replaced by fanciful images reified by the materializing imagination.

And so, a mind abandoned to the imagination is a mind abandoned to the body. Imagining, said, Descartes, "is a way of thinking specially suited to material things"; it is "simply contemplating the shape or image of a corporeal thing," and those who rely on their imaginations "never raise their minds above things which can be perceived by the senses."[50] Having delivered himself over to the corporealizing imagination, an Enthusiast "so farre sinks into Phantasmes" that he "thinks" on a level more sensational than ideational. When the Modern Author of *A Tale of a Tub* argues that effective public speaking requires "a *superior Position of Place*" because words are "Bodies of much Weight and Gravity, as it is manifest from those deep *Impressions* they make and leave upon us; and therefore must be delivered from a due Altitude, or else they will neither carry a good Aim, nor fall down with sufficient Force,"[51] he is not thinking so much as seeing: ideas have been reduced in his mind to their corporeal concomitants—emotional response becomes physical impression, intellectual gravity becomes something of material weight—and he draws conclusions on the basis of how things look rather than what they mean. In the mind of an Enthusiast, an idea is so concretized as a physical image that the image no longer acts as a sign but as a thing itself. There is no ideational kernel; there is only the physical husk.

Moreover, the imagination ensnares the Enthusiast in the body in a second and much more powerful way, a way articulated most strikingly by Swift. An Enthusiast, according to Swift's formulation, begins by rejecting his senses, *"lifting up . . . the Soul or its Faculties above Matter,"* but he always ends thoroughly immersed in matter, driven by the squalid kinetics of his body, by his vapors and flatulence, completely governed by the energies of the body welling up from below.[52] However, this is not as paradoxical as it seems. "All Objects from without, being wholly, or in a great measure shut out and excluded," says Trenchard in his analysis of Enthusiasm, "we must submit" to "Images within us" springing from the fancy. And these images, already corporealized by virtue of their being of the imagination, sink us further and further into matter because, more often than not, they themselves spring from "the agitations and motions of the internal parts of our own Bodies." For the imagination, notoriously, was in league with the passions and the appetites, energies which were "material, corporall, and depending upon some bodilie instruments." The passions and the appetites used the imagination to articulate desire in concrete, compelling images and thus to persuade the higher powers, such as the understanding and will, to submit to their direction. Thus, the "imagination is the common carrier of passions, by whose means they work and produce many prodigious effects." Through the imagination, the energies of our lower strata seize our whole being, controlling "the rudder of this our ship, which reason should steer, but overborne by phantasy cannot manage, and so suffers itself and this whole vessel of ours to be over-ruled, and often overturned."[53]

The senses, whatever their deficiencies, at least kept a person anchored to external realities. But, rejecting the images of the senses, the Enthusiast was left with nothing but the corporeal images of his fancy, which, as representations of the corporeal energies of his passions and appetites, immerse him entirely in his own body as the only reality. Swift expressed these complexities with extraordinary economy simply by appropriating the scholastic aphorism, *"the Corruption of the Senses is the Generation of the Spirit,"* for the proposition on which

Enthusiasm has erected itself: what the Enthusiast perceives as the motions of the immaterial Spirit are in fact the motions of the physiological spirits, now ascendant because the senses have been rejected, allowing images of the fancy (controlled by the energies of the body through the agency of the spirits) to predominate. This process, particularly after Swift pressures the language downward with his examples drawn from physiology, is entirely a corporeal one, a "mechanical operation," akin to the generation of a gas from the decomposition of organic matter.[54]

Hogarth fashioned *Cunicularii* within the genre of anti-Enthusiastic satire because he saw the corporealizing imagination as the source of the confusion in the bagnio on 4 December. The three doctors, driven by their ambitions, become fools to the kind of knavery they themselves perpetrated because their imaginations confuse them, making them experience, as through the senses, a reality that is untrue. For an Enthusiast is both a knave, motivated by his self-serving impulses and appetites, and a fool: unable to "distinguish betwixt [his] own Fancies and reall Truths," he is "befooled in his own conceit" and becomes a dupe to his own knavery.[55] And this context of Enthusiastic confusion explains the more significant confusion the print portrays, the confusion suggested by the joke of making the events of 4 December a parody of the Adoration of the Magi. The subtitle, "The Wise Men of Godliman," alludes on the one hand to the proverbial stupidity of the "Wise Men of Gotham," for certainly the doctors in consultation in this print are meant to be just as foolish; but the phrase also points to those other three Wise Men who were present at a miraculous birth. Similarly, Hogarth's label for Mary Toft, "The Lady in the straw," points two ways: it is a slang term for "a woman in delivery" and at the same time it refers to another birth in the straw by another Mary. And visually, *Cunicularii* is an obvious parody of the Adoration. One doctor is bowing in reverence—and delivery; the second raises his hands in wonder; and the third dances for joy and says, with comic equivocation, "A Great Birth." In *Cunicularii,* a divine moment is reenacted as a gross, wholly physical parody.

At the heart of Hogarth's *Cunicularii,* then, is a vision of the corporealizing imagination, hyperbolized (as so often in the manner of the Mary Toft satires) and made entirely disproportionate to its cause: Mary Toft is portrayed as a woman who has the power to reduce the spiritual to the physical. The sacred mystery of the birth of Christ, the infusion at that moment of the human body with the divine spirit, becomes—to use the phrase of another observer of the Mary Toft episode—a "filthy miracle"[56] which has lost all traces of the divine moment it parodies. Here is a mocking image of the sacred, reproduced in foul matter.

This theme of the siphoning off of the spiritual, the transformation of the immaterial downward to the purely corporeal, is at the center of almost all anti-Enthusiastic satires, especially those of Butler and Swift, both of whom charged the Enthusiasts with confusing mind and body, spirit and matter, religion and self-interest, transforming the "Mystical" into the "Mechanick." Indeed, Swift, whose vision of Enthusiasm is based on his perception of how easily "a Pruriency, . . . with due Management, hath been refined from a Carnal, into a Spiritual Extasie," portrays the essence of Enthusiastic thinking as the wholesale replacement of the spirit by its physical parody, so that divine inspiration becomes belching and flatulence, *caritas* carnal lust.[57]

This corporealization of the spiritual occurs because the imagination is driven by the energies of the body and the passions working up a chain of mediation: these corporeal drives figure themselves to the mind as images which the Enthusiast misinterprets as divine when in fact they are grossly physical. "When the blood and spirits run *high,* inflaming the brain and imagination," wrote Lavington, "it is most properly *Enthusiasm.*"[58] He was not speaking metaphorically; this is a medical description of the disease. For the etiology of Enthusiasm was derived from medical explanations of Melancholy, and so it was considered a psychosomatic disease, one which originated in a physiological disorder but which manifested itself mentally. The body worked up through the hierarchy of intermediaries to the imagination, which, lying on the "narrow Suture" of mind and body, effected the crossing from the corporeal to the mental. In terms of humoral pathology, Enthusiasm was caused when bodily fluids, usually bile in the spleen, gave off melancholic vapors which pressed on the animal spirits, which in turn worked on the imagination, provoking visions, delusions, and bizarre mental distortions. Sometimes the body's impingement on the mind was attributed to different agents or routed through different chains of intermediaries, and by the eighteenth century it was much simplified, such as in Trenchard's vague and muddled description: "When Melancholy is once heated, it is like Boiling Water, and transcends the Flame of Fire, and then Sulphurious Exhalations flying up to the Brain, fill the Mind with lively Imaginations, . . . and when heated to a great degree cause Ravings, Frenzy, and Madness." Yet even in this simplified version, Enthusiasm retains that central feature of its nature: an Enthusiast, by "a sort of natural Mechanism," is "intoxicated with Vapours ascending from the lower Regions of his Body."[59]

This sense that for an Enthusiast there is "a very free Communication between the Superior Faculties and those below" stands behind Swift's formulation of Enthusiasm as a "Phœnomenon of Vapours, ascending from the lower Faculties to over-shadow the Brain, and thence distilling into Conceptions."[60]

The Enthusiast misinterprets these physiological movements as spiritual ones and attributes them to a supernatural source. "The agitations and motions of the internal parts of our own Bodies," Trenchard concluded, come to be taken for "Visons and revelations." More, who thought of Enthusiasm as "a kind of *naturall inebriation*," reached the same conclusion:

> The *Spirit* . . . that wings the *Enthusiast* in such a wonderful manner, is nothing else but that *Flatulency* which is in the *Melancholy* complexion, and rises out of the *Hypochondriacal* humour upon some occasional heat, as *Winde* out of an *AEolipila* applied to a fire. Which fume mounting to the Head, being first actuated and spirited and somewhat refined by the warmth of the Heart fills the Mind with a variety of *Imagination,* and so quickens and inlarges *Invention,* that it makes the *Enthusiast* to admiration *fluent* and *eloquent,* he being as it were drunk with new wine drawn from that Cellar of his own that lies in the lowest region of his Body, though he be not aware of it, but takes it to be pure *Nectar,* and those waters of life that spring from above.[61]

And thus, since "naturall fervency [was] mistaken for supernatural," Enthusiasm was essentially parodic. The images produced by the corporealizing imagination were physical, not spiritual, and they sprang from the mechanics of physiology, not from divine revelation or spiritual insight. Because an Enthusiast was utterly knotted into his body, Enthusiasm itself was, as More said, a "notorious Mockery" of true spirituality, rooted as it was in the grossly physical: "There is nothing better then *Nature* in it." What an Enthusiast interpreted as religious zeal could be traced to "the lowest regions of his Body." And what an Enthusiast claimed to be divine love was also nothing but a "mysterious mockery": "it was the fumes of Melancholy that infatuated the fancie of the late new-fangled *Religionist,* when he sat so kindly by a gipsie under a hedge, and put his hand into her bosome in a fit of devotion, and vaunted afterwards of it as if it had been a very pious and meritorious action."[62]

IV

Actually, Hogarth was not the only satirist to see in the Mary Toft affair the presence of Enthusiasm. Every satirist we have examined who focused on the confusion of those involved in the affair linked that

confusion, sometimes briefly and obliquely, sometimes quite forthrightly, to the imagination's confounding of the mind and the body
typically associated with Enthusiasm. In "Mr. P— to Dr. A———t,"
Manningham's mental disarray manifests itself as the creation of a specious religious miracle by utterly confusing (in several ways) spirit and
matter, the divine and the sexual:

> You know *Vagina* means a Case,
> It is dear Knight a tempting Place,
> Where you have shewn great Inclination
> To Bring in Transubstantiation.

"A Shorter and Truer Advertisement" portrays this confusion even
more explicitly as a moment of religious Enthusiasm. Its subtitle is "Dr.
Douglas in Exstacy," and when Douglas goes out of his senses, as his
diction betrays, he enters a religious vision of the miraculous:

> Have I my Fingers? and have I my Eyes?
> Or are my Senses fled through much Surprise?
> . . . .
>
> A Birth! A Birth! is now at hand
>   Come in without delay
> Nay, Come good sirs, this Moment in
>   Or I will run away.
>
> Unless you all come in and see
> This *Wondrous Birth,* this *Prodigy*
> I never more Belief shall find,
> Amongst my Brethern or Womankind
> Therefore come in, with one Consent
> For I am all *Astonishment.*

When Pope and Pulteney depicted the confusion of Molyneux in "The
Discovery," they were quite obviously writing within the tradition of
anti-Enthusiastic satire, for the virtuoso-astronomer by this time had
become the stock representative of the Enthusiast. And by using his
telescope as a grotesque phallic displacement, they were making
explicit the central theme of anti-Enthusiastic satire, the confusion of
higher modes of thought with lower drives, the confusion of body and
mind.

When Mary Toft said that she was giving birth to rabbits, she
invoked the power of the maternal imagination to shape the fetus, and
when she invoked this power, she could not help but to invoke the
power of the corporealizing imagination to shape the self, that power
which manifested itself most radically as Enthusiasm. They were the
same power. "Many Children are observed to bear on their Faces the

Marks and Traces of the Idea that affected their Mother":[63] in monstrous birth, the imagination violates the boundary between the body and the mind, translating an immaterial "Idea" into a corporeal "Mark." And this is the process of Enthusiasm, too. The mind and the body contaminate each other because the imagination translates the one into the other across that "narrow Suture" that separates them, and hence it misshapes the self just as the maternal imagination misshapes the fetus. "And even as slime and durt in a standing puddle, engender toads and frogs, and many other unsightly creatures," commented Thomas Nashe, describing the physiological processes of ascending vapors that Swift would later point to as the cause of Enthusiasm, "so this slimie, melancholy humor still thickening as it stands still, engendreth many mishapen objects in our imaginations."[64] The "misshapen" conceptions in the mind "engendered" by the imagination were not spoken of in the language of birth and teratogenesis because the relationship between monstrous birth and monstrous thinking was merely metaphoric. To the contrary, the delusions of the imagination—its power of "producing many monsters and prodigious things," its ability to "breede *Chimeres* and Monsters" in the mind—were described in the language of monstrous birth because the two processes were thought of as the same process.[65] In *Cunicularii,* Hogarth can so easily parallel the "false conception" of Mary Toft's rabbits to the "false conception" in the minds of the three Enthusiastic doctors because monstrous birth and Enthusiastic thinking play out in different keys the concretizing process of the imagination, its fall into matter, its movement down to the one dead level of the body. Both are psychosomatic disorders of the imagination whose dynamics are identical. In both, the imagination blurs and then disastrously transgresses the boundary between mind and body so that things of the mind are transmogrified into things of the body, the spirit materialized as a deformed, mocking image of itself in flesh. In the mind of the Enthusiast, the demands of "the lowest regions of his Body" are imaged as the highest spiritual impulses, his grossest passions as ideas, but these images are corporeal and represent drives that are corporeal, and by following these demands, the Enthusiast abandons his mind and sinks into his body, lured downward by a corporeal parody of the spirit, not the spirit itself. It is the same in monstrous birth, for when the idea in the mother's mind is imprinted on the flesh of her child, the ideational content of the image evaporates, leaving the physical image as a "mysterious mockery":

> For it must be well observed, that those impressions that stir up Sentiments of Piety in the most Devout Mothers, do not communicate it to their unborn Infants; and that, on the contrary, the Traces which excite the Ideas

of sensible Things, and which are followed with Passions, fail not to communicate to the Infants the Sensation and Love of Sensible Things.

A Mother, for Instance, who is excited to love God by the Motion of the
Spirits, which accompany the Trace of the Image of a venerable Old Man,
because this Mother has united the Idea of God to this Trace of the Old
Man; . . . This Mother, I say, can only produce in the Brain of her Child the
Trace of an Old Man; and an inclination for Old Men, which is not the love
of God wherewith she was affected; For, indeed, there is no Traces in the
Brain, which can of themselves stir up any other Idea's than those of Sensible Things, because the Body is not made to instruct the Mind, and speaks
not to the Soul as to it self.[66]

Monstrous births were rare, and few of those who responded to the
Mary Toft incident, I think, would consider themselves in danger of
becoming Enthusiasts. And so the sources of the anxieties provoked by
Mary Toft probably were not the literal fears of giving birth to
deformed offspring or of becoming possessed by Enthusiastic madness.
But even though both monstrous birth and Enthusiasm were extreme
and rare, they were still manifestations of a power of the imagination
that did affect everyone, substantively and every day. The imagination
had as a quotidian power the capacity to make us vulnerable to the
pressures of the body and the passions, to confuse us utterly about our
experience, to distort monstrously our sense of reality. The imagination embruted us deeply in our corporeality. In "Mr. P— to Dr. A——
—t," when he is asked to summarize the moral of the Mary Toft affair,
the speaker replies with a triple pun:

> Hence learn the Ladies have a Place
> That makes the Wisest Man an Ass.

The real power of a woman like Mary Toft—whether it lay in her ability to convert a human fetus into an animal, to provoke sexual desire,
or to make a man a fool—was to draw man lower than he was, to make
him a beast in some way, to transform him downward to body. I think
the threat many people intuited in Mary Toft was the possibility that
mind, spirit, and consciousness, the very grounds of our sense of identity, could be reduced to the one dead level of the body by the corporealizing imagination, that the imagination could lay us open to those
alien energies from below, which could well up and assimilate the self,
now impotent before their power, and turn us out as shapeless as monsters. And this, I suspect, is why many people were "angry at the
Account" of Mary Toft's births and demanded "that if it be a fact, a
Veil should be drawn over it, as an imperfection of human Nature."
When she gave birth to seventeen rabbits, this "fact" implied how
deeply humans were trammelled in their own physiologies.

The ability of the imagination to provoke these anxieties was not isolated to this one incident in 1726. Some thirty years after the Mary Toft affair, Sterne published *Tristram Shandy,* a novel in which the hero is beset by impotence and the tyranny of the corporeal and is precipitated into a perpetual whirl of confusion that threatens to swamp his identity, all because, at the moment of his conception, the imaginations of his parents were disordered, which set the animal spirits cluttering like hey-go-mad.

4

WE BEG LEAVE TO ASSURE YOU
THAT WE ARE, &C.

When Mary Toft claimed to have given birth to seventeen rabbits, I believe, she provoked apprehensions about the imagination's ability to translate motions of the passions and the body into motions of the spirit, blurring sensation and idea and corporealizing the mind. If I am correct, two additional points about the responses to the incident need to be explained.

The first point is that odd disjunction I have repeatedly called attention to, the way in which the anger, fear, and anxiety expressed during the incident seem out of proportion to what apparently provoked them. Even if my speculation is right that people were responding to the power of the imagination, not as it occasionally was manifested in its ability to misshape the fetus but rather as it was manifested in all of us, daily, in its ability to erase the boundaries between body and mind—even, I say, if this speculation is right, it is still difficult to explain the intensity of the responses to the incident. Since it was a piece of moral orthodoxy that our imaginations could make us act like beasts by subjecting us to the impulses of our sensuous, passionate, bodily natures, something must have transformed this unexceptionably commonplace notion into an unusually unsettling anxiety.

There is a second point that needs to be clarified. The imagination's being a boundary-blurring faculty, one that obscures fundamental distinctions between mind and body, sensation and idea, reality and fantasy, suggests why so many people turned to images of collapsing structures (such as the fall of kingdoms, the breakdown of language) to express their sense of the threat of Mary Toft. It explains, too, why so many of those who responded to the incident focused on confusion, and specifically on the kind of confusion the imagination was thought to precipitate, the confusion between what was experienced as a concrete, palpable reality and what was created as a fantasy. What is not self-evident, however, is how this fear of the imagination is related to the other patterns of anxiety in the responses to the incident—the fear of the loss of identity, often figured under the powerful images of a self becoming impotent, then assimilated into the mother, and then transformed into a monster. In the responses to Mary Toft, confusion almost always eventuates in the loss of identity, as if that initial moment when the imagination is taken as a palpable reality is the first step in a process that necessarily ends in the complete unstructuring of the self and the dispersion of identity. If, then, Mary Toft represented the threat of the imagination, the second point that needs to be explained is how the imagination's opening the self to the upwelling energies of the body and the passions caused a loss of identity and the dispersion of the self into a monstrous shapelessness.

Both of these points, I believe, are closely related. I think that people responded with such intensity to Mary Toft because the notion of self-identity was profoundedly unsettled in early eighteenth-century England, and it was muddled in uncertainties and vexations largely because people feared that their bodies exercised a prominent but indefinite power, one that called into question the integrity of the self. Since the imagination caused an irruption of the body into a realm that normally gave us our identities, the realm of spirit and mind, it was seen as an agent that threatened our very identities.

The lineaments of these issues are revealed in the teratological debates between Daniel Turner and James Blondel, historically the most important of the responses to the Mary Toft incident.

I

The Mary Toft incident prompted the first serious, systematic questioning of the medical theory that the mother's imagination had the power to misshape or make monstrous the body of the child she was carrying. Five months after Mary Toft was exposed, James Blondel put out *The Strength of Imagination in Pregnant Women Examin'd,* a work "published," he said later, "upon the Occasion of the Cheat of *Godalming.*"[1] He used Mary Toft's imposture to attack wholesale the belief in the prenatal influence of the imagination. Daniel Turner suspected that Blondel's real target was his own *De Morbis Cutaneis,* originally published in 1714 and just recently reissued, in the twelfth chapter of which he had argued for the power of the imagination. Turner responded to Blondel's *Strength of Imagination* as if it were a personal attack, vindicating himself in 1729 in *A Defence of the XIIth Chapter of . . . De Morbis Cutaneis.* Blondel answered immediately, publishing that same year *The Power of the Mother's Imagination Over the Fœtus Examin'd.* In 1730, Turner replied, more truculently than ever, with *The Force of the Mother's Imagination upon her Fœtus in Utero . . . in the Way of a Reply to Dr. Blondel's Last Book.*

Blondel died shortly thereafter, but the debate the two men initiated was carried on by others well into the next century, and today their exchange is recognized as a watershed in the history of teratology.[2] Doubts about the power of the imagination occasionally had been aired earlier, but no one had attacked it so vigorously or so methodically as Blondel did. He brought to the issue a serious investigative temperament, a firm empirical skepticism, and a strong commitment to contemporary embryological thought. And when he attacked the theory, he attacked it at its very foundation.

The theory of the power of the mother's imagination was founded on the notion of mediation. The mother could shape the fetus because the imagination was thought to be a Janus-faced faculty situated at that "narrow Suture" between the mind and body. The mind could work on the body, the body on the mind, because the imagination translated their effects one on the other by using the "proper and peculiar *Mediums,*" those various faculties, humors, spirits, fluids, and tissues which were ranged in a hierarchical continuum from the grossest to the most ethereal. This chain of intermediaries binding the mother's mind and her own body also bound the mother to her fetus. Malebranche, for instance, explained that "Children in their Mothers Bellies . . . [are] united with their Mothers in the strictest manner that can be imagined." "Mothers are capable of impressing upon their children all the same Sensations they are affected with" because "the body of an Infant makes but one with that of the Mothers, the Blood and Spirits are common to both, and sensations and Passions are the Natural Consequence of the Motions of the Spirits and Blood, which Motions necessarily communicate themselves from the Mother to the Child."[3]

Blondel denied the power of the mother's imagination by denying the existence of such a chain of intermediaries binding the mother to her fetus. There was no interchange of fluids, humors, or spirits between the mother and her fetus, he argued, and hence there was no way for the mother's imagination to exercise its power. The fetus was, to use Blondel's favorite word, an "individuum," and throughout its development "the *Fœtus,* in respect of the Mother, is all along no more to her than a child, that is in a Nurse's Arms, and at her Breast, by which it receives Nourishment, but is not reputed to be Part of her Body."[4]

Blondel examined all stages of fetal development, and at no point did he find any communication between the mother and the fetus. In the ovary "the *Ovum* is only lodged in the *Vesicula* as a Ball in a Socket, and having no stronger Tyes than those of *Contiguity,* I see no Reason, though it is inclosed in the Mother's Body, why it should not be reputed to be originally a *distinct Individuum,* upon which her *Imagination* has no Power, nor Authority." In the Fallopian tube, "the *Fœtus* is an *individuum,* distinct, and separate from the Mother's Body," and "the several Functions relating to Life are performed independent on the Mother." Nor is there any communication in the womb. Nothing circulates between the mother and the fetus through the placenta, whose sole function, according to Blondel, is to anchor the fetus to the womb, preventing it from being tossed to and fro:

> If, in this *Stage,* the *Fœtus* is reputed to be part of the Mother, 'tis in the same Sense, that an *Ivy-tree* is said to be part of the Tree, or of the Wall, which it cleaves to, and from which it cannot be separated, without some Trouble and Difficulty. . . . There is no common Circulation of blood between [the mother and the fetus], no Communication of Animal Spirits, they have not the same Sensation; what the Mother feels is nothing to the *Fœtus,* one may be in pain, when the other is easy; one sleeps, and the other is awake; and very often the Mother is dead, when the Child is still alive.[5]

"There's no *immediate* Communication of Blood and Spirits between the Mother and the Child, without which 'tis not possible for the Mother's Imagination to act upon the *Fœtus,"* Blondel concluded. By denying the existence of these intermediaries, he destroyed the theory of the mother's imagination at its foundation. For, without them, "Whence then shall come that dreadful Inundation of Spirits, that Father *Malbranche,* and some others speak of? How can the Mother's Imagination reach the *Cerebrum* of the *Fœtus* and disturb it?"[6]

Turner sneered at Blondel's argument, particularly at what he called his opponent's "modish mechanic way" of thinking, his readiness to explain all phenomena as resulting from "Causes under the Force of mechanic Powers."[7] And, in fact, Blondel *is* "modish" and "mechanic," for his argument about the independence of the fetus, his belief that it is an "individuum" incapable of being affected by the mother, is extrapolated from the most up-to-date embryological theory, and one that was thoroughly mechanistic.

The embryological theory that is at the heart of Blondel's argument is the theory of pre-existence, which had been formulated in the last quarter of the seventeenth century and, by the 1720s, had become the prevailing explanation of reproduction.[8] According to this theory, the fetus existed even before fecundation, and it existed as a miniature, predelineated being, "an entire Animal, furnished with all its proper Instruments for Life, Motion, and Procreation, and also the Fluids whereby it is nourished, though indeed so small, that no Power of human Imagination seems capable of being extended to [it]."[9] Opinion was divided about where this being was lodged, the ovists arguing that it was contained in the ovum, the animalculists that it was in the spermatazoon. But both ovists and animalculists believed that it did exist fully predelineated, and that, therefore, there was, strictly speaking, no development. What we perceive as development was really just an uncoiling and augmentation of whole pre-existent beings, "nothing else but a gradual unfolding and Expansion of their Vessels, by a slow and progressive insinuation of Fluids adapted to their Diameters; until, being stretched to the utmost Bounds appointed them by Providence at their Formation, they attain their State of Perfection, or, in other Words, arrive at their full Growth."[10]

Since every fetus was a completely preformed entity before fecundation, there was no creation *de novo* by human beings. All individuals had been created at the same time, all simultaneously with Adam and Eve, and each individual "Must of necessity derive its origin from God himself, and from no less Cause," "*Formed ab origine Mundi,* by the *Almighty Creator.*"[11] Thus, the succession of generations could be explained only by *emboîtment:* each egg—or each spermatazoon, if one were an animalculist—contained a preformed being, and within that was another, and in that another . . . and so on. Encapsulated one within another, all were contained in the beginning of history within the body of either Adam or Eve, nestled one in another like a set of Chinese boxes, continually diminishing in size, but each as perfect and complete as the being that contained it. "Thus ADAM's Loins contained his large Posterity, / All people that have been, and all that e'er shall be."[12] What we perceive as the birth of one generation from the previous is actually the successive emergence of individuals all of whom had their existence from the beginning of the world, "so that the whole species to be afterwards produced, were really all formed in the first, and enclosed therein; to be brought forth and disclosed to view in a certain time, and according to a certain order and oeconomy."[13]

Pre-existence had a startling consequence. If "you and I did once exist and swim together, in the real, corporeal, literal Loins of our first Parent Adam," if, as Blondel argued, "there's not a single *Fœtus* at this Time, but has been successively in the *Ovary* of Two Hundred and Fifty Persons at least,"[14] then the concept of human parentage was absurd. Before pre-existence, all theories of generation had argued that the fetus was made up in some way of the very stuff of the parents, such as the coagulated menstrual blood of the mother or representative particles drawn from all parts of both parents. But pre-existence relegated parents to mere containers of a being to which they contributed nothing: "the parents conduce nothing but a convenient Habitation, and Suitable Nourishment to [the fetus], till it be fit to be trusted with the Light, and capable of receiving the Benefits of the Air."[15] Although the fetus was contained in the parents, it was in no sense of them. "It passes indeed *through* the bodies of the parents, who afford a transitory habitation and subsistence to it: but it cannot be *formed by* the parents, or *grow out* of any part of them."[16] It was, in short, at all stages of its existence, a perfect "individuum."

Blondel buttressed his case against the power of the imagination with a number of collateral arguments, but the main line of his attack rested squarely on pre-existence. "What I maintain is grounded upon a principle universally received, *viz.* That there is no new Creation, and that the *Rudiments* of *all* Vegetables, and of *all* Animals now in Being, are *a Principio.*" And if all human beings were formed simultaneously with Adam and Eve, then it followed that each fetus was an "individuum" at every stage of its existence, an independent being from the beginning of time. "There's no Child born," said Blondel, "but the *Lineaments* of its Body have been *somewhere* from the first Creation. . . . The Opinion, which is now generally received, is, that the *somewhere* was in a *primitive Ovum,* which had several *Ovula* involved one within another." And since "the Parts of the *Fœtus* are all existent somewhere before *Conception,*" it is "consequently a distinct, and separate *Individuum,*" utterly incapable of being influenced by the mother's imagination and its chain of intermediaries:

> By what Means can the Mother's *Imagination* on a sudden, without her knowledge, or Consent, and contrary to her Inclination, obliterate the Lineaments of the *Fœtus,* which were pre-existent to Conception, and subsisting, even since the Creation of the World, and, in an Instant, produce *new* Limbs, with *new* Articulations, new Arteries and Veins, new Glands with *Lymphaticks* and other *Excretory* Vessels, such as we see often in some monstrous Births, when the Woman is entirely ignorant of the Structure of the Body?[17]

This line of thinking, as Turner saw quite accurately, is "Reasoning from mechanick Powers." And Blondel would agree. "My Opinion implies no Absurdity," he asserted. "'Tis clear and intelligible, and easily deduced from the Laws of Motion, which God has established amongst Bodies."[18] For Blondel, as well as for the majority of thinkers in the eighteenth century, the doctrine of pre-existence was thoroughly mechanistic, a doctrine in which biological processes were conceived as subject to the same mechanical "Laws of Motion" that governed the physical universe. Indeed, pre-existence was not a hypothesis created to explain specific observations or data patiently collected over years of research but, to the contrary, was created out of metaphysical presuppositions about the mechanical nature of the universe, and it was appealing to the eighteenth century not because it answered to a body of facts but because it validated prior philosophical assumptions about the way the universe operated.[19]

Pre-existence was an intellectual product of a world view that envisioned physical nature as made up of passive and inert matter governed by simple and inviolable mechanistic laws set in motion and sustained by God, and that world view applied to organic nature the same universal laws of mechanical causation that held sway over the inorganic world. The kind of complexity and order one witnessed in the processes of generation could have arisen only out of forces ultimately derivable from the Creator, following "the eternal and unalterable Laws established at their first Creation."[20] Generation, like the physical universe itself, was so systematically ordered yet so complex that we "must resolve it finally, as Sir *Isaac Newton* has done the whole *course of nature,* into the immediate, tho' regular and uniform impulse of the first mover, and the divine will and pleasure exerting itself at all times by certain laws of its own establishing, thro' the infinitely wide extend of its dominion."[21] Original creation—the act that formed these embryos, encased them one within the other, and then set in motion the dynamic forces that would govern their unfolding—was God's. But the gradual unfolding itself of each embryo and the liberation of each successive generation from its encasement was an entirely mechanical process.

Having envisioned the processes of generation and gestation as taking place according to the universal laws of physics, Blondel placed monstrosity itself within the "wonderful *Uniformity*" of a mechanically ordered universe. "There's nothing," he concluded, "but what is according to the Course of Nature." Rather than being produced by something lawless and arbitrary like the imagination, deformities were the result of more mundane and mechanical causes: an accidental bruise to the pre-existent being that may have occurred as much as four-thousand years earlier, disease or physical violence done to the fetus while in the womb, a constriction of blood vessels that caused disproportionate growth of some parts over others. And as for the notorious mulberries, strawberries, and plums, they were simply gatherings of blood vessels close to the surface of the skin, defects perfectly within the normal limits of variations one expects to find in individuals. All monsters proceed from "the usual Accidents which do naturally follow the Laws of Motion."[22]

II

Turner's reply to Blondel is fascinating, for it hints at the kind of anxieties latent in much of the thinking about monstrosity in the eighteenth century.

Turner repeatedly attacked Blondel's argument for its "modish mechanic way" of explanation, and yet for all that, it is not quite accurate to see the debate between the two as a debate between a non-mechanist who supported the power of the mother's imagination and a mechanist who denied it. The situation is considerably more messy. For bafflingly, in *De Morbis Cutaneis* (the very work Turner thought Blondel was attacking) Turner himself not only appealed to mechanistic causes to account for the imagination's power but boasted that mechanism alone was a sufficient explanation. "All this," he said, referring to the entire process of the imagination's marking the fetus, "all this is transacted by mechanic Laws, at first settled by the most adorable and supreme Being, and continued still by his general concurring Power and Providence":

> In some Curious Piece of Mechanism, when the Artist has given the finishing Stroak, and wound up the *Machine;* we find it capable of performing various Motions, and of delighting our Eye with Variety of strange Appearances, whilst it hath no Consciousness of its own Performance, brought to pass by the due order of its Springs and Wheels, adapted and wisely connected according to the Idea the Maker of it had conceived, as necessary and subservient to the Uses he expected and intended it should perform: Unassisted by other Helps, when once set a going, than its own Structure or the Parts of its Fabrick.
>
> In like Manner, if Physicians would not overlook the First (and as bad as they are represented, I know some of them do not) I see not why they should be reproach'd as *Atheistical,* because they do not substitute a second Cause called *Nature,* if they mean other or more thereby than the Motion of Blood and Spirits, together with a due Conformation of the Parts of the Body, as to its Pores, Vessels, Fibres, &c. which of themselves so excellently constituted at first by their Omniscient *Architech,* and endow'd with a Power of propagating their Species, are able to answer the Ends appointed them, without Recourse to subordinate or fictitious Beings; . . .[23]

In light of Turner's own mechanistic thinking (he later refers his readers to Descartes and Willis for a further elucidation of his own views!), on what grounds could he later have attacked his opponent, sarcastically characterizing Blondel's efforts as "the Secrets of Generation explained and made easy by the principles of Mechanics"?[24] Did Turner think that his own explanation of the imagination's working mechanistically through the "Motion of Blood and Spirits" was somehow less mechanistic than the mechanism of the "Laws of Motion" which Blondel extrapolated from pre-existence?

There is, I think, no rational explanation at all, and this is precisely what is so revealing about the controversy. Turner's use of a "modish mechanic way" in his own original explanation, and then his turning on Blondel, attacking him for *his* "modish mechanic way" of explanation, seems not to arise from a logically consistent position but from a moment of anxiety in which Turner suffers a failure of nerve, as if he has found himself halfway down a path he himself has chosen and suddenly discovers how dangerous it is. This is clearly seen in the one and only moment in the entire, long controversy when Turner tries to explain the actual operations of the mother's imagination on her fetus:

> Whatever calls off her thoughts from all other Objects, and employs as it were the whole *Systasis* of the Soul; whatever determines the Bend, as I may say, of the Mind entirely to one thing; to dwell upon an Object either belov'd or dreaded, may, through Intenseness of her Thought about the same, so operate upon the *Plastic Power,* or, if this be Jargon, so determine the Blood and Spirits as well of the Mother on the one side, as of the *Foetus* on the other, now at work and unfolding the parts, as to new-model certain Particles, which like Dough or Paste at this time are capable of the Impression; and to insculp or delineate the terrible or delightful Object, or depict in a manner what was so earnestly coveted, yet perhaps could not be obtained, at least till too late to obviate the Accident.[25]

The phrase "so operate upon the *Plastic Power,* or if this be Jargon, so determine the Blood and Spirits" is remarkable. When at last he is going to elucidate the operation of the imagination, he retreats from the mechanistic causes he had argued earlier were the sufficient explanation for the phenomenon. By appealing, even speculatively, to the *"Plastic Power,"* he is turning to a neo-Platonic, quasi-immaterial force that had been posited in reaction to the materialistic threat of mechanism, a power so dated the moment it was fabricated that it could not hold its own in the modern world of mechanistic explanation.[26] Turner knows this, of course: that is why he says, "or, if this be Jargon," a statement in which he defensively acknowledges that such old-fashioned mentalistic powers are now dismissed as so much scholastic mystification. But the phrasing is defensive only in part. What is so interesting about it is how Turner converts this defensiveness into a gesture of contemptuous dismissal and thereby gains his whole point. For by referring first to the "*Plastic Power*" as the intermediary between the mother's imagination and the body of the fetus and then to the mechanism of the "Blood and Spirits," as if it were a matter of indifference, his sarcasm suggests that it *is* a matter of indifference because both explanations are a kind of "Jargon," both pretending to explain a phenomenon that is in fact beyond explanation.

And it is this fact of our sheer incomprehension, the fact that the "mysterious Intercourse" between the mother and the fetus is "impenetrable to the humane intellect," that Turner made the center of his argument against Blondel. He continually admitted his ignorance about how the imagination exercised its power—and made it clear that he did not consider it a particularly important question. "*Causes extraordinary* produce *extraordinary Effects*," he explained in a defiant tautology. "If you ask me . . . the *Cause* of these several *Phaenomena,* you must not take it ill, if, in Matters thus transacted out of Sight, and by inscrutable Agents . . . I should confess I know not how the same is brought about."[27]

Blondel was extremely annoyed at this line of argument. People who argue like Turner, he said, "confess that they have nothing to say for their Opinion, but that '*tis so,* because 'tis so." He demanded a more precise explanation. Turner bristled at Blondel's demand. The "*Modus* is hidden from us," he shot back; "our Maker has placed such a relationship between certain Causes and their Effects, that the latter shall result from the former, under certain Modifications, or when disposed to their Production."[28] Blondel's demand was perverse, Turner thought, for to ask how a mother's mind could cause a physical deformity in the fetus was simply to ask how the mind was related to the body. And it astonished Turner that Blondel implied that if the specific operations could not be explained then the phenomenon itself could not occur. Of course such a relationship could not be "explained," but the fact that such a relationship existed was indisputable, for all one had to do was to point to the obvious interaction between the body and the mind, between sense and thought, between intention and act, all bound together by various mediating faculties, or by the plastic powers, or by the blood and spirits, or by whatever—it really did not matter what. "The great Influence of [the] Passions over our Blood and nervous Fluid, and consequently the whole Body" was a self-evident fact, just as was "the mutual Commerce it hath pleased our Maker to establish between outward objects and the . . . Spirits; that at the mere Beck of the Will . . . they should straight flow into these or those Muscels of the Body, by which we may best prosecute the desired Good, or avoid the feared Danger." In the end, Turner defended his position in one blunt statement: "But you say . . . that the Imagination in respect to the Mind is only Thought; tho' in respect to the Body, Motion. And when you tell me how this Thought can produce Motion in the Body, I may resolve you how *Imagination* may work on the Fœtus."[29] Turner's case rests on the aggressive proclamation of mystery. That the bodily mechanisms and mental activity impinge one upon the other is a self-evident fact. How they impinge one on the other is inexplicable.

What made Turner shift from his initial statement that "all this is transacted by mechanic Laws" to his declaration that it was all shrouded in mystery? Why did he find his original mechanistic explanation of the "Motion of Blood and Spirits" acceptable (up to a point) but Blondel's mechanism of pre-existence not? And at what point exactly did the mechanism of blood and spirits cease to be an acceptable explanation, and why? Perhaps Turner had in his own mind well-defined positions that made such shifts and such distinctions logical and consistent. But, if he did, he never once stated them, and frankly I do not think that he did, for his argument is consistently muddled, largely ad hoc and reactive, and often capricious. What we see in his argument is not a rigorous exfoliation of a cogent metaphysics but, I think, the bob and wheel of a mind under the pressure of an anxiety. He begins his course of thinking by accepting the fact that man is, at least in part, a corporeal mechanism, but when pressed to consider how that mechanism interacts with the mind, he had to have asked himself *to what degree* man is a mechanism. For if the matter of the body is subject to a chain of necessary mechanical causes, and if mental activity parallels physiological activity, then the mind might well be seen as determined by the mechanisms of the body itself. Was there not a line that had to be drawn somewhere, a line beyond which mechanism was no longer operable, or else man in his totality, and not just his body, becomes a mechanism of matter in motion? And so Turner drew the line, established a point beyond which mechanism must yield to the irreducible mystery of the mind and to the mystery of the mind's union with the body. Turner felt that Blondel had crossed that line, and perhaps he felt that he himself had, too, in the unconsidered broadness of his statement that "all this is transacted by mechanic Laws." It was a line he could not quite put his finger on for he himself had no certain knowledge where exactly that line was, and although this prevented him from clearly defining that line, it did not prevent him from expressing his sense of the transgression and from scrambling to mystery as a defense.

III

More and more, those who argued for the power of the mother's imagination appealed, like Turner, to incomprehension and mystery, simply declaring that the fancy shaped the fetus and leaving the actual operation of the imagination unexplained. "The *Imagination* is the strongest and most efficacious of all the SENSES," observed Maubray, but his discussion immediately dwindles into bare assertion and a rather offhanded confession of ignorance:

> It works upon, and affects *others* as well as *ourselves,* and operates in the very *Soul,* as well as Body of Man; moving the Powers of all the *Passions* of the Mind.
>
> And besides, this IMAGINATION hath not only such power over the body, but also over the very *Soul* of Man; which Power of the *Soul,* hath its respective influence upon the *Body.*
>
> However *That be,* I know very well that when the *Soul* is elevated and inflamed with a fervent IMAGINATION, it may not only affect its own proper Body, but also *That* of ANOTHER.
>
> For the *Longing* of a *Woman* that has conceiv'd, acts upon *Another's Body,* when it *marks* the *Infant* in her WOMB with the *Figure* or *MARK* of the *Thing* long'd for.[30]

Even before Turner, Sennert, who thoroughly believed in the power of the imagination, confessed that there was no fully convincing explanation of the phenomenon: "But how the imagination makes a change in the fetus is so obscure that all the most learned men are at a loss on this point when rendering a cause."[31] Daniel de Superville, writing after the first heat of the Turner-Blondel controversy, acknowledged his own ignorance:

> It is said, that it is incomprehensible how the Soul of the Mother can have the Effect on the Child. I own I do not Comprehend it neither. It does not follow from thence, that we ought to reject as false all that our Reason cannot penetrate into. When once the existence and Nature of the Soul has been demonstrated, when once we have perfect Knowledge of the Manner how an immaterial Being acts upon Matter, we shall then reason in Consequence about what the soul can do, and cannot do. Daily Observations demonstrate to us, that the disordered and disturbed Imagination of Woman hurts the Infants. . . .[32]

When de Superville looked forward to the time when he would have "a perfect Knowledge of the Manner how an immaterial Being acts upon Matter," he was looking in the wrong direction. The explanations were in the past, and the future would have few to offer. The reason that he and Turner before him could offer no real explanation of how the mother's imagination affected her fetus was that, as Blondel's line of argument instanced, those systems of mediation which once had explained the transits across the "narrow Suture" of body and soul were simply melting away. In the extraordinary ferment of knowledge in the seventeenth century, Aristotelianism and scholastic philosophy, which had formulated the terms which had made mediation intelligible, collapsed; Galenic thinking, which had provided the principles and the physiology that buttressed this mediation, foundered; new systems of physiology and new ways of conceiving of the relationship between mind and body proliferated, and while none was broadly accepted singly, collectively they eroded the old certainties. By the eighteenth century, gone, or near fatally wounded, were the divisions of the soul, a clear sense of the nature and function of the faculties, the humors, even the spirits—that whole stock of powers and substances that for hundreds of years had been drawn from to construct explanations of the transactions between mind and body.

This loss of a system of explanation, however, was symptomatic of a more thoroughgoing helplessness. When one of the defenders of the mother's power over her fetus found himself incapable of explaining how the imagination could manipulate matter, he simply wrapped that problem within another riddle, the riddle of the relationship between the mother and the fetus, and then placed both riddles within the largest enigma of all: "The Union of the child with its Mother, I take to be such a Mystery, that I can compare it to nothing else, than to the Union of the Body and the Soul."[33] Here was the root of the problem that bedeviled Turner and prevented him from bringing any cogent arguments against Blondel, the problem that bedeviled almost all of Turner's contemporaries: the relationship between the body and the mind had become inexplicable. When the ancient mind-body division was restated in the seventeenth century by the Cambridge Platonists in England and by Descartes on the continent, they consigned mind and body to two ontologically independent and incompatible realms: mind was an immaterial substance, a *res cogitans;* body was an extended substance, material and solid. Thus conceived, any interaction between the two was impossible to comprehend. For how could there be any interaction between two substances so thoroughly antithetical? Even had not the systems of mediation failed, they would have been of no help within such a stark dualism. They could be only magical explanations, based on the illusion that if you sublimated the body fine enough or corporealized the mind to the necessary degree of physicality, you could bridge a gap that was ontologically unbridgeable. But no matter to what degree of rarity the body was sublimated, it was body still, and the mind, no matter how corporealized, was mind; you could proliferate intermediaries endlessly and never would an immaterial impinge upon a material substance.[34]

Pressed to explain how the physical, external world could cause perceptions and ideas in the mind and how the volitions of the mind could be translated into the responses of the body, Descartes was at a loss. Our notions of the body and mind, he confessed, are obscure. Metaphysics allowed us to clearly distinguish the two but not to understand their union. And yet, he concluded, the two obviously did interact, for experience proved it so. Descartes' explanation, in short, was the same as Turner's: it was all mystery.[35]

In fact, for nearly every thinker in the eighteenth century, it was all mystery:

> The Manner whereby the Soul and Body are united, and how they are distinguished, is wholly unaccountable to us. We see but one part, and yet we know we consist of two; and this is a Mystery we cannot comprehend, any more than that of the Trinity.

The sentiment was echoed by a contemporary:

> Impressions made on the retina by rays of light, I think I understand; and motions from thence continued to the brain may be conceived, and that these produce ideas in our minds, I am persuaded, but in a manner to me incomprehensible.

The first statement is by Swift, delivered in a sermon, and his contempt for metaphysics and his belief that his parishioners might spend their time more profitably by pursuing practical morality than by trying to solve insoluble puzzles make it easy to dismiss. But the second statement is John Locke's and his puzzlement indicates how thoroughly the eighteenth century was living amidst the wreckage of explanation.[36]

It is within this larger historical context of the growing inability to explain the relationship between the body and the mind, I think, that we can find some of the roots of the anxiety that made Turner back away from his own original mechanistic explanations and that made the Mary Toft incident so disquieting to so many people. For this inability to explain the interaction between body and mind had created an intellectual vacuum that was being filled with new explanations, most of them, to the orthodox mind, reducing man to a corporeal mechanism. Descartes had argued for both a material and immaterial substance in the human constitution, it is true, but by exploring in such detail and with such enthusiasm the mechanisms of the body, by showing that many of the activities of the body were carried out auto-

matically, by severely limiting the *res cogitans* to an unextended thinking substance, and by failing to account satisfactorily for the relation
between the two, he gave the impression that a human being was
largely like a "clock or other automaton" which, by the "arrangement
of its counter-weights and wheels," acted independently of the mind.
To most of the orthodox, he seemed to claim for physiology processes
traditionally assigned to the mind.[37] Leibniz had tried to explain the
relationship between body and mind by taking the embryological doctrine of pre-existence to its most radical metaphysical formulation,
arguing for not only a pre-existent body but also a pre-existent soul,
both fitted together in a pre-established harmony. But to the orthodox,
all Leibniz had done was to "make *Men* be thought as *mere Machines*"
and to make us doubt whether there was "any thing more than mere
Matter in Men at all." He had so fettered the mind to the body's mechanisms that men's souls themselves had become "automates."[38] If
Descartes and Leibniz seemed to be edging the mind out of the body
and blurring the distinction between man and machine, others seemed
to have abolished the mind altogether. Spinoza, it was thought, had
excised spirit from the universe, and Hobbes had reduced all phenomena to matter and motion, maintaining, in the words of one critic,
"that *Cogitation, Intellection,* and *Volition,* are themselves really Nothing else, but *Local Motion* or *Mechanism,* in the inward *Parts* of the
Brain and *Heart*" and that, therefore, men were "Really Nothing else,
but *Machines,* and *Automata.*"[39] Locke, at a loss to understand fully the
properties of matter or mind and to explain the relationship between
the two, had speculated "that God can, if he pleases, superadd to matter a faculty of thinking."[40] The orthodox exploded in anger at his
conjecture, especially since it was being appropriated by Free-thinkers
like Anthony Collins and argued not as a speculation but as a fact.
Here, under a new guise, was one more attempt to extirpate the
immaterial from human beings and to reduce us to mere thinking
matter. Such a notion could only mean that what "we call our Souls,
may be nothing but the contexture of several parts of our Bodies to
perform those feats of Motion, which for an honourable kind of Distinction we call Thoughts, tho really they are only the Operations of
Matter, qualified with the knack of thinking." One had to conclude
that a human being "is only a *finely organiz'd* and well shap'd
Machin."[41]

Locke and thinkers like him had "almost discarded *Substance* out
of the reasonable part of the World"[42]—that is to say, they had discarded *immaterial* substance, the ground of mind and soul. Nor was it
the philosophers alone who were making man into a corporeal mech-

anism. The revelation by anatomical research of our exquisite bodily systems, the rise of iatromechanism, the general tendency to assimilate biological phenomena into the quantifiable mechanics of the physical sciences, all these threatened to reduce the psychological-physiological parallelism into mere physiology, presenting the spectre that human beings could be wholly explained as systematically organized parcels of matter, that thinking was a product of the brain, not the mind. Human beings had become "a Species of Machins."[43] *"The Whole System of Modern Infidelity,"* Humphrey Ditton concluded, has utterly materialized the world. The modish, mechanic thinkers "have made the whole *Universe* a meer Lump of Matter; and *Man,* the most elegant and lovely Creature of all; they have complimented no higher, than to give him the Title of the best and finest Piece of *Clock-work.* They have divested us of all our *Intellectual* Powers, and made up our very *Souls* of *Wheels* and *Springs;* so that we are only a Set of Moving pratling Machines."[44]

Surrounded by evidence and arguments for a corporeal mechanism that seemed to encroach more and more on the domain of the spirit, those who upheld the orthodox position that human beings possessed an immaterial substance found themselves in much the same situation Turner found himself in.[45] For the terms of the debate did not present a simple, clear-cut choice between immaterialism and material mechanism. Like Turner, the orthodox accepted the truth of mechanism—to a degree. Human beings were corporeal mechanisms: they had bodies, and it was obvious that these bodies were subject to the same mechanistic laws that governed the physical universe. Indeed, the fact of this mechanism provided for the orthodox one of their strongest arguments that man possessed an immaterial substance. For if matter were passive and inert and therefore incapable of self-direction or self-activity, it ultimately had to depend on a nonmechanical, immaterial force for its operation. In the mechanism of the cosmos, matter was moved, shaped, and presided over by an immaterial Intelligence, God. So, analogously, in man the mechanism of the body required an immaterial substance—a mind, a soul—to set it in motion and give it direction. Consequently, the fact of their corporeal mechanism demonstrated that human beings must necessarily possess immaterial substance.

And, in the eyes of the orthodox, human beings must possess immaterial substance for another reason. If humans had no immaterial substance, they had no identities at all. An "individual cannot subsist without the notion of a spiritual substance."[46] To be an individual, to have an identity, meant that one had to possess a selfhood that was a unitary thing persisting through time, and therefore individual identity had to be grounded in a substance that was itself indivisible and unchanging. Identity, in short, had to be grounded in an immaterial substance: immaterial substance alone "secure[d] a Principle of *Personal Identity*," for it alone was ontologically immutable and indivisible.[47]

The alternative—to ground the self in the material substance of the body—was unthinkable. If that which "is properly called, *I My Self*" is "an *Unextended* and Indivisible Unity, . . . one *Self-Active, Living Power, Substantial*, or *Inside-Being*, that Containeth, Holdeth, and *connecteth* all together," it could not possibly inhere in "the *Extended Bulk* of the Body, which is not *One* but *Many Substances*."[48] For the body was extended, and what was extended had parts, and what had parts could be divided and changed. To try to ground *one* identity in a thing which was, by definition, *many* would lead to manifest absurdities.

Indeed, when the Free-thinker Collins made just such a heterodox claim, asserting that individual identity was a kind of epiphenomenon of the mechanics of the body, that "several Particles of Matter, when united in one System, [may] become an individual Being," Samuel Clarke derided him. A self grounded in the mechanical systems of the body could not be an "individual Being" because the material substance it was grounded in was "in perpetual flux and change," and "it is a manifest Contradiction that the *Consciousness* of [my action's] being done by *me*, by *my own individual self* in particular, should continue in me after my whole Substance is changed": "So if a Man at Forty Years of Age, has nothing of the same Substance in him . . . that he had at Twenty; he may be called the *same Person*, by a mere *external imaginary Denomination*. . . . But he cannot be really and truly the same person."[49]

The orthodox divine Joseph Butler, too, attacked this modern, mechanistic conception of the self by drawing a similar picture of what such a self must necessarily be. Such a conception, he said,

> when traced and examined to the bottom, amounts, I think, to this: "That personality is not permanent, but a transient thing: that it lives and dies, begins and ends continually: that no one can any more remain one and the same person two moments together, than two successive moments can be one and the same moment: that our substance is indeed continually changing; . . ."[50]

Identifying the self with the mechanical systems of the body had a second consequence, and one just as destructive of personal identity as the first. As Clarke pointed out, "*Matter* being a divisible Substance, consisting always of separable, nay of actually separate and distinct parts," a self constituted of matter could not possibly cohere as a single thing, an individual:

'Tis plain . . . no System of [matter] in any possible Composition or Division
can be an individual Conscious Being. For, suppose three or three hundred
Particles of Matter, at a Mile or at any given distance from one another; is it
possible that all of those separate parts should in that State be one individual
Conscious Being? Suppose then all these particles brought together into
one System, so as to touch one another; will they thereby, or by any Motion
or Composition whatsoever, become any whit less truly distinct Beings,
than they were at the greater distance? How then can their being disposed
in any possible System, make them one individual Being?[51]

A self that was merely thinking matter would not be single, for any
material "Particle may be divided into distinct Parts," and it followed
that such a self would be "two distinct Consciousnesses"—indeed,
since matter was infinitely divisible, a corporealized self would be "a
Multitude of distinct Consciousnesses added together."[52]

Those mechanists who argued against this orthodox position—
Collins in particular—are made satiric targets in the *Memoirs of Martinus Scriblerus.*[53] The Society of Free-thinkers sends Martin a letter in
which they broach the problems of personal identity. Man has no
immaterial substance, they claim (the soul is a "Theological Non-enti-
ty"). He is of a single substance, matter. But "notwithstanding the flux
state of the Particles of matter that compose his body," he nevertheless
has an identity; indeed, the "great noise about this Individuality" is
amenable to "an easy *mechanical Explication.*" The Free-thinkers insist
that identity resides in his self-consciousness, which they (like Collins)
argue *can* "inhere in [a] system of Matter," for self-consciousness is but
"several modes or qualities" that "result from the mechanical composition of the whole Animal"—just as a "*meat-roasting* Quality" inheres in
the mechanical arrangement of the chains, weights, and wheels of a
roasting-jack. The Free-thinkers end their letter to Martin with these
words: "We wait with the utmost patience for the honour of having
you as a member of our society, and beg leave to assure you that we are,
&c." Indeed, they need to assure him that they "are," for having denied
immaterial substance, they have denied the grounds for an identity.[54]
In the absence of an immaterial substance, identity perforce can be constituted only by what is left, the "&c." of our corporeality: the self
becomes the very "flux state of the Particles of matter that compose
[the] body," the "I" subsumed into the heterogeneities of appetites,
impulse, desire, and the body's mechanisms. Uprooted from an immaterial substance, the "I" becomes "but a transient thing . . . that . . . lives
and dies, begins and ends continually," a thing that is not a single thing,
but a "Multitude." Since "identity . . . cannot subsist with diversity of
substance," the more the self becomes the body, a (physical) thing, the

more it becomes a (metaphysical) nothing, a thing that has no identity at all.[55] One is reminded of Corinna, Swift's beautiful young nymph. As a prostitute, she is defined and has defined herself as a body, and consequently her identity is so ephemeral that it can be dismantled in parts and then gathered up again and put back together.

In their battle against the mechanists, the orthodox staked out a clear chain of logic. The mechanists were right to the extent that men do have bodies and their bodies "are mere engines or machines, whatsoever souls may be united to them."[56] But, the orthodox metaphysicians went on to argue, the very fact of this mechanism proves that men do have souls and that these souls are united to the machine of the body, for inert matter can be moved and directed only by impulses of an immaterial substance. Consequently, man must be a creature of two substances, the material and the immaterial, and in him these two are linked in some intimate, though mysterious way. But, though linked, each substance remains separate and distinguishable from the other. "We allow that a Spirit may act and cogitate in Matter, and be so united to some Systems of it, there may be a reciprocation of Actions and Passions betwixt them, according to the Laws of their Union. But still all these cogitations are the Powers of the Spirit, not of the Matter."[57] Viewing man as a union of material and immaterial substances, to be sure, cleaved him in two, making him, as Arbuthnot said, "Essence divine, with lifeless clay allayed, / By double nature, double instinct swayed." But this doubleness also guaranteed that he was, in part, "Essence divine," and this in turn guaranteed an immaterial ground for a persisting, unitary personal identity. Man's doubleness, then, meant that he might be "swayed," but his identity itself could not be uprooted, for the "I" was not the body, but the unchanging, persistent immaterial substance, the mind, the soul:

> Am I but what I seem, mere flesh and blood;
> A branching channel, with a mazy flood?
> The purple stream that through my vessels glides,
> Dull and unconscious flows like common tides:
> The pipes through which circling juices stray,
> Are not the thinking I, no more than they:
> The frame, compacted, with transcendant skill,
> Of moving joints obedient to my will;
> Nursed from the fruitful glebe, like yonder tree,
> Waxes and wastes; I call it mine, not me:
> New matter still the mouldering mass sustains,
> The mansion changed, the tenant still remains:
> And from the fleeting stream repaired by food,
> Distinct, as is the swimmer from the flood.[58]

The "I" remains an "I" because it is grounded in an immaterial substance; it is a "thinking I," utterly "Distinct" from the mechanisms of the body. The body is merely "mine," not "me."

But, in arguing in this way, the orthodox metaphysicians found themselves in much the same discomfiting position Turner found himself in. If the two substances of man's double nature are so intimately united that, even in the eyes of the orthodox, mind and body "interpenetrate and dissolve in each other, so that while life flourishes, wherever there is mind there is body, and wherever body, mind";[59] and if the relationship between mind and body is, as Swift and Locke said, "wholly unaccountable" and "incomprehensible"; and if the claims of corporeal mechanism have become more and more encompassing, more and more compelling: with what confidence can one assert that the "Powers of the Spirit" are, in fact, powers of the spirit and not powers of the body, especially when no one can explain the "Laws of their Union"? Where does one draw the line, and having drawn it, how does one defend the line's being drawn just there? How does one defend the line's being drawn at all? And yet the line has to be drawn. For once the "I" ceases to be "Distinct" from the body, once the body is no longer "mine" but "me," the "I" becomes what the body is, something that "Waxes and wastes," a "fleeting" thing that is ever "New" because it is ever "changed." The "I" dissolves into the "&c." of the body.

This threat of corporeal mechanism and its spectre of the annihilation of identity is, I think, the specific historical pressure that made not only the Mary Toft incident, but the imagination and the figure of the monster, too, resonant fields, rich in ambiguities, tensions, and anxieties. From a comfortable intellectual distance, Mary Toft's birth of rabbits, though it might be an unpleasant reminder of human corporeality, should not have been particularly disturbing. In fact, it might have been even oddly comforting, just as the theory of the maternal imagination appears to have been for Turner. For both monstrosity and the power of the mother's imagination were proofs of a "mysterious Intercourse" between mind and body and, hence, of the existence of both in human nature. Turner's repeated insistence on mystery, his constant refrain that the causes of monstrosity, the operation of the imagination, and the relationship between the mind and the body are all "impenetrable to the humane intellect," his aggressive touting of his own ignorance: these are signs of how crucial the truth is that Turner is trying to protect, the truth manifested in the birth of monsters, the truth of human doubleness.

But this aggressiveness is a sign, too, of Turner's sense that this truth is under serious attack, and it is probably a sign of his sense that his appeal to mystery, while it hedged away the threat, simultaneously robbed his arguments against it of their cogency. For monstrous birth might not indicate, in fact, the existence of the immaterial and its mysterious union with the body. Rather, monstrous births might betoken the very opposite, the very threat that Turner found so disconcerting. And, in the specific case of Mary Toft, it might betoken this threat in a powerfully literalistic way. For monstrous birth, and Mary Toft's in particular, might be seen as emblems of the other, nightmarish possibility, the possibility of the triumph of the corporeal, the possibility that the material could swamp the immaterial entirely, that the body could annihilate identity.

IV

In the summer of 1708, one of the most celebrated monsters of the eighteenth century was exhibited in London, attracting huge crowds and inspiring enthusiastic handbills:

> At Mr. John Pratt's at the Angel in Cornhil . . . are to be seen two Girls, who are one of the greatest Wonders in Nature that ever was seen, being Born with their Backs fasten'd to each other, and the Passages of their Bodies are both one way. These Children are very handsome and lusty, and Talk three different languages; they are going into the 7th year of their Age. Those who see them, may very well say, they have seen a Miracle, which may pass for the 8th Wonder of the World.[60]

The two girls were Helena and Judith, twins from Hungary, bound together at the buttocks and sharing a single vagina and a single rectum. Their mother attributed their deformity to the fact that, in the early months of her pregnancy, her imagination had been agitated by the sight of a monstrous two-headed dog.[61]

Swift was in London at the time, and he reacted somewhat more dryly than the crowds or the writers of the handbills. "Here is the sight of the two girls joined together at the back, which, in the news-monger's phrase, causes a great many speculations; and raises abundances of questions in divinity, law, and physic."[62] There were, in fact, "abundances of questions in divinity, law, and physic." For nearly a month, *The British Apollo* had to respond to a flow of queries from their readers concerning the puzzles of her identity: Did the twins have one or two souls? If one were guilty of a capital crime, how would she be punished? If someone were to marry one of the twins, would he be committing incest? Could they bear children and, if so, how could each mother know her own child? At the Resurrection, would each rise in her own individual body?[63] How weighty Swift and his fellow Scriblerians thought these questions were is revealed in the *Memoirs of Martinus Scriblerus,* where the satirists transform this incident into the episode of Lindamira-Indamora, Bohemian sisters joined at their backs and sharing "common parts of Generation"[64] and turn those "questions in divinity, law, and physic" which were seriously posed in *The British Apollo* into pure intellectual farce.

The Double-Mistress episode is an exuberant satiric fantasia, the Scriblerians poking fun at such disparate targets as the conventions of romances, virtuosi's passion for curiosities, and the bottomless pit of the law. But, increasingly, the satire focuses on the concern raised by the case of Helena and Judith, how to "determine the *constituent Principle* and *Essence* of *Individuality*" (157). In fact, the Double-Mistress episode climaxes this concern, for the question of what "the Essence of Unity and Individuality should consist in" (160) is present throughout much of the *Memoirs,* and in exploring it, the Scriblerians directly engage the issue that so preoccupied the metaphysicians of their age, the issue of the corporeal mechanism of human beings and the degree to which this mechanism threatens our personal identities.[65]

"Unity and Individuality" are challenged early in the *Memoirs.* When Cornelius tries to teach the fundamentals of metaphysics to his son and his son's companion, Crambe,

> Crambe would tell his Instructor, that All men were not *singular;* that Individuality could hardly be prædicated of any man, for it was commonly said that a man *is* not the same as he *was,* that madmen are *beside themselves,* and drunken men *come to themselves;* which shews, that few men have that most valuable logical endowment, Individuality. . . . When he was told, a *substance* was that which was *subject to accidents;* then Soldiers (quotes Crambe) are the most substantial people in the world. Neither would he allow it to be a good definition of *accident,* that it could be *present or absent without the destruction of the subject;* since there are a great many accidents that destroy the subject, as burning does a house, and death a man. (119)

The Scriblerians introduce here two themes that become increasingly important in the *Memoirs.* First is the rejection of individuality as something that "could hardly be prædicated of any man." Second is the concretization of the ideational and the abstract into physical entities: the metaphor "to be beside oneself" takes on a bizarre literalness in Crambe's mind, just as the metaphysical categories of "substance," "subject," and "accident" are conceived by him as physical things. The point the Scriblerians make throughout the *Memoirs* is that the first is a consequence of the second: like the orthodox metaphysicians and divines, they see that the more the self is conceived of as a physical object, the more it loses its identity.

This is why it is so appropriate that the search after the truth of the "great noise made about this Individuality" (138) should be conducted by Martin, a man whose mind is incapable of raising itself to abstraction ("Martin's understanding was so totally immers'd in *sensible objects,* that he demanded examples from Material things of the abstracted ideas of Logic" [119]). He is a fitting guide to what Turner called the "modish mechanic way" of thinking which had so perplexed the question of personal identity.

Typical is Martin's first attempt to understand human nature. He begins with the unarguable commonplace "that the Soul and Body mutually operate on each other." But he immediately corporealizes human beings by conceiving of "*Virtues* and *Vices* as certain Habits which proceed from the natural Formation and Structure of particular parts of the body." It is an easy step from this proposition to a mechanical manipulation of morality. Since pride and arrogance "were mark'd by tossing the head, and bending the body backwards,"

> in the proud and insolent there was a great over-balance of strength in the Extensors of the Neck and Muscles of the Back, from whence they perform with great facility the motion of *tossing,* but with great difficulty that of *bowing,* and therefore have justly acquir'd the title of stiff-neck'd. In order to reduce such persons to a just balance, he judg'd that the pair of Muscles call'd *Recti interni,* the Mastoidal, with other flexors of the head, neck, and body must be strengthen'd; their Antagonists, the *Splenii Complexi,* and the Extensors of the Spine, weaken'd: For which purpose Nature herself seems to have directed mankind to correct this Muscular Immortality by tying such fellows *Neck-and-heels.* (131–32)

Increasingly, Martin materializes the human soul. He next decides that there is "nothing so necessary as an Enquiry after the *Seat* of the *Soul*" (137). Knowing that the soul is defined as an immaterial substance, he thinks of "substance" as a material entity and assumes that therefore it must, like a material substance, have a physical place:

> Sometimes he was of opinion that it lodg'd in the Brain, sometimes in the Stomach, and sometimes in the Heart. Afterwards he thought it absurd to confine that sovereign Lady to one apartment, which made him infer that she shifted it according to the several functions of life: The Brain was her Study, the Heart her State-room, and the Stomach her Kitchen. But as he saw several offices of life went on at the same time, he was forc'd to give up this Hypothesis also. He now conjectured it was more for the dignity of the Soul to perform several operations by her little Minister, the *Animal Spirits,* from whence it was natural to conclude, that she resides in different parts

according to different Inclinations, Sexes, Ages, and Professions. Thus in Epicures he seated her in the mouth of the Stomach, Philosophers have her in the Brain, Soldiers in their Hearts, Women in their Tongues, Fidlers in their Fingers, and Rope-dancers in their Toes. (137)

Denied its immateriality, increasingly identified with the physical mechanisms of the body, human identity finally evaporates into nonexistence. For "these enquiries into the *Seat* of the *Soul* gave occasion to [Martin's] first correspondence with the society of *Free-Thinkers*," who drive Martin's corporealization of the human to its logical conclusion. Man *is* his body. What is "commonly call'd the *Soul*" is a "Chimera." The "power of thinking, self-moving, and governing the whole Machine" of the body resides in consciousness, which is itself but "the result from the mechanical composition of the whole Animal." This conception ends exactly as Arbuthnot says it would end in "Know Yourself." If the "thinking I" is just thinking matter, something coterminous with the "pipes through which the circling juices stray," with "mere flesh and blood," then the "I" is really just a "mouldering mass" that "Waxes and wastes." Corporealized, the self has no identity. If, as the Free-thinkers argue, man is simply "a *Congeries* of Glands," then we must conclude, as they do, that identity is a fiction, "to be understood in no other sense than the maxim of English Law, that the *King never dies*" (138–41).

And yet, in all these attacks on mechanistic materialism, the Scriblerians set at work a countermovement of irony that complicates the issue of identity. Thus, while it is fatuous for Martin to consider "*Virtues* and *Vices* as certain Habits which proceed from the natural Formation and Structure of particular parts of the body," it is true that the "Muscular Immorality" of the proud and arrogant tends to be cured by "tying such fellows *Neck-and heels*." And it is utterly impossible to gainsay Martin's clinching proof: "Castration abates Lust" (131). Though the Scriblerians probably would agree with Clarke when he says that to corporealize the mind leads to the absurd conclusion that "there must be several incoherent *consciousnesses*,"[66] they certainly agree with Crambe that a man can be beside himself (and with Martin, when he discovers that the narcissistic nobleman has split himself in two and has become "the object of his own adoration" [136]). To place human identity in the "flux state of the Particles of matter that compose his body" means, as Butler saw, that "the self or person of to-day, and that of to-morrow, are not the same";[67] but again, Crambe is right in concluding that "a man *is* not the same as he *was*." Humans are deeply implicated in their bodies, and in spite of what the metaphysicians say, the contours of identity are shaped as much by the laws of physics as by the laws of metaphysics. Although it is a metaphysical impossibility, it is a point of fact that the self can become the locus of this or that bodily drive, now this, now that jerk of an organ. Thus, Epicures do behave as if the soul were "seated . . . in the mouth of the Stomach, Philosophers . . . in the Brain, Soldiers in their Hearts, Women in their Tongues, Fidlers in their Fingers, and Rope-dancers in their Toes." The Scriblerians mock the Free-thinkers' corporealization of the human, but when the Free-thinkers claim that they have actually constructed a mechanical man, the Scriblerians turn their irony to show that, in fact, man does live down to these impossibilities:

> We are so much persuaded of the truth of this our Hypothesis, that we have employ'd one of our Members, a great Virtuoso at Nuremberg, to make a sort of an Hydraulic Engine, in which a chemical liquor resembling Blood, is driven through elastic chanels resembling arteries and veins, by the force of an Embolus like the heart, and wrought by a pneumatic Machine of the nature of the lungs, with ropes and pullies, like the nerves, tendons and muscles: and we are persuaded that this our artificial Man will not only walk, and speak, and perform most of the outward actions of the animal life, but (being wound up once a week) will perhaps reason as well as most of your Country Parsons. (141)

The form of irony in the *Memoirs* is the same as that in *Mechanical Operation of the Spirit* and *A Tale of a Tub,* where Swift uses various mechanical explanations of Enthusiastic madness—rising vapor, corrupt semen, flatulence, spirits—to shadow forth important intuitions (that the mind and body are interpenetrating, that often the lower drives press on the higher modes of thought, that Enthusiasts in particular are controlled by the energies of their bodies) as well as to satirize the all-embracing systems of explanation typical of Enthusiasts and their inability to think beyond the material. Swift's irony allows him to have it both ways at once, exploding the reductionism of mechanistic thinking and at the same time showing that it is an adequate description of how in fact human beings do behave. So in the *Memoirs,* the Scriblerians attack the mechanists who have reduced the "thinking I" to an automaton and then reveal that human beings behave as stupidly as the reductionistic theories have proposed.

All this play climaxes in the Lindamira-Indamora episode, where monstrosity becomes a figure the Scriblerians use to give shape to the puzzles of identity. When Martin marries Lindamira, he causes legal disputes about property, theological squabbles about the seat of the soul, and metaphysical debates about the nature of personal identity. All these debates are unresolvable, and they are unresolvable because the very systems of definition and determination (law, theology, metaphysics) implode when confronted with the enigma of Lindamira-Indamora. The sheer fact of her monstrosity causes these systems of explanation to fold in on themselves, to reveal the limitations of their own premises by terminating in self-contradictions and absurdities. For instance, when Mr. Randal, the owner of the twins, tries to regain his property, he charges that Martin, in taking possession of Lindami-ra, "might be sued for a *Rape* upon the body of her Sister"; but he is "quaintly disappointed" to discover that the law *also* provides that Martin "claim'd nothing but his own; and if another person had fix'd herself to his Wife, he must not for that cause be debarred the use of his Property" (155).

Thwarted, Mr. Randal arranges a secret marriage between Indamo-ra and the Black Prince. The resulting legal battles between Martin and the Black Prince over twins who share a common vagina occasion suits and countersuits that hinge on determining "the *constituent Prin-ciple* and *Essence* of *Individuality*" (157). The monstrosity of the twins so perplexes this issue of individual identity that here, too, no resolution is possible. What the cases do reveal, however, is how insufficient our conception of identity is.

Dr. Penny-feather, Martin's lawyer, argues that two are one, that Lindamira-Indamora is the "individual wife" of Martin because she "makes but one individual Person." He begins by reasoning along orthodox lines: the "*constituent Principle* and *Essence* of *Individuality*," he says, is "one simple identical soul, in one simple identical body." But then, like his client, Martin, he veers in a materialist direction. For, having to determine what constitutes "one simple identical body" in the problematic case of the twins, he concludes that the "individuality, sameness, or identity of the body, is not determin'd (as some vainly imagine) by one head, and a certain number of arms, legs, and other members; but in one simple, single . . . member of Generation." And then he clinches his point (again, by following a materialist line of thought) by arguing that the "organ of Generation is the Seat of the Soul; and consequently, where there is but one such Organ, there can be but one Soul" (156–58).

Against Dr. Penny-feather's argument that two are one, Dr. Leatherhead, the lawyer for the Black Prince, insists that "*One is Two*" (156). He takes a much more orthodox line of argument to prove that "though there were but one Organ of Generation, yet are there but two distinct persons":

> Neither the individual Essence of mankind, nor the Seat of the Soul, doth reside in the Organ of Generation; . . . for unreasonable indeed must it be, to make that the Seat of the rational Soul, which alone sets us on a level with

beasts; or to conceive, that the Essence of Unity and Individuality should consist in that which is the source of Discord and Division. In a word, what can be a greater absurdity, than to affirm Beastiality to be the Essence of Humanity, Darkness the Centre of Light, and Filthiness the Seat of Purity?

Having demonstrated that one is two, Dr. Leatherhead concludes that Martin's marriage to Lindamira "render[s] him plainly guilty of Bigamy, Rape, or Incest" (160–61).

But, as in the earlier episodes in the *Memoirs,* countercurrents of irony are set in motion which subvert the positions taken by both sides and which utterly perplex the question of identity. For both arguments reveal their own inadequacies. Dr. Leatherhead's championing of the "rational Soul" as the constituent essence of personal identity, so pious and orthodox on the face of it, leads him into a ludicrous theological fantasy that rests on an impossible vision of human nature. Arguing against Dr. Penny-feather's notion that the organ of generation is the seat of the soul, he attempts to prove "that personal individuality did subsist, when there was no generative Carnality":

> It hath been strenuously maintained by many holy Divines (and partic-ularly by Thomas Aquinas) that our first parents, in the state of Innocence, did in no wise propagate their species after the present common manner of men and beasts; but that the propagation at that time must have been by Intuition, Coalition of Ideas, or some pure and spiritual manner, suitable to the dignity of their station. And though the Sexes were distinguish'd in that state, yet it was plain it was not by parts, such as we have at present; since, if our First parents had any such, they must have known it; and it is written, that they discover'd them not till after the Fall; when it is proba-ble those parts were the immediate Excresence of Sin, and only grew forth to render them fitter companions for those Beasts among which they were driven. (161)

To conceive of personal identity as grounded in a "rational Soul," to argue, as Dr. Leatherhead does, for *"Intuitive Generation,"* is to sepa-rate our identities from our bodies, to ludicrously unsex and decorpo-realize the self.

On the other hand, the argument of Dr. Penny-feather, patently ridiculous in its reduction of human identity to the organ of genera-tion, turns out, like the equally ridiculous arguments of the Free-thinkers, to be an adequate description of human behavior in spite of all its metaphysical absurdity. "When we behold this one member," Dr. Penny-feather reasons, "we distinguish the Sex, and pronounce it a *Man,* or a *Woman*" (157). "This our Doctrine," he continues,

> is confirm'd by all those Experiments, which conspire to prove the absolute Dominion that part hath over the whole body. We see how many Women,

who are deaf to the persuasions of the Eloquent, the insinuations of the Crafty, and the threats of the Imperious, are easily governed by some poor Logger-head, unfurnish'd with the least art, but that of making immediate application to this *Seat of the Soul.* The impressions made by the Ear are so distant, and transmitted thro' so many windings, that they lose their Energy: But your Honour, by immediately applying to the Organ of Generation, acts like a bold and wise Petitioner, who goes strait to the *very Throne and Judgment-Seat* of the Monarch. (158–59)

And to the objection that, if Lindmira-Indamora is but a single individual, she has two wills, Dr. Penny-feather is unfazed, for observation confirms that he has lighted on an empirical truth:

> And whereas it is objected that here are *two Wills,* and therefore *two* different *Persons;* we answer, if multiplicity of Wills implied multiplicity of Persons, there are few Husbands but what are guilty of *Polygamy,* there being in the same Woman great and notorious deversity of Wills: . . . (159)

What generates these ironic perplexities and prevents them from being resolved is the question the monster raises, whether "*One* is *Two*" or two are one. Given the monstrosity of Lindamira-Indamora, one is two—and two are one. This singleness-and-doubleness, this straddling the borders between one and two, throws all conventional categories created by law, theology, and metaphysics into confusion and baffles our attempts at definition. And, to the end, the monster remains single-and-double, creating riddles impervious to solution, for the court declares that both Martin and the Black Prince may perform their "Conjugal Duties," but it leaves them with this impossible injunction: "Consider also by how small Limits the Duty and the Trespass is divided, lest, while ye discharge the duty of Matrimony, ye harmlessly slide into the sin of adultery" (163). Those "small Limits" are, in fact, no limits at all. Duty cannot be distinguished from trespass because Lindamira-Indamora occupy the very limits themselves, the very borders that distinguish one thing from another, and hence they blur all distinctions and identities. She is (they are!) a liminal creature, inhabiting the borders between categories, suggesting the possibility that the categories themselves are ambiguous, permeable.

Thus, Lindamira-Indamora is a fitting climax for the theme of identity in the *Memoirs.* For her singleness-and-doubleness is the singleness-and-doubleness of humanity itself, and it is the fact of human singleness-and-doubleness that generates the irony of the discussion of identity in the *Memoirs.* Man is single in that, metaphysically considered, he has a self with a single, unified identity: he is a "rational Soul," a "thinking I," and his identity is grounded in an immaterial substance. This is what grants him his status as an individual and what guaran-

tees a persisting identity. But man is also double in the sense that he is
an immaterial substance *and* the body to which it is fastened in vital
union, and therefore he is subject to the body and its mechanics. And
so, he has a self—"self" in its more commonplace usage, meaning the
totality of human drives, appetites, and instincts—which is not singular or unified, but which is heterogeneous, always in flux, a bundle of
incoherent, self-contradictory impulses, energies, and inclinations.
And it is the human estate to be one-and-two: an individual with a persisting identity as well as an "&c.," an automaton that is a "nothing."

Such a single yet heterogeneous self can be pictured only by paradox
or by statements subjected to continual redaction, such as Pope's
"glory, jest, and riddle of the world" or such as Swift's unstable trian-
gulation of the human self using the unfixable points of Gulliver, the
Yahoos, and the Houyhnhnms. Or such a self can be suggested by the
form of irony played out in the *Memoirs*. The mechanists are wrong
because they want to make that which is one-and-two *just* one by
reducing humanity to the body. Therefore, the orthodox metaphysicians are right in their demand that man has an identity that is rooted
in an immaterial substance. He does, as Dr. Leatherhead insists, have a
"rational Soul," and thus, "what can be a greater absurdity, than to
affirm Bestiality to be the Essence of Humanity, Darkness the Centre
of Light, and Filthiness the seat of Purity?" But the metaphysicians are
wrong, too, for it is precisely this "greater absurdity" that humanity
finds itself in. Though it is true that "the *constituent Principle* and
Essence of *Individuality*" is immaterial substance, it is also true that we
are substance in the less metaphysical meaning of the word, what
Crambe means when he says that substance is *"subject to accidents."*
The self *is* subjected to its own accidents, it is embruted in the matter of
its own body, a sexed and corporeal thing, a *"Congeries* of Glands," and
in this way the mechanists are right even in their being wrong. For
although it is true, as the metaphysicians argue, that the self is indivisible by virtue of its soul, it is also true, as the mechanists claim, that it is
divisible: we can be besides ourselves; we can have two wills; our selves
can become scattered, dispersed, and portioned out into so many centers that our personalities become like the "flux state of the Particles of
matter that comprise [the] body" (140). Our identities, far from partaking of the immaterial substance which is their ground, can be reduced
to an organ of the body, or, like the automaton constructed by the virtuoso at Nuremberg, become a mindless thing.

Besides paradox, continual redaction, and the kind of irony we see
in the *Memoirs,* such a self can be portrayed one further way: it can be
portrayed as a monster. For all monsters, and not just Lindamira-

Indamora, are creatures of the borders. As distortions or amalgams of forms, they simultaneously have and do not have an identity, and hence they baffle our attempts to settle on a definition of what they are. And this is why the Scriblerians settled on a monster to climax the theme of identity in the *Memoirs*. Lindamira-Indamora's monstrosity is the mysterious singleness-and-doubleness of humanity, and her monstrousness confirms the truth and reveals the falsity of the definition of human kind by the metaphysicians and mechanists alike. And she reveals the falsity of both because she embodies the undefinability of human identity, its sheer mystery. In the *Memoirs,* the language of monstrosity, like the monsters themselves, has become a purely liminal phenomenon, one-and-two, unresolvable.

What is remarkable about the *Memoirs* is how in the hands of the Scriblerians the figure of the monster becomes a way simultaneously to articulate a vision of corporealized human nature and to deny it. On the one hand, the monster Lindamira-Indamora represents humanity as a divided being, driven by the body, a creature of indeterminate identity. On the other hand, her monstrosity means for the Scriblerians precisely what monstrosity meant for Turner. For in the *Memoirs,* the monster Lindamira-Indamora is a symbol of mystery, specifically (as with Turner) the mystery of the inexplicable union of body and mind, and therefore it mocks the absurdity of the mechanists, who have attempted to define something that by its very nature eludes definition. Like Turner, the Scriblerians have converted the vulnerability of orthodoxy—its inability to bring cogent arguments against the case of the mechanists—into an aggressive weapon of satire.

And yet, the fact that the Scriblerians use monstrosity to figure forth the disintegration of identity into corporeal mechanism *as well as* to articulate its counter-meaning, the mystery of human nature, is suggestive. For the aggressiveness of Turner's use of monstrosity to express the mystery and unknowableness of human nature is an index to his defensiveness in the face of mechanism, and I suspect that the Scriblerians' language of monstrosity, which articulates a meaning and also a defense against this meaning, grows out of a similar anxiety.

V

At the risk of being somewhat repetitious, let me summarize what I think happened when Mary Toft claimed that she gave birth to seventeen rabbits. Her declaration stirred disquiet and apprehension because, if it were true, she possessed a power that was deeply feared. That power was the power of the imagination—not its power, literally, to misshape offspring, but rather that very same power as it manifested itself in our everyday lives, minute by minute. The imagination was a great leveller: ideas, sensations, fantasies, passions, all were reduced in the imagination to quasi-corporeal images, one as seemingly solid and real as another. What we fabricated in our fancies had the same texture and weight as what we experienced of the external world through our senses. The images that represented the demands of the body and the passions, to the eye of the mind, had the same substantive presence as images of ideas. Everything in the mind—sensation and idea, fantasy and reality, the commands of reason and the demands of passion, the movements of the body and the movements of the mind—spun in a phantasmagoric dance of images that had been drawn down to the one dead level of corporeality. Just as the imagination deformed a fetus by incorporating mind in body, so the imagination in this quotidian operation blurred the boundaries of the material and the immaterial and thus knotted the mind more and more inexorably into the body that contained it. The result of this process in one instance was monstrous offspring, in the other, monstrous confusion, a moment in which the imagination, concretized as corporeal images, blanked out reality, became reality—a moment, in short, when the body began to incorporate the mind.

In this moment of confusion (so suggest the patterns of responses during the Mary Toft incident), personal identity began to collapse: the self lost its contours and became a shapeless thing, a monster. The logic of this loss of identity is explained, in part, by the dynamics of the imagination as it was conceived during the early eighteenth century. The self mistakes the fantasy constructs of the passions and the mechanisms of the body for the ideas of the mind, for voices of the spirit, and abandons itself to their promptings. Hence, the self is corporealized by the imagination. For, when one abandons oneself to the imagination, one abandons oneself to the energies welling up from the lower strata, from the passions and the body. The self, to use the images that so often recur in the Mary Toft satires, is made impotent and then transformed by being assimilated into these energies: the self loses its identity because it is absorbed into the endless flutter of the senses, the restless thrust and heave of the body's mechanisms, and the shapeless ferment of the passions. The self *becomes* the amorphous energies it abandons itself to. It takes on the lineaments of a monster, for a self delivered over to its body is incapable of identity: it becomes the flux, the "&c." of its own energies.

The threat to self-identity posed by the body's impingement on the mind by way of the imagination was intensified by the impasse that had developed in thinking about mind and body, by the increasing inability to explain the interaction between the two, and, consequently, by the growing menace of corporeal mechanism. In a parodic attack on Free-thinking, one of hundreds that were written during this period, "Isaac Alogist" writes "a *Mechanical Essay on the Operations of the Mind*" to prove that a human being is nothing but a "*Machine*." Significantly, he attributes to this automaton only two faculties, imagination and memory (which, since it is conceived of as a storehouse of images, is an extension of the imagination). The assumption behind this piece is clear: to the extent that someone allows his mental operations to be governed by his imagination, to that degree he becomes the corporeal machine that is his body.

> First then I lay down, as an undeniable Truth, that we have in common with other Animals *a certain Machine* of a curious and exquisite Workmanship, the principal Springs whereof are *Imagination* and *Memory.* If we carefully examine this *Machine,* we shall find it exactly the same in Men and Beasts, every thing being done in both in a manner meerly *passive* and *necessary.* To be convinced of this, let us but consider that all outward Objects do, by the exterior Organs of Sensation, send into the Brain *certain Images,* which meeting with the animal Spirits *aptly disposed,* excite in the *Machine* some determined Motion or other. The *Machine* itself is incapable of any Choice, but is always actuated by the strongest Impression, which generally depends on the Disposition it is in at the very Instant it receives it. . . .
>
> I now proceed to *Memory,* which is nothing but the same *Imagination* acting without the assistance of exterior Objects. To explain this, we must consider that the first Image which an outward Object imprints on our Brain is very slight; it resembles a thin Vapour which dwindles into nothing, without leaving the least track after it. But if the same Object successively offers itself several times, the *Image* it occasions thereby increases and strengthens itself by degrees, till at last it acquires such a consistency (if I may so call it) as makes it subsist as long as the *Machine* itself. A Stock of *Images* having thus been acquired, they each have their respective little *Cell* or *Lodge,* where they go and hide. Yet we must not suppose that they are continually in their Retirement; they would become useless if they were so. But, on the contrary, great Numbers of them are always going to and fro; and if one of them chances to go by the *Cell* or *Lodge* of another which has the least real or imaginary conformity with it, out pops the retired *Image,* and immediately joins the wandering one. This never so obviously happens, as when a *new Image* is introduced into the Brain, who as soon as he appears, occasions great Commotions among all the *old Inhabitants,* who either have, or think they have, any resemblance or relation to the *new Comers.*
>
> Now, according to my supposition, there being no *active intelligent Being,* who, by his Presence and Superintendency, governs and directs the course of those *vagabond Images,* every thing in the Brain resembles the *fortuitous concourse of Atoms.* Two *Images* meet, and unite to each other, these

two meeting with a third, it unites to them in the same manner: and this Meeting and Union continuing for some time, at last occasions a most monstrous Aggregation, very like the *Chaos* of the Poet, where *Frigida cum calidis pugnant, humentia siccis.*[68]

Much of the pattern of response to the Mary Toft incident can be found in miniature in this passage. Once our *"active intelligent Being"* is abandoned, nothing is left in our minds but a train of images. These are more sensational than ideational, always threatening to becomes physical objects, "acquir[ing] . . . a consistency," as if they were corporeal particles moved by the law of physics. The self becomes impotent before them, unable to will self-direction since thinking has become an automatic response to the physical stimuli of mental images ("every thing being done . . . in a manner merely *passive* and *necessary*"). And so, the *"vagabond images"* spill through the mind like a *"fortuitous concourse of Atoms."* All the while, of course, it is *we* who have become this *"Chaos,"* our very identities reduced to the "monstrous Aggregation," which is the body the imagination has delivered us to. This is a fall into matter, and this, I am arguing, is the threat Mary Toft represented.

There were, as we saw, defenses against this spectre of encroaching corporeality. "Man is a Creature of so mix'd a Composure, and of a Frame so Inconsistent and Different from *Its* self, that it easily speaks his Affinity to the highest and meanest Beings," wrote Steele; "that is to say, he is made of Body and Soul, he is at once an *Engine* and an *Engineer.*" Even though this divides a human being and presupposes a "Soul . . . Imprison[ed] in Sense and Matter," it is still a very comfortable thought. For division into two implies some degree of independence of the one from the other, and hence the Engineer may never be caught in the machinery of the Engine he supervises:

Tho' indeed both that Body and Soul act in many Instances separate and independent of each other: For when he Thinks, Reasons and Concludes, he has not in all that Work the least Assistance from his Body: His finest Fibres, purest Blood, and highest Spirits are as brute and distant from a Capacity of Thinking as his very Bones; and the Body is so mere a Machine, that it Hungers, Thirsts, Tastes and Digests, without any exerted Thought of the Mind to command that Operation: Which when he observes upon himself, he may, without deriving it from Vapour, Fume or Distemper, believe that his Soul may as well Exist out of, as in that Body from which it borrows nothing to make it capable of performing its most perfect Functions. This may give him hopes, that tho' his Trunk return to its native Dust he may not all Perish, but the Inhabitant of it may remove to another Mansion; especially since he knows only Mechanically that they have, not Demonstratively how they have, ev'n a present Union.[69]

The appeal in the last sentence to mystery—we know that the body and soul are united, but we know not how, for it is utterly impossible that they can be—seals the boundary between body and mind and guarantees the existence of a stable identity and an autonomous self.

This was the same mystery that the Scriblerians appealed to in the *Memoirs* under the figure of the monster, and it seems to have served the same function of diffusing the potentially explosive anxiety of the mind's incorporation in the body. The tone of the *Memoirs* is all "Frolick Mirth."[70] The sheer ease and good humor with which the Scriblerians acknowledge the limitations of orthodoxy and deflate the pretentions of the mechanists but admit something of the truth of their bleak vision suggests that they have accepted human singleness-and-doubleness with equanimity. That man's being strung between a self that has an identity and one that is driven by the processes of the body toward the "&c." of atomization and nothingness might be a matter of tragedy or the cause of maddening pain is not even broached in the *Memoirs*.

Yet individual Scriblerians rehearsed these same issues with considerably more bitterness and sting than we find in the *Memoirs*. In the *Dunciad*, Pope envisions the possibility of a world reduced to the "one dead level" of corporeality and mechanism, a world in which humans become things and (therefore) nothings, their identities dispersed and then extinguished, and he explores this possibility under the figure of the monster. In spite of a good many moments of high comedy in the poem, Pope's view is much less sanguine than that expressed in the *Memoirs*.

And so, too, is Swift's. At the very end of his analysis of Enthusiasm in *Mechanical Operation*, he concludes: "Too intense a Contemplation is not the Business of Flesh and Blood; it must by the necessary Course of Things, in a little Time, let go its Hold, and fall into *Matter*." Much of his work, of course, is a scarifying exploration of how frail the boundary is between mind and body, "how near the Frontiers of height and Depth border upon each other,"[71] and how horrifying it is when those frontiers give way and one falls into matter. And in *Gulliver's Travels*, he returns to the themes of the triumph of corporeality and the loss of identity, themes which he, like Pope, expresses under the figure of the monster, and the tonal strains in his satire suggest that these anxieties are not as easily domesticated as they were in the *Memoirs*.[72]

In order to explore further the complex relationships among the notions of monstrosity, the imagination, and self-identity, I want to turn, first, to *Gulliver's Travels*, then to the *Dunciad*, and finally to the trajectory of Pope's poetic career, a career, I will argue, shaped by anxieties about monstrosity, the imagination, and self-identity.

5

A LUMP OF DEFORMITY

 The most obvious joke in the title of Swift's *Travels into Sever-al Remote Nations of the World* is that what purports to be a chronicle of several excursions to remote nations turns out to be a satiric anatomy of English attitudes and values. But there is a second joke. Many of the sights Gulliver observes in these far-away nations, sights which he regards as utterly singular and alien, in fact could have been seen in London. I am referring here to something more than those few buildings, institutions, and ceremonies that have obvious analogues to ones in England: the temple in Lilliput where Gulliver is imprisoned, which is like Whitehall; the Grand Academy of Lagado, which is similar to Gresham College (and even more similar to Bedlam); the exercises of the Brobdingnagian militia, which resemble the daily parade of the Horse and Grenadier Guards near Mews Gate. What I am referring to is the fact that a large portion of the supposedly unfamiliar and exotic sights Gulliver sees in his sixteen years and seven months of wandering in remote nations, and even the radically altered perspectives from which he sees them (as diminutive landscapes, giant people, intelligent animals, and so forth), could have been seen or experienced in a few days by any of his countrymen at the tourist sights, public entertainments, shows, spectacles, and exhibitions in the streets and at the fairs of London.

Gulliver himself senses that the wonders he sees in remote nations resemble popular entertainments back home in England when he notes that the capital city of Lilliput "looked like the painted Scene of a City in a Theatre."[1] And other popular entertainments would allow Londoners to see many of the same sights Gulliver saw in Lilliput. A Londoner could experience what a miniature city looked like to the giant Gulliver by going to see the papier-mâché and clay architectural and topographical models displayed at fairs and in inns, some of which were extraordinarily elaborate and detailed, such as the model of Amsterdam exhibited in 1710, which was twenty feet wide and twenty to thirty feet long, "with all the Churches, Chappels, Stadt house, Hospitals, noble Buildings, Streets, Trees, Walks, Avenues, with the Sea, Shipping, Sluices, Rivers, Canals, &c., most exactly built to admiration."[2]

Miniature people, as well as miniature landscapes, could be seen in one of the most popular diversions in London, the peepshows, which were enclosed boxes containing scenes made out of painted boards, paper flats, and glass panels and given the illusion of depth by mirrors and magnifying glasses. All of this was seen through a hole bored in one side. Among the most popular scenes were interiors, particularly palace interiors of European royalty, and so there is a direct analogy between peering in the hole of a peepshow and Gulliver's looking into the palace in Lilliput: "I applied my Face to the Windows of the middle Stories, which were left open on Purpose, and discovered the most splendid Apartments that can be imagined. There I saw the Empress, and the young Princes in their several Lodgings, with their chief Attendants about them. Her Imperial Majesty was pleased to smile very graciously upon me, and gave me out the window her Hand to kiss" (31). The Queen's movements could have been seen in the peepshows, too, for clockwork animating the figures was introduced early in the century.[3] And much the same illusion of a living, miniature world could be found in another popular diversion, the "moving picture," a device in which cut-out figures were placed within a frame and activated by jacks and wheels. This curiosity fascinated contemporary Londoners: "The landscape looks as an ordinary picture till the clockwork behind the curtain be set at work, and then the ships move and sail distinctly upon the sea till out of sight; a coach comes out of town, the motion of the horses and wheels are very distinct, and a gentleman in the coach that salutes the company; a hunter also and his dogs, &c. keep their course till out of sight."[4] Swift saw this same moving picture, or one very much like it, and was impressed.

When the Brobdingnagian king first saw Gulliver, he thought that he "might be a piece of Clock-work . . . contrived by some ingenious Artist" (87). The little world of Lilliput—or the little Gulliver among the Brobdingnagians—has another analogue in the numerous clock-work automata which were exhibited at inns and fairs. By the eighteenth century, these had reached remarkable levels of complexity and craftsmanship, depicting entire villages, panoramas of forests and countrysides, and detailed interiors, all filled with animated miniature figures, both human and animal.[5]

But most obviously, "Pygmy Actors" moving in diminutive settings could be seen daily in the London puppet shows. Indeed, the Lilliputians are introduced to us as if they were puppets, for they first address Gulliver in their "shrill" voices from "a Stage erected about a Foot and a half from the Ground, capable of holding four of the Inhabitants" (6–7). And, in less obvious ways, the entire episode in Lilliput recalls a puppet show. The mock-heroic, always implicitly present in book 1, is a tacit dimension of any puppet show simply by virtue of the fact that human actions are mimicked so accurately by such inconsiderable mechanisms. Addison had already exploited its mock-heroic potential in his poem, "Machinæ Gesticulantes," where he satirized human self-importance by describing puppets practicing court manners and engaging in wars, much as Swift does in his description of the Lilliputian court. This mock-heroic potential was enhanced by the increasing range and sophistication of early eighteenth-century puppet shows, especially those mounted by Martin Powell, who showed his puppets for many of the years Swift was in London. Powell presented puppet dramas in which noble and royal personages were engaged in signal actions in the midst of elaborate, often spectacular sets, shows in which the puppets played out classical heroics, and shows which represented modern heroic action in miniature (such as Marlborough's victory at Malplaquet). And three specific pieces of business in Powell's productions have very close parallels in *Gulliver's Travels:* puppet rope-dancers; palaces in flames in *The Destruction of Troy;* and live animals intermixed with the puppet actors (which recalls Gulliver's adventures with large animals in book 2).[6]

Among the curiosities Gulliver brought back to England were his miniature livestock from Lilliput; he made "a considerable Profit by shewing [them] to many Persons of quality, and others" (63–64). When Swift was in London, there was exhibited a "little Horse, 2 Foot Odd Inches high, which performs several wonderful Actions by the Word of Command, being so small that it's kept in a Box."[7] Almost all of the other curios Gulliver brings home could have been seen by a Londoner in that favorite show place for curious sights, the Royal Society. The comb "contrived out of the Stumps of the King's Beard" (130) easily could have found a place among the Indian combs displayed in its cabinets. Gulliver's four wasp-stings could have been seen along side the "TOOTH of the . . . *Bahama-Spider,*" "the CLAW of a SCORPION," and the "TAIL of another, with the *Sting* at the end." And although the Society did not have a tooth to match that of the Brobdingnagian footman (to see the tooth of a real giant, a Londoner would have to rummage through the gimcracks at Don Saltero's Coffee House), they did have a large collection of teeth. A Londoner could even find displayed at the Society the "Sun-Dial upon the great Weather-Cock" (165) Gulliver saw at the Grand Academy of Lagado—Wren's ingenious "weather-clock," a device which automatically recorded wind direction by means of a weather-cock attached to a pendulum-driven clock.[8]

Gulliver's Travels is filled with the sights, shows, and diversions of London. Although no Londoner could see a politician perform on a rope, he could see rope-dancers themselves at Charing Cross or in any of the city's fairs—performers like the celebrated Jacob Hall,[9] or "the two famous French Maidens" who had "gain'd the highest Applause from all the Nobility and Gentry, for their wonderful performance on the Rope, both with and without a Pole," or "the Italian Scaramouch," who danced on the rope "with a Wheel Barrow before him with two Children and a Dog in it, and with a Duck on his Head." And even though Gulliver claims that the leaping and creeping of the politicians under a stick was a performance he had "not observed the least Resemblance of in any other Country of the old or the new World" (23), such performances, though not by politicians, could have been observed daily in the tumblers who "Lay head and heel to creep through Hoope."[10] The beggar Gulliver sees on the street in Lorbrulgrud "with a couple of wooden Legs, each about twenty Foot high" (97) could be seen in the stilt-walkers who frequented the fairs. The form of swearing an oath in Lilliput (Gulliver is required "to hold my right Foot in my left Hand, to place the middle Finger of my right Hand on the Crown of my Head, and my Thumb on the Tip of my right Ear" [26–27]) recalls the contortions of the posture-masters who exhibited their skills at London's fairs. The "ingenious Doctor" at the School of Political Projectors in Balnibarbi, who had found out the most "effectual Remedies for all Diseases and Corruptions, to which the several Kinds of public Administration are subject" (171), in both the extravagance of his claims and the outrageousness of his cures resembles nothing so much as the mountebanks who plied their trade at the fairs and in the streets of London. The Laputans, or at least someone who shared their strange appearance, could have been seen simply by going to the Ram's Head Inn where the *"Bold Grimace Spaniard"* made his living by demonstrating his extraordinary powers of facial contortion, "turn[ing] his Eyes in and out at the same time." Londoners would never see one of the immortal Struldbruggs, to be sure, but they could go to Covent Garden and gawk at the man "suppos'd to be a Hundred and Fifty Years Old."[11] And they could experience, too, something of what Gulliver felt in Glubbdubdrib when he was surrounded by the ghosts of the famous and infamous of the past simply by visiting the wax-works at a booth in Bartholomew or Southwark Fair or at the permanent exhibits of Du Puy or the Salmons. As in Glubbdubdrib, they portrayed the heroes and villains of history, both ancient and modern ("the Effigies of Mark Anthony, naturally acting that which rendered him remarkable to the World: Cleopatra, his Queen; one of her Egyptian Ladies. Oliver Cromwell in Armour: the Count Tollemach: with many others too tedious here to mention").[12] The incomprehensible music Gulliver heard in Brobdingnag could be heard in the cacaphonous music booths at Bartholomew Fair.[13] The horses in Lilliput, trained to take Gulliver's "Foot, Shoe and all" (24), could be seen at the Fair, too, where vaulting acts recently had been introduced.

Had the Lilliputians followed through on their plan to kill Gulliver, "leaving the Skeleton as a Monument of Admiration to Posterity" (55), their descendants would have seen little more than Londoners saw in 1702 when the skeleton of a whale caught in the Thames was displayed in a field near King Street, Bloomsbury. And the Lilliputians' anxiety about the stench of Gulliver's carcass was realized when, ten years later, another whale exhibited on a barge near Blackfriars had to be auctioned off quickly because of its smell.[14]

Something of the topography of Laputa—the "most delicious Spot of Ground in the World" at the center of which is "the *Astronomer's Cave;* situated at the depth of an Hundred Yards beneath the upper Surface of the Adamant" (149, 151)—could have been seen at a favorite tourist haunt, Greenwich, whose "pleasant *Park* . . . afford[ing] a delectable Prospect" had at its center its own astronomer's cave, "a deep Well, to make Observations in."[15] And at another tourist spot, Londoners could see the machine the projectors of Lagado built to pipe water uphill, a "curious Engine" at London Bridge, "which by the *Flux* and *Reflux* of the Tide, raises the Water to such a Height, as to furnish most Parts of the City."[16] The amazement the Lilliputians felt on seeing Gulliver's watch, enclosed in "some transparent Metal" and making "an incessant noise like that of a Water-Mill" (19), could be experienced by a Londoner at the top of St. Paul's, one turret of which had its clock encased in glass for curious spectators.[17] If a Londoner wanted to see the contrivance Gulliver built to entertain the Lilliputian nobility, setting up a "rim quite round, of five inches high, to prevent Accidents," within which "Coachmen would gently drive . . . round my table" (49), he merely had to visit the Ring in Hyde Park.[18] And although Gulliver had to go to the "chief Temple" in Brobdingnag to find among the "Gods and Emperors cut in marble" a "little Finger which had fallen down from one of those Statues, and lay unperceived among some Rubbish" (98), a tourist in London merely need go to Westminster Abbey, where, notoriously, the statues were in the same condition. Ward lamented that in this "Magnificent Temple" the "Monuments should be defac'd, some with their hands off, and some with their Feet off, lying by them without Reparation."[19]

But it is not these miscellaneous details scattered throughout *Gulliver's Travels* that call up the presence of the sights and shows of London so much as it is the book's frequent allusions to one of the most common of all popular diversions, the exhibitions of prodigies and monsters. In the opening chapters of book 2, the matter is quite explicit, for Gulliver is shown "as a Sight," and he expresses his resentment at "the Ignominy of being carried about for a Monster" and being "exposed for Money as a publick Spectacle to the meanest of the People" (80–81). The details of his early tour of Brobdingnag—his being trundled from town to town, carried in a box, and exhibited publicly in inns and privately to the wealthy in their homes—are drawn from the actual practices of showing monkeys and dwarfs in eighteenth-century England. And so too are the "diverting Tricks" (81) he is forced to perform. He pays his "humble Respects" to the company, drinks "a Thimble filled with Liquor," and then uses a straw "exercised as a Pike" (82). Handbills show that monkeys performed precisely these same tricks: a "Noble Creature, which much resembles a Wild *Hairy Man* . . . pulls off his Hat, and pays his Respects to the Company" and then "drinks a Glass of Ale"; a "Man Teger" takes "a glass of Ale in his hand like a Christian, Drinks it, also plays at Quarter Staff."[20]

But monster shows, particularly as practiced at Bartholomew Fair, are omnipresent in *Gulliver's Travels*. For Bartholomew Fair had become a place "for Recreation chiefly; *viz.* To see Drolls, Farces, Rope dancing, Feats of Activity, Wonderful and Monstrous Creatures, wild Beasts made Tame, Giants, Dwarfs, &c."[21] Precisely these "Wonderful and Monstrous Creatures, wild Beasts made Tame, Giants, Dwarfs, &c." inform much of the structure of *Gulliver's Travels,* made up as it is of little people, big people, intelligent animals, and bestial men, the four most typical monsters exhibited at the Fair.

The giants exhibited in London were not as tall as Gulliver when he was among the Lilliputians (they averaged between seven and eight feet), so no person, let alone an army, could walk with ease between their legs, though one giant who showed himself at Southwark Fair in 1684 remarked in his handbill that "his late Majesty was pleased to walk under his Arm, and he has grown very much since."[22] Giants of another sort—large strongmen—were common too. The feats they performed were fairly uniform. All lifted heavy objects, usually barrels or men; they bent iron bars; and the "*Southwark Sampson,*" William Joyce, "snaps Cables like Twine Thread, and throws Dray Horses upon their backs with . . . ease." Gulliver performs most of these: he can lift horses, men, and the "largest Hogsheads" (8) effortlessly, and he "twisted three . . . Iron Bars together" (35) with no difficulty. He had more trouble, however, snapping cables—he had to cut the cables of the Blefuscudian ships—and from the beginning he is a signal failure at the one feat most strongmen performed easily, lifting heavy objects by their hair. Joyce's handbill proclaimed "HIS STRENGTH PROV'D before the KING," a claim that was made by almost all the giants and strongmen who were exhibited, and so in this way, too, they are like Gulliver, who is asked to perform numerous diversions before the king of Lilliput and is invited by the Court of Blefuscu "to shew them some Proofs of [his] prodigious Strength, of which they had heard so many Wonders" (38).[23]

Even more popular than giants were dwarfs. If we are to trust their handbills, they too were regularly exhibited before royalty. And they appeared to be valued not only because of their size. First, a premium was put on a dwarf who was well-proportioned. The dwarf who attracted an audience (judging from handbills and the reactions of spectators) was one who was "straight, well proportioned and well-made in every way," one who, as John Wormberg boasted of himself in his handbill, "is so very well proportioned to his bigness that all that sees him, admires him." Secondly, dwarfs had to display some intelligence and an ability to interact with the audience—thus the "Woman Dwarf but Three Foot and one Inch high, who discourses excellently well"; the dwarf "not above eighteen inches long," who "hath all her sense of Admiration, and Discourses, Reads very well"; and the "Little Scotchman," who "discourses of the Scriptures, and of many Eminent Histories, very wisely." These are the very qualities in Gulliver that so fascinate the Brobdingnagians. The farmer advertises Gulliver as "exactly shaped in every Part like a human Creature" and as having "the finest Limbs in the World" (80). Gulliver's show itself—conversing with Glumdalclitch and the spectators and delivering "Speeches [he] had been taught" (82)—displays his intelligence and his skill at "discourse," just like the shows of the dwarfs at Bartholomew Fair. And the Brobdingnagian king's desire to get "a Woman of [Gulliver's]

own Size" so that he might "propagate the Breed" (123) was anticipat-
ed by the sensation of the winter of 1711–12. The "Black Prince," a
three-foot dwarf from the West Indies, and his pregnant wife, "the
Fairy Queen . . . the least woman that ever was with child in Europe,"
were shown daily at Charing Cross. Her condition was avidly reported
in the press, as were the details of her delivery in March of 1712.[24]

Along with giants and dwarfs, the third popular attraction at the
Fair were creatures which blurred the distinction between men and
beasts. Apes and monkeys were taught to mimic human actions, and
other animals were trained so that they appeared to have the skills or
intelligence of men: an elephant that could raise a flag and shoot a gun,
a troop of eight dancing dogs, dressed in the newest French fashions,
who appeared at Southwark Fair in the early eighteenth century and
later performed before Queen Anne, the single dog Evelyn saw "that
seemd to do many rational actions."[25] And an almost unbroken succession of Clever Mares. None of these was as virtuous as the Houyhnhnms nor, I suspect, as intelligent, but all of them were smart enough to
count, to ferret out hidden objects, to tell time, and to perform "many
things to admiration,"[26] some of which, if we are to trust the handbills,
were "past human Faith to believe unless seen done."

At the other end of the spectrum were human beings who seemed to
have degenerated into animals: the "Northumberland Monster," who
had "the head, the maine, neck and forefeet exactly like a horse, all the
rest of the body directly like a man"; a boy who was covered with fish
scales from his neck downward; another boy, "a fresh lively country
lad just come from Suffolk who is all cover'd all over his Body with
Bristles like a Hedge Hog as hard as horn which shoot off yearly";
another, exhibited at May Fair, "born with a Bear growing on its back
alive, to the great Admiration of all Spectators"; and the tantalizingly
unspecified monster shown at Moncress's Coffee House in June 1698,
"being Humane upwards, but Bruit downwards, wonderful to
behold." Other humans were exhibited who, though they retained
their human shape, like Yahoos had degenerated to savagery: the
"Cannibal Indian or Man Eater who was taken in a Skirmish near
South Carolina"; the man who had been "brought from Bilboa and
lived fifteen years among wild Creatures in the mountains and is said
to have been reared by them. . . . His former natural Estrangement
from human Conversation oblig'd Mr. *Cornwell* to bring a Jackanapes
over with him for his Companion, in whom he takes great Delight and
Satisfaction"; Peter the Wild Boy, taken from the woods of Germany
and put under the care of Dr. Arbuthnot. Particularly popular were
those whose descent into bestiality was physically obvious, such as the

"Wild and Hairy Irishman," whose "Body and Arms were covered with Long thick Black Hair," and the "Tall Black Wild Man," exhibited in London in 1711, who "had Been taken savage in the Woods near Bengall in the East Indies[.] he was stark Naked and he run very swiftly[.] he was Covered all over the Body, Arms and Hands with very Thick Long Black Hair." The "Wild Monstrous Hairy Man" Paris saw in London in May 1710 could have stood as a model for Swift's Yahoos: "The Hairs of his Head and Beard were . . . Black but longer than those that Covered his Body all over, from Head to toe, Excepting the inside of his Hands and the soles of his feet where their was no Hairs at all. he spoke High Dutch very Unperfectly, and with a Rude and Disagreeable accent, he had no manner of Education, he eat Roots, Herbs and fruit, very greedily, and also Raw flesh, he slept better upon Boards than upon a soft Feather bed, he was never Baptized, having no Manner of religion, he knew Neither Father nor Mother nor the Place of his Nativity."[27]

Swift makes these popular diversions, and particularly the popular diversion of monster-viewing, the imaginative center of *Gulliver's Travels*. And, by making monstrosity the central experience of his book, he engages that whole nest of problems, anxieties, and issues associated with monstrosity which was at work in the Mary Toft episode.

II

Swift's usual reaction to popular diversions—I include for the moment everything from tourist attractions to puppet shows and spectacles to the exhibition of monsters—was a dry amusement that sometimes shaded into contempt. In a letter to John Barber, Swift wryly commented that Matthew Pilkington should come to London a few weeks before assuming his duties as Lord Mayor's chaplain "to prepare him for his business, by seeing the Tower the Monument and Westminster Abbey, and have done staring in the streets."[28] The opposition between "business" and "staring," between the thoughtful conduct of life and the inattentiveness of blank wonder, is often at the back of Swift's comments on popular diversions. Such spectacles were profitless. They were, after all, mere "sights": they appealed to the eye, and if they worked on the mind at all, they raised only wonder and useless speculations.

Swift's attitude was common in the early eighteenth century. Almost all "men of taste" deplored the mindlessness of popular diversions, which they found epitomized in the Fair. Catering to the eye's demand for spectacle, the Fair provided sights that were dazzling but devoid of thought; like *"Fire Works,"* the diversions there "rarely do any Body good, but those who are concern'd in the *Show*." The sights of Smithfield titillated the eye, their sole purpose being to "make the wond'ring idiot's gaze." To Ned Ward, the fair-goers were the "unthinking Mob," the "gazing Multitude," the "gaping Throng." Swift described his own irrational attraction to the monster shows at Charing Cross as being "fasten'd by the Eyes."[29] Worse yet, the addiction to staring was not confined to the Fair. The high arts and rational amusements had become infected by the popular diversions of the streets of London and the booths of Smithfield. "Bartholomew Fair," said Tom Brown, "revives in . . . the playhouses. Poetry is so little regarded there, and the audience is so taken up with show and sight, that an author need not much trouble himself about his thoughts and language." Others were equally gloomy. The Fair's rope-dancers and tumblers had been introduced on stage "to entertain that Part of the Audience who have no Faculty above Eyesight"; pantomimes were brought in from Smithfield because "they are no Objects of the Understanding. . . . The Eye only is necessary." The theatres had capitulated to the demand for an audience that was "given up to the shallow Satisfaction of the Eyes and Ears only. . . . The Understanding has no Part in the Pleasure."[30]

Swift was disturbed by the decline of the arts, which he too attributed in part to the influence of popular diversions, but he saw in the appeal of sights and shows something far more pervasive, something akin to what Pope saw in them in the *Dunciad*. In the *Dunciad,* the spectacles, sights, and shows of Smithfield do signal the degeneration of the high arts, of course, but as the poem implicates more and more spheres of human life, it reveals that the forces of Dulness are loose everywhere, infecting every cultural, political, intellectual, social, and personal relationship, and popular entertainments become a way for Pope to spell out symbolically what is responsible for this general collapse of society: man's native predisposition for thoughtlessness. In the *Dunciad,* sights and shows define a world given over to staring ("staring," "gaping," and "gazing" are the most common responses of the Dunces), a world in which the intelligent perception of life and the responsible participation in it are abandoned for the pleasures of sheer mindlessness, the comforts of unconsciousness, and the diverting flicker of images on the eye.

It was man's bottomless capacity for thoughtlessness that Swift, too, saw in the attraction of popular entertainments. They were diversions, and quite literally so, for they played on man's desire to divert his attention from the business of life. Thus their danger. By encouraging the audience to lose itself in wonder, sights and shows fostered a state of mind in which simple discriminations no longer were made and fundamental values were lost. For the month of August, Bickerstaff predicts the state affairs of France and Poland with the same gravity with which he claims that "much Mischief will be done at *Bartholomew* Fair, by the Fall of a Booth." And these diversions catered to more fatal propensities. The Fair, said Swift, appeals to "a corrupted Tast," one that finds pleasure in seeing Nature "Inverted," and hence it abetted willful self-delusion, an active escape from reality.[31] In this respect, Swift's sense of the Fair is similar to Hogarth's. Hogarth's *Southwark Fair,* overcharged with images of flight and fall, of pathetic play-acting and false appearances contrasted to grim human limitations and realities, suggests that the Fair attracted its audience precisely because it could induce vertiginous fantasies that blanked out the actualities of their lives, encouraging them to indulge in appearances that were pleasing but self-defeating. Similarly, when Swift seeks images to point to self-destructive flights of delusion, he turns to the Fair. To suggest Godolphin's false sense of his infallible power, he compares his staff of office to the "glitt'ring Tinsel of *May*-Fair."[32] In "The Wonder of All Wonders," Swift portrays the Bank as a Fair conjuror. He is satirizing the cheating dexterity of the Bank, but the fact that the satire is in the form of a Fair handbill points to a more disturbing perversity: the audience is so dazzled by his tricks (the conjuror performs "to the great Surprise and Satisfaction of all Spectators") that they have become eager, thoughtless spectators to their own destruction.[33] And the Fair supplied Swift with an image for the unnatural, self-deluding, and self-destructive energies of the Whigs:

> A DOG loves to turn round often; yet after certain *Revolutions,* he lies down to rest: But Heads, under the Dominion of the *Moon,* are for perpetual *Revolution;* Besides, the *Whigs* owe all their Wealth to *Wars* and *Revolution;* like the Girl at *Bartholomew*-Fair, who gets a Penny by turning round a hundred Times, with Swords in her Hands.[34]

Popular entertainments are present in *Gulliver's Travels,* as they are in the *Dunciad,* as evidence of man's thoughtlessness. Literal-minded and superficial, Gulliver travels through the world like the stereotypical tourist, staring at everything and seeing nothing: "The great Oven [in Brobdingnag] is not so wide by ten paces as the Cupola at St. *Paul's:* For I measured the latter on purpose after my Return" (98). So much for St. Paul's: dwindled to a mere sight, its religious significance has evaporated. Diverted by the sights he sees around him, Gulliver empties his experience of meaning. The moral efficacy of public executions, even the value of human life, become lost in the sheer entertaining spectacle of a beheading: "The Veins and Arteries spouted up such a prodigious Quantity of Blood, and so high in the Air, that the great *Jet d'Eau* at *Versailles* was not equal for the Time it lasted" (103–4).[35] And everywhere, Gulliver, like the fair-goers in *Southwark Fair,* dwells on the surface of the sights and shows he sees so he can entertain himself in the delusion of his own importance. *Gulliver's Travels,* as much as the *Dunciad,* portrays a world sinking to "one dead level" of Dulness. With their eyes ever open to diversion, men have reduced the business of life, even the ultimate horrors of war, to mindless spectacle. "And to set forth the Valour of my own dear Countrymen, I assured him, that I had seen them blow up a Hundred Enemies at once in a Siege, and as many in a Ship; and beheld Bodies drop down in Pieces from the Clouds, to the great Diversion of all the Spectators" (231).

Like other "men of taste," then, Swift looked on sights, shows, and popular entertainments with irony and contempt. When he could not distance himself in these ways, he mocked himself:

> I went afterwards to see a famous moving Picture, & I never saw any thing so pretty. You see a Sea ten miles wide, a Town on tothr end, & Ships sailing in the Sea, & discharging their Canon. You see a great Sky with Moon & Stars &c. I'm a fool.[36]

And yet the strength of Swift's mockery of his own response to the moving picture can have been only equal to the strength of his attraction to it. For all his professed contempt for sights and shows, he willingly laid out one shilling four pence to see a couple of dwarfs.[37] Given the sheer number of his references and the detail of his descriptions, he was a careful viewer of popular entertainments, and probably an avid one. When he wrote about his first meeting with Harley, Swift pictured himself in what he clearly meant to be a characteristic posture:

> Some few Days after HARLEY spies
> The Doctor fasten'd by the Eyes,
> At *Charing Cross,* among the Rout,
> Where painted Monsters are hung out.

Swift licenses his fascination here by the special dispensation of satire, for by watching the "painted Monsters" he is practicing his moral and artistic metier.[38] And the passage itself justifies this license, for the first object of Swift's satire is himself: he is no different from the vulgar ("among the Rout"), and he too is capable of being gripped by the powerful, irrational hold of monsters. Viewing monsters, it turns out, is valuable—or at least it can be valuable to the degree to which the viewer becomes mindful of the very mindlessness the spectacle produces in him.

Precisely this same sense of the potentials of sights and shows is addressed in the description of the puppet show in "Mad Mullinix and Timothy," Swift's longest sustained description of any popular entertainment.

> Observe, the Audience is in Pain,
> While *Punch* is hid behind the Scene,
> But when they hear his rusty Voice,
> With what Impatience they rejoice.
> And then they value not two Straws,
> How *Solomon* decides the Cause,
> Which the true Mother, which *Pretender,*
> Nor listen to the Witch of *Endor;*
> Shou'd *Faustus,* with the Devil behind him,
> Enter the Stage they never mind him,
> If Punch, to spur their fancy, shews
> In at the door his monstrous Nose,
> Then sudden draws it back again,
> O what a pleasure mixt with pain!
> You e'ry moment think an Age,
> Till he appears upon the Stage.
> And first his Bum you see him Clap,
> Upon the Queen of *Sheba's* lap.
> . . . .
>
> *St. George* himself he plays the wag on,
> And mounts astride upon the *Dragon.*
> He gets a thousand Thumps and Kicks
> Yet cannot leave his roguish Tricks;
> . . . .
>
> There's not a Puppet made of Wood,
> But what wou'd hang him if they cou'd.
> While teizing all, by all he's teiz'd,
> How well are the Spectators pleased!
> Who in the motion have no share;
> But purely come to hear, and stare;
> Have no concern for *Sabra's* sake,
> Which gets the better, Saint or Snake.
> Provided *Punch* (for there's the Jest)
> Be soundly mawl'd, and plagues the rest.[39]

Having "purely come to hear, and stare," the audience learns nothing from the puppet show. Not only do they ignore the simple moral distinctions the show itself makes, but they fail to learn a more important lesson, one about themselves. For Punch has called out in them the very same irrational, destructive impulses he embodies. As the amoral, antisocial spirit of aggression that overturns everyone and everything, Punch releases this same energy in the audience, who take joy in his subversions and delight in his destructiveness, so much so that in the end they become even more aggressive, directing their energy against the Lord of Misrule himself ("Provided *Punch* . . . / Be soundly mawl'd, and plagues the rest"). The puppet show's lesson that each member of the audience harbors the blind, destructive energies of a Punch is an important truth, but it is a truth no one in the audience sees.

And so the puppet show potentially is valuable, just as was the monster show where Swift stood "fasten'd by the Eyes" and came to a moment of humiliating but profitable self-recognition. Perhaps all popular sights and shows have the potential to become occasions for knowledge. True, given the premium they place of spectacle, they can just as easily provoke mindless wonder, but when that is the case, the fault lies less in the spectacle than in the spectator. The Modern Author of *Tale of a Tub,* for instance, sees the same "painted Monsters" Swift saw, but he learns nothing of what Swift did:

> For I have always lookt upon it as a high Point of Indiscretion in *Monster-mongers* and other *Retailers of strange Sights;* to hang out a fair large Picture over the Door, drawn after the Life, with a most eloquent Description underneath: This hath saved me many a Threepence, for my Curiosity was fully satisfied, and I never offered to go in.[40]

Like the audience at the puppet show, the Modern Author finds it easier to slip into a comfortable superficiality than to recognize his alliance with the monsters he is staring at.

In *Gulliver's Travels,* Swift is alive to both the possibilities and failures of popular diversions. He himself is willing to tease out the meanings in sights and diversions (such as in book 1, where he uses the puppet show to reveal our pretentiousness, our mechanical obeisances to power, our willingness to be manipulated). But he is just as interested in the failure of these shows to mean anything—that is, in the refusal of the spectators to overcome their predisposition to gaze thoughtlessly at them. Much of the satire in *Gulliver's Travels,* I think, is devoted to this fact and to an analysis of the motives of an audience who "purely come to hear, and stare."

III

The popular diversion Swift turns to most often in *Gulliver's Travels* is the monster exhibit, and if I am correct that he uses sights and shows to satirize the failure of human beings to respond adequately to the business of life, then he probably had in mind the specific kinds of failure in their reactions to monster shows in particular. But how *did* his contemporaries react to monster shows, and why did they respond to them the way they did?

These are difficult questions to answer. Monster shows appealed to all social strata, but the bulk of the audience, the lower classes, left no testimony, and most of the records that have survived express the perspectives peculiar to the higher class that left them. Further, those who did leave records do not spell out their reactions in any great detail. Comments are terse and unrevealing. On seeing a giantess in 1677, Hooke remarked: "saw the Dutch woeman in Bartholomew fair, very strange."[41] "After dinner with Mr. Gale," wrote Thoresby; "walked into Southwark to see the Italian gentleman with two heads; that growing out of his side has long black hair." His language suggests little excitement, scarcely even a tremor of interest, and yet Thoresby was fascinated enough to memorialize his visit ("I bought his picture").[42] Pepys was infatuated with monsters. The jumpy rhythms of his account of a bearded lady betray the depth of his fascination—her beard, he says, "is now as big as any man's, almost as ever I saw. I say bushy and thick"—but when he turns to specify the source of his excitement, he is utterly unhelpful: "It was a strange sight to me, I confess, and what pleased me mightily."[43] James Paris hunted down every monster he could find and chronicled each one in words and pictures, and he left as his life's work a lengthy manuscript, *A Short History of Human Prodigies & Monstrous Births*. It is the record of an obsession, but it is a strangely mute record. He details all the minutiae of the monsters' physical deformities, but not once does he record his own reaction to them or speculate about the reasons for his extraordinary interest.

This absence of self-analysis is not altogether surprising. The records that are left us, after all, are the records of men imbued with the spirit of Baconian science. The diarists to whom we are most indebted for our knowledge of the monsters exhibited during this period—Pepys, Evelyn and Thoresby—were all members of the Royal Society, and James Paris considered his collection as a contribution to scientific learning, for when poverty forced him to sell it, he turned first to Sloane as a buyer. In this scientific climate, there was nothing remarkable about an interest in monsters, and hence there was no need to speculate about one's own fascination with them. Such an interest was expected. Bacon had urged that "a collection . . . must be made of all monsters and prodigious births of nature," for "he that knows [Nature's] deviations will more accurately describe her ways." And, too, Bacon probably constrained the way in which monsters were reported. For knowing that previous histories of monstrosities had been sullied by falsehoods and extravagant fancies, he cautioned that such a collection be done "with the strictest scrutiny" and insisted on "grave and credible history and trustworthy reports."[44] Hence the comments of the diarists are filled with neutral observations and with details to make their reporting creditable: weights, measurements, places and times of birth, where they were seen, corroborating witnesses. "With Sir Henry Piers and the Swede, to see le grand Maximilian Christopher Miller, born at Leipsic 1683," wrote Thoresby; "he is (as I measured him) seven feet and three or four inches tall."[45]

And yet there may be another dimension to this fascination with monsters and the lack of interest in examining the roots of the fascination, another dimension to the whole Baconian project that had legitimized a careful examination of monsters but had prescribed a particular way of looking at them. Swift seems to think so, for he satirizes this mentality again and again in book 2, where Gulliver is always playing the miniature virtuoso. Confronted with a monstrousness that is frightening, disgusting, and humiliating, Gulliver reacts by weighing and measuring. When he sees a "monstrous Breast," he is disgusted—"nothing could appear more nauseous"—but he is mindful "to give the curious Reader an Idea of its Bulk, Shape and Colour" (75).[46] He is driven to the "utmost Terror" by wasps, so he kills and then measures them: "I took out their Stings, found them an Inch and a half long, and as sharp as Needles" (94). After killing the rat, even though "it went against [his] Stomach to drag the Carcass off the Bed," he nevertheless "measured the Tail . . . and found it to be two Yards long, wanting an Inch" (77). The lice he sees on the beggars "were the first I had ever beheld; and I should have been curious enough to dissect one of them, if I had proper Instruments (which I unluckily left behind me in the Ship) although indeed the Sight was so nauseous, that it perfectly turned my Stomach" (97).

At these moments, I believe, Swift is dramatizing the psychology of monster-viewing in the eighteenth century. Gulliver learns something in his encounters with the monstrous, but something negligible (the length of rats' tails), and his limited scientific knowledge is acquired at the cost of a more valuable wisdom, the knowledge of his own weakness and insignificance. His fascination with monstrosity is an unquiet dance of attraction and avoidance, of desire and distance. He desires to know monsters, but he must manage what he knows about them in order to defend himself against the humiliating knowledge they offer about himself, so he shunts his desire into the comfortable parameters of scientific observation, which allows him to push away the frightening and disgusting even while approaching it.

And why do monsters exercise a fascination that so powerfully attracts but that must be carefully managed so that it is distanced even as it is approached? The "Double Mistress" episode of the *Memoirs of Martinus Scriblerus* suggests the beginnings of an answer. There, it will be remembered, the intransigent singleness-and-doubleness of Indamora-Lindamira threw all conventional definitions into chaos because the twins occupied the borders that distinguish one thing from another; hence, they blurred all categories and dispersed identities. This blurring of boundaries and collapsing of identities, I believe, is at the heart of the experience of monstrosity. Indeterminate amalgams of forms, monsters make us experience a dispersion of identity. They are liminal creatures, straddling boundaries between categories we wish to keep distinct and separate, blurring distinctions, haunting us with the possibility that the categories themselves are ambiguous, permeable. A giant or a dwarf challenges our everyday sense of human size and human power and status. Androgynous monsters such as hermaphrodites and bearded ladies perplex the normally distinct identity of the sexes. Feral children, humans disfigured so that they resemble animals, or animals that ape human action and intelligence—all these blur the boundaries between the bestial and the human. Seeing monsters, then, must call up a complex response. Because of their abnormality, they appear not to be us at all. They are different. And yet, as boundary creatures, they are not wholly different. They are also recognizably human, recognizably and disturbingly the same. Monsters answer to suspicions we may have about our own identities, those comfortable, flimsy identities of our everyday lives. They point to a hidden shape of the self we may intuit or fear lies hidden beneath the convenient fictions of our quotidian identities; they call into question the extent of our power and status, the contours of our sexuality, the nature of our "humanity." They are, in this sense, us, which means that it is *we* who are different—different, that is, from the way we typically think of ourselves. And out of this play of sameness and difference, this dissolving of identity, our encounters with monsters offer us knowledge of what we really are beneath our quotidian identities. Hence our fascination. But such knowledge is horrifying and painful self-knowledge, a recognition of the self that causes our illusory identities to melt away. Hence our horror, our need for distance, our desire to manage, as Gulliver does, the sight of monsters.[47]

This dynamic of attraction and avoidance structures the internal economy of monster exhibits, an economy evident in John Evelyn's account of his visit to a bearded lady:

I saw the hairy Maid. . . . : her very Eyebrowes were combed upward, & all her forehead as thick & even as growes on any womans head, neately dress'd: There come also tw[o] lock[s] very long out of Each Eare: she had also a most prolix beard, & *mustachios,* with long locks of hair growing on the very middle of her nose, exactly like an Island Dog; . . . & for the rest very well shaped, plaied well on the Harpsicord, &c.[48]

Now, why would this woman play the harpsichord? Surely her hirsuteness was enough to draw spectators. And yet, this ordinary act of playing the harpsichord *was* part of her draw. Indeed, most of the monsters that were exhibited did something ordinary like the Hairy Maid. Again and again, what we see in the exhibitions of eighteenth-century monsters is this peculiar emphasis on the ordinary in the midst of the monstrous.

Take, for instance, giants and dwarfs. When Pepys went to view the tall Dutchman, one of the few comments he made was that "He is a comely and well made man." Such remarks were made frequently. Evelyn saw a monstrously tall woman who kept an ale house in Lincoln and noted that she was a "well proportioned woman."[49] Paris saw the two-foot, two-inch Anne Royale when she put herself on exhibit in London in 1690 and remarked that she was "very well shap'd, well Proportion'd and very Strait." Handbills for giants and dwarfs touted these characteristics as well. "The Living Collosus" was advertised as "almost eight foot in height and every way proportionable." The dwarf John Wormberg "is so very well proportioned to his bigness that all that sees him, admires him." The "little *German Woman*" advertised herself as "no ways Deform'd, as the other two women are, that are carried about the Streets in Boxes from House to House, for some years past."

Since many giants were disfigured by acromegaly and dwarfs by achondroplasia, to be well proportioned was to be something of a curiosity among curiosities. Yet, this does not seem to be a sufficient explanation for the fascination with which well-proportioned dwarfs and giants were viewed. If one is attracted to the monstrous, then why not be attracted to total deformity, to monstrosity in figure as well as size? No, the exhibition of well-proportioned dwarfs and giants follows the same economy as that of the Hairy Maid and her harpsichord: it is not the merely monstrous that draws the viewers; rather it is the *frisson* that comes with seeing how closely the monstrous verges on the normal, the human, the everyday. And the exhibitors of monsters seemed to understand this pleasure. For they showed monsters in such a way as to engage the play of difference and sameness in viewing them, to titillate the audience by blurring even more those lines that monsters already blur, to make even more tantalizingly ambiguous the boundaries between them and us.

Consider how in the following advertisement of a woman exhibited in London in the opening years of the eighteenth century the attractions progress from extraordinary monstrosity to compensatory feats of dexterity to what in other circumstances might be considered the bathos of the quotidian: "A Woman about thirty-five years of age, ALIVE, having two heads, ONE ABOVE THE OTHER, the upper face smooth. She has no fingers nor toes, yet can dress and undress, knit, soe, read, sing and do several sorts of work. Very pleasant and merry in her behavior." Or consider the famous John Wormberg. Since he was a "man of the least stature that has been seen in the memory of any, being but two foot and seven inches in height," one would think that he would attract spectators by virtue of his small size alone; yet his advertisements added that he "has a very long beard and sings well." The "Little Scotchman," a two-foot six-inch dwarf exhibited in London in 1682, "was marry'd several years, and had Issue by his wife, two sons (one of which is with him now.) He Sings and Dances with his son, . . . He formerly kept a Writing school; and discourses of the Scriptures, and of many Eminent Histories, very wisely; and gives great satisfaction to all spectators; and if need requires, there are several Persons in this town, that will justifie that they were his Schollars, and see him Marry'd." Another dwarf advertised himself as two-feet nine-inches high and as having been born jointless in his wrists and double-jointed in his ankles: "When he sleeps he puts his head between his two feet to rest by way of a pillow and his great toes in each ear, which posture he shews." But his handbill concluded, "He performs the beat of a drum in a surprising degree and sings with a loud voice at the same time." They all advertised abilities of this same sort. One dwarf "discourses excellently well." Another "Discourses, Reads very well, Sings, Wistles, and all pleasant to hear." The dwarf Hannah Warton "Could sing, Dance, and Play with the Castanets Excellently well."

Likewise, a monstrous human was exhibited that had "one Body, Two Heads, four Armes and Hands, four Legs and Feet with Toes and Fingers, having Nails upon them very perfect; but that which is most remarkable and Amazing, is this, that it was Born with Teeth in each Mouth, which are plain and Visible to all Spectators." To be "Born with Teeth" is rare, very rare, in fact, but it is not, it seems to me, what is "most remarkable and Amazing" about this monster, its two heads, four arms, and four legs surely counting for something more. But this displacement of amazement from spectacularly monstrous deviations to a relatively minor anomaly is revealing, for the teeth, in spite of their anomalousness, titillatingly draw the completely aberrant into the realm of the normal, just as do those other objects of fascination, the "very perfect" nails: both are signs of the monster's being identifiably human, their almost irrelevant triflingness confirming its intimate and thorough rootedness in the human race. This same kind of displacement is obvious in the fascination with the pregnancy of the "Fairy Queen." She and her husband, the Black Prince, captivated all of London in the winter of 1711–12 simply because of their extraordinarily normal act of getting married and begetting a child.

Just as "wild men" were shown to call attention to their animality (excessive hair, monkeys for companions, eating and sleeping habits appropriate to beasts), so animals were exhibited precisely because they so provocatively blurred the lines between men and beasts. Thus, all the Clever Mares that could count and tell time, the elephant that could shoot guns and raise flags, the dog who, according to Evelyn, "seemed to do many rational actions," and the dancing dogs from France, shown at Bartholomew Fair and later at Hampton Court and Richmond, who were made to appear as human as possible, "their dresses, as well as their dances, being entirely after the French mode particularly Miss Depingle in her Hoop petticoat and leading strings."[50] But the blurring is seen most especially in the ubiquitous monkey- and ape-shows. For when the animals could not be touted as being physically similar to humans ("from their Heads downward they resemble Humane Nature, having Breasts, Bellies, Legs and Arms like a Man or Woman"), they were trained in such a way as to appear to be on the verge of humanness: drinking glasses of ale, smoking pipes of tobacco, dancing the Cheshire Rounds, taking off their hats and paying their respects to the company "like a Christian." One monkey was taught the elaborate mimicry recorded by Ned Ward: "At last out comes an Epitome of a Careful Nurse, drest up in a Country Jacket, and under her Arm a Kitten for a Nurslin, and in her contrary Hand a piece of Cheese; down sits the little Matron, with a very Motherly Countenance, and when her Youngster mew'd, she Dandled him, and Rock'd him in her Arms, with as great Signs of *Affection* as a Loving Mother could well shew to a disorder'd Infant; then bites a piece of Cheese, and after she had mumbled it about in her Mouth, then thrust it in with her Tongue into the Kittens, just as I have seen Nasty Old Sluts feed their own Grand children." (This is the Fair show Gulliver remembers with such humiliation after he is force-fed by the monkey in Brobdingnag: "He took me up in his right Fore-foot, and held me as a Nurse does a Child she is going to suckle; just as I have seen the same Sort of Creature do with a Kitten in *Europe*" [106]).[51]

But this appeal to the audience's intuition of a hidden identity with the monsters was all titillation. For at the same time the exhibitions blurred the boundaries between viewers and monsters, they firmly drew the lines again, comfortably distancing the audience by emphasizing the monsters' sheer difference. Displayed in a circumscribed part of the city set aside for the purpose, placed on a stage, shown during holidays, exhibited precisely because of their anomalousness, the monsters were, in the end, not us at all but just freaks in a fair booth. The intuition of identity that attracted the audience in the first place, instead of being allowed to ripen into conscious self-awareness, was diverted into the mindless pleasures of spectacle. And so the economy of monster exhibitions answers perfectly to the dance of attraction and avoidance. What begins as titillation ends as mere entertainment, to the infinite satisfaction of an audience who "purely come to hear, and stare."

In 1635, a minister in Plymouth complained, "The common sort make no further use of these Prodigies and Strange-births, than as a matter of wonder and table-talk."[52] Nor was this mental sloth an attribute of the "common sort" alone. The mindless wonder of the vulgar was played out in its own key in the responses of the virtuosi. Pepys, Evelyn, Thoresby, and Paris, too, distanced themselves from the full lesson of monsters. Like Gulliver, who manages the knowledge monsters offer by turning his attention to matters of "Bulk, Shape, and Colour," these men left unexamined their attraction by placing it within the comfortable justifications of Baconian science. Nearly everyone, vulgar and virtuoso alike, could look at monsters without the slightest perturbation. Monsters had been dismissed, neutralized of their power to jolt us out of our complacent assurances and everyday certainties. One remembers Gulliver's reaction upon reading the Brobdingnagian book that "treats of the Weakness of Human kind." The Brobdingnagians had reached their humbling self-knowledge after their own experience with monstrosity, their discovery of the bones of giants larger than themselves. But Gulliver is unsettled neither by the book nor by the giants in front of him: "I could not avoid reflecting, how universally this Talent was spread of drawing Lectures in Morality, or indeed rather Matter of Discontent and repining, from the Quarrels we raise with Nature" (121). Behind this specious wisdom is an imperturbable smugness. Gulliver has seen monsters, and they have done nothing but convince him of the fitness of things—and the fitness of himself.[53]

But not everyone in the eighteenth century dismissed monsters and boundary-blurring creatures. Here is Congreve: "I could never look long upon a Monkey, without very Mortifying Reflections; thô I never heard of any thing to the Contrary, why that Creature is not Originally of a Distinct *Species*."[54] Congreve's reaction, I think, is the sort of reaction Swift is trying to provoke in the readers of *Gulliver's Travels*. For a satirist like Swift, the best possible outcome of monstrosity's play of difference and sameness was this: brought face-to-face with the monstrous, the viewer would see in it a grotesque likeness that would reveal uncomfortable but salutary truths about the self. The falsity of our quotidian identities would be revealed, and a more disfigured but truer shape of the self—its identity with the monster—would be made manifest. This was, for instance, the possibility Swift saw in the puppet show. The viewers who strongly responded to Punch—whose swollen belly and humped back, of course, made him a monster among puppets—should see in the anarchistic aggression Punch provoked in them their own secret identity with him.

But real viewers of real monsters almost always declined this invitation to self-discovery. They wished to be diverted. And since Swift is less interested in diverting his readers than in vexing them, he recreates in *Gulliver's Travels* the exhibition booths of Bartholomew Fair, but he recreates them in such a way that we cannot stare stupidly at its monsters, or, like the Modern Author of *Tale of a Tub,* turn away satisfied that we have seen enough. For Swift dramatizes the shifts and scams we go through to avoid becoming conscious of the uncomfortable truths monsters have to tell us. He presents us with the reactions of the "gaping Mob"—our reactions—exposes their insufficiencies, and, in doing so, re-engages us in the true dialectic of monster-viewing, with all of its attendant "Mortifying Reflections."[55]

IV

When Gulliver first appears on the shores of the several remote nations he visits, the inhabitants respond to his monstrosity much as Londoners responded to monsters at Bartholomew Fair. The Lilliputians show "a thousand Marks of Wonder and Astonishment" (8) when they first see him, and when he rises to his feet, "the Noise and Astonishment of the People . . . [were] not to be expressed" (12). In Brobdingnag, Gulliver "was shewn ten Times a Day to the Wonder and Satisfaction of all People" (83). The Laputans "beheld [him] with all the Marks and Circumstances of Wonder" (143). Not even the rational Houynhnhnms are immune to astonishment: "The Horse started a little when he came near me, but soon recovering himself, looked full in my Face with manifest Tokens of Wonder" (208).

These first reactions give way to another, equally mindless response. Astonishment and wonder are succeeded by a desire to be diverted—

most obviously in Brobdingnag, where Gulliver is trundled around the country as dwarfs were in England, but also in Lilliput where the king uses Gulliver as the kings of Europe used giants, as a way of "diverting himself" and of "entertaining the Court" (26, 25). And the Houyhnhnm master, Gulliver reports, "brought me into all Company, and made them treat me with Civility, because, as he told them privately, this would put me in good Humour, and make me more diverting" (222).

Turning Gulliver into a diversion is a way of neutralizing the threat of his monstrous difference, a way of managing the radically alien so that it does not disrupt the comforting assurances of the usual. Tied down in Lilliput, Gulliver is addressed by one of the officials: "I saw a Stage erected about a Foot and a half from the Ground, capable of holding four of the Inhabitants, with two or three Ladders to mount it: From whence one of them, who seemed to be a Person of Quality, made me a long Speech, whereof I understood not one syllable" (7). This a deliciously ludicrous moment. To give a "long Speech" to a monster who obviously does not understand a word of it is to insist on the unexpungeable truth of the normal with a tenacity that verges on the solipsistic. But this is the strategy of the inhabitants in all the lands Gulliver visits. They effortlessly assimilate him into their societies, preserving their quotidian realities unperturbed.

To be sure, very occasionally some of the creatures are willing to see Gulliver as a monstrous Other whom they allow, if not radically to critique or disrupt their own familiar reality, at least to comment on it. Like the Brobdingnagian king before him, the Houyhnhnm master is willing to listen to Gulliver because he thought "that it was no Shame to learn Wisdom from Brutes, as Industry is taught by the Ant, and Building by the Swallow" (257). But even the Houyhnhnms have their limits. They do learn from Gulliver the technique of castration which they can apply to their local problem of pest control, but they appear to learn nothing at all about the confines of their own structures of thought and values which are exposed by the fact that the mere existence of Gulliver causes unprecedented puzzlement and disagreement. And so, in the end, all the creatures turn from his monstrosity and ignore what he might have to tell them about themselves.[56]

In *his* encounter with monsters, Gulliver's reactions are more complex and varied. However, he tends (though this is not invariable) to react to the monstrous inhabitants he visits in a manner just the opposite from the way the inhabitants react to him, their monstrous visitor. If they assimilate him, thus leaving intact and unquestioned their own sense of the normal, he tends to take the monsters as normative and to assimilate into himself their realities. And yet, for all of this apparent openness to their difference, he gains no more self-knowledge from his dealings with monsters than they do from their dealings with him.

Gulliver achieves no awareness because in his dealings with monsters he is always anxious about his own identity, always caught up (like the gawkers at Bartholomew Fair) in the various strategies of defense against humiliating self-knowledge. Something of a paradigm of his psychology is revealed when he first sees the Brobdingnagians in the beginning of book 2:

> I bemoaned my desolate Widow, and Fatherless Children: I lamented my own Folly and Wilfulness in attempting a second Voyage against the Advice of all my Friends and Relations. In this terrible Agitation of Mind I could not forbear thinking of *Lilliput*, whose Inhabitants looked upon me as the greatest Prodigy that ever appeared in the World; where I was able to draw an Imperial Fleet in my Hand, and perform those other Actions which will be recorded for ever in the Chronicles of that Empire, while Posterity shall hardly believe them, although attested by Millions. I reflected what a Mortification it must prove to me to appear as inconsiderable in this Nation, as one single *Lilliputian* would be among us. But, this I conceived was to be the least of my Misfortunes: For, as human Creatures are observed to be more Savage and cruel in Proportion to their Bulk, what could I expect but to be a Morsel in the Mouth of the first among these enormous Barbarians who should happen to seize me. (70–71)

There are several peculiar features in this passage, not the least of which, given the context, is Gulliver's use of the word "mortification." For at this moment he is on the brink of a literal death, fearful that he is about to be made "a Morsel in the Mouth" of the Brobdingnagians, who, like Grim Reapers, are advancing on him "with Reaping-Hooks in their Hands, each Hook about the largeness of six Scythes" (70). But in the face of this death, Gulliver dwells on another kind of "mortification," and the fact that the two are linked by association in his mind (and by etymology in Swift's) is suggestive. For Gulliver's encounter with monsters at this moment causes anxieties about his personal identity. The sight of the Brobdingnagians causes him to swing hysterically from fears of the loss of his identity, "mortification," the "death" of the self, to hypertrophied fantasies of immortality (he thinks his actions "will be recorded for ever in the Chronicles of that Empire"). And he swings so violently because he has delivered his sense of his own identity over to others. He is as he is perceived. To be "mortified" is to be seen as "inconsiderable"; to be "the greatest Prodigy" is to be so "attested by Millions." And the double meaning of "Prodigy" reveals both the direction Gulliver takes to achieve a comfortable identity and the cost he is willing to pay to achieve it: in order to be distinguished, he is willing to play the monster.

For these reasons, it seems to me that throughout the book most of Gulliver's misperceptions of the significance of the creatures and events he witnesses, his inability to see any important relation between them and himself, and his partial judgments and skewed misinterpretations seldom arise from naiveté or stupidity. For if his encounters with monsters provoke a blurring of his identity, these varieties of misseeings become ways, often unconscious, by which he re-constructs a sense of himself that he finds pleasing.

This strategy is most obvious in book 1. Gulliver quickly loses any sense of the Lilliputians' monstrosity, accepting their perceptions and finally their values as normal, for to see the world as the Lilliputians see it is to see himself to considerable advantage. He can think of himself as having "performed ... Wonders" (8) simply by eating and drinking, and he can take pride in urinating, watching with awe that "Torrent which fell with such Noise and Violence from me" (9). And so he willingly plays the monster. He begins "entertaining the Court with . . . Feats" (25). He is pleased that he can find a way to "divert" the emperor and nobility "after a very extraordinary Manner" by turning his handkerchief into an exercise field (24). He willingly yields to the king's "fancy of diverting himself" (26) by acting the colossus. The longer he stays in Lilliput, the more he can entertain fantasies of what "so prodigious a Creature ... I must appear to them" (8). And the more deeply he implicates himself in the Lilliputian point of view, the more he can see himself as superior not only physically but socially as well. He fails to see the patent physical absurdity in the charge that he has had an affair with a Lilliputian lady not because he is stupid but because it is more flattering to mis-see it in this way: he can revel in visions of himself at the center of court society ("I have often had four Coaches and Horses at once on my table full of Company") and as an important player in Lilliputian social and court politics ("I had the Honour to be a *Nardac,* which the Treasurer himself is not; for all the World knows he is only a *Clumglum*" [49–50]).

One can see Gulliver's strategy in little in the scene in which the Blefuscudian ministers ask him "to shew them some Proofs of [his] prodigious Strength, of which they had heard so many Wonders." Gulliver readily complies. "When I had for some time entertained their Excellencies to their infinite Satisfaction and Surprize, I desired they would do me the Honour to present my most humble Respects to the Emperor their Master, the Renown of whose Virtues had so justly filled the whole World with Admiration, and whose Royal Person I resolved to attend before I returned to my own Country. Accordingly, the next time I had the Honour to see our Emperor, I desired his general licence to wait on the *Blefuscudian* Monarch" (38). First, Gulliver has normalized the monsters, fully assimilating himself into their point of view ("our Emperor"). He then attributes to them an inflated stature which is in no ways theirs ("whose Virtues had so justly filled the whole World with Admiration"). He then performs before them, seeing himself as he fancies they see him ("I entertained their Excellencies to their Infinite Satisfaction and Surprize"). From this he reaps "Honour" and "Admiration"—indeed, the honor and admiration mean something only because he has previously attributed to the monsters a worthiness that makes their honor and admiration worth receiving.

The specific context of this passage is the common practice of showing monsters before the king. (The language is a pastiche of the language used by giants in their handbills: William Joyce's proclaimed "HIS STRENGTH PROV'D before the KING," and the handbill of the "tall BRITAIN" boasted that he had "Travelled abroad, and has been shown before all the Foreign Kings and Princes in Christendom; . . . and had the Honour to have been shown before Her Present *Majesty of Great Brittain* and her Royal Consort the *Prince to the Great Satisfaction of all* Spectators that have seen him.")[57] To be distinguished, Gulliver has made a spectacle of himself. He has not engaged in the dialectic of monstrosity at all. Refusing to see in the Lilliputians their monstrosity, their sheer difference, he cannot see their monstrous sameness to humans. And not recognizing in their pettiness, vainglory, and power hunger this monstrous identity, Gulliver allows himself to be governed by precisely these same passions and hence becomes a monster—literally, by "entertaining the Court with . . . Feats" and allowing the king to use him as a way of "diverting himself," and morally by allowing his vanity to seduce him into the inanities of the Lilliputian social hierarchy and, even worse, into becoming an engine of war.

Gulliver's encounters with monsters are never this simple again. In Brobdingnag, he is so obviously treated as a monster that he himself complains of "being exposed for Money as a publick Spectacle" and of "the Ignominy of being carried about for a Monster." After Lilliput, Gulliver is increasingly mortified. His sense of his identity is continually under attack: he is "mortified" that the "smaller Birds" were not afraid of him, acting as if he were "no Creature at all" (102); he feels his "most Uneasiness" among the Maids of Honor, who treated him "like a Creature who had no Sort of Consequence" (103). The Struldbruggs are "the most mortifying Sight" (198) he has ever beheld. And among the Houyhnhnms, he is always haunted by his sense of identity with that "ugly Monster" (208), the Yahoo. He is made so conscious of monstrosity both without and within that he can no longer deal in the easy self-deceptions by which he had fashioned his identity in Lilliput.

Still, he does manage his mortifying encounters with monsters by drawing from a repertoire of defenses. At times, he uses simple denial. It is not until he leaves Brobdingnag that he calls his travelling box what it really is, a "Dungeon," instead of what he usually calls it while he is in Brobdingnag, a "convenient Closet" (127, 122), and he never does allow himself to become aware that Glumdalclitch has treated him like a doll. At other times, he simply converts his mortification into anger against others. "Mortified" by the dwarf (91), Gulliver attacks him for his small stature. Classed among the "little odious Vermin" by the king of Brobdingnag, Gulliver condemns the king's "*Short Views*" for refusing the secret of gunpowder (116, 119).[58]

Gulliver even continues to try to play the monster, which worked so well in Lilliput. He voluntarily performs for his royal patrons, pleased that the Brobdingnagian queen was "agreeably entertained with my Skill and agility" when he performed his "Diversion" of rowing a boat (104), pleased that it was "her Diversion . . . to see me eat in Miniature" (90). His stunts, particularly his flourishing his sword ("wherein my Dexterity was much admired" [93]), jumping over cow dung, playing a musical instrument, and even dressing himself, recall the compensatory feats deformed dwarfs performed at Bartholomew Fair (such as John Valerius, born without arms or completely formed feet, whom Paris saw in 1714: "he Combs a Perriwig very well; Shaves himself, Dresses and Undresses Himself. . . . He Fences with a Single Rapier, he darts a Sword with a Great Strength in a deal Board at a mark, he Beats a Drum, he Charges and fires a Pistol or gun or any other fire Arms, and Shoots at a Mark; Jumping and Vaulting are his masterpieces"). Such diverting tricks have their rewards. Gulliver thinks that he has "become a Favourite" (90) and fancies that he is "esteemed among the greatest Officers" (97). He even entertains the extraordinary notion that he "might live to do his Majesty some signal Service" (111).

And yet such defenses become more and more insufficient. "I was the Favourite of a great King and Queen, and the Delight of the whole Court," he says of his tenure in Brobdingnag; "but it was on such a Foot as ill became the Dignity of human Kind" (123). Increasingly, Gulliver seems incapable of silencing the voices of the monsters, and he begins to entertain "Mortifying Reflections." He realizes that the Brobdingnagians are a reproach to the petty pride of Europeans, including himself. By the end of his stay in Brobdingnag, having been surrounded by "such prodigious Objects," Gulliver "could never endure to look in a Glass . . . because the Comparison gave me so despicable a Conceit of my self" (131).

Gulliver's self-loathing and misanthropy culminate in book 4, of course, and to all appearances he seems to enter into the full dialectic of monsters, recognizing in the Yahoos their secret alliance with himself. Initially, he sees the Yahoo as a complete Other: "singular" and "deformed," an "ugly Monster" (207), it appears to be a species other than man. Even after Gulliver recognizes in the Yahoo the "perfect human Figure," he resists identifying it with himself, insisting on distinguishing it from "my own Species" (214). But Gulliver's certitude about what constitutes "my own Species" begins to erode. The more he observes the Yahoos, the more the two species begin to merge in his mind, and in spite of his attempt to keep them separate, he quietly elides them, so that he unselfconsciously begins to call humans Yahoos, and before too long, when he refers to "my own Species," he means "*European Yahoos*" (269). By the end of his stay with the Houyhnhnms, Gulliver believes that humans *are* Yahoos, and it is within the Yahoo species that he finally classifies himself ("I [am] a poor *Yahoo*," he tells the Portugese crew when they find him on the island [269]). His final assessment of man is that he is a "Lump of Deformity" (280), exactly like the "deformed" and "ugly Monster," the Yahoo. His identification of the two species is complete, and he appears to be consumed by self-disgust: "When I happened to behold the Reflection of my own Form in a Lake or Fountain, I turned away my Face in Horror and detestation of my self; and could better endure the Sight of a common Yahoo, than of my own Person" (262).

And yet, for all of his mortification, Gulliver never once truly entertains those "Mortifying Reflections" Congreve did. Gulliver's apparent acknowledgment of the identity between the Yahoos and himself, it turns out, is his most elaborate defense. Indeed, Gulliver's willingness to see an identity between the two species is suspicious, if for no other reason than that, after his first gestures of resistance, he begins to pursue it with so much relish. Initially, of course, he is appalled. He hears the Houyhnhnms call him Yahoo "to my everlasting mortification" (213). In Brobdingnag, when Gulliver was "mortified," his first impulse (in fantasy, at any rate) was to make himself singular in order to distinguish himself. And this is his initial reaction among the Houyhnhnms. Mortified to learn that the master Houyhnhnm identifies him with that species of monsters, Gulliver conceals the secret of his clothing "in order to distinguish myself as much as possible, from that cursed Race of *Yahoos*" (220).

But soon, Gulliver no longer tries to distinguish himself. In fact, he presses for the identity. When he is assaulted by the female Yahoo, the incident becomes "Matter of Diversion to my Master and his Family, as well as of Mortification to my self" (251)—but this is a "Mortification" that Gulliver has sought out (and one, significantly, that has led to someone else's "Diversion"). For, he has purposefully titillated himself by toying with the identification, much as the monster-mongers in London titillated their viewers with the promise of a hidden identity between them and the monsters: "And I have Reason to believe, [the Yahoos] had some Imagination that I was one of their own Species, which I often assisted myself, by stripping up my Sleeves, and shewing my naked Arms and Breast in their Sight" (249). It is an identity he seeks with enthusiasm:

> As I ought to have understood human Nature much better than I supposed it possible for my Master to do, so it was easy to apply the Character he gave of the *Yahoos* to myself and to my Countrymen; and I believe I could yet make farther Discoveries from my own Observation. I therefore often begged his Honour to let me go among the Herds of *Yahoos* in the Neighbourhood. (249)

Armed with his observations, Gulliver returns to teach his master Houyhnhnm the truth that man is a Yahoo.

But why would Gulliver "give so free a Representation of my own Species, among a Race of Mortals who were already too apt to conceive the vilest Opinion of Human Kind, from that entire Congruity betwixt me and their *Yahoos*" (242)? The answer becomes clearer and clearer as book 4 draws to a close:

> At first, I did not feel that natural Awe which the *Yahoos* and all other Animals bear toward [the Houyhnhnms]; but it grew upon me by Degrees, much sooner than I imagined, and was mingled with a respectful Love and Gratitude, that they would condescend to distinguish me from the rest of my Species. (262)

"To distinguish me from the rest of my Species": here is the motive for Gulliver's misanthropy and self-loathing. In order to be distinguished, Gulliver must first identify himself with the Yahoos; once having done that, he can then distinguish himself from the identity he himself has created by conspicuously doing those things Yahoos cannot do: be self-critical, judge himself, loath his own nature. By identifying himself with the Yahoos, and then by attacking both them and himself, Gulliver distinguishes himself not only from the Yahoos but from the "self" he claims to be, for he makes himself superior to that "self" by condemning it.

In book 4, Swift reveals that self-loathing can become a mechanism of self-love, that self-love can turn the dialectic of monster-viewing into a parody where the identification of the self with monsters becomes a way to deny any truly "Mortifying Reflections." But for all of its knotted intricacy, Gulliver's final construction of his identity is merely a variation on all his earlier constructions. When he takes leave of the master Houhynhnm, Gulliver "was going to prostrate myself to kiss his Hoof, but he did me the Honour to raise it gently to my Mouth," and Gulliver is besmitten "that so illustrious a Person should descend to give so great a Mark of Distinction to a Creature so inferior as I" (266). From the beginning, Gulliver has been driven by this desire for "Distinction," and throughout he has been willing to play the monster in order to be distinguished. In so doing, he really does become a monster. For Gulliver is proud that he "passed for a Prodigy" (240) among the Houyhnhnms, proud that they "looked upon it as a Prodigy, that a brute Animal should discover such Marks of a rational Creature" (218). And he makes sure that he continues to pass for a prodigy by identifying himself with the monstrous Yahoos in order to distinguish himself from them. In the end, he becomes to the Houyhnhnms, as well as to himself, the "wonderful Yahoo" (219, 256), the epithet recalling all those wonderful monsters that were on show at Bartholomew Fair.

Back in England, when he is laughed at for imitating the Houyhnhnms' gait and whinny, he can "hear [himself] ridiculed . . . without the least Mortification" (263) because he has perfected an identity that has put him beyond mortification. Of course, in doing so, he has had to define himself out of the human species (as he reveals with the slip of his pen in the very last sentence he writes when he tells Sympson that he fears he shall be corrupted by continuing to associate with "your Species" [xxxvi]). Gulliver, therefore, becomes, like a Yahoo, a true monster, utterly "singular," outside all species. And so it is appropriate that when he returns to England he, like all monsters, is plagued by "the Concourse of curious People coming to him at his House in *Redriff*" (xxxvii).

V

In delineating the trajectory Gulliver travels in formulating an identity during his encounters with monsters, I have assumed that Gulliver in fact has a self and that in the book he functions as a character—not, to be sure, a character in the Jamesian sense, one created to give the illusion of a fully nuanced and textured personality, but a character nevertheless, a character with enough of a center and enough coherence that

I have been able to speak of lines of development, of defenses, of unitary drives, and of unconscious motives. Such an assumption on my part goes against the grain of much of the most insightful criticism about how Swift typically uses speakers in his satires and how he uses Gulliver in *Gulliver's Travels*. Critics increasingly have come to recognize the baffling fluidity of Swift's satire, and especially the discontinuities of the voices which tell Swift's tales, all attached to nominally particular speakers, but to speakers who, because of "their crudeness, their heavy adaptability to the twists and turns of ironic self-expression, their transparently two-dimensional quality," "flout our most elementary expectations of character consistency." In any Swift satire, rather than one voice, there appears to be "an array of clearly distinguishable but quite temporary voices" which Swift "moves deftly into and out of . . . , seemingly untroubled by the way they contradict one another." It is folly, then, to search in the voice for evidence of the character of the speaker. For Swift "habitually manipulates his narrators (or speakers) with little regard for psychological or dramatic consistency," and the speaker's consistency "is sacrificed . . . for immediate comic or satirical ends." Consequently, for many critics, Gulliver does not exist at all except as a kind of rhetorical exigency: "he has no character, he is a cipher"; "he is, in fact, an abstraction, manipulated in the service of satire."[59]

Yet, granted that Gulliver is not a novelistically consistent character, is it true that his voice is defined moment by moment according to the ever-shifting demands of local effects and particular satiric intentions? Is it true that we hear in *Gulliver's Travels* merely a chorus of voices, one voice coming to the surface, becoming articulate, and then sinking, to be succeeded by another, quite different voice? Our experience of reading *Gulliver's Travels,* it seems to me, is more complex and altogether more vexing than this. For we enter *Gullliver's Travels* expecting a voice with a stable identity. Such an expectation is hardly, as some critics have argued, one we anachronistically have foisted on *Gulliver's Travels* because of our experience with nineteenth-century novels. The expectation of a coherent voice was not created by the fiction of high realism; it was already to be found in the kind of non-fictional writing that Swift habitually turns to for the forms of his satiric parodies—literary criticism, religious controversy, benevolent social proposals, political tracts and, of course, travel accounts—in all of which we expect the boundary between the written voice and the self that has written it to be very thin and in which, therefore, we expect the voice to incarnate a minimally stable self that articulates itself through it.

On the basis of this expectation, Swift leads us to assume larger integrities of character. For out of the voice of Gulliver, Swift is always precipitating intimations of a coherence. The voice of Gulliver keeps falling into well-known literary types or roles or characters (in the Theophrastian sense) or broad social stereotypes, all of which recur repeatedly and consistently throughout the work: Gulliver the "prostitute Flatterer"; Gulliver the patriot, who "perpetually dins our ears with Praises of his Country, in the midst of Corruptions"; Gulliver the latter-day Timon, the foolish ingénu betrayed into misanthropy by his own susceptibility to flattery; Gulliver the stolid middle-class Englishman; Gulliver the satiric surgeon, the critical observer and anatomist of man's ills; Gulliver the satirist satirized; Gulliver the court fool.[60] Not only do these roles and types tease us with the promise of at least some coherence and stability, but they often slide neatly into each other to intimate a more complex, layered self (for instance, Gulliver's role as a middle-class Englishman gives a concrete social and psychological context to his literary role as the foolish ingénu, and together they suggest a set of plausible, concrete motives for his bedazzlement at foreign courts and his becoming the flatterer). Often Swift creates chains of situations which imply a sustained continuity of feeling, attitude, and motive (for instance, the extraordinary care Swift takes to lead up to Gulliver's offer of gunpowder).[61] And often these roles and types and situations dovetail across the whole expanse of the book, creating such complexities of character as I have argued for in explaining Gulliver's playing the monster. In short, Swift encourages us to *think of* Gulliver as a character, to expect to hear in his voice the lines of a coherent selfhood. And then, having half fulfilled this expectation, Swift half defeats it. For, because of their typicality and literariness, we are always aware that these roles are just roles, and though often they slide together into coherency, they just as often rub against each other, create unresolvable contradictions, become unstable, and collapse into incoherency. The effect of Swift's play with the discontinuities *and* continuities of voice is to create in us as we are reading a sense of a self in Gulliver, but a jerry-built self, one continually constructing itself and continually losing its coherence, dissolving, its identity slipping away before our eyes.

This effect, of course, is similar to the effect created by the Modern Author of *A Tale of a Tub*. There, too, we hear an ever-shifting voice, a voice which continually controverts itself, pulled this way and that by the motion and countermotion of ideas, emotions, and intentions at cross-purposes with themselves, spinning apart in its contradictions and instabilities, often at the edge (and often over the edge) of coherence, a voice of a self in the perpetual process of dissolving under the pressures of its own centrifugal energies.

I wanted to call attention to this resemblance because I think that Swift returns in *Gulliver* to his grand theme in the *Tale,* the dissolution of identity, and that in both works he traces this dissolution to the same source. The Modern Author of the *Tale* is always fragmenting himself because he is always articulating himself at the leading edge of the present moment, often clause by clause, driven by the "great Design of an everlasting Remembrance, and never-dying Fame."[62] He must play to the ever-shifting and ever-contradictory expectations of the Modern audience, thrusting himself forward in an ever-present now in order to dominate them and shape their opinion of him, making a spectacle of himself to establish his superiority, abandoning any continuity or durability of self-identity for the sake of the immediacy of effect. Consequently, his identity becomes "eternally momentary."[63] And this is precisely Gulliver's motive and fate. Gulliver bobs and wheels through poses and attitudes, performing for his various audiences, driven, like the Modern Author of the *Tale,* by an insistent self-assertion, a desire to distinguish himself. Because his audience (both in his head and in the lands he visits) is always changing and always variegated, he too must play to them in a kind of eternal present, constantly shifting stances, feelings, beliefs, and standards, constantly reformulating an identity to suit the context of whatever monstrous world or monstrous moment he happens to find himself in. In the *Tale,* the dissolution of the Modern Author's identity is figured in that work's central symbol: the Modern Author becomes a tub, all surface surrounding an empty space. In *Gulliver,* Gulliver's dispersion of identity is figured in what I have been arguing is that work's central symbol: Gulliver becomes a monster, dissolving into the shapeless, incoherent gestures of the ego's desire to distinguish itself.

Gulliver's encounters with monsters make him anxious about his identity, and in reacting to this anxiety, he unwittingly enters into a trajectory that ends in his losing his identity and becoming a monster himself. Thus *Gulliver's Travels* repeats the basic pattern of the Mary Toft affair. But this is only to be expected, for Swift is working with the same complex of ideas and following out the same network of associations that undergirded the anxieties of those who responded to Mary Toft. In fact, it turns out that the psychological mechanism responsible for the dispersion of Gulliver's identity is precisely the same one blamed in the responses to the Mary Toft affair: the imagination. Swift is quite explicit about this at the end of the book, when he reveals the reasons for Gulliver's final, and most disastrous misjudgment, his abandoning the human race for the Houyhnynms:

> I must freely confess, the Sight of [my family] filled me only with Hatred, Disgust and Contempt; and the more, by reflecting on the near Alliance I had to them. For, although since my unfortunate Exile from *Houyhnhnm* Country, I had compelled myself to tolerate the Sight of *Yahoos,* and to converse with Don *Pedro de Mendez;* yet my Memory and Imaginations were perpetually filled with the Virtues and Ideas of those exalted *Houyhnhnms.* (273)

And it is not just the imagination, but the corporealizing imagination, with its train of material images, that possesses Gulliver, so much so that his admiration for the Houyhnhnms finds its source and expression in the physical itself: the only human he can tolerate when he returns to England is the groom ("I feel my spirits revived by the Smell he contracts in the Stable" [274]), and although he claims that he is dazzled by the Houyhnhnms' "Virtues," what he actually does is "imitate their Gait and Gesture, . . . Voice and manner" (263). Any values more immaterial, any values like "*Friendship* and *Benevolence,*" for instance, "the two principle Virtues among the *Houyhnhnms*" (252), are unimaginable.

Though named only at the end, the imagination has been Gulliver's problem from the beginning. Swift repeatedly places before us instance after instance of the kind of confusion we have seen the eighteenth century thought was caused by the imagination. Consider this example from the first paragraph of the narrative proper:

> But the Charge of maintaining me (although I had a very scanty Allowance) being too great for a narrow Fortune; I was bound Apprentice to Mr. *James Bates,* an eminent Surgeon in *London,* with whom I continued four Years; and my Father now and then sending me small Sums of Money, I laid them out in learning Navigation, and other Parts of Mathematics, useful to those who intend to travel, as I always believed it would be some time or other my Fortune to do. (3)

Did or did not Gulliver intend to travel? True, he set aside money in order to learn those things useful to those "who intend to travel," but at the same time, he implies that whether or not he will travel will be determined not by his own will but by an impersonal, implacable force, "Fortune." What happens in this sentence is that a mind partly reveals itself and then quickly tries to revise what it has just revealed. For this opening paragraph is a variation on the conventional situation of the son's running away to sea in violation of his father's injunctions to pursue goals that will lead to a more secure and gainful life, the same dramatic situation with which *Robinson Crusoe* opens. It *was* Gulliver's intention to travel, an intention he is somewhat embarrassed by, given the straitened financial situation of his father, the sacrifice he and other members of the family have made (all greatly detailed in this paragraph), and given the fact that Gulliver perversely has chosen the least respected and least remunerative branch of a not particularly respectable or well-paid profession. And so, having briefly let slip his motives, he quickly attempts to obscure his responsibility with the comforting excuse of "Fortune."

But, whom is Gulliver attempting to deceive here, us or himself? Or, to phrase the question in both a more accurate and a more illuminating way: what is Gulliver, a fool or a knave? Is he driven, not only here but everywhere in the book, by an egocentricity which he tries to hide from us, or has he duped himself while trying to fool us, so that he sincerely thinks that his motives are not dishonorable? Surely he is both: like the doctors in Hogarth's *Cunicularii,* like Molyneux, Manningham, and Douglas in the Mary Toft satires, like Butler's Hudibras, Ralpho, and Sidrophel, like the Modern Author of *A Tale of a Tub,* Gulliver is in the midst of a confusion in which he is both a fool and a knave, a confusion caused by the imagination. For Gulliver's lineage is that of an Enthusiast; his imagination has made it impossible for him to "distinguish betwixt [his] own Fancies and reall Truths," and he is therefore "befooled in his own conceit."[64] Everything Gulliver tells us is the truth (for Gulliver "was so distinguished for his Veracity, that it became a sort of Proverb among his Neighbours at *Redriff,* when any one affirmed a Thing, to say, it was as true as if Mr. Gulliver had spoke it"), but it is a truth that is, as his enemies charge, "a meer Fiction out of [his] own Brain," a truth that says the thing which is not, a truth which is "a Dream," Pedro de Mendez speculates, "or a Vision" (xxxvii, xxxvi, 271). The interior texture of an Enthusiast's life is brilliantly embodied in the style of *Gulliver's Travels,* a style which allows the exfoliation of the most outrageous fantasies within a dead-pan circumstantial realism, so that what we see is the wildly fertile invention of an untamed imagination, but we see, too, that this imagination is experienced not as an insubstantial phantasmagoria but rather as a palpable reality, having all the chaste logic and autonomy of the empirical world. Gulliver experiences his fiction of "Fortune" not as something he has made up but as a fact as solid and as real as that other "Fortune," the sums of money sent to him by his father.

What is liberated by the corporealizing imagination, of course, are all the energies from below, symbolized by the corporeal, egocentric Yahoos. Abandoning himself to his imagination, Gulliver becomes those very energies that work through it, and thus he loses his identity and becomes a "Lump of Deformity." From its beginning in the corporealizing imagination to its end in the dissolving of identity, Gulliver's travels recapitulate the trajectory of anxiety revealed in the Mary Toft affair.

And *Gulliver's Travels* appears to recapitulate, too, the Lindamira-Indamora episode of the *Memoirs* and to concur with its assessment of human nature as a mystery, an unknowable "&c." Swift uses the presence of monsters in his book as a way to press us toward larger questions about human identity, and these questions are unanswerable, for by the end of *Gulliver's Travels,* what is meant by "human species" is unascertainable. Within the fictional world of the book, the human species appears to include the Yahoos, who live along the energy of their egocentric drives and brutish appetites, naked, unconscious of themselves and unashamed of their nature. But the species also includes Gulliver, whose impulse is to "hide [his] Nakedness" (221) because he is as acutely conscious of his own nature as the Yahoos are blithely unconscious of theirs, as naturally ashamed as the Yahoos are naturally unashamed. Human beings comprise the "stark naked" (268) natives Gulliver encounters when he leaves the Houyhnhnms, who attack him unprovoked, as well as the crew of the Portugese ship who save him from the savages and treat him "with great Humanity" (270)—the phrase comes as a giddy shock after the apparently definitive equation between humanity and the Yahoos that has just occurred in Houyhnhnmland. Man has the capacity, like Gulliver, to use the skins of his own kind to clothe himself or, like Pedro de Mendez, to give a fellow being the shirt off his own back. We are as petty and as vicious as the Lilliputians and as capable of moral restraint and humane intelligence as the king of Brobdingnag. We can be misled by mindless innovations like the Laputans as easily as we can be brought to venerate the common forms like a Lord Munodi. And so on. Gulliver's final definition of man is "a Lump of Deformity," and in a way he does not understand, this is accurate enough: the human species cannot be defined, for it is a deformed monster, shapeless because it is an undefinable chaos of energies, capacities, tendencies, and drives, an "&c." that is too varied to be defined, too much "a Bundle of Inconsistencies and Contradictions"[65] to have a completely knowable shape.

Gulliver's Travels ends exactly as the *Memoirs* ends, whose final chapters about the monster Indamora-Lindamira portray not only the undefinable monstrosity of the human species but also the folly of trying to define that which defies definition. And if it is true that humanity defies definition, then it is less important what man the species *is* than what each individual *does* with whatever he is: how he represses and channels and fashions all these energies and tendencies to create an individual identity out of this "Lump of Deformity"—how he fashions himself into a king of Brobdingnag, a Lord Munodi, a Pedro de Mendez, shaping a specific human identity from the shapeless monstrosity of his variegated potential.

And yet, *Gulliver's Travels* does not press this solution with any conviction, nor does it have anything like the sense of resolution that the *Memoirs* has. The *Memoirs* implies not merely that uncertainty can be lived with but that uncertainty itself, the very unresolvableness of our singleness-and-doubleness, is a principle of reality on which one can erect a workable ethos that will allow us to manage a humane and intelligent life through self-awareness and a good-humor that distances us from the immediacy of our needs and desires.

This resolution is something of a humanist commonplace. Shaftesbury, for instance, played with the same paradoxes of our singleness-and-doubleness when he argued that we could achieve an identity and integrity of selfhood only by "becoming plural," actively seeking to "discover a certain duplicity of soul, and divide ourselves into two parties." What he means is that, being by nature an "&c.," we can move toward integrity only by embracing our multiplicity to rise above it. A person must "multiply himself into two persons and be his own subject." And what he must be conscious about when he becomes his own subject is his very multiplicity. Then he can enter into "a sort of soliloquy" with himself, acting as speaker and critical listener, performing a "self-dissection" in which he is both "pupil and preceptor," in which "he teaches, and he learns." By splitting himself apart in this way, he can begin the process of moving toward a single identity. For once having seen the heterogeneity of the self, he can construct from it an integrity by a continual interrogation of the self and a control of the heterogeneous impulses and energies that have been uncovered by this interrogation. Such a self-interrogation will "teach us ourselves, keep us the self-same persons, and so regulate our governing fancies, passions, and humours, as to make us comprehensible to ourselves, and knowable by other features than those of a bare contenance." By subjecting ourselves to ourselves, by a continual process of questioning, judgment, and regulation, integrity is fashioned and the self creates its identity:

> As cruel a court as the Inquisition appears, there must, it seems, be full as formidable a one erected in ourselves, if we would pretend to that uniformity of opinion which is necessary to hold us to one will, and preserve us in the same mind from one day to another. . . . We hope that our patient . . . will consider with himself that what he endures in this operation is for no inconsiderable end, since 'tis to gain him a Will, and ensure him a certain

resolution, by which he shall know where to find himself; be sure of his own meaning and design; and as to all his desires, opinions, and inclinations, be warranted one and the same person to-day as yesterday, and to-morrow as to-day.[66]

Pope often argued similarly. He takes up the theme of our singleness-and-doubleness, for instance, in the opening of book 2 of *An Essay on Man:*

> Know then thyself, presume not God to scan;
> The proper study of Mankind is Man.
> Plac'd on this isthmus of a middle state,
> A being darkly wise, and rudely great:
> With too much knowledge for the Sceptic side,
> With too much weakness for the Stoic's pride,
> He hangs between; in doubt to act, or rest,
> In doubt to deem himself a God, or Beast;
> In doubt his Mind or Body to prefer,
> Born but to die, and reas'ning but to err;
> Alike in ignorance, his reason such,
> Whether he thinks too little, or too much:
> Chaos of Thought and Passion, all confus'd;
> Still by himself abused, or disabus'd;
> Created half to rise, and half to fall;
> Great lord of all things, yet a prey to all;
> Sole judge of Truth, in endless Error hurl'd:
> The glory, jest, and riddle of the world![67]

Pope implicitly defines man as a monster here, so self-contradictory that the self can be understood only as something that "hangs between." For such a monstrously heterogeneous creature to have any integrity, as Shaftesbury saw, he would have to be in perpetual dialogue with himself. In other words, given our singleness-and-doubleness, our identity is a never-ending process of constructing but never fully achieving integrity, the always fashioning of a self out of our monstrosity. Like the importance of uncertainty and mystery that the Scriblerians recognized in the *Memoirs of Martinus Scriblerus,* or like the unceasing dialectic Swift wanted between the self and the monster it sees, Pope in this passage realizes that the dynamic process of creating a self can be sustained only by living, as he repeatedly says, "in doubt." To accept the illusion of certainty is to risk being seduced by our pride and imagination and to bring the process of self-creation to a halt. In sum, our human identity is created by our admission of our monstrousness, our unwillingness to remain monstrous, and our skepticism about ourselves as we go about moving away from our monstrosity to an integrity; we triangulate ourselves out of our monstrosity

by simultaneously assenting to three mutually contradictory propositions: that we are the jest of the world; that we are the glory of the
world; and that, in spite of the truth of both of these definitions, we are
an undefinable riddle.

But *Gulliver's Travels* seems less sanguine about this resolution
because Swift doubts that a mind can sustain itself "in doubt." Uncertainty, as we have seen, was used to underwrite a vision of the self as
singleness-and-doubleness and to argue for the possibility of self-identity. *Gulliver's Travels* shows that uncertainty can be so vexing that it is
more likely to cause us to end in our losing ourselves. Gulliver cannot
remain "in doubt," and so he calls an end to all dialogue with himself
by giving definitive answers to the questions, What is man? What am
I? The jest that he is, his own monstrosity, is too intolerable. The vision
of the glory he might be is too tempting. The uncertainty, the hanging
between, is too tormenting. Unable to live by performing the endless
dialogue that is required if we are to create an identity out of our monstrously variegated selves, Gulliver yields to his imagination and thus
loses the lineaments of a selfhood to become the wonderful monster he
does.

6

THE MIGHTY MOTHER, AND HER SON

I

The Mary Toft affair culminated in December 1726. Pope knew of the incident, of course, wrote at least one poem making fun of it, and then appears to have dismissed it from his mind. But a little over a year later, in May 1728, he published the first version of the *Dunciad*. At the center of the poem is a mother who prolifically brings forth monsters.

The Mary Toft incident did not occasion the *Dunciad*. Pope was at work on the poem as early as October 1725, and, except for an allusion in a single couplet added many years later, there is no explicit trace in the poem of Mary Toft or her rabbits.[1] And yet, the fact that the *Dunciad* was published and the Mary Toft incident took place in a space of little more than a year seems more than a felicitous historical coincidence.

I think that it was more than a coincidence. The Mary Toft episode fascinated and alarmed many in the eighteenth century because it worked on already existing preoccupations and anxieties. These preoccupations and anxieties were Pope's, too, and when he wrote a poem which dealt with them, he turned naturally, for reasons I will explain, to the symbol of the monster-breeding mother to give them shape. If this is so, the Mary Toft incident may be a valuable guide to Pope's poem. Mary Toft was perceived as a threat to personal coherence and autonomy, as a force which dissolved the boundaries of identity by swamping the self in matter. The power she represented was the power of the imagination. At the heart of the *Dunciad* is a vision of the mind so invaded by the mechanisms of the body that the boundaries of self-identity give way to incoherence. And the force which threatens personal identity, the force embodied in the goddess Dulness, I will argue, is the imagination.

My equation of Dulness and the imagination may be surprising, for probably our most immediate impulse on reading the poem is to attribute the "uncreating word" (4.654) of Dulness to an utter absence of the imagination.[2] And it may be surprising for another reason. In the *Dunciad,* Pope portrays Dulness as the systematic antithesis to the imagination as he characterized it elsewhere, particularly in his "Preface" and commentary to his translation of *The Iliad.* "Homer is universally allow'd to have the greatest Invention of any Writer whatever," Pope begins his "Preface," and it is this energy, an energy that makes Homer the sheer opposite to the torpid goddess of the *Dunciad,* that Pope sees as characteristic of Homer's imagination. Homer's "vast *Invention*" is so expansive that "None have been able to enlarge the Sphere of Poetry beyond the Limits he has set"; so lush is the "generous Profusion" of his imagination that, "like the *Nile,*" Homer "pours out his Riches with a boundless Overflow." With this energy of his imagination come associated powers: heat, motion, life, vigor, fertility, variety. Homer can "comprehend the vast and various Extent of Nature" because his work is like "a wild Paradise":

> 'Tis like a copious Nursery which contains the Seeds and first Productions of every kind. . . . If some things are too luxuriant, it is owing to the Richness of the Soil; and if others are not arriv'd to Perfection or Maturity, it is only because they are over-run and opprest by those of a stronger Nature.

Homer wrote with "unequal'd Fire and Rapture," creating poetry "of the most animated Nature imaginable," poetry in which "everything moves, every thing lives, and is put into Action." In his "*Expression,* we see [his] bright Imagination . . . shining out in the most enliven'd Forms." "He was the only Poet who had found out *Living Words.*" His numbers, "always in motion, and always full," sound "with so much Force and inspiriting Vigour, that they awaken and raise us like the Sound of a Trumpet." His measures, "instead of being Fetters to his Sense, were always in readiness to run along with the Warmth of his Rapture."[3]

The "Preface" reads like a point-for-point counter-manifesto to the aesthetics of Dulness. For Homer's expansiveness, we have the Dunces' contraction: "Bounded by Nature, narrow'd still by Art, / A trifling head, and a contracted heart" (4.503–4). For his "bright Imagination," the warmth of his raptures, we have the Dunces' night and their emotional coldness. For his fertility and variety and life, his energy and motion, we have the Dunces' sterility, sameness, death, their sinking into stasis. For Homer's "Poetical Fire, this *Vivida vis animi,*"[4] we have Dulness's "*Vis inertiæ of Matter*" (4.7n). Homer's poetry can "awaken and raise us"; the Dunces' art sends us to sleep, drawing us down to "one dead level" (4.268).

The energy of his imagination has one final attribute that makes Homer the great antithesis of Dulness, and Pope's admiration for this attribute pervades his commentary.

> If we observe his *Descriptions, Images,* and *Similies,* we shall find the Invention still predominant. To what else can we ascribe that vast Comprehension of Images of every sort, where we see each Circumstance of art and Individual of Nature summon'd together by the Extent and Fecundity of his Imagination; to which all things, in their various Views, presented themselves in an Instant, and had their Impressions taken off to Perfection at a Heat.[5]

That important phrase—"all things, in their various Views, presented themselves in an Instant"—is remarkable. It expresses Pope's assessment of Homer as well as his own sense of the possibilities of the imagination and of imaginative art. This is the "creating word." Here the imagination gathers the minute particulars of reality, perceives each from multiple perspectives, and shapes them all into a whole of intricate relationship:

> This strong and ruling Faculty was like a powerful Star, which, in the Violence of its Course, drew all things within its *Vortex.* It seem'd not enough to take in the whole Circle of Arts, and the whole Compass of Nature to supply his maxims and reflections; all the inward Passions and Affections of Mankind to furnish his Characters, and all the outward Forms and Images of Things for his Descriptions; but wanting yet an ampler Sphere to expatiate in, he open'd a new and boundless Walk for his Imagination, and created a World for himself in the Invention of *Fable.*[6]

By virtue of his imagination, Homer is the poet of relatedness and wholeness.

"They who would take Boldness from Poetry," Pope remarked on Homer's daring to encompass the whole of reality by means of his imagination, "must leave Dulness in the room of it."[7] To a great extent, Dulness is that particular kind of dullness which results from the failure to achieve the possibilities of the Homeric imagination. For the Dunces can connect nothing with nothing, can draw nothing into the vortex of relationship: it is they who are "gently drawn" to Dulness, "Roll in her vortex, and her pow'r confess" (4.83–84). Applied to Homer, circles symbolize comprehensiveness and perfection. His understanding of "the whole Circle of Arts" and of "the whole Compass of Nature" is fused perfectly into the "ampler Sphere" created by his imagination. For the Dunces, the sphere symbolizes confinement ("'I meddle, goddess! only in my sphere'" [4.432]), and the circle sym-

bolizes imprisonment and exclusion, ceaseless activity that has no purpose, and the destruction of relatedness. A Dunces' circle is the optic
field of his own "microscope of Wit," in which he "Sees hair and pores,
examines bit by bit" but never understands "How parts relate to parts,
or they to whole" (4.233–35). When Homer "created a world for himself," it was "ampler" and "boundless," comprehending and mirroring
the complexity of life; the world the Dunces create for themselves is the
"new World" (4.15) of Dulness, a cramped, little world that explains
nothing and is related to nothing.

Dulness and Homer, it is obvious, are sheer contrarieties, but just
because Dulness's uncreating mind exactly inverts the Homeric imagination, it does not follow that what Dulness represents can be defined
as the absence of the imagination. The imagination was a power that
could lead to Homer's vision of relatedness—or, as we have seen, it
could precipitate the collapse of all structures and end in Duncical
chaos.

Pope was certainly acquainted with the other side of the imagination. In spite of his enthusiasm for Homer's fancy in the "Preface," he
knew that the imagination was potentially a dangerous power. Indeed,
he himself experienced the imagination in its negative mode, and
much of his experience, I think, he embodied in his portrait of Dulness.
In 1712, he wrote to John Caryll, Jr.:

> While you are pursuing the Sprightly Delights of the Field, springing up
> with activity at the Dawning Day, rouzing a whole Country with Shouts
> and Horns, & inspiring Animalls and Rationalls with like Fury and Ardor;
> while your Blood boils high in ev'ry Vein, your Heart bounds in your
> breast, & as vigorous a Confluence of Spirits rushes to it at the sight of a Fox
> as cou'd be stirrd up by that of an Army of Invaders; while the Zeal of the
> Chace devours the whole man, & moves him no less than the Love of our
> Country or the Defence of our Altars could do. While—I say, (& I think I
> say it like a modern Orator, considering the Length of my Period, and the
> little Sence that is to follow it) while you are thus imployed, I am just in the
> reverse of all this Spirit & Life, confind to a narrow Closet, lolling on an
> Arm Chair, nodding away my Days over a Fire, like the picture of January
> in an old Salisbury Primer. I do believe no mortal ever livd in such Indo-
> lence & Inactivity of Body, tho my Mind be perpetually rambling (it no
> more knows whither than poor Adrian's did when he lay adying)[.] Like a
> witch, whose Carcase lies motionless on the floor, while she keeps her airy
> Sabbaths, & enjoys a thousand Imaginary Entertainments abroad, in this
> world, & in others, I seem to sleep in the midst of the Hurry, even as you
> would swear a Top stands still, when tis in the Whirle of its giddy motion.
> 'Tis no figure, but a serious truth I tell you when I say that my Days &
> Nights are so much alike, so equally insensible of any Moving Power but
> Fancy, that I have sometimes spoke of things in our family as Truths & real

accidents, which I only Dreamt of; & again when some things that actually happen'd came into my head, have thought (till I enquird) that I had only dream'd of them. This will shew you how little I feel in this State either of Pleasure or Pain: I am fixt in a Stupid settled Medium between both.

But possibly some of my good Friends, whom we have lately spoke of in our last letters may give me a more Lively Sense of things in a short time, & awaken my Intellects to a perfect Feeling of Myself & Them.[8]

In the "Preface," Pope described the imagination as an instrument of engagement with the world, the means by which Homer ranged through all existence and grasped reality entire. In this letter, however, Pope conceives of his own imagination wholly in terms of withdrawal. It is a solipsistic, alienating force that separates him from his friends, from a true perception of himself and his obligations, even from a "Lively Sense of things"—in short, from any engagement with the world at all. Hence, Pope contrasts Caryll's animation to his own "Indolence & Inactivity." Caryll is fully awake, invigorated, generating heat, exuding life ("your Blood boils high in ev'ry Vein, your Heart bounds in your breast"). Pope, drawing a pittance of heat from outside, languishes in chill, stillness, and sleep ("lolling on an Arm Chair, nodding away my Days over a Fire, like the picture of January in an old Salisbury Primer"). Caryll directs his attention outward, alert and eager in his possession of the external world, vigorously pursuing the "Sprightly Delights of the Field." Pope is closed in on himself, "confind to a narrow Closet." Sinking toward one dead level of emotional and physical stasis, he becomes "fixt in a Stupid settled Medium" between pleasure and pain and "stands still" as a top.

This symbol of the top, however, discloses a central paradox of Pope's experience of the solipsistic imagination. Under the spell of fancy, the mind only *seems* to stand still and sink toward sleep. In truth, like a spinning top, it is "in the midst of the Hurry," caught up in a "Whirle of . . . giddy motion." For, in the place of the external world it has withdrawn from, the imagination creates a new world, an internal world so vast and boundless that the mind can be "perpetually rambling" in it. In this new world, the mind is liberated into a preternatural wakefulness and vigorous movement, as much as Caryll is liberated into the "Sprightly Delights of the Field," so that Pope becomes "Like a witch, whose Carcase lies motionless on the floor, while she keeps her airy Sabbaths, & enjoys a thousand Imaginary Entertainments abroad, in this world, & in others."

Pope's activity is, of course, parodic of Caryll's, for it is "Imaginary," occurring in the confines of his mind. Like a top, the movement of his imagination is wholly self-centered, sustaining its energy by turning round itself in defiance of the forces of the outside world. And like a boy with a top, to be enchanted by this "giddy motion" is mere child's play, all idleness and trifling, a retreat from adult concerns and responsible behavior. (A few months before his letter to Caryll, Pope published in *The Spectator,* under the name of "Samuel Slack," a piece condemning "Indolence and Inactivity" and the "Encroachments of Idleness," all of which he attributed to the imagination. "I please my self with the Shadow, whilst I lose the Reality," he complained. The idleness nurtured by the fancy "undermines the Foundation of every Virtue. . . . And it is to no Purpose to have within one the Seeds of a thousand good Qualities, if we want the Vigour and Resolution necessary for the exerting them.")[9]

If Pope's imagination parodies Caryll's animation and energy, it parodies, too, the real possibilities of the imagination Pope found in Homer. The creative energies opened for Homer "a new and boundless Walk for his Imagination." But there is a great difference between Homer's "boundless Walk" and that vast space of the fancy in which Pope found himself "perpetually rambling." The capacious new world Pope experienced in his imagination was a "wandring Maze of Thought," "Fancy's Maze," as he called it much later,[10] seemingly as boundless as Homer's, but in truth an enclosed circuit, its expansiveness, like a maze's, an illusion caused by space folded back on itself. Homer's imagination was a "Walk" that directed him toward truth. Pope's sent him "rambling" aimlessly in a maze with no clew. "I do believe no mortal ever livd in such Indolence & Inactivity of Body," Pope had remarked in his 1712 letter, contrasting his own directionless wandering to the straightforward pursuit of Caryll's hunting, "tho my mind be perpetually rambling (it no more knows whither than poor Adrian's did when he lay adying)." The imagination led Homer to a vision of relatedness, heightening his perception of order and his comprehension of reality. The solipsistic imagination sets Pope wandering in a confusion that ends in a diminished sense of the actual. When he becomes subject to "the Whirle of its giddy motion," the boundaries between the real and the phantasmal become uncertain and ambiguous, his very "Sense of things" perplext, his mind chaotic. "I have sometimes spoke of things in our family as Truths & real accidents, which I only Dreamt of; & again when some things that actually happen'd came into my head, have thought (till I enquird) that I had only dream'd of them."[11]

This confusion of "Truths & real accidents" with things "only Dreamt of" is something we have seen before. It is the same confusion Gulliver experienced and the same confusion pointed to so often in the

Mary Toft satires, a confusion that was an almost inevitable consequence of the Enthusiastic fancy as explained by the traditional theories of the imagination. And, although Pope obviously experienced
such a dislocation for himself, he experienced it and understood it
within this conceptual framework that that tradition had handed
down to him.[12] His two opposing views of the dynamics of the imagination—its Homeric, centrifugal drive outward to an expanded
awareness of reality, and its solipsistic, centripetal pull inward to confusion—both flow from the concept of the imagination which he was
heir to. As a mediating faculty at the boundary of sense and thought,
the imagination could either raise the thought to insight or plunge it
into blindness. Since the imagination was linked to the senses, it could
turn the mind outward to the world, and since it could rise above the
contingencies of time and space, the imagination was able to range
through the whole of experience, seeking resemblances, perceiving
relationships, making connections, and then pass on its findings to the
further ordering processes of the intellect. Working at its highest pitch,
the imagination culminated in the Homeric vision of relatedness, a
vision that was coherent, whole, and rooted in the real order of things.

But, inhabiting this boundary of sense and thought, the imagination
could just as easily perform the opposite, corporealizing transactions.
Rather than sublimating sense experience into the stuff of the intellect,
it might give to the specious, airy fabrications of the mind the weight
and feel of reality, the vividness, immediacy, and substantiality that we
experience in our perception of the things of the world, and thus
impute to fancies the title and authority of reality that belongs by right
only to God's created world. Seduced by the corporealizing imagination further and further inward, the mind would finally let go of the
external world, which faded into insubstantiality (Pope loses his "Lively Sense of things"), supplanted by corporealized fancies, things "only
Dreamt of," which were now so palpable that they appeared as "Truths
& real accidents."

In spite of the high claims he made for the imagination in the "Preface" of his translation of The Iliad, in spite of the example of Homer
himself, whose poetry vindicates the worth of the fancy, Pope also was
apprehensive about this other possibility, this capacity of the imagination to corporealize things "only Dreamt of," to create a world which
was seemingly real but which actually was constructed from "so many
shadow images and airy prospects, which arise to us but so much the
livelier and more frequent as we are more overcast with the darkness,
wrapt in the night, and disturbed with the fumes of human vanity." He
thought that he himself was particularly susceptible to the solipsistic

appeal of the fancy ("it takes me up so intirely," he confessed, "that I scarce see what passes under my nose, and hear nothing that is said about me"), and he often generalized his misgivings about the self-engrossing imagination to extend to all of poetry:

> I never had so much cause as now to complain of my poetical star, that fixes me at this tumultuous time, to attend the gingling of rymes and the measuring of syllables: To be almost the only trifler in the nation; and as ridiculous as the Poet in *Petronius,* who while all the rest in the ship were either labouring or praying for life, was scratching his head in a little room, to write a fine description of the tempest.

As in his 1712 letter to Caryll, Jr., where he associated the imagination with being "confind to a narrow Closet," here too the poetic fancy is "a little room," and to live in the imagination is to confine himself in an illusion of life and action, indulging himself in the "Indolence & Inactivity" of being a "trifler," amusing himself by describing a fictitious tempest rather than "labouring or praying" to deal with the real one. And thus, when he defended poetry (at least until he substantially reformulated his aesthetics in the early 1730s), Pope was diffident. In the "Preface" to his 1717 *Works,* he shied away from making any important claims. Poetry was merely an "affair of idle men who write in their closets, and of idle men who read there," too unaffiliated to the real concerns of life, too self-involved to be taken seriously. Perhaps one ought to be "ashamed to consume half one's days in bringing sense and rhyme together."[13]

This strain of skepticism about the imagination often colored Pope's feelings about poetry. "I am really so fatigued with scribbling," he wrote while he was at work on the translation of *The Iliad,*

> that I could almost wish, in the Scripture phrase, that *my hand had forgot its cunning.* . . . If I out live this task, . . . I shall be capable of being everything that I am now hindered from being,—I mean I shall be a better man, a better friend, a better correspondent, &c. I am now like a wretched man of business, who regards only himself and his own affairs.[14]

Pope's opposition here between "a better man, a better friend, a better correspondent" and a "wretched man . . . who regards only himself" has grown out of his earlier dichotomy in his 1712 letter to Caryll, Jr., where he had set the wretched self-absorption of a man possessed by his imagination against the proper self-regard of a better man, that "perfect Feeling" for the self which sprang from the recognition that the higher good of an individual lay in his pursuing goals outside the egocentric world created by his imagination, that the soul had duties to attend to, that one had moral obligations to friends and to society. The

"Indolence & Inactivity" Pope decries is not physical laziness but the moral idleness that results when the self-enclosure of the imagination prevents a man from seeing that he is part of a web of moral and social responsibilities that exists outside the confines of his own skull. Pope's sense of his obligations to reality—to his friends, to the public good, to his own highest interests—made him often think of his poetry as an "idle trade," a self-contained pleasure that could easily seduce him to abandon "all more serious employment" and to "give up all the reasonable aims of life":

> I should be sorry and ashamed to go on gingling to the last step, like a waggoner's horse in the same road, to leave my bells to the next silly animal that will be proud of them. That man makes a mean figure in the eyes of reason who is measuring of syllables and coupling rhymes, when he should be mending his soul and securing his own immortality.

"One goodnatured action or one charitable intention," he wrote, "is of more merit than all the rhyming, jingling faculties in the world."[15]

This strain of skepticism in Pope is, of course, only a strain. It occasionally surfaces in such remarks as we have just seen, but often it nearly vanishes in his more ebullient moods, and often it is only silently present, exerting subtle pressures against his other views and prodding him to qualify his more optimistic ideas about poetry. And sometimes it simply lies alongside other attitudes, unresolved and oddly discordant:

> To write well, lastingly well, Immortally well, must not one leave Father and Mother and cleave unto the Muse? Must not one be prepared to endure the reproaches of Men, want and much Fasting, nay Martyrdom in its Cause. 'Tis such a Task as scarce leaves a Man time to be a good Neighbour, an useful friend, nay to plant a Tree, much less to save his Soul.[16]

The contradiction—we can hear in this passage Pope's conviction that poetry is a quasi-divine art worth the very "Martyrdom" he complains against—does not mean that he is insincere in his grievance. This is a contradiction Pope could not avoid: it is a contradiction that arose from the doubleness of the imagination as it was traditonally conceived, a doubleness which made the imagination both a vehicle of Homeric insight and a temptation to self-indulgent idleness.

Pope's feelings about the imagination were very unsettled throughout the first half of his career. The problem of the fancy preoccupied him, and his sometimes confusing statements and his often ambiguous tones suggest that he was trying to sort out the contradictions of the imagination (the danger of its temptation to solipsistic idleness as well as its possibilities for creative insight are central themes in *Windsor-Forest, Eloisa to Abelard,* and *Rape of the Lock,* for instance).[17] But by the early 1730s, his need to reconcile a vocation he deeply feared was idle and self-indulgent with the obligations he thought required of any moral creature drove him to announce publicly a redirection of poetic energy to more acceptable ends. He opens *An Essay on Man* (a poem he wrote, he said, in conscious rejection of the "vanity" of his earlier work and as an attempt to turn his poetry toward "some honest and moral purposes") with those images he had revolved in his mind for at least a decade and a half in his effort to get a purchase on the problem of the imagination, poetry, and ethical obligations:

> Let us (since Life can little more supply
> Than just to look about us and to die)
> Expatiate free o'er all this scene of Man;
> A mighty maze! but not without a plan;
> .   .   .   .
>
> Together let us beat this ample field,
> Try what the open, what the covert yield;
> The latent tracts, the giddy heights explore
> Of all who blindly creep, or sightless soar;
> Eye Nature's walks, shoot Folly as it flies,
> And catch the Manners living as they rise; . . .[18]

Here Pope commits himself to a direction he knew as early as 1712 he should take but which he had not been able to commit himself to earlier, so perplexed was he by the contradictory tendencies of the imagination. But from now on, like Caryll, Jr., he would join the hunt. He had, he confessed a little later, "wander'd" in "Fancy's Maze" too long, and consequently he had produced but "many an idle Song." But now he rejected that solipsistic maze of fancy for the "mighty maze" of Nature herself, and there would be no more pleasing but directionless "perpetually rambling" in "a wandering Maze of Thought." The maze of Nature was "not without a plan," and he would hunt it down not by wandering but by following "Nature's walks."[19]

It is not at all surprising that in the end Pope should reconcile his vocation and his ethical obligations by making poetry an instrument of engagement with the moral, social, and political realities of the world. But what is surprising, particularly given Pope's enthusiasm for the possibilities of the Homeric imagination, is the way he reaches this reconciliation by turning away, at least in his public pronouncements, from the fancy, as if he judged it too problematic to serve as the foundation of his art. From the early 1730s on, Pope founds his art and his career on a completely different principle. To pick a single instance among many, at the end of *An Essay on Man* he thanks Bolingbroke: "urg'd by thee, I turn'd the tuneful art / . . . from fancy to the heart."[20]

Pope's motives for turning from the "fancy" to the "heart" are complex, and I shall focus on them in my next chapter. All I want to point out here are a few, more simple lessons that we can draw from this material. First, the question of the imagination preoccupied Pope well into the early 1730s. Secondly, he saw the imagination as possessing both Homeric and Enthusiastic modes, and about the latter he had well-developed ideas and strong opinions. Thirdly, though in the "Preface" to *The Iliad* Pope had brilliantly defended the Homeric imagination as a faculty that engaged the poet with the world outside of himself, he appears to have been so suspicious of the fancy as an instrument of idleness and withdrawal that when he radically redefined his career in the 1730s, he publicly founded his poetry on an entirely different principle—indeed, on an explicit rejection of the fancy.

In the *Dunciad,* then, when Pope systematically contrasts Dulness to Homer, he does not mean that she lacks imagination. The antithesis to the Homeric imagination is not no imagination at all, but rather the imagination closed in on itself. This was the distinction that had been ripening in Pope's mind for over a decade before he wrote the first *Dunciad.* Dulness, Pope cautions, "is not to be taken contractedly for mere Stupidity, but in the enlarged sense of the word, for all Slowness of Apprehension, Shortness of Sight, or imperfect Sense of things . . . : a ruling principle not inert, but turning topsy-turvy the Understanding, and inducing an Anarchy or confused State of Mind" (1.15n). A "ruling principle not inert" that leads to an "imperfect Sense of things" and induces a "confused State of Mind": in his letter of 1712, Pope described his own solipsistic imagination as a "Moving Power" that deprived him of a "Lively Sense of things," subverted his understanding, and induced an anarchy of mind, a "Whirle of . . . giddy motion." I think that, to the degree that she can be said to represent any single thing, Dulness in fact represents the Enthusiastic imagination.

II

The dynamics of the imagination that Pope detailed in his 1712 letter to Caryll, Jr. and elsewhere reappear as the central patterns of the *Dunciad.*

The most pervasive images in the poem are those of obscurity and darkness. Dulness is a "clouded Majesty" (1.45), surrounded by a "veil of fogs" (1.262), and she keeps her children in "solid darkness" (3.226), spreading "a healing mist before the mind" to secure them in their "native night" (1.174–76). This darkness and obscurity suggest a mental obtuseness, a moral opacity, perhaps even an alliance with the powers of evil, but at base they and their variations (physical enclosures, such as vapors, clouds, fogs, mists, shades, curtains, veils, caves, cells, recesses, closed rooms, dark valleys, engulfing waters, and smothering mud; and states of mental insensibility, such as unconsciousness, drunkenness, and sleep) represent a withdrawal of consciousness from contact with the external world, a retreat into solipsism.

In their solipsism, the Dunces suffer the same consequences Pope did when he withdrew into his imagination. Like him, they lose first all "lively Sense of things":

> Here, in a dusky vale where Lethe rolls,
> Old Bavius sits, to dip poetic souls,
> And blunt the sense, and fit it for a skull
> Of solid proof, impenetrably dull.
>
> (3.23–26)

The Dunces' fundamental tie to the external world, the senses, is stultified. At best, they perceive a distorted reality—sometimes the fogs that surround them clear just enough to "magnify the scene" (1.80)—but more often they "See Nature in some partial narrow shape" (4.455), or worse yet, only "bit by bit" (4.234). Unable to perceive "How parts relate to parts, or they to whole" (4.235), the Dunces are incapable of understanding the coherence and purpose of the world. They are no longer fit "to proceed beyond *Trifles,* to any useful or extensive views of Nature, or of the Author of Nature" (4."Argument"). They reach the point Pope himself reached when he was possessed by the imagination: with a "Shortness of Sight," all "lively Sense of things" decays, the relationship among things begins to unravel, and the intricate order of the world is "uncreated," undone in a giddy whirl.

Unable to see the relationships among things, the Dunces are incapable of seeing how they themselves are related to the world. Pope had charged the solipsistic imagination with idleness because it enticed a person inward so that he lost all living touch with reality and hence ceased to be or act in the world. The ties of affection, obligation, and need that bound humans together ceased to matter. Seduced by his own imagination, Pope lapsed into a "Stupid settled Medium" of no emotion, and he no longer performed his duties to society, to his friends, to God, losing even the "perfect Feeling" for his own better self. In his 1712 letter to Caryll, Jr., Pope figured this insensibility with images of stillness, chill, stasis, and sleep. The same images, of course, pervade the *Dunciad,* and they signify the same stupor and impassivity, for the Dunces "all Relation scorn" (4.479); they are drawn away from any engagement with the world, and each "forgets his friends, / Sire, Ancestors, Himself" (4.518–19).

Idleness pervades the *Dunciad* from the opening announcement that "the Goddess bade Britannia sleep" (1.7) to the yawn that brings the poem to a close, and this sinking into sleep turns out to be every bit as paradoxical as the withdrawal into the solipsistic imagination that Pope described in his letters. Just as for Pope the "Indolence & Inactivity" of the imagination opened up a boundless internal world that liberated him into a preternatural energy and animation, so the Dunces, sinking into sleep and stupefaction, are released into unconfined, feverish activity. Dulness narrows each Dunce and encourages him to "meddle . . . only in [his] sphere" (4.432)—in such things, say, as the study of moss. But, under her aegis, such limited spheres magically expand. Moss becomes a "wilderness of Moss," so extensive that a Dunce can "wander" in it forever (4.450). The Dunces pray to the goddess to "spread a healing mist before the mind" to "Secure us kindly in our native night," but this enclosure, as it turns out, is emancipating, for the Dunces become "All-seeing in [her] mists" (4.469). Cibber is carried from the real world "on Fancy's easy wing" (3.13) and inexorably cut off from it by Lethe and "th' oblivious Lake" (3.44). This, too, proves liberating. Instead of settling into blank unconsciousness, he perceives all the past, the present, and the future ("shadow images and airy prospects," Pope had remarked, "arise to us so much the livelier and more frequent as we are more overcast with the darkness, wrapt in the night, and disturbed with the fumes of human vanity"). Confined to a stage, the Dunces create a cosmos where

> Gorgons hiss, and Dragons glare,
> And ten-horn'd fiends and Giants rush to war.
> Hell rises, Heav'n descends, and dance on Earth:
> Gods, imps, and monsters, music, rage, and mirth,
> A fire, a jigg, a battle, and a ball,
> 'Till one wide conflagration swallows all.
>   (3.235–40)

When Dulness looks into herself in the opening of book 1, she sees not a straitened, narrow world, but one that is spacious and teeming, a "wild creation" (1.82) that in its fertility, variety, and sheer vitality rivals the real world it has replaced. And, like Pope himself, who seemed to "stand still" and yet was in a "Whirle of . . . giddy motion," the *Dunciad* as a whole sweeps forward in a paradox of stasis and movement. Dulness is a maternal goddess, her tendencies all quietistic. She is the "Great Tamer of all human art" (1.163), always pacifying and comforting her children, gently moving them to rest and sleep, and yet what we actually see in the *Dunciad* is that she unleashes a ferment of energy. Under her influence, the Dunces become a frenetic, "industrious tribe" (2.33) who move through the poem in an explosive rush of activity, running, diving, floundering in the mud, erupting into parades, heroic games, and wildly chaotic stage plays.[21]

For Pope, withdrawal into the imagination resulted in a moment of giddiness, by which he meant a moment when the identity of a thing suddenly became problematic. Giddiness for Pope was preeminently a moment of boundary ambiguity. The fancy, whose function was to join things which were separate in nature and to separate things which were joined, and whose corporealizing power gave to the fabrications of the mind the heft and feel of the objects of nature, perforce weakened the boundaries of things and muddled the sense of the actual. When the solid lineaments defining the identities of things began to weaken and dissolve, things themselves were transformed and took on new identities. The self was caught in a "Whirle of . . . giddy motion," perplexed by confused realities and merged identities. For Pope (as well as for the confused doctors poked fun at in the Mary Toft satires, for Hudibras and Ralpho, for Gulliver, for the Modern Author of *A Tale of a Tub,* and for the whole tribe of Enthusiasts who had sunk into their imaginations), "Truths & real accidents" became something "only Dreamt of" and dreams were transformed into truths and real accidents.

It is precisely this experience of giddiness, in the very particular sense he defined it in his letter of 1712, that is at the center of Pope's portrayal of "giddy dulness" (3.294) in the *Dunciad*. Dulness, like the giddy imagination itself, is a transformative power who blurs the boundaries that distinguish things and give them their identities. Hence, the *Dunciad* is a world in perpetual mutation. "Cook shall be Prior, and Concanen, Swift" (2.138), Dulness commands, and they become so, transformed by her fiat:

> Three wicked imps, of her own Grubstreet choir,
> She deck'd like Congreve, Addison, and Prior,
> . . . .
> Curl stretches after Gay, but Gay is gone,
> He grasps an empty Joseph for a John:
> So Proteus, hunted in a nobler shape,
> Became, when seiz'd, a puppy, or an ape.
> (2.123–24, 127–30)

The force which rules the world of the *Dunciad* is "ductile dulness" (1.64)—ductile because Dulness assumes a variety of shapes to infiltrate all levels of eighteenth-century life, and ductile, too, because Dulness makes all things malleable, setting off monstrous metamorphoses: she "turns Learning into Air"; under her transformative power, "Beeves ... to jelly turn / ... Hares to Larks"; "Now to thy gentle shadow all are shrunk, / All melted down, in Pension, or in Punk"; "Prologues into Prefaces decay, / And these to Notes are fritter'd quite away" (3.78; 4.551, 554, 509–10; 1.277–78). The metamorphoses end in things whose identities are ambiguous and equivocal and whose boundaries are inde-finable, in "Prose swell'd to verse, verse loit'ring into prose," in "A past, vamp'd, future, old, reviv'd, new piece, / 'Twixt Plautus, Fletcher, Shakespear, and Corneille," in "a monster of a fowl, / Something be-twixt a Heideggre and owl" (1.274, 284–85, 289–90). The *Dunciad* is lit-tered with things whose shapes have become ambiguous and indefinable (clouds, fogs, mists, smoke, wafting vapors, veils, puddings, custards, running lead, bogs, excrement, vomit, ooze, quaking mud, foam), with the definite degenerating into the formless (rags, tattered ensigns, scraps of paper, patch-work clothing, hacked and torn pages), and especially with noises sunk just beneath the articulate (cackling, roars, hisses, cat-calls, chatterings, brayings, twangs, jabberings, din, moans, bellows, bawls, screams, howls, murmurings, titterings, warblings).

This feeling of giddiness—the sense of boundaries giving way, of transformation in progress, of identities becoming so equivocal that it is impossible to know whether something is one thing, or another, or both—shapes the whole of the *Dunciad*. When the ghost of Settle comes before Cibber, he appears to be "another yet the same" (3.40). The phrase could stand as an epigraph for the entire poem. For, throughout the work, Pope creates the sense of things being them-selves and something else too, so that the *Dunciad* becomes a world of metamorphosis, transmogrification, and unstable identities. The poem tumbles forward in a bewildering jumble of genres and *topoi*—bits and snatches of *successio* poetry, sessions poetry, *translatio studii,* epic, pastoral, farce, progress pieces, prospect pieces—so that the very con-tours of narrative action become blurred, begin yawing toward the amorphous, the "plot" moving in the same deliquescent rhythms of fantasies and dreams.

And this giddiness of shifting identities is replicated, too, in the quirky texture of the poem's verse. Consider, for example, this couplet attacking Lord Hervey:

> Narcissus, prais'd with all a Parson's power,
> Look'd a white lilly sunk beneath a show'r.
> (4.103–4)

The couplet starts out straightforwardly enough, the allusion to Narcissus tagging Hervey as an egotist. But this is unsettlingly transformed by the backward pressure exerted on "Narcissus" by the "white lilly" of the simile. Is "Narcissus" to be understood as that figure from classical myth or as the white flower, the narcissus? The confusion is compounded by the lilly's being "sunk beneath a show'r," for if the unexpected appearance of the "white lilly" suggests the "Narcissus" is not the figure from classical myth, the fate of the lilly, so appropriate to the drowning Narcissus, half gives back what has been half taken away—but only half, for Narcissus sank in a pool of water, while the white lilly contains a pool of water and sinks under its weight. The result is delightful confusion, a kind of anarchy of identity. What is Hervey? Is he a knave, so possessed with vanity that he has repeated the sin of Narcissus? or is he, as the image of the narcissus suggests, a weak fool, a victim so frail that he is overwhelmed by the sycophantic praise of someone with a stronger personality than his? In fact, his identity is caught up in a "Whirle of . . . giddy motion."

This giddiness, it seems to me, is the essential fact of the style of the *Dunciad,* a style which, mutatis mutandis, is the style of *Gulliver's Travels.* Like *Gulliver's Travels,* the *Dunciad* interweaves the minute particulars of a palpably quotidian and empirical reality with the patently bizarre and phantasmagoric. So intricate is the amalgam of the historic and the fictional, the real and the imagined, that all things in the poem exist as confused and equivocal identities. (The whole of book 3, in fact, is built on this ambiguity, for the events of that book are, according to its dramatic fiction, an insubstantial vision of the hero, "no more than a Chimera of the Dreamer's brain" [A.3.5n]; yet the grotesqueries, so appropriate to the mental confusion of the hero, are drawn from the contemporary facts and events.) Scraps of historical fact rapidly shade into hyperbole, metaphors cease to be wholly metaphoric because they have been dramatized and made so concrete that they take on the aura of actuality, allegory swells beyond the allegoric because it, too, has one foot in real events. As a result, the reader is precipitated into the world as an Enthusiast must have seen it, as Gulliver, driven by his fancy, saw it—or as Pope saw it when, possessed by his imagination, he was unable to distinguish "things that actually happen'd" from things "only Dreamt of."[22]

III

Other patterns in the poem point to the link between Dulness and the imagination. At the end of the *Dunciad,* Dulness, through the power of her "uncreating word," dissolves the world and obliterates all creation in "Universal Darkness." The power of the poem's spectacular vision of the triumph of nothingness can easily make us forget that Pope speaks of this apocalypse quite differently elsewhere in the poem.

> Then rose the Seed of Chaos, and of Night,
> To blot out Order, and extinguish Light,
> Of dull and venal a new World to mold,
> And bring Saturnian days of Lead and Gold.
>
> (4.13–16)

Dulness is the "Seed of Chaos, and of Night"—meaning, of course, that she is the daughter of Chaos and Old Night, but meaning also that she is their generative origin and that her restoration of chaos and darkness is not simply a process of annihilation and negation, but a calling into being, an act in some way as creative as the act which causes a creature to spring from its seed. Although she does "blot out" creation and extinguish its light, this act is not wholly destructive: she will "mold" a new order, create a "new World," and bring new "days," substituting one light for another, a second creation for the one she has destroyed.

Dulness uncreates the world by fabricating a new one to replace it. Through her power, "a new world to Nature's laws unknown, / Breaks out refulgent" (3.241–42). She is not, as Pope said, "to be taken contractedly for mere Stupidity," and when he charges her with being "uncreating," he does not mean that she represents a cessation of thought or a blank dormancy. Dulness is "a ruling principle not inert," a power of mind that acts. And, even though Pope speaks of Dulness as if she were a force of sheer negation bringing stasis, death, nothingness, and uncreation, when we actually get a glimpse of her internal workings, we see something else entirely:

> Here she beholds the Chaos dark and deep,
> Where nameless Somethings in their causes sleep,
> 'Till genial Jacob, or a warm Third day,
> Calls forth each mass, a Poem, or a Play:
> How hints, like spawn, scarce quick in embryo lie,
> How new-born nonsense first is taught to cry,
> Maggots half-form'd in rhyme exactly meet,
> And learn to crawl upon poetic feet.
> Here one poor word an hundred clenches makes,
> And ductile dulness new meanders takes;
> There motley Images her fancy strike,
> Figures ill-pair'd, and Similes unlike.
> She sees a Mob of Metaphors advance,
> Pleas'd with the madness of the mazy dance:
> How Tragedy and Comedy embrace,

> How Farce and Epic get a jumbled race;
> How Time himself stands still at her command,
> Realms shift their place, and Ocean turns to land.
> Here gay Description Ægypt glads with show'rs,
> Or gives to Zembla fruits, to Barca flow'rs;
> Glitt'ring with ice here hoary hills are seen,
> There painted vallies of eternal green,
> In cold December fragrant chaplets blow,
> And heavy harvests nod beneath the snow.
>
> (1.55–78)

Dulness is lavishly, generously creative. In this passage, she shares with God his formative causes, with nature the power of spontaneous generation and the cyclical regeneration of the seasons, and with humans their sexuality. And what she creates is neither static, nor dead, nor "nothing": she brings forth sheer matter, living things that assert their existence with an impudent corporeality, things tumultuously alive.

These contradictions in Dulness's uncreation are epitomized by the interplay of two images, the one opening, the other closing the poem. The *Dunciad* concludes with an emblem of Dulness's destructive power, her yawn, symbolizing the triumph of nothingness and death; she is the devouring mother, absorbing back into herself her own creation. But this image of annihilating emptiness has a counterpart in the opening of the poem:

> One Cell there is, conceal'd from vulgar eye,
> The Cave of Poverty and Poetry.
> Keen, hollow winds howl thro' the bleak recess,
> Emblem of Music caus'd by Emptiness.
> Hence Bards, like Proteus long in vain ty'd down,
> Escape in Monsters, and amaze the town.
> Hence Miscellanies spring, the weekly boast
> Of Curl's chaste press, and Lintot's rubric post:
> Hence hymning Tyburn's elegiac lines,
> Hence Journals, Medleys, Merc'ries, Magazines:
> Sepulchral Lyes, our holy walls to grace,
> And New-year Odes, and all the Grub-street race.
>
> (1.33–44)

The "Cell" and the "Cave" are imagistic parallels to the yawn at the end of the poem (in fact, in the first version of the poem, the cave was a "yawning ruin" that "nods" [A.1.28]). But if the yawn which closes the *Dunciad* is a devouring tomb, here, the gaping voids are prolific wombs, the matrices of vital creation. Instead of swallowing all into nothingness, they pour forth a profusion of matter in a furious birth.

There is an inextricable alliance between creation and destruction at the heart of Dulness's activity (she presides over that place "Where things destroy'd are swept to things unborn" [1.242]). If her yawn brings chaos and death, it is a destruction oddly leagued with creativity, for it ushers in the "all-composing Hour" (4.627). "Music caus'd by Emptiness" refers not only to Dulness's miraculous creation of something out of nothing but also to the more mundane fact of her flatulence, and thus conflates birth and excretion, generation and annihilation. Dulness gives birth—through the agency of the imponderable sexuality of "Curl's chaste press, and Lintot's rubric post"—bringing forth whole generations of things, "lines" of poems and "all the Grubstreet race." And yet death and nothingness haunt these strange births, for the "lines" are, literally, the death songs of Tyburn, and the poems are "Sepulchral."

A void which is also a plenum of being, a movement toward death which is at the same time an act generative of life, the destruction of all creation which is simultaneously the creation of a "new World": the "uncreating" power of Dulness is paradoxical because Dulness represents the imagination, and the imagination, as we have seen, is informed by these paradoxes, for it blanks the world to a nothing and envelops the self in a deadened stasis, but it uncreates the world by creating a "new World," an internal world instinct with life and erupting in activity.[23]

The *Dunciad* is heir to the anti-Enthusiastic tradition of Butler and Swift, a tradition whose object was to depict the aberrations of the imagination. The withdrawal of the Dunces from the external world, their entering a paradoxical state of stasis and sleep on the one hand and of explosive, hyperkinetic activity on the other, their consequent blurring of distinctions that brings chaos and induces a giddy whirl of confused identities—all of these suggest that in his portrayal of Dulness Pope had in mind the specific aberrations of the imagination which tradition taught him to expect and which he himself experienced.

IV

Because the complexities and contradictions of the uncreating imagination could not be contained in the simple negations of death, stasis, and nothingness, Pope turned to the resonant symbol of the monster-breeding mother. Monstrous, defective, and perverse births, of course, pervade the poem from beginning to end, and with them Pope figures forth the complex etiology of the imagination, an etiology which is most strikingly depicted in the passage in which Dulness reviews all her Dunces and singles out Cibber for special notice:

> In each she marks her Image full exprest,
> But chief in BAYS'S monster-breeding breast;
> Bays, form'd by nature Stage and Town to bless,
> And act, and be, a Coxcomb with success.
> Dulness with transport eyes the lively Dunce,
> Remembring she herself was Pertness once.
> Now (shame to Fortune!) an ill Run at Play
> Blank'd his bold visage, and a thin Third day:
> Swearing and supperless the Hero sate,
> Blasphem'd his Gods, the Dice, and dam'd his Fate.
> Then gnaw'd his pen, then dash'd it on the ground,
> Sinking from thought to thought, a vast profound!
> Plung'd for his sense, but found no bottom there,
> Yet wrote and flounder'd on, in mere despair.
> Round him much Embryo, much Abortion lay,
> Much future Ode, and abdicated Play;
> Nonsense precipitate, like running Lead,
> That slipp'd thro' Cracks and Zig-zags of the Head;
> All that on Folly Frenzy could beget,
> Fruits of dull Heat, and Sooterkins of Wit.
>
> (1.107–126)

Here, as elsewhere in the poem, much of the meaning springs from the giddy whirl of confused identities. The confusion begins with the phrase, "an ill run at Play," meaning either that Cibber has had poor luck at the gaming table or that one of his dramas has failed. Of course, it means both: Pope conflates the two to imply that for Cibber writing is a kind of gambling, that when he sits down to write a play he abandons himself to chance. His dashing of the pen to the ground, a gesture recalling his earlier throwing of the dice, continues the parallel, and it is sustained by the downward movement that governs the rest of the passage. For next the process of thinking itself begins a haphazard descent, the verbals "Sinking ... Plung'd ... flounder'd" emphasizing actions which perhaps began as intentional but which continue as the result of a surrender of will and direction. Finally, the very products of his thought are, like "running Lead," freed from intentionality, resigned to the shaping forces of gravity and chance.

This movement downward to chance is simultaneously a process of corporealization. The rapid shift from the dashing of the arm to the sinking of thought to the tumbling out of the final product has the effect of dissolving one into the other, blurring the act of thinking with the fall of the pen and the toss of the dice, so that as a result mental activity comes to be equated with physical movement. (Similarly, we learn that Cibber is "supperless," then watch him gnaw his pen, and

finally see how he "sipp'd" and "suck'd all o'er," plundering other literature to produce his own, leaving "half-eat scenes" [1.128–31].) Hence,
the image that culminates this movement downward, "Nonsense precipitate, like running Lead, / That slipp'd thro' Cracks and Zig-zags of
the Head," is an image that stresses not only the formlessness and inde-
terminacy of what Cibber produces but its utter physicality. From first
to last—from the "ill Run" that begins the process to the "running
Lead" that is its issue—Duncical creativity, its motive, its excution, and
its product, is a matter of chaos and the body. (The allusion to Satan's
fall through Chaos in these lines also identifies this downward movement as a movement toward corporeality and chance, for Satan falls
from spirit to body and from order to disorder.)

The grand movement of the *Dunciad* as a whole is the movement
played out in little in this passage, the movement of all things down to
"one dead level." What is significant about this passage, and about the
Dunciad as a whole, is how thoroughly Pope associated this double
descent into disorder and the body with monstrous birth. Cibber's
"Embryo," "Abortion," and "Sooterkins"—all that Folly and Frenzy
could "beget"—are metaphoric equivalents to the "running Lead" (as,
a few lines earlier, Dulness's own perverted births, her hints which
"scarce quick in embryo lie," her "new-born nonsense," her "half-
form'd" "Maggots" that "crawl upon poetic feet," represent the chaotic
formlessness and physicality of *her* creativity). In the *Dunciad,* "monster-breeding" is a process that must end in chaos and corporeality, and
it symbolizes the dynamics of the Enthusiastic imagination.

In *Cunicularii,* Hogarth conflated the misshapen conceptions of
monstrous birth with the false conceptions of the imagination, and
Pope does so, too, in the *Dunciad.* Both men could figure the imagination's plunge into shapelessness and corporeality as a kind of teratogenesis because they were drawing from a common tradition that had
conceived of biological and imaginative creation as parallel.

From antiquity, the processes of thought had been identified with
conception and childbirth. The analogy was probably intuited in pre-
literate days, and it found expression in a myriad of ways, from
Socrates' description of himself as the "midwife" of other's thoughts to
Harvey's speculation that, given the resemblance between the structure
and tissue of the womb and those of the brain, man must "conceive"
ideas in a way fundamentally similar to the way in which a woman
conceives a child. The equation of childbirth with the processes of
imaginative creation, not simply with thought in general, is almost as
ancient as the broader analogy. Probably its first, and certainly its most

influential, annunciation was in the *Symposium,* where Plato spoke at length about how a work of art was the "child" of the artist. After the *Symposium,* the metaphor became a trope in Western literature. By the time Pope came to write the *Dunciad,* it had become pretty much a cliché, lending itself to extensive elaboration. Poetic creativity was said to spring from a "pregnant fancy," and the Muse—often a "lab'ring Muse"—was a "fruitful *Mother.*" A poet might have "to lye in of a Poetical Child for at least two Months" before he delivers his "Offspring" to the world. If he is a neophyte poet, his poems are sure to be the "First Children of the imagination," or his "youngest Infant," or perhaps the "early offspring of a VIRGIN-WIT." If his poetic work comes easily, he "bring'st forth sons without a mother's pain." But often his creativity is stifled, and, after "painful labour," the poet, "great with child, and helpless in [his] throes," produces "th' issue of's brain . . . with trouble and pain." And it might all come to nought. He might "labour to be deliver'd of the great burden of nothing," or perhaps bring forth some unfinished thing, an "Embrio of a Play" or some other "Weak, short-lived issues." In such a case, he might want to "disown that Child of his Wit" because such "conceptions . . . are better Stifled in the Birth, or thrown away when they are born, as not worth bringing up." But most likely, he will look on them with paternal fondness, for all men are "no perfecter Judges of their own Writings than Fathers are of their own Children."[24]

Obviously, the analogy was susceptible to an extraordinary range of embellishments. But from the Renaissance through the first half of the eighteenth century, it tended to be extrapolated along the lines of the logic of a single idea, the idea of mimetic representation. The imagination performed the crucial function of representing accurately the truth of nature, reproducing in the mind an object's "true height, or declination, / For understandings cleare intelligence." But the imagination was just as capable of distorting: it "hath her variation," and it can reproduce objects "too foule, or faire; / Not like the life in lineament, or ayre." When the imagination ceased to represent the "appearances of things . . . according to their very truth," said Puttenham, "then doth it breede *Chimeres* & monsters."[25] The proper function of art, too, was to "represent the Worlds true image." When it produced something for which there was "no such thing in Nature," it produced a "Monster which the world ne'er saw"—"Monsters and Births of Mischance" which ought to be "stifled and huddled out of the way, like *Sooterkins.*" "Poets are Limners," wrote another, "And Nature is their Object to be drawn"; but when artists are "void of Art" and turn away from the "just proportions" of nature, they

Gygantick forms and monstrous Births alone
Produce, which Nature shockt disdains to own.[26]

In the *Dunciad,* Pope portrayed monstrosity as the inevitable result of an imagination that turns away from the world to indulge itself in solipsistic pleasures. Cowley, too, thought that men would create "Monsters" once they shut themselves up "in their own private Studies," where they would be unable to "grasp, or lay hold on, or so much as touch Nature, because they catcht only at the shadow of her in their own Brains." "Not guided by sensible Objects," he concluded, "we shall compound where Nature has divided, and divide where Nature has compounded, and create nothing but . . . Deformed Monsters." Swift's Criticism is a monster herself as well as the prolific mother of "a Crew of ugly Monsters" because she is utterly solipsistic, "her Eyes turned inward, as if she lookt only upon herself" and her "Diet . . . the overflowing of her own *Gall.*" Henry Reynolds attacked self-enclosed poetasters who had "scarce suffered themselves to look beyond the dimension of their own braine":

> What can wee expect then of the Poems they write? or what can a man, mee thinks, liken them more fitly to than to *Ixion's* issue? . . . What does he more than imbrace assembled cloudes with *Ixion,* and beget only Monsters?[27]

In *Peri Bathous,* his first full-scale attack on Dulness, Pope used monstrosity in this traditional way to point to the chaos of the solipsistic imagination. A Dunce, scorning to be a "servile copyer after Nature," closes himself in his imagination, and by this *"anti-natural* way of thinking" creates the monstrous: he mingles "bits of the most various, or discordant kinds, landscape, history, portraits, animals," connecting them "with a great deal of flourishing, by Head or Tail, as it shall please his imagination."[28]

But Cibber's fall to "one dead level" is not simply a fall into formlessness, but a fall into corporeality, and here, too, the tradition sanctioned Pope's use of monstrous childbirth as a symbol for the misconceiving imagination. For monstrosity was freighted with Aristotelian notions of generation. Aristotle had argued that the menstrual blood of the female was the "prime matter" from which the child was wrought. Passive and formless, this mass of blood was shaped by a formal cause, an immaterial "principle of movement," the "form," or the "Soul" carried by the male semen. According to Aristotle, monstrosities occurred when, for a variety of reasons, this "soul-principle" failed to fashion the material to its perfect form.[29]

"I have a young conception in my brain: / Be you my time to bring it to some shape."[30] The speaker here is Ulysses in Shakespeare's *Troilus and Cressida,* but the voice behind him is Aristotle's. Like childbirth, mental activity was thought of as a movement from the amorphous to the formed, a working of the mind on inchoate material to "bring it to some shape." "The first materials of unfashion'd thought" remain "Yet dim and undigested," wrote Christoper Pitt,

> till the mind,
> Big with the tender images, expands,
> And, swelling, labours with th' ideal birth.[31]

To reproduce the true image of nature, one had to do more than merely turn one's attention outward. One had to enter into the real "labour" of thinking, shaping the prime matter of the imagination to bring it to "th' ideal birth"—that is, the birth of the idea. The order and proportion of nature was not something perceived, but something conceived. The images of nature that lay in the imagination had to be worked on by the higher faculties of the intellect and wrought to true shape, or else nature remained just brute, material phenomena. Monsters were created, as Montaigne explained, when the labor of thought was avoided and the shapeless imagination was not forced into an idea:

> They are shadows and *Chimeraes,* proceeding from some formlesse conceptions, which they cannot distinguish or resolve within, and by consequence are not able to produce them, in asmuch as they understand not themselves: And if you but marke their earnestnesse, and how they stammer and labour at the point of their deliverie, you would deeme, that what they go withall, is but a conceiving, and therefore nothing neere downelying; and that they doe, too, but licke that imperfect and shapeless lump of matter.[32]

Poetic creativity is the imposition of form by the mind on the shapeless matter of the imagination. First, "Fancy lab'ring for a Birth, / With unfelt Throws brings its rude issue forth"; and then "imperfect shapeless Thought / Is by the Judgment into Fashion wrought." Monstrous poetic birth, then, resulted when the fancy was not shaped into thought. Fielding confessed that his own early works were the "unshaped monsters of a wanton brain" because, though "his fancy pleased, his judgment failed."[33] Monsters were bred when the mind failed to bring to form the "shapeless," corporeal issue of the imagination, leaving fancy stalled in what Dryden called its "first work" ("when it was only a confused mass of thoughts, tumbling over one another in the darkness; when the fancy was yet in its first work, moving the sleeping images of things towards the light, there to be distinguished, and then either chosen or rejected by the judgment").[34] It is fancy in its first work that we see in Dulness's internal "Chaos dark and deep" where "nameless Somethings in their causes sleep," where poetry lies in a "mass," "scarce quick in embryo." And the "Embryo" and "Sooterkins of Wit" Cibber gives birth to are the first work of his fancy, too, for he does not apply the rigors of thought and judgment to his imagination.

To say, as Aristotle said, that monstrosity was caused by the soul's inability to inform prime matter and shape it to its potential end was to say that "the material does not get mastered," that "the 'formal' nature has not gained control over the 'material' nature." Monstrosity, in other words, was the triumph of the corporeal, the body's defeat of the mind. A monster was matter that remained mere matter.[35]

These implications were irresistible to satirists. Monstrous births implied that the jumble of corporeal images in the imagination had not been mastered by the mind (Montaigne's "imperfect and shapeless lump of matter") and that, through the undisciplined imagination, the energies of the passions and of the body had found vent (Dryden mocked MacFlecknoe as a "kilderkin of wit . . . from whose Loyns recorded *Psyche* sprung"; his shapeless "Issue" reveals an imagination utterly sunk in matter).[36] Monstrosity was creation at degree zero, creation as a mindless, entirely physical process.

Pope used monster breeding as a symbolic equivalent to Cibber's descent to "one dead level," then, because traditionally the monstrous figured forth a process of the imagination whose issue was both shapeless and physical. Cibber, like all the Dunces, by turning away from nature and abandoning himself to his solipsistic imagination, enters "Fancy's Maze," and out of the maze of his own fancy he projects an image of the world, but it is a monstrously distorted image, one merely reflecting his own internal disorder. And it is a monstrous image, too, because it is corporeal, and unless it is informed by the intelligence, the imagination can produce only sensual images. The solipsistic imagination does not attend to the continuity and order of nature, and hence images enter the mind as unrelated things which point to nothing higher than their own discrete physicality. Unordered and unconceptualized by the mind, they mass, never raised to ideas, for as we have seen repeatedly, the imagination reduces all things to corporeal images, things bereft of thought, spirit, and meaning. (In a cancelled line, Pope called the products of Duncical minds "Unideal thoughts," that is to say, unideational ideas.)[37] And so, for a Dunce, all experience becomes a flow of images through the mind, chaotic and physical. Thus Cibber "creates," but he creates matter, matter that is never mastered, and therefore matter which remains shapeless. He creates monsters.

V

The reduction of spirit, mind, and meaning to shapeless corporeality is present everywhere in the *Dunciad,* but it is the explicit theme of the lengthiest and most complex scene of perverse and monstrous birth in the poem, the Annius-Mummius episode. The episode begins when Annius, an antiquarian dealing in coins, most of them counterfeit, approaches Dulness and asks that he be granted the power over a group of "ever-listless Loit'rers" to turn them into virtuosi and thus customers for his false coins:

> But Annius, crafty Seer, with ebon wand,
> And well dissembled em'rald on his hand,
> False as his Gems, and canker'd as his Coins,
> Came, cramm'd with capon, from where Pollio dines.
> Soft, as the wily Fox is seen to creep,
> Where bask on sunny banks the simple sheep,
> Walk round and round, now prying here, now there;
> So he; but pious, whisper'd first his pray'r.
> "Grant, gracious Goddess! grant me still to cheat,
> O may thy cloud still cover the deceit!
> Thy choicer mists on this assembly shed,
> But pour them thickest on the noble head.
> So shall each youth, assisted by our eyes,
> See other Cæsars, other Homers rise;
> Thro' twilight ages hunt th' Athenian fowl,
> Which Chalcis Gods, and mortals call an Owl,
> Now see an Attys, now a Cecrops clear,
> Nay, Mahomet! the Pigeon at thine ear;
> Be rich in ancient brass, tho' not in gold,
> And keep his Lares, tho' his house be sold;
> To headlesss Phœbe his fair bride postpone,
> Honour a Syrian Prince above his own;
> Lord of an Otho, if I vouch it true;
> Blest in one Niger, 'till he knows of two."
> Mummius o'erheard him; Mummius, Fool-renown'd,
> Who like his Cheops stinks above the ground,
> Fierce as a startled Adder, swelled, and said,
> Rattling an ancient Sistrum at his head.
> "Speak'st thou of Syrian Princes? Traitor base!
> Mine, Goddess! mine is all the horned race.
> True, he had wit, to make their value rise;
> From foolish Greeks to steal them, was as wise;
> More glorious yet, from barb'rous hands to keep,
> When Sallee Rovers chac'd him on the deep
> Then taught by Hermes, and divinely bold,

> Down his own throat he risq'd the Grecian gold;
> Receiv'd each Demi-God, with pious care,
> Deep in his Entrails—I rever'd them there,
> I bought them, shrouded in that living shrine,
> And, at their second birth, they issue mine."
>   "Witness great Ammon! by whose horns I swore,
> (Reply'd soft Annius) this our paunch before
> Still bears them, faithful; and that thus I eat,
> Is to refund the Medals with the meat.
> To prove me, Goddess! clear of all design,
> Bid me with Pollio sup, as well as dine:
> There all the Learn'd shall at the labour stand,
> And Douglas lend his soft, obstetric hand."
>   (4.347–94)

The logic behind this bizarre fantasia of alimentation, coin collecting, and monstrous male-childbirth can be understood if we place this episode in the context of the earlier poem from which Pope reworked a number of these lines, "To Mr. Addison, Occasioned by his Dialogues on Medals." In "To Mr. Addison," Pope also attacked the folly of coin-collecting virtuosi:

> To gain Pescennius one employs his schemes,
> One grasps a Cecrops in ecstatic dreams;
> Poor Vadius, long with learned spleen devour'd,
> Can taste no pleasure since his Shield was scoured;
> And Curio, restless by his Fair-one's side,
> Sighs for an Otho, and neglects his bride.

The triviality of this pursuit by the virtuosi is contrasted to the more cultivated use of coins by Addison:

> Theirs is the Vanity, the Learning thine:
> Touch'd by thy hand, again Rome's glories shine,
> Her Gods, and god-like Heroes rise to view,
> And all her faded garlands bloom a-new.[38]

Pope draws his distinction between the virtuosi and Addison from Addison's own defense of numismatics in his *Dialogues Upon the Usefulness of Ancient Medals,* the occasion of Pope's poem. Addison had argued that the coins "give a very great light to history, in confirming such passages as are true in the old authors, in settling such as are told after different manners, and in recording such as have been omitted. In this case a cabinet of medals is a body of history." Coins—or medals, for "formerly there was no difference between money and medals"— are "abridgments of history": "What a majesty and force does one meet in these short inscriptions! Are you not amazed to see so much history gathered into so small a compass, you have often the subject of a volume in a couple of words."[39]

For Pope, like Addison, the true value of medals lay in the fact that they were "abridgments of history." In its "narrow orb," a medal condensed the triumphs and glories of the ancient world and transmitted them through time ("The Medal, faithful to its charge of fame, / Thro' climes and ages bears each form and name"). A medal was more than a curiosity from a dead culture: it was a potential progenitor in the present of the values of the past it preserved on its face. To someone who could read them right, someone like Addison, medals were things to "Stand emulous" before. He would reanimate the values embossed on the coins as "living medals," make the values of the past reborn in the present so that "all her faded garlands bloom a-new."[40]

In the Annius-Mummius episode, coins are both money and medals, and how they are perceived tells us about the perceiver. For Annius, who makes his living selling them, they are (a bit too literally, it turns out) filthy lucre, and for the Duncical virtuosi who collect them, becoming "rich in brass, tho' not in gold," they are something even less useful, meaningless objects in the mindless business of antiquarianism. But for Pope, they are medals which purvey ethical values, and he continually contrasts the true worth of the medals—their celebration of family, love, and devotion to country—to the physical objects the Dunces have reduced them to:

> And keep his Lares, tho' his house be sold;
> To headless Phœbe his fair bride postpone,
> Honour a Syrian Prince above his own.

Mummius "like his Cheops stinks above the ground": here is another image of something which should be preserved through time becoming an object of physical corruption. It is an image of death-in-life, just as Annius's "canker'd" coins are, and it points to the fact that the Dunces leech from medals all intellectual, moral, and spiritual values and thus destroy their potential for conveying meanings which can be reanimated to "bloom a-new" in the present. They fail to stir their culture to life and preserve the hereditary line of value from the past by making it be born again in the present. Here, as everywhere in the poem, the Dunces reduce everything to the "one dead level" of corporeality. They transmogrify medals into coins whose meaning is stillborn in mindless physicality. Hence, in the most stunning metaphorical transformation in this episode, defecation is collapsed with childbirth, the child becomes waste, possible renewal mere destruction.

Childbirth here, as throughout the poem, is a symbol of the fancy, and, in this episode, the process that has turned medals to money is the corporealizing imagination and its capacity to reduce all to mere matter. This is why Annius is presented as a type of artist, a "Seer, with ebon wand" (he even has his own "Pollio" as patron). His power is an artistic one. Like all artists, he deals in deception, magically raising imaginary scenes that enrapture his audience:

> "So shall each youth, assisted by our eyes,
> See other Cæsars, other Homers rise;
> Thro' twilight ages hunt th' Athenian fowl,
> Which Chalcis Gods, and mortals call an Owl,
> Now see an Attys, now a Cecrops clear,
> Nay, Mahomet! the Pigeon at thine ear; . . ."

Coin-minting was a traditional metaphor for the creative, shaping power of the artist, and Pope probably had this in mind throughout the episode.[41] Certainly when Annius promises to "refund the Medals," he is not simply promising to give them back, but to "re-found" them, that is, creatively reshape them, downward of course, following the course the corporealizing imagination always takes, downward to body.[42]

Annius's audience is particularly receptive to this seduction by the imagination. In the allegory of the episode, Annius begs of Dulness power over *"Indolent Persons abandoning all business and duty, and dying with laziness . . . intreating her to make them Virtuosos, and assign them over to him"*:

> a lazy, lolling sort,
> Unseen at Church, at Senate, or at Court,
> Of ever-listless Loit'rers, that attend
> No cause, no Trust, no Duty, and no Friend.
> Thee too, my Paridel! she mark'd thee there,
> Stretch'd on the rack of a too easy chair,
> And heard thy everlasting yawn confess
> The Pains and Penalties of Idleness.
> (4."Argument" and ll. 337–44)

The lineage of these "ever-listless Loit'rers" can be traced all the way back to Pope in 1712, when he himself experienced the "Pains and Penalties of Idleness," seduced into "Indolence & Inactivity" by his imagination, which created a fanciful world where he lost all "lively Sense of things" and abandoned friendship and his own better self for the pleasures of "Imaginary Entertainments," attending "No cause, no Trust, no Duty, and no Friend" because idle dreaming has replaced actively engaging himself in the real world, "labouring" for the social good.

It is because the source of the danger is the idleness of the imagination, I think, that Pope names his chief idler after Spenser's Paridell.
In *The Faerie Queene,* Paridell and Britomart meet at Malbeccon's castle and tell each other of their lineage. Paridell, as his name suggests,
is descended from Paris, and even while he tells the tragic story of the
fall of Troy, he seduces his host's wife, Hellenore, "This second *Hel-
lene,*" and steals her away from her husband. Paridell sees the past, but
it has no meaning for him; rather than "reuiue the sleeping memorie"
of the values of the ancient world and thus make its glory live in the
present, he recapitulates its nightmare.[43] The idle virtuosi in the
Annius-Mummius episode repeat the same failure: they do not reanimate the values signified on the medals; rather, they substitute the
mere images of home, love, and duty for the real things, selling their
estates to possess a pictured Lares, forsaking a bride for a headless
Phoebe, honoring a Syrian prince but never appearing "at Church, at
Senate, or at Court." Just as Paridell's failure causes him to repeat the
tragedy of the past, so the failure of these virtuosi, the poem suggests,
is causing in Britain the same collapse that overtook Rome and
Greece. And the fact that this failure is figured as perverse childbirth,
as a failure to preserve the hereditary line of the past by bringing it to
birth in the present, shows how deeply Pope felt that the imagination
was the source of the cultural collapse not only of this episode but of
the whole of the *Dunciad.* For this episode—indeed, the whole of the
Dunciad—plays out the fear Pope articulated in 1712 that the idleness
of the imagination "undermines the Foundation of every Virtue," and
it plays it out in the very same image of childbirth that Pope had used
to articulate his anxiety:

> To-Morrow is still the fatal Time when all is to be rectified: To-Morrow
> comes, it goes, and still I please my self with the Shadow, whilst I lose the
> Reality; unmindful that the present Time alone is ours, the future is yet
> unborn, and the past is dead, and can only live (as Parents in their Children)
> in the Actions it has produced.[44]

Since the corporealizing imagination could "refund" the world,
recasting it as a merely physical object no longer containing the spiritual values it once embodied, Pope ends this episode in parody. When he
has Mummius "revere" the coins lying in Annius's stomach, he is doing
more than literalizing the man's worship of wealth. The entire birth
sequence, from the intervention of the god Hermes, to Annius's receiving "each Demi-God . . . / Deep in his Entrails," to Mummius's vener-
ating them "shrouded in that living shrine," to the anticipation of their
"second birth" before a group of learned men, is a parody of the

Annunciation, Conception, and Visitation of the Virgin Mary and of the birth of Christ. And Duncical creation is a parody of divine creation and the Incarnation: instead of infusing the earthly with the spirit, the Dunces siphon off the divine, leaving a dead physical mass.[45] This is why it is Douglas who is there to lend his "soft, obstetric hand." It is not simply because Annius's, too, is a monstrous birth, one performed, like Mary Toft's, by deception. Mary Toft's births were from the beginning connected with the corporealizing imagination. In Hogarth's *Cunicularii,* Mary Toft's monstrous birth was also a parody of the birth of Christ because it represented the imagination's ability to reduce spirit to body: it was the "filthy miracle" of the corporealizing imagination, the filthy miracle that parodies the true miracle of the union of body and spirit in Christ. Indeed, as we have seen, in the anti-Enthusiastic tradition, the imagination always ends in a grossly physical parody of the spiritual—just as the *Dunciad,* everywhere, is a parody, mostly through *Paradise Lost,* of the divine creation of the world and the Word's becoming Flesh.

VI

The central action of the *Dunciad* is the transformation of everything downward to "one dead level." The goddess Dulness is the agent of this transformation, and in this she is cast in precisely the same role as Mary Toft. Both Dulness and Mary Toft are feminine forces who possess the terrifying power to subvert language, civilization, and the very structures of thought. Presiding over a process of corporealization, they dissolve distinctions, blur boundaries, and precipitate the mind into a giddy whirl of a confusion that descends into chaos and the body and ends in parody. Their power of destruction is located, paradoxically, in their monstrous creativity.

If I am right that it was the anxieties about the imagination that provoked the responses to the Mary Toft incident, and if, as I have argued, it was the imagination Pope was writing about when he wrote about the power of dullness in the *Dunciad,* these parallels should not be at all surprising. When Pope came to write his poem, he naturally turned to the figure of a monster-breeding mother because monstrosity was the traditional metaphor for the dangers of the imagination and was the most remarkable instance of the perversity and power of the human fancy. Pope's misgivings about the imagination were by and large those of his culture, and so his portrayal of the goddess Dulness came, in this round about way, to echo the responses to the Mary Toft episode.

If all of this is true, the Mary Toft incident may illuminate the *Dun-*

ciad in one more way. I have said that the anxiety at the heart of the Mary Toft episode was an anxiety about the imagination's power to dissolve the identity of the self, a fear that expressed itself in images of impotence and assimilation. These two images are, of course, central to the *Dunciad,* and I think they, too, express Pope's fear that personal identity can be destroyed by the imagination.

Impotence permeates the *Dunciad,* from the first line of the first version, where "Books and the Man" is ironically linked to Virgil's "Arma virumque" (we find out later that the troops of Dulness carry only "blunted Arms" [4.25]) to the yawn that concludes the poem. The power of Dulness is defined as a passive power, a "Force inertly strong" (4.7). Dulness will bring a revolution. She will "rock the throne" (1.312). But the pun reveals that her power will be established not by aggression but by pacification, by a kind of disarmament that will allow the goddess to "suckle Armies, and dry-nurse the land" (1.316).

When Pope changed "Books and the Man" of the original version to "The Mighty Mother, and her Son," he was emphasizing that "the *Mother,* and not the *Son,* is the principal Agent of this Poem" (1.1n), and throughout the poem, all the Dunces are reduced to powerless children, passive objects moved by a stronger agent. The Dunces' quiescence before the power of Dulness is emblematic of their relation to their own imaginations. In fact, this impotence is implied in the symbol of monstrous birth. The satiric use of birth as a symbol for artistic creativity (even normal, let alone monstrous birth) inevitably stressed passivity. Poetry was something that happened to the poet. Like a pregnant woman, a poet was caught up in a process that was undergone, a process beyond the control of reason, intention, or consciousness.[46] Monstrous childbirth underscored this impotence even more. Since monstrosities were produced by the imagination, and since the imagination was subject to the control of the higher faculties, monstrous birth signaled a yielding to the power of fancy, an abdication of one's responsibility to think, to exercise judgment, and to practice some self-control. Monsters were produced by choosing to acquiesce to the working of the imagination.[47] "A Poet is not to leave his reason," Rhymer warned, "and blindly abandon himself to follow fancy: for then his fancy might be monstrous . . . ; but reason is to be his guide, reason is common to all people, and can never carry him from what is Natural."[48] Cibber produces his monstrous "Sooterkins of Wit" because, writing in the same way he throws dice, he has chosen to "blindly abandon himself to follow fancy."

"I have been lying in wait for my own imagination this week or more," Pope wrote to a friend, "and watching what thoughts of mine came up in that whirl of fancy that were worth communicating." For Pope, the true use of the imagination did not lie in passively yielding to its pressures. Pope is "lying in wait" to pass judgment on what the "whirl of fancy" produced. True genius must be active, make discriminations, exercise the full faculties of the mind to discover what "worth" there is in the chaotic whirl. When Pope praised Homer's imagination, it was specifically "Invention" that he singled out as the quality that made him a great poet: that active search through the field of impressions tossed up by the imagination to find what was "worth communicating." When we see Cibber, "Sinking from thought to thought," it is specifically *his* attempt at "Invention" we witness. But, unlike Pope or Homer, Cibber is passive: he forsakes all guidance of a directing intelligence and allows himself to be driven by the chaotic energies of the imagination. He is "the Instrument" of Dulness (1."Argument"). His giddy floundering and plunging is an oxymoron of movement, really, exertion within passivity. His only true action is his initial decision to remain impotent by delivering himself over to "Fancy's easy wing"—"easy" because such willed impotence rids him of all the pain of consciousness, judgment, and intellect.

As it happens, Pope himself had experienced something of Cibber's sinking into the chaos of the imagination, and he knew firsthand the monstrous consequences of this, the terminal stage in the etiology of the Enthusiastic imagination:

> I have been lying in wait for my own imagination this week and more, and watching what thoughts of mine came up in the whirl of fancy that were worth communicating to you in a letter. But I am at length convinced that my rambling head can produce nothing of that sort; . . .
>
> You can't wonder my thoughts are scarce consistent, when I tell you how they are distracted! Every hour of my life, my mind is strangely divided. This minute, perhaps, I am above the stars, with a thousand systems round about me, looking forward into the vast abyss of eternity, and losing my whole comprehension in the boundless spaces of the extended Creation, in dialogues with Whiston and the astronomers; the next moment I am below all trifles, even grovelling with Tidcombe in the very center of nonsense: now am I recreating my mind with the brisk sallies and quick turns of wit, which Mr. Steele in his liveliest and freest humours darts about him; and now levelling my application to the insignificant observations and quirks of grammar of Mr. Cromwell and Dennis.
>
> Good God! what an Incongrous Animal is Man? how unsettled in his best part, his soul; and how changing and variable in his frame of body? The constancy of the one, shook by every notion, the temperament of the other, affected by every blast of wind. What an April weather in the mind! In a word, what is Man altogether, but one mighty inconsistency.[49]

Pope conceives of his experience of his own imagination here within his customary framework of hunting, rambling, and the maze. He begins by "lying in wait," like a watchful hunter, the metaphor suggests, and then he begins "rambling," and finally he falls into a giddy maze of confusion. Initially, he experiences the imagination as an autonomous force, independent of the self, the "I" sitting in judgment over the fancy as if it were an alien and external power. But gradually the self becomes impotent before the fancy. And then the self is absorbed into the imagination, and the "I" becomes the "whirl of fancy" it once contemplated (thus Pope moves from a position where there is a clear distinction between the "I" and the imagination to a position where the two are identified, the self incorporated into the non-self: "lying in wait for my own imagination . . . watching what thoughts of mine came up in the whirl of fancy . . . my thoughts are scarce consistent . . . they are distracted . . . I am above the stars"). Assimilated into the giddy whirl of the imagination, the self is tossed willy-nilly in its chaotic energies, now "above the stars," now "below all trifles," like Satan in his progress through Chaos—or like Cibber in his precipitate plunge through his own mind.

To be assimilated into the imagination is to become a "mighty inconsistency" and thus to lose a definable human identity. Abandoning themselves to the imagination, the Dunces become monsters ("Bards, like Proteus long in vain ty'd down, / Escape in Monsters, and amaze the town"). They become as protean as the giddy whirl of the imagination they are swallowed up in. A Dunce is "This Mess," this "growing lump" (1.222, 102). Appearing in "a thousand shapes" (1.42n), every Dunce loses his identity and disintegrates into a "nameless name" (3.157).

Cibber, as the most monstrous of the Dunces, shifts shapes more than any of the others. He is something of everything: a poetaster, dramatist, actor, stage-manager, apologist for his life. As hero of the poem, he is pointedly contrasted to that other shape-shifting, protean hero of the *Dunciad,* Swift:

> O Thou! whatever title please thine ear,
> Dean, Drapier, Bickerstaff, or Gulliver!
> Whether thou chuse Cervantes' serious air
> Or laugh and shake in Rab'lais' easy Chair, . . .
>
> (1.19–22)

The difference between a Swift and a Cibber lies in one word, "chuse." Swift chose to assume a number of roles and titles, shrewdly shaping his own life and art in response to the shifting demands of a complex world. Behind his protean surface lies a controlling personality and intelligence. But Cibber's proliferation of roles indicates not a complexity of character, but a dispersion of identity. He and all the Dunces abrogate their wills from the beginning, refusing to "chuse" anything, abandoning themselves to the chance movements of their fancies.

Impotent before their own imaginations, they become assimilated into its unruly energies, they *become* its unruly energies. And since the solipsistic imagination is merely a field of physical sensations, the only self a Dunce retains is the corporeal residue left when the mind abandons itself to the body. The pervasive sinking to "one dead level" in the *Dunciad* is the reduction of the human intellect to lower, always more corporeal orders of existence. The minds of the Dunces obey the primitive, impersonal rhythms of physical nature: digestion ("here he sipp'd . . . / and suck'd all o'er, like an industrious Bug" [1.129–30]), spontaneous generation (their works come to life on "a warm Third day" [1.57]), vegetative growth (the opinions of the Dunces are apt to change "at different seasons" ["Testimonies of Authors," p. 23]), meteorological phenomena (their works are bred "from some bog below, / Mount in dark volumes, and descend in snow" [2.363–64]), the mechanics of matter in motion (a Dunce's head is a weighted "bowl" that we see "Obliquely wadling to some mark in view" [1.170–72]). What passes for thought among the Dunces is some effort vaguely situated between physics and flatulence:

> As, forc'd from wind-guns, lead itself can fly
> And pond'rous slugs cut swiftly thro the sky;
> As clocks to weight their nimble motions owe,
> The wheels above urg'd by the load below.
>
> (1.181–84)

A Dunce is "a bulk" with "A brain of feathers, and a heart of lead," a thing which, appropriately enough, can "find / Congenial matter in the Cockle-kind" (2.39, 44; 4.447–48). They are "Dry Bodies" (1.152). Settle is known not by his character, but by "his broad shoulders . . . and length of ears" (3.36). At the end of the poem, we can find their names listed in the "Index of THINGS (including AUTHORS)." Like passive matter, the Dunces act only in the sense that they obey the laws of falling bodies:

> The young, the old, who feel her inward sway,
> One instinct seizes, and transports away.
> None needs a guide, by sure Attraction led,
> And strong impulsive gravity of Head:
> None want a place, for all their Centre found,
> Hung to the Goddess, and coher'd around.

> Not closer, orb in orb, conglob'd are seen
> The buzzing Bees about their dusky Queen.
>   The gathering number, as it moves along,
> Involves a vast involuntary throng,
> Who gently drawn, and struggling less and less,
> Roll in her Vortex, and her pow'r confess.
>   (4.73–84)

From his own experience, Pope knew that the "I," gazing on the giddy whirl of the fancy, could be engulfed in its energy and hence transmuted into an impersonal, alien, and shapeless "it." This is what he dramatizes in the *Dunciad*. Allowing themselves to sink into the corporeal imagination, the Dunces are reassimilated into the rhythms of the material world which constitutes the imagination, absorbed into the matrix of the imagination which gave them birth. They become anonymous bodies.

Assimilated into the impersonal physical forces of their imaginations, the Dunces lose all lineaments of individual identity and come to resemble one another. They sink to "*one* dead level." (Pope's greatest insult to Cibber was not making him the hero of the 1743 *Dunciad,* but making him the hero and scarcely changing the 1727 text, as if he and Tibbald were so indistinguishable as to be interchangeable.) "Three College Sophs, and three pert Templars came, / The same their talents, and their tastes the same" (2.379–80). "Behold yon pair, in strict embraces joined; / How like in manners, and how like in mind!" (3.179–80). "Contending Theatres our empire raise, / Alike their labours, and alike their praise" (3.271–72). "Christians, Jews, one heavy sabbath keep, / And all the western world believe and sleep" (3.99–100). By the end, personal identity has melted down to homogeneity. The Dunces increasingly move through the poem in nameless "crowds on crowds" until, "all tun'd equal," they "send a gen'ral hum" and join in a "long solemn Unison" (4.135, 2.386, 4.612). Personal identity simply disappears as Dunce merges with Dunce. "Another Durfey, Ward! shall sing in thee" (3.146).

The anxiety that the imagination would dissolve the boundaries of identity was expressed in the Mary Toft incident under the image of Mary Toft's swallowing men and transforming them into herself. Dulness, like Mary Toft, assimilates the Dunces and destroys their identities by transforming them into monster-breeders like herself. This is the threat announced at the very beginning of the poem, in the epigraph, "Tandem Phœbus adest, morsusque inferre parantem / Congelat, et patulos, ut erant INDURAT hiatus." And this is the threat fulfilled at the end when the yawn of Dulness "Wide, and more wide . . .

spread o'er all the realm" (4.613), encompassing all the Dunces and all creation.

This final loss of identity by assimilation into the forces of the undisciplined imagination is played out in the poem in the symbol of childbirth, and particularly in the poem's concern with dynastic lines. The *Dunciad* is a succession poem. Cibber assumes the kingship on the death of Eusden and thus insures that "Dunce the second reigns like Dunce the first" by "sure succession" (1.6, 98). But the *Dunciad* is also a restoration poem which chronicles the reestablishment of Dulness's "old Empire" (1.17). Succession poems and restoration poems, of course, are mutually contradictory, but they can be conflated so easily in the *Dunciad* because of the peculiar metamorphoses monstrous birth plays on individual identity and dynastic lines. The poem opens with Dulness "revolving the long succession of her Sons (1."Argument"); and "revolving" suggests that Dulness gives birth to a line of offspring only to revolve them back into herself. When Cibber succeeds to the throne, he is really restoring Dulness, for Cibber no longer exists. As her monstrous offspring, his self has been so utterly extirpated that he has become nothing but an empty container of the image of Dulness:

> She saw, with joy, the line immortal run,
> Each sire imprest and glaring in his son:
> So watchful Bruin forms, with plastic care,
> Each growing lump, and brings it to a Bear.
> She saw old Pryn in restless Daniel shine,
> And Eusden eke out Blackmore's endless line;
> She saw slow Philips creep like Tate's poor page,
> And all the mighty Mad in Dennis rage.
>   In each she marks her Image full exprest,
> But chief in BAYS'S monster-breeding breast.
>   (1.99–108)

Lineage, succession, and birth signal the extinction of identity here. The Dunces are born as featureless repetitions of others' works ("And Eusden eke out Blackmore's endless line") or blank slugs on which are stamped the identities of their forebearers ("Each sire imprest and glaring in his son"). And all of them, fathers, sons, and works, revolve back into the mother. For "She marks her Image": meaning not simply that she sees herself in her children but that she sees herself in them because she "marks" them with her image in the way that a mother, like Mary Toft, disfigures her offspring in the course of monstrous birth by impressing on them the forms of her imagination. Lineage, instead of being a succession of individual identities, becomes a chain of tautological genesis, the production of a line of repeatable, indistinguishable objects, the endless replication in matter of the mother's imagination.

And so succession is restoration. When Cibber mounts the throne by climbing onto the lap of Dulness, his succession brings on her restoration. For Cibber is no more. Since Dulness is "full exprest" in him, he has no identity: he has become the very image of his mother, assimilated back into the matrix that bore him. He is a true monstrous birth, a product of the imagination.[50]

7

WHAT THE BODY SAYS

All men, Plato said in the *Symposium,* long for immortality, and most fulfill their longing by begetting children. Some, however, long more intensely, more spiritually, desirous of "the progeny which it is the nature of the soul to create and bring to birth." These men are artists, and their longing can be fulfilled only by creating works of art, which "surpass human children by being immortal."

Plato's notion quickly became a trope in Western literature, and writers routinely spoke of poems as "children whose qualities have won immortal fame and glory for their parents." Poets begot immortal poetry, and this poetry bestowed immortality on their begetters: "Time on their off-spring hath no power, / Nor fire, nor fate their Bays shall blast." In the *Dunciad,* of course, time *can* blast the Dunces, and fire's effect on the Dunces' "children" is, alas, more Aristotelian than Platonic:

> Adieu my children! better thus expire
> Un-stall'd, unsold; thus glorious mount in fire
> Fair without spot; than greas'd by grocer's hands,
> Or shipp'd with Ward to ape and monkey lands, . . .
> (A.1.197–200)[1]

When his children "glorious mount in fire," they do not enter Eternity, purged of mortal dross. They are reduced to ash, and whatever claim Tibbald had on immortality goes up in smoke.

Throughout the *Dunciad,* Pope uses teratological birth to invert the Platonic trope. The Dunces beget "momentary monsters" (1.83). Their art is not immortal but as short-lived as monsters notoriously were, "sure to die as soon as born" (A.3.175n). There is no immortality for a Dunce; when his works disappear, they take him into oblivion with them, a "nameless name."

But in their monstrousness, the Dunces, like Gulliver, suffer another mortification, perhaps one as painful as death. According to the Platonic trope, the work of art immortalizes its creator by figuring forth
his identity. A poem is a "Child" wherein "you can trace, / Throughout, the Sire's transmitted face." "Look how the father's face / Lives in
his issue," Ben Jonson wrote in his elegy on Shakespeare:

> even so, the race
> Of Shakespeare's mind and manners brightly shines
> In his well turnèd, and true filèd lines.[2]

And so in the *Dunciad,* although the works of the Dunces are only
"momentary monsters," during their brief lives they do incarnate the
identities of their progenitors—but mortifyingly, shamefully. Each
monstrous "Sooterkin of Wit" *is* an accurate embodiment of its
author's identity, the very image of his moral and psychological monstrosity ("Look, and find / Each Monster meets his likeness in thy
mind" [3.251–52]). But since this identity, having been delivered over
to the incoherent energies of the imagination, is no longer an identity, a
Dunce has, like his "nameless name," a kind of identityless identity.
And this paradoxical turn also is captured in the figure of teratological
birth, where the mother "marks her Image full exprest" in her progeny: such monstrosity signals that the identity of the self has been assim-
iliated into the imagination and has been transformed into an unnameable amorphousness.[3]

This capacity of the imagination to make the self monstrous and
then disperse identity was not its only capacity, nor did this power necessarily lessen the value of the imagination—if the imagination was
used properly. As we have seen, Pope himself drew complex distinctions between what I have called the Homeric and the Enthusiastic
imaginations, and in the *Dunciad* he asserts the value of the Homeric
imagination continually. For with every abuse of the imagination by
the Dunces, we are reminded, by virtue of the poem's allusiveness, of
Homer, Virgil, Milton, and scores of other poets who have used the
imagination to create something of value and who have begotten
immortal works which have incarnated their identities with credit and
honor.

And yet, in spite of his many explicit commendations of the the
imagination, and in spite of his tacit defense of the imagination in the
very allusiveness of the *Dunciad,* a surprising thing happened in the
course of Pope's life-work. After writing the *Dunciad,* Pope reevaluat-
ed his career, in large part because he was concerned with the way his
personal identity was to be formulated in his poetry. As a result, he redi-

rected his poetic energies and began reshaping his identity—not, as we might expect, by dedicating himself to the Homeric imagination but expressly by rejecting the imagination as a central force in his poetry.

I want to examine now how the writing of the first *Dunciad* provoked Pope to reformulate his career. This change, I shall argue, was shaped by the complex interplay of Pope's notions of identity, monstrosity, and the imagination.

I

In October 1725, Pope sent Swift "a very good conclusion of one of my Satyrs." The passage he sent Swift attacked Ambrose Philips and was later worked into the *Dunciad*. Swift replied by expressing his own attitude to the kinds of fools Pope was attacking: "Drown the World, I am not content with despising it, but I would anger it if I could with safety. I wish there were an Hospital built for it's despisers, where one might act with safety and it need not be a large Building, only I would have it well endowed. . . . I am no more angry with ——— Then I was with the Kite that last week flew away with one of my Chickins and yet I was pleas'd when one of my Servants Shot him two days after." He concluded with the witty observation: "Take care the bad poets do not outwit you, as they have served the good ones in every Age, whom they have provoked to transmit their Names to posterity[.] Maevius is as well known as Virgil, and Gildon will be as well known as you if his name gets into your Verses."[4]

A few weeks later, Pope wrote back to Swift:

> But I am much the happier for finding (a better thing than our *Witts*) our *Judgments* jump, in the notion of entirely passing all Scriblers by in silence: To vindicate ones self against such nasty Slanders, is as much wise, as it was in your Countryman when people said he was besh— to show the contrary by showing his A— so let Gildon and Philips rest in peace. What Virgil had to do with Mævius, that he shou'd wear him upon his Sleeve to all eternity, I don't know? but I think a bright author should put an end to the Slanders only as the Sun does to Stinks; by shining out, exhale 'em to nothing. . . .
>
> I wish as warmly as you, for the Hospital to lodge the *Despisers of the world* in, only I fear it would be fill'd wholly like Chelsea with Maim'd Soldiers, and such as had been dis-abled in *its* Service. And I wou'd rather have those that out of such generous principles as you and I, despise it, Fly in its face, than Retire from it. Not that I have much Anger against the Great, my Spleen is at the little rogues of it: It would vexe one more to be knockt o' the Head by a Pisspot, than by a Thunderbolt. As to the great Oppressors (as you say) they are like Kites or Eagles, one expects mischief from them: But to be Squirted to death (as poor Wycherley said to me on his deathbed) by *Potecaries Prentices,* by the under Strappers of Under Secretaries, to Secre-

taries, who were no Secretaries—this would provoke as dull a dog as Ph—
—s himself.

But I beg your pardon, I'm tame agen, at your advice. I was but like the
Madman, who on a sudden clapt his hand to his Sword of Lath, and cry'd,
Death to all my Enemies! when another came behind him and stopt his
wrath, by saying, *Hold! I can tell you a way worth twenty on't: Let your Enemies alone, and they will dye of themselves.*[5]

I have quoted this letter at length because it is Pope's most dramatic
revelation of the anxiety and doubt he had about writing the *Dunciad.*
So anxious was he, in fact, that he erroneously thought Swift had suggested he abandon the poem—which Pope eagerly agreed to, "at your
advice"—misunderstanding completely the tenor of Swift's letter and
overlooking the fact that Swift was encouraging the writing of the
poem ("I hope in a few months to see it all," Swift had written).[6]

Pope was deeply troubled by the very conception of the *Dunciad.*
And the rhythms of his anger and contempt, his restless circling of the
problem of trying to find a way of dealing with the Dunces, suggest
that his perplexity was caused by the very lowness and impotence of
those he wanted to attack: "Not that I have much Anger against the
Great, my Spleen is at the little rogues." Because the Dunces are so low
and seem so impotent—they can only irritate by tossing a "Pisspot,"
not do real damage by hurling a "Thunderbolt"—Pope ends in a
quandary. Emotionally, he is strung between rage and disdain, and he
vacillates from the one to the other. Angered at their "nasty Slanders,"
he desires to "Fly in [the world's] face" for harboring the Dunces, to
cry *"Death to all my Enemies!"* But to feel such anger is to be like a
"Madman." For he cannot help but be contemptuous of the "little
rogues." Their dullness is self-defeating, their stupidity makes them
powerless and harmless. They are little nothings, "the under Strappers
of Under Secretaries, to Secretaries, who were no Secretaries," whom
he can, "by shining out, exhale . . . to nothing." *"They will dye of themselves."* But if they will die of themselves, if they are truly as contemptible as he says, why attack them? Baffled by the contradiction
between his anger and his contempt, Pope involves himself in deeper
perplexity. If the Dunces truly are trivial and harmless, he cannot be
outraged by them, only amused, and if he responds to them with anything more than contemptuous amusement, his motives and integrity
can be called into question.[7]

In other letters from the years surround the writing and publication
of the *Dunciad,* we witness Pope issuing disclaimers, expressing
doubts, even showing some embarrassment as he tries to articulate a
consistent and acceptable attitude toward the Dunces. He writes to

Swift in a pose of unconcern that the Dunces have no significance, that *he* certainly is not concerned about them: "As for those Scribblers for whom you apprehend I would suppress my *Dulness*, . . . how much that nest of Hornets are my regard, will easily appear to you when you read the Treatise of the Bathos." The *Dunciad,* he says loftily, "will rid me of those insects." In a later letter to Swift, he deprecates not only the Dunces but any work that takes cognizance of them: "Would to God we were together the rest of our lives! The whole weight of the Scriblers would just serve to find us amusement, and not more. I hope you are too well employed to mind them." In 1731, he told Aaron Hill that he would never write anything like the *Dunciad* again, and his snooty tone suggests that he felt he had done something quite beneath himself: "Be assur'd, no little Offenders ever shall be distinguish'd more by me."[8]

Such a pose was difficult to maintain. To see the Dunces as trifling souls scarcely worth consideration was tantamount to admitting that the *Dunciad* was motivated more by personal spite than by a feeling for the public good. When Pope persuaded Burlington to act as publisher of the poem, he pointed out that by putting his name to the piece Burlington would be "in some degree Author & Proprietor of my Follies, or (which perhaps is worse) Partaker & Promoter of my Resentments."[9] The humor here is not entirely comfortable, and it suggests that Pope had the uneasy suspicion that he had transgressed some moral limit, that his personal spite had gotten the better of his judgment, that he had betrayed himself into "showing his A——," as he had said to Swift, "when people said he was besh——." A sense of culpability and a concern for his reputation would certainly explain Pope's efforts to persuade his friends to contribute to the poem's prose apparatus and to share credit publicly for the work. And these feelings would also account for the remarkable statement to Sheridan in which he placed as much distance between himself and the poem as possible by claiming that "my Friend the Dean . . . is properly the Author of the Dunciad: It had never been writ but at his Request, and for his Deafness: For had he been able to converse with me, do you think I had amus'd my Time so ill?"[10]

At other times, unwilling to trivialize the *Dunciad* or to half-acknowledge the morally suspect motivations that may have prompted it, Pope defended his writing of the poem:

> That strict neutrality as to publick parties, which I have constantly observ'd in all my writings, I think gives me the more title to attack such fools, that slander and belye my character in private, to those who know me not. Yet even this liberty I will never take, unless at the same time they are Pests of

private society, or mischievous members of the publick, that is to say, unless
they are enemies to all men as well as to me.

But this unequivocal statement was made well over five years after the
publication of the *Dunciad,* from a perspective that had quieted the
doubt and had obscured, perhaps, the complex origins of the poem.
While he was writing and arranging for the publication of the poem,
his views were much less settled and he was much less self-assured.
Thus, when he defends himself to Caryll by charging that there *is*
something dangerous about the Dunces, that the poem *is* concerned
with the public welfare, he cannot do it straightforwardly: instead, we
find a tangle of disclaimer, doubt, moral perplexity, a more serious purpose hinted at, but obscurely, even questioningly:

> You will laugh sometimes when you read the notes to the *Dunciad,* and
> sometimes you will despise too heartily to laugh (there is such an edifying
> mixture of roguery in the authors satirised there). The poem itself will bear
> a second reading, or (to express myself more justly and modestly) will be
> better borne at the second than first reading, and that's all I shall say of it.
> My friends who took so much pains to comment on it, must come off with
> the public as they can. All I wish to have your opinion of in relation to their
> part, is as to the morality and justifiable design in the undertaking, for of
> what is honest and honorable no man is a better judge.[11]

Most of the notes, of course, were by Pope himself.

The letters that span the writing and publication of the *Dunciad* are
a record of Pope's genuine uneasiness. He knew that the *Dunciad*
sprang in part from motives that would not bear moral scrutiny, and he
knew that much of the poem's sheer destructive energy could not be
explained away by his assertions that he had a purely moral end in
view when he wrote. And knowing these things, at times he simply
had to own up to the consequences of writing the *Dunciad.* In 1729,
when he sent the Earl of Burlington a copy of the *Dunciad Variorum,* its
frontispiece picturing an ass with its pannier loaded with the works of
the Dunces, Pope concluded his letter with this postscript: "I beg my
Lady Burlington's Patronage of the Ass & the Dunciad, me and my
burden."[12]

I do not want to overemphasize the degree of anxiety that Pope had
about the *Dunciad.* He did, after all, publish the poem, he continued to
republish it throughout his life, and his final four-book version is in
many ways the culmination of his poetic career. Still, it would not do to
dismiss his misgivings. The monstrous births in the *Dunciad* point to
Pope's own conviction that a poet's identity was incarnated in his art,
that his character was mirrored in it just as a father's image is mirrored

in his child. Even when he joked about it—such as when he visited Oxford and described the pleasure of "seeing myself seated with dignity on the most conspicuous Shelves of a Library" and remarked that it was "the only place where I make a good figure"—the humor is a bit rueful, and one can hear behind it a warmth of feeling that springs from a regard for how art could embody the ideal identity of the artist. Authors left traces of their "own images in their writings," and thus their works were their "best monuments"—meaning not simply that their works preserved a name but, as on eighteenth-century tombs, they preserved an image of the "character" of the dead, an epitome of the self. A library was the only place, as Pope said, where he could "make a good figure," because only there could he reveal what was most true about his invisible selfhood, freed from the accidentals of his everyday life, freed from his monstrous figure.[13]

To the degree that Pope was driven by the belief that the "most Sacred Part" of any man was "his Character," and to the degree that he wished the image of his own character to be embodied in poetry so that he would become "immortal for [his] Morality,"[14] he could not help having some misgivings about having written the *Dunciad* and about what he had revealed about his character in writing it. For one of Pope's greatest ambitions was to beget "such Sons upon the Muses, as I hope will live to see their father what he never was yet, an old and good Man":

> No Child of mine (but a Poem or two) is to live after me. I never had any ambition, but this one, that what I left behind me (if it chanced to survive me) should shew its parent was no Dishonest, or Partial, Man, who owed not a six pence to any Party, nor any Sort of advantage to any Mean or mercenary Methods.

But Pope knew he also ran the risk of producing a monstrous "child" that would embody the image of the equally monstrous parent. This anxiety lies just beneath the humor in his comment to Caryll (Pope is speaking about his letters, but his feeling applies equally well to all his writings): "You have proved yourself more tender of another's embryos than the fondest mothers are of their own, for you have preserved every thing that I have miscarried of. Since I know this I shall be in one respect more afraid of writing to you than ever at this careless rate, because I see my evil works may again rise in judgment upon me."[15]

It is significant that almost immediately after the publication of the first *Dunciad,* Pope began to announce, in both his poems and his letters, a real dissatisfaction with the poetry he had written and to express a need to transform his career. He repeatedly characterized this transformation as a rejection of "Fancy." His motives for repudiating the fancy were complicated, I believe, but at heart they were deeply implicated in his desire to create a new kind of poetry which would embody an identity he wanted to be seen as possessing. And to do this, the imagination had to be rejected. It was, as the *Dunciad* dramatized, simply too dangerous a power. Its capacity to swamp the self in egocentric energies, to confuse high principles with low drives, undid the very character it gave birth to by making the poet monstrous, destroying his integrity and his self-identity by subjecting him to the deforming pressures of the passions. Pope feared that he had enmeshed himself in his own imagination in writing the *Dunciad.* He feared that he, like those whom he attacked, had blurred the boundaries of the public and the private, had confused self-interest and principle, had acted on his own private "Resentments," had exposed his own "Enormities," and had revealed himself to be as egomaniacal, as mean, as vicious, in short, as monstrous, as the Dunces. "My Brother Dunces,"[16] Pope called his enemies a few months after the publication of the *Dunciad Variorum,* betraying an apprehension, beneath the humor, that his was an ancestry he had hoped to refute by writing the poem. He feared that he had not fathered an artistic "child" that would make immortal his identity as a good man. He feared that he had been delivered by his own imagination into the monstrous and short-lived lineage of the Dunces.

II

Another fact increased his apprehension that in writing the *Dunciad* he had revealed himself to be something like the monsters he portrayed in that poem. Pope, of course, *was* a monster. Tuberculosis of the spine had left him twisted and stunted, and it subjected him to both physical pain and emotional humiliation. He usually maintained a good-humored if not entirely convincing show of equanimity, joking about "my Evil Forme," about "that little Alexander the women laugh at," speaking about himself as "the Least Thing like a Man in England," and even calling himself a "monster,"[17] and he did so in the face of a life-long stream of abuse from enemies who would not let him forget that he was "A rude, mishapen Lump" whose deformity was "Visible, Present, Lasting, Unalterable, and Peculiar to himself" and whose twisted body, "That wretched little Carcass," as Lady Mary called it, was a punishment from God and proof that he was an offspring of the devil.[18] Pope was pained by these attacks, but they were so witless and clumsy, so obviously motivated by the desire to humiliate him as cruelly as possible, that he rarely complained about them, wisely letting them die of themselves.

A great number of attacks on Pope's physical deformity, however, had a more ambitious reach. These used his monstrous body as a figure for a more significant inner deformity:

> That Mind so suited to its vile Abode,
> The Temple so adapted to the God,
> It seems the Counterpart by Heav'n design'd
> A Symbol and a Warning to Mankind:
> As at some Door we find hung out a Sign,
> Type of the Monster to be found within.[19]

Such attacks, one might suppose, are to be taken no more literally than those attacks which used his body as evidence that he was the offspring of the devil. His body is merely a "Symbol," a "Sign," a "Type"—a convenient object for Pope's enemies to exercise their wits on. But in point of fact, many of these satirical equations between Pope's body and mind were meant to be taken quite literally. Rather than the body's being a sign of an inward monstrosity, his enemies say, it is the *cause:*

> No wonder! that his Muse should tread awry,
> When guided by such proud Deformity,
> Or that his Wit, so learnedly refin'd,
> Should with such spleen and arrogance be join'd,
> Since a distemper'd Body oft corrupts the Mind.[20]

Usually, the causal relationship between Pope's physical monstrosity and his twisted character is not stated as explicitly as it is here, and for good reason: the relationship was so deeply assumed that it did not need to be stated. Although the eighteenth century had freed itself from such superstitions that bodily deformity was a punishment from God, it had not freed itself from the stereotype about what the "character" of a human monster was, what shape his personality must take as a consequence of his misshapen body. And it is this which angered Pope and about which he would not keep silent. To jeer at his misshapen body was one thing. But to infer from his physical deformity the shape of his internal self was something else.

This stereotype of what the character of a monster must be like, I will argue, not only heightened Pope's sensitivity about the dangers of the imagination and sharpened his fears that he had betrayed himself in writing the *Dunciad,* but it also charted the specific direction he took when he transformed his career.

What character did the eighteenth century think a monster must have? Bacon drew such a character (in the Theophrastian sense) in his

essay "Of Deformity"; and there were two memorable literary depic-
tions of the deformed—Thersites in *The Iliad* and especially Shakespeare's portrait of that "lump of foul deformity," Richard III. Taken
together, these three were the touchstones of what the eighteenth century "knew" monsters to be.[21]

Physical deformity, said Bacon, must be understood "not as a
sign, . . . but as a cause" of deformity of character, a cause "which seldom faileth of the effect." Specifically, a disfigured body almost
inevitably caused a person to become *"void of natural affection."* A
deformed person feels, as Richard III confesses of himself, "neither
pity, love, nor fear."[22] For a disfigured body provokes scorn, and
because he is scorned a defomed person becomes, Bacon claimed,
"envious of all." His envy is so enormous that it drives out of him all
"natural affection[s]" but anger and the desire for revenge. (Johnson
explained that Richard's wickedness "proceeded from his deformity,
from the envy that rose at the comparison of his own person with others, and which incited him to disturb the pleasures he could not par-
take.")[23] Hence the three images most commonly applied to the
deformed: the toad, the spider, and the mad dog. The toad was the traditional emblem of envy, and since its froth was thought to be venomous, it was seen as a creature overflowing with the destructive malice that sprang from envy; and both the spider and the rabid dog bit
indiscriminately out of the depth of their malice. (All three images are
repeatedly applied to Richard, "that bottled spider," that "poisonous
bunch-backed toad," that rabid dog who "when he bites / His venom
tooth will rankle to the death.")[24]

Objects of contempt, the deformed wished, Bacon said, "to free
themselves from scorn," and often they did so by directing scorn at
those the world held in high esteem. The *locus classicus* was the portrait
of Thersites in *The Iliad*. "Scorn all his Joy," Thersites was "studious to
defame" and to "lash the Great":

> His Figure such as might his Soul proclaim;
> One Eye was blinking, and one Leg was lame:
> His Mountain-Shoulders half his Breast o'erspread,
> Thin Hairs bestrew'd his long mis-shapen Head.
> Spleen to Mankind his envious Heart possest,
> And much he hated All, but most the Best.
> *Ulysses* or *Achilles* still his Theme;
> But Royal Scandal his Delight supreme.[25]

But defaming the great was not enough for the deformed. They
themselves must become great. "Whoever hath any thing fixed in his
person that doth induce contempt," Bacon reasons, "hath also a perpet-

ual spur in himself to rescue and deliver himself from scorn." Thus, the deformed are driven by a compulsion for "rising," "advancement." "Counting my self but bad till I be best," Richard confesses, he will not rest until he rises to become the "grand tyrant of the earth":

> . . . since this earth affords no joy to me
> But to command, to check, to o'erbear such
> As are of better person than myself,
> I'll make my heaven to dream upon the crown;
> And, whiles I live, t'account this world but hell,
> Until my misshap'd trunk that bears this head
> Be round impaled with a glorious crown.[26]

But the deformed rarely advance themselves honorably or decently. They "watch and observe the weakness of others," says Bacon, and then use these weaknesses to destroy them. Such behavior leads to their own "advancement," of course, but just as importantly, it satisfies their malice. And they are willing to be obsequious, too, for according to Bacon, "they that are envious toward all are more obnoxious [i.e., deferential] to one"—that is to say, to the one above them in power. But this is all duplicity, for when the occasion is ripe, they turn on those they have been obsequious to and destroy them with the same pleasure they destroy everyone else. "Take heed of yonder dog!" says one of Richard's victims. "Look when he fawns, he bites; and when he bites / His venom tooth will rankle to the death."[27]

In all their dealings, in fact, the monstrous are duplicitous, which is why Bacon remarks that they are "good spials [i.e., spies] and good whisperers." Envious and malicious, they advance themselves by spreading scandal, gossip, and lies. Richard boasts, "I am subtle, false, and treacherous," and he takes joy in working through "Deceits," "Plots," "libels," and "secret mischiefs" which are lain "unto the grievous charge of others." But all of this is conducted under a mask of friendship, virtue, and sanctity. "I clothe my naked villany," says Richard, "And seem a saint, when most I play the devil":

> Why, I can smile, and murder while I smile,
> And cry "Content!" to that which grieves my heart,
> And wet my cheeks with artificial tears,
> And frame my face to all occasions.[28]

When Richard is pictured as (merely) a "diffus'd infection of a man," his entire identity is reduced to nothing but the envy and malice that possess him; *"void of all natural affection,"* there is nothing to connect him to the human family. The deformed, it turns out, *are* monstrous, singular, and repugnant to our common humanity:

> Then, since the heavens have shap'd my body so,
> Let hell make crook'd my mind to answer it.
> I have no brother, I am like no brother;
> And this word "love," which greybeards call divine,
> Be resident in men like one another,
> And not in me: I am myself alone.

In that closed and circular illogic that governs so many stereotypes, bodily deformity, which Bacon said was a cause and not a sign of an inner deformity, once again becomes a sign, a sign of a self so monstrous that it is to be cast out as not of our species, like Richard, that "foul misshapen stigmatic, / Mark'd by the Destinies to be avoided, / As venom toads."[29]

This "character" of a monstrous person is precisely the character that was attributed to Pope. This was the stereotype, for instance, that Dennis was drawing from in 1716 when he claimed that Pope's deformity, like Richard's, was "the mark of God and Nature upon him, to give us warning that we should hold no Society with him, as a Creature not of our Original, nor of our Species." And it was this same stereotype that Lady Mary and Lord Hervey called up when they claimed that, as a consequence of his singular monstrosity, Pope was an "Outcast, and alone":

> . . . as thou hate'st, be hated by Mankind,
> And with the Emblem of thy crooked Mind,
> Mark'd on thy Back, like *Cain,* by God's own Hand;
> Wander like him, accursed through the Land.[30]

His critics' minute dissection of motives and feelings they had no way of perceiving, their perverse misinterpretations of much of his behavior, their groundless allegations, the tedious similarity of their points of attack against him are to a great extent explained by the fact that Pope's character came to them prepackaged in the stereotype of the deformed. Pope's enemies charged that he was "born to hate" and that he was "by *Nature* shap'd to ill," and they should be taken to mean what they literally say, that the monstrosity of his character was caused by his monstrous body. When Edmund Curll set out to publish anecdotes of Pope's behavior as a schoolboy, he wrote in his advertisement that the incidents from Pope's early life were "Proof of that Natural Spleen which constitutes Mr. Pope's Temperament, (as my Lord Bacon observes of Deformed Persons) and from which he has never yet deviated." Curll went on to reprint in its entirety Bacon's "Of Deformity," which he subtitled "A *Looking-Glass* for Mr. Pope."[31]

The attacks on Pope are almost entirely shaped by this stereotype of a monster. In fact, the single most common charge brought against him is the principal accusation brought against the deformed: he is consumed by envy and malice. Pope is an "envious Dwarf," a "mishapen Lump of Malice and Ill-nature," "a *Waspish* Thing / . . . Replete with Malice, Spleen, and Spite." He possesses "a malignant Heart and envious Mind"; he is completely "abandon'd to the worst of Principles, feeding on Malice and inglorious Envy"; he writes his poetry out of "Ill-nature, the Petulancy of Malice, and the Wantonness of a bad Heart." "Spleen fill my Heart and *Head,*" he is made to say, "*and so I write.*" The *Dunciad* was written "only to gratify a malicious Temper," and his earlier works were similarly motivated: "*Windsor Forest,* [was] writ in Envy of Sir *John Denham*'s Poem upon *Cooper's Hill;* . . . *Temple of Fame,* writ in Envy of *Chaucer*'s Poem; . . . and . . . the Ode on *Cæcilia*'s Day, writ in Envy of Mr. *Dryden*'s Feast of *Alexander.*"[32]

The source of Pope's envy and malice, just as Bacon had explained, is the contempt brought on him by his monstrous body, and so his greatest desire is to "free himself from scorn" by "rising." Like Richard, Pope lusts for a crown: he will not be satisfied until he has advanced "into the Front part of the Sons of *Parnassus.*" "He . . . usurps / A Sovereign Rule, and, in *Apollo*'s stead, / Becomes the Tyrant of his fellow Bards." Obsessed with his need to be preeminent, Pope has become another Thersites, whom he resembles "both in Shape and Malice," eager to "impeach with stedfast Hate / What-e'er is God-like, and what-e'er is Great." He has

> endeavoured to make Asses, Owls, Fools, Blockheads, Blunderers, Coxcombs, Rogues, Rascals and Scoundrels of many Gentlemen of superior Rank and Figure, eminent for their Learning and universal Accomplishments, as well as their high Stations, thereby maliciously attempting to level the Best and Greatest of Men with the Worst and Weakest, in Expectation that his own Character would stand and remain the Brighter by such a Procedure.

Even early in his career, he had distinguished himself by "attacking several Persons of a Hundred times greater Merit than himself; and who had given him no Provocation, but by surpassing him." Moved "by his natural Envy and Malice, (the Deformity of his *Mind* answering to that of his *Body*)," Pope "has endeavoured to decry and calumniate every Author who has excelled him."[33]

But it was not only those who were better than he was in station, merit, or talent whom Pope envied and hated. As Bacon had explained, the deformed were scorned by all and therefore they envied all and hated all. Pope is so tormented by his jealousy of everyone that, like Richard, he counts himself bad until he is best. "Here's the Center

and Fountain of his Malice. Truly he can bear no Character in Competition with his own." He is "jealous of Fame, and envious of every
Rival, grasping at the smallest Shadow of Reputation, all of his Attention fix'd to one Point, raving after imaginary Honours." Pope
"haste[s] to mount Immortal Envy's Throne, / To crush all Merit, that
disputes [his] own." Driven by "restless Envy," he tries to "stigmatize
all Merit but [his] own," for he is "afraid others should rise above him,
and so he endeavours to blast their Characters." His envy and hatred
are so profound, so irrational, that he is a bottomless well of venom,
always overflowing, having no single object: he "slanders *all* Men"; his
"ranc'rous Arrows fly, / At Good and Bad, at Friend and Enemy." He
aims his "pointed Satire . . . alike at All." He "omits no Occasion of
showing his Malice," for his desire is to "libel all Mankind." Driven by
"the gross *Lust* of Hate," he spews his "universal Rancour" everywhere, "Without Distinction": "The Object of thy Spleen is Human
Kind." So possessed is he by "ungovernable Spleen [and] Envy" that he
has "attack'd such Numbers of People at one Time as no one before
him ever did in any Nation." One critic drew up a list of sixty-two targets of Pope's malice, headed by "ALMIGHTY God" and descending
through the king, the queen, both houses of Parliament, the Privy
Council, the current ministry, Shakespeare, Sir William Temple,
Samuel Garth, and dwindling at last in Edward Ward.[34]

Devoid of every natural affection, Pope, like Richard, feigns human
ties only to advance his career, and when his friends are no longer of
use, he turns on them and betrays them viciously. He is "Base to his
Foe, but baser to his Friend." Those who have "ventur'd to be familiar
with him, have severely suffer'd for it, by his Perfidiousness," for "he
has fallen upon none so foully as his friends and Benefactors"; indeed,
he has "at one Time or other, *Betrayed* or *Abused* almost every one he
has conversed with":

> No sooner did the Town take notice of him, but he began to fancy himself a
> very great Man, and treated those Gentlemen who had rais'd him from
> nothing with the utmost Contempt, taking all the vile methods he could
> think of to do them Injuries; nay, he was so much lost to Shame, that he
> wrote a Work on purpose to abuse them.

He betrayed Gay, he betrayed Congreve, he betrayed Steele and Addison; he attacked Philips at the same time he "smil'd on him, embrac'd
him, and called him Friend"; he "fell foul on his first and greatest
Benefactor," Wycherley, "by ridiculing him behind his Back"; he
betrayed the Duke of Chandos.[35]

In fact, all of Pope's behavior is marked by a malicious duplicity and underhandedness. This is, after all, how the deformed act. Had not Bacon said that they made "good spials and good whisperers," and had not Richard confessed that he was "subtle, false, and treacherous," secretly destroying others by slander and libel (the favorite weapons, too, of Thersites) but always covering his "naked villany" by contriving to "seem a saint"? So, too, Pope. He is "a little affected Hypocrite" who will attack anyone "in a clandestine manner with the utmost Falshood and Calumny," having "nothing in his mouth at the same time but *Truth, Candor, Friendship, good Nature, Humanity,* and *Magnanimity.*" "He has been many Years a Spy," secretly gathering information to spread in slander. "My Eyes pry ev'ry where," he is made to say, "my Tongue *repeats* / The falsest Slanders; I forment all *Heats.*" And when he cannot find gossip to spread, he simply "invents the basest Calumnies." Like Richard, he excels in "Lyes and Slander," "Fictions, Cheats," "false Aspersions"; he "Coins and disperses Lies thro' all the Town." These he uses as "clandestine Weapons," for he never spreads his lies openly, but "Sculking, the Scandal privately disperse[s]." All this is done behind a carefully contrived mask of "outward Sanctity," friendship, and especially (as Bacon had warned) obsequiousness. His is a "flatt'ring Heart." He is "servile, scraping," but he is, "When most oblig'd, most ardent to abuse!" He "Grins lowly fawning, biting as he whines." Indeed, he "seldom does one fawning line impart, / But when some Mischief's broiling in his Heart."[36]

Since his character is derived from the stereotype of the deformed, it is not surprising to see the poet imaged as those animals used to signify the monstrosity of Richard III. Pope is often pictured as a "distracted" dog, "Poison flashing from his Eyes": "He bites, he snaps at all, disgorging Foam." He is a "venomous . . . hunch-back'd Toad" who "Spits his Venom thro' the Town," the same toad that in Aesop's fable "swell'd / And burst with Envy, 'cause he was excell'd." And he is the monstrous spider, as in "The Butterfly and Spider," a poem whose formulaic repetition of nearly every feature the deformed were reputed to have shows how thoroughly Pope was conceived of within the stereotype of the monster:

> Oft have I, mov'd with Anger, seen,
> Sad Object of envenom'd Spleen,
> A painted Butterfly unfold
> Its spangled Wings, bedrop'd with Gold;
> And basking in a Summer's Day,
> The Glories of its Plumes display:
> While issuing from his mazy Cell,
> With Rage replete, a Spider fell,
> Indignant views the pretty Form,

And spits upon the painted Worm.
So *Pope,* of Spider Kind and Make,
A monstrous Form, all Legs and Back,
Crawls hateful from his Hole obscure,
Nor lovely Object can endure,
But views, with Envy, Pride, and Hate,
The shining Honours of the Great,
'Till squeezing forth his pois'nous Steam,
The subtle still malignant Stream
Blackens, infectious as it flows,
Heroes and Statesmen, Belles and Beaus:
He rails and bids the World despise
Whate'er his ugly Self outvies.[37]

III

Even while he was writing the first *Dunciad,* Pope worried that he inadvertently had delivered himself over to his monster-breeding imagination and had exposed his monstrosity to the world. This anxiety would have been intensified because his character increasingly was being defined as that of a monster. The confluence of his apprehensions about the teratogenic imagination and his victimization by the stereotype of monstrosity, I believe, provoked Pope to transform his career after the first *Dunciad* and greatly determined the precise direction that transformation took. Pope announced this transformation publicly in his poetry and disclosed it privately in his letters, but perhaps because he spoke out his feelings piecemeal and never drew them together into a coherent manifesto, we have not grasped how deeply this transformation was implicated in his anxieties about monstrosity.

"As to your question, if I am writing," Pope wrote to Caryll a few years after the publication of the first *Dunciad,*

> I really very rarely dip my pen. The vanity is over: and unless I could hope to do it with some good end, or to a better pitch than I've hitherto done, I would never return to the lists. But the truth is, it is now my hopes (God knows whether it may prove in my power) to contribute to some honest and moral purposes in writing on human life and manners, not exclusive of religious regards, . . .[38]

The meaning of the "honest and moral purposes" and "vanity" is obvious enough, though the deeper ramifications are revealed when Pope restates this dichotomy, formulated slightly differently. "Be one Poet's praise," he announces, at once apologizing for his earlier career and committing himself to a new direction,

> That not in Fancy's Maze he wander'd long,
> But stoop'd to Truth, and moraliz'd his song: . . .
> (*Epistle to Dr. Arbuthnot*, 336, 340–41)

"Fancy's Maze": we have heard this language before. This is the language Pope used to describe the solipsistic, Enthusiastic imagination, the kind of imagination he figures as Dulness herself. The Enthusiastic imagination is an agent of idleness. It draws us away from the world and from our proper duties in the world. It is "vanity," for to abandon oneself to fancy is to allow oneself to be completely absorbed in the pleasures of the closed world of the self. And so, to reject "Fancy's Maze" is automatically to commit oneself "to some honest and moral purposes in writing on human life and manners," since to reject the self-sufficiency of the imagination is to submit oneself to the moral imperatives of the human community, to the "Truth" outside the self.

Pope is being entirely self-consistent when he explains to Swift why he has rejected the fancy and disciplined himself to work within the confines of moral poetry: "My system is a short one, and my circle narrow. Imagination has no limits, and that is a sphere in which you may move on to eternity; but where one is confined to Truth (or to speak more like a human creature, to the appearances of Truth) we soon find the shortness of our Tether."[39] Imagination is a "sphere in which you move on to eternity" because it is a sphere entirely within the mind, a sphere which (like a "Maze") gives the illusion of infinite space because reality is not allowed to impinge on it. Hence, the Enthusiastic imagination is a "vanity" in a second sense: it encourages us to wander forever in delusion, keeping us forever far from truth.

The dichotomies Pope uses to formulate the redirection of his career, then, seem consistent and straightforward. There is, on the one hand, the possibility of indulging oneself in egocentric idleness, the "vanity" of "Fancy's Maze," a maze that has "no limits" because it exists only in the unreal infinity of the solipsistic mind; and, on the other hand, the task of disciplining the self to the "narrow" limits of "Truth," acknowledging the real existence of human life outside of our imaginations, recognizing our "religious" obligations and "moral purposes" in that life, and contributing to the good by engaging ourselves in the web of social and human responsibilities.

But how do these dichotomies jibe with Pope's most trenchant formulation of the nature of the change in his career, his assertion in *An Essay on Man* that he has

> turn'd the tuneful art
> From sounds to things, from fancy to the heart?
> (4.391–92)

His repudiation of the empty "sounds" of fanciful poetry for the solid "things" of Nature is of a piece with his repudiation of the internal world of "Fancy's Maze" for "Truth," the empirical world of other people and the human community. But what about that second dichotomy, the opposition between "fancy" and the "heart"?

To explore what Pope may have meant by "heart" and how this dichotomy between "heart" and "fancy" is related to his other pronouncements about transforming his career, let me turn to William Hay, an almost exact contemporary of Pope, and, like the poet, deformed. "I am scarce five Feet high," he wrote of himself; "my Back was bent in my Mother's Womb; . . . in Person I resemble . . . Mr. Pope."[40] In 1754, Hay published *Deformity: An Essay,* a remarkable inquiry into the plight of the monstrous and a (sometimes unconscious) revelation of the strategies the deformed created to subvert the vicious social stereotypes that denied them their identities.

"Bodily Deformity," wrote Hay, "is visible to every Eye; but the Effects of it are known to very few; intimately known to none but those, who feel them; and they generally are not inclined to reveal them." And so, if the stereotype encouraged people to make egregiously stupid assumptions about their characters, the first act a deformed person must perform to contest this stereotype is to make visible the hidden self, thus demonstrating that his identity was not shaped by what his body said:

> I do not pretend to be so ingenious as *Montaigne;* but it is in my power to be as ingenuous. I may with the same *Naïveté* remove the Veil from my mental as well as personal Imperfections; and expose them naked to the World. And when I have thus anatomized my self, I hope my Heart will be found sound and untainted, and my Intentions honest and sincere.[41]

And *Deformity: An Essay* is, in fact, a self-anatomy Hay undertakes in order to make visible his "Heart" and to prove that it is "sound and untainted." Hay begins his self-anatomy by confronting directly the stereotype as articulated by Bacon, and particularly the claim that deformed people are *"void of natural affection"*:

> If by natural Affection is here meant universal Benevolence, and Deformity necessarily implies a want of it, a deformed Person must then be a complete Monster. But however common the Case may be, my own Sensations inform me, that it is not universally true. If by natural Affection is meant a partial Regard for Individuals; I believe the Remark is judicious, and founded in human Nature. Deformed Persons are despised, ridiculed, and

ill-treated by others; are seldom Favourites, are commonly most neglected by Parents, Guardians, and Relations: and therefore, as they are not indebted for much Fondness, it is no wonder, if they repay but little. It is the Command of Scripture, *Not to set our Affections on Things below:* it is the Voice of Reason, not to overvalue what we must soon part with: and therefore, to be fond of others, as not to be able to bear their Absence, or to survive them, is neither a religious or moral Duty; but a childish and womanish Weakness: and I must congratulate deformed Persons, who by Example are early taught another Lesson. And I will now lay open my own Heart to the Reader, that he may judge, if Lord *Bacon*'s Position is verified in me.

I hope it proceed not from Malignity of Heart; but I never am much affected with the common Accidents of Life, whether they befall my self or others. I am little moved when I hear of Death, Loss, or Misfortune: I think the Case is common,

(Tritus, & e medio fortunae ductus acervo:)

As it is always likely to happen, I am not surprised when it does. If I see a Person cry out or beat his Breast on an such Occasion, I cannot bear him Company, but am not *Democritus* to laugh at his Folly. I read of Battles and Fields covered with Slain; of Cities destroyed by Sword, Famine, Pestilence, and Earthquake; I do not shed a Tear: I suppose it is, because they are the usual Storms, to which the Human Species are exposed, proceeding from the just Judgments of God, or the mistaken and false Principles of Rulers. I read of Persecutions, Tortures, Murders, Massacres; my Compassion for the Sufferers is great, but my Tears are stopped by Resentment and Indignation against the Contrivers and Perpetrators of such horrid Actions. But there are many Things, that bring Tears to my Eyes, whether I will or no: and when I reflect, I am often at a Loss in searching out the secret Source from whence they flow. What makes me weep? (for weep I do) when I read of Virtue or Innocence in Distress; of a good Man, helpless and forsaken, unmoved by the greatest Insults and Cruelties; or courageously supporting himself against Oppression in the Article of Death. I suppose it is, to see Vice triumphant, and Virtue so ill rewarded in this Life. . . . When I read of *Regulus* returning to Torment, and *John* of *France* to Imprisonment, against the Persuasion of Friends, to keep Faith with their Enemies; I weep to think, there is scarce another Instance of such exalted Virtue. Those, who often hear me read, know, that my Voice changes, and my Eyes are full, when I meet a generous or heroic Saying, Action, or Character, especially of Persons, whose Example or Command may influence mankind. I weep when I hear a *Titus* say, That he had lost the Day in which he did no Good.[42]

Hay's characteristic rhetorical gesture, which he makes repeatedly in this passage and throughout *Deformity,* is to appear to acquiesce to the vile charge of the stereotype but, by doing so, to turn that accusation into a vindication of himself. We can see this in small in a single sentence. "I read of Persecution, Tortures, Murders, Massacres; my Compassion for the Sufferers is great, but my Tears are stopped. . . ," and here he seems to demonstrate the truth of Bacon's charge that the deformed are *"void of natural affection."* But the sentence goes on, and he reveals that his apparent lack of sympathy results not from a lack of natural affection but, to the contrary, from a plethora of emotions: " . . . but my Tears are stopped by Resentment and Indignation against the Contrivers and Perpetrators of such horrid Actions."

This, too, is the rhetorical pattern of the passage at large. "I will now lay open my Heart to the reader, that he may judge, if Lord *Bacon's* position is verified in me," says Hay, and almost immediately he seems to prove Bacon right. "I am little moved when I hear of Death, Loss, or Misfortune: I think the Case is common. . . ," and then, even more monstrously, he confesses, "I read of Battles and Fields covered with Slain; of Cities destroyed by Sword, Famine, Pestilence, and Earth-quake; I do not shed a Tear. . . ." But then, just when he appears to have exposed an utterly deformed heart the stereotype claimed he had, he reveals that, in fact, he is acting on the basis of noble principle.

Why has Hay taken this tack? Part of the answer is that by seeming to acquiesce, he is able to redefine the charges the stereotype brings against the deformed and thereby deny its most damaging allegations. "I do not shed a Tear," says Hay, inviting the accusation that he, like all monsters is an "Out-cast, and alone," so imprisoned in his ego by his envy and malice that he is devoid of all natural affection and thus shares nothing in common with the rest of humanity. But to have a "heart" in this conventional sense, to shed a tear for those who have brought their sufferings upon themselves or who have been caught in the inescapable toils of the human condition, is at best only to demon-strate "a partial Regard for Individuals." No, Hay has deep feelings for his fellow humans, but they are feelings guided by "the Command of Scripture" and "the Voice of Reason": and his *not* shedding a tear is proof that he does have a heart, "heart" redefined now to mean the capacity to allow his feelings to be guided by virtue, by his knowledge of the proper end of man, and by his commitment to humanity's best interest. His not shedding a tear shows a profound commonality with the human race: this is proof of a "universal Benevolence," a feeling of a heart not only liberated from egocentric self-regard but so disciplined by virtue that it rejects the secret self-satisfactions of sentimentality, weeping with "partial Regard for Individuals." When Hay weeps, as weep he does, he weeps for "exalted Virtue."

Bacon, at the end of his essay on deformity, said that the deformed could liberate themselves from the determinism of their distorted bod-ies in only one way: "by virtue." Since a monster is devoid of natural affections and enclosed in his ego, he could free himself only by following the impulse of his heart out of the self, following the heart as it knotted itself, "by virtue," into the larger good of the human community. It is precisely this capacity of the heart that Hay is laying claim to. And, by committing his heart to virtue and "universal Benevolence," he is proving that he is not monstrous at all. His is the common case.

The heart Hay exposes in this self-anatomy, as any reader of Pope will immediately recognize, is in its broad lineaments the "heart" that Pope exposes in his poetry of the 1730s. And Hay is valuable because he helps us understand two facts about what Pope meant when he said that he had turned "from fancy to the heart." First, Hay suggests just how thoroughly Pope's redirection of his career, whatever its other motives, was rooted in his monstrosity. Hay felt compelled to expose his heart because he was living under the weight of a stereotype that denied that he had a heart and that he could ever think or feel beyond the confines of his ego. Pope, too, suffered under the same stereotype. His "Character as an honest Man," he complained, had been impugned by those who had no "personal Knowledge of my Heart, or the Motives of my Conduct." Thus, like Hay, Pope found himself under "the Necessity to say something of *Myself*," to "publish my own heart." His poetry increasingly would become, as he wrote to Arbuthnot, a "Memorial . . . of my own Character."[43]

The second thing Hay reminds us of is what "heart" means in the eighteenth century and how it gathers under a single rubric intentions and acts we normally think of as quite disparate. "Heart" means not merely the capacity for strong feelings. As Hay reminds us, the heart connects us with our fellow human beings by means of "universal Benevolence," not by "a partial Regard for Individuals": we feel for others and work for their good as we understand that good within the context of the well-being of the whole and the proper end of human beings (as defined by "the Command of Scripture" and "the Voice of Reason"). "Heart," in short, is the commitment to "Virtue," the only reliable guide to human happiness and fulfillment.

Pope's claim that he turned "from fancy to the heart" is made in the last verse paragraph of *An Essay on Man,* where it acts as a coda to the climax of his argument in the previous verse paragraphs that the "boundless heart" (4.355) finds its proper bliss only by cherishing virtue and universal benevolence. And if the heart cherishes virtue, we can comprehend how Pope's rejection of "fancy" and his embracing of the "heart" is of a piece with his other ways of speaking about his redirection of his career in the 1730s. For to speak from the heart, in this context, *is* to moralize his song and to "contribute to some honest and moral purposes in writing on human life and manners." And it is to reject the fancy, too, for the heart commits him to a pursuit of virtue and benevolence that, of necessity, draws him further and further out of the maze of egocentricity and idle self-absorption.

The poetry that Pope writes in the 1730s, then, truly is poetry written from the heart, expressive equally of both public and personal drives. *An Essay on Man,* the *Moral Essays,* and especially the *Imitations* are different from his earlier poetry (even his close friends did not recognize *An Essay on Man* as his when he published it anonymously): more discursive, more didactic, more explicitly concerned with moral, social, and political matters—matters, in short, of "human life and manners," matters addressed from a pointedly ethical perspective in order to "contribute to some honest and moral purposes." At the same time, of course, this very public poetry, to an extent never seen before in English poetry, is extraordinarily personal, articulating the poet's individual identity by focusing on his character, his sensibility, and his ethical struggles.[44] Pope redirects his career toward *apologia* and self-portrayal, writing poetry which testifies to the honesty of his motives, to his integrity, and to a heart which is "sound and untainted."

Pope's rejection of the fancy and his embracing of the poetry of the "heart," of course, is only one dimension of his poetic career, and it is not at all the thoroughgoing revolution he often wanted to give the impression it was. For all of his anxiety about how he had revealed himself to be a monster by writing the *Dunciad,* he continued to republish and enlarge the poem throughout his life; and, in spite of his fear about what it may reveal about his heart, he went on to write scathing satire. Still, the transformation of his poetry was genuine and profound. For, though he wrote satire, it was (so he dramatized publicly in the satires themselves) satire motivated by unselfish high-mindedness and love of virtue—satire, in short, written from a generous and benevolent heart. And by the time he came to publish the *Dunciad* for the last time at the end of his career, it had been so thoroughly transformed that in it (as in all of his satirical poetry of the 1730s) Pope could convincingly present himself as a poet who spoke for virtue and benevolence, not a poet driven, as a monster was, by envy, malice, and a lacerated ego.

IV

"The libel'd Person, and the pictur'd Shape," Pope confessed, set him on that "awkward . . . Task," "the Necessity to say something of *Myself.*"[45] Just how profoundly his anxiety about his monstrosity prompted him to cultivate new modes of poetry in which he simultaneously addressed the ethical dimension of "human life and manners" and laid open his heart to the readers can be seen in *An Epistle to Dr. Arbuthnot.*

In fact, when one turns to the earliest extant manuscript, one can see that much of the generative impulse of the poem lies in Pope's attempt to deal explicitly with the question of how much his character was determined by his physical monstrosity. In the early manuscript, the poem concludes with Pope's dramatizing how he is flattered: "Even to my Person some will make their Court / I cough like Horace, & am thick, & short; / Ammon's great Son one shoulder had too high, / Such Ovid's Nose!" He is, he admits, "A monstrous mixture" of defects. And this explicit naming of his monstrosity forms the transition to the climax and conclusion of the poem as it then stood.

> But Friend! this Shape wch you & Curl admire
> Came not from Ammon's Son, but from my Sire;
> And for my Headake (you'l the truth excuse)
> I had it from my Mother, not the Muse:
> Happy! thrice happy, had I heir'd as well
> The Christian Kernel, as the crazy Shell
> Meek was my Sire, & held it for a rule
> It was a Sin *to call our Brother Fool;*
> My Mother judgd no wedded Wife a *Whore;*
> Hear this, & spare my Family, James M-re!
> And cou'dst thou think my Father was unknown
> Meerly because thou dost not knowe thy own?
> Known he shall be! & lov'd, and honord long,
> If there be Force in Virtue or in Song.
> Of gentle blood, part shed in Honor's Cause
> (While yet in Albion Honor had applause)
> The Good man sprung: his Fortunes were his own
> And better gain'd than from th' ungrateful Throne:
> Unlearn'd, his morals were not taught by Art;
> One Language, but that Language of the Heart:
> By Genius honest, & by Nature wise;
> Healthy, by Temp'rance & by Exercise:
> Who Wine's mad transports never deignd to try;
> Who ne'er risqu'd an Oath, nor dar'd a Lye:
> Who ne'er knew Law Suit, or domestick Strife,
> Religious Contest, or mad Party-Life:
> Nor Courts wd know, no Great Mans Friendship try,
> Nor ever riskd an Oath, or dar'd a Lye.
> Whose days, tho full, to Sickness were unknown;
> Whose Death was instant, & without a Groan:
> O grant me thus to live, & thus to dye!
> Who sprung from Kings shall know less bliss than I.[46]

Pope's response to his own monstrosity is a bit muddy. On the one hand, he seems to reject outright the stereotype that the characters of the deformed are determined by their bodies simply by making a dichotomy between the "Christian Kernel" and "crazy Shell." But the absoluteness of that dichotomy is subverted by a pun: "Happy! thrice happy, had I heir'd as well / The Christian Kernel, as the crazy Shell." His "crazy Shell," he "heir'd" from his father (presumably, Pope is thinking of his father's orthopedic problem, which he thought was the predisposing cause of his own deformity),[47] but he also "erred" from his parents, deviated from the "Christian Kernel" of his parents' good nature and simple virtue (Pope calls attention to this in the very next lines, "Meek was my Sire, & held it for a rule / It was a Sin *to call our Brother Fool*": this in a poem in which Pope continually calls a fool a fool).[48] In a single couplet, then, Pope seems to protest against the easy accusations about monstrosity and at the same time to admit that there is something monstrous in his behavior.

Indeed, Pope repeatedly points to how greatly he has "erred" from his father's model. His father was plain and unassuming: "Nor Courts wd know, no Great Mans Friendship try." Pope, of course, was quite well acquainted with the Court, and he knew many a great man—he knew the Great Man himself, for even into the early 1730s he was on good enough terms with Walpole to dine with him and ask favors (in the published version of *Arbuthnot* itself he says, "I condescend / Sometimes to call a Minister my Friend" [265–66]).[49] His father never knew "Religious Contest, or mad Party-Life." Strictly speaking, this is true of the son, too, but only if we interpret the phrase quite literally, for though Pope himself studiously avoided religious and party controversy, much of the animosity directed against him was motivated by either party or religion and was often expressed in those terms. And again, strictly speaking, Pope, like his father, "ne'er knew Law Suit, or domestick Strife." But just a few months earlier, Pope had presented himself as having taken up satire as a "Weapon" and, thus "arm'd for *Virtue*," declared himself willing to "perish in the gen'rous Cause."[50] Given the tenor of constant acrimony and strife throughout his career, which *Arbuthnot* documents in some detail, to see any true similarity between his life and his father's requires an almost mindlessly literal reading of these lines.

Thus, by the time he comes to the end of the poem, the contrast between him and his father has grown enormously:

> Whose days, tho full, to Sickness were unknown;
> His death was instant, & without a Groan:
> Oh grant me thus to live, & thus to die!

The prayer is ludicrous if read literally. His father's life is "to Sickness ... unknown" whereas the poet's life, of course, has been "this long Disease" (133), and this return to the topic of his body at the end of a long passage which shows how much Pope has "erred" from his father's virtuous character suggests once again how central to this poem is the question of the relation between his twisted body and the deformity of his conduct of his life.

Pope's intention in the early draft of *Arbuthnot* and in the final version of the poem, too, is to explore the relationship between inheritance and monstrosity. He wants to show where and why he has "erred" from his parents' examples so that he can clear his character of any serious imputation of monstrosity by revealing that, in spite of appearances, he is the true "heir" of their virtue. And it is important for him to do so precisely because of his bodily deformity. Pope described his early draft of *Arbuthnot* as a poem "wherein the Question is stated, what were, & are, my Motives of writing."[51] His father was a "good Man" who "walk'd innoxious thro' his Age," speaking nothing but "the Language of the Heart" (395, 399), and the most obvious way in which Pope has "erred" from his father is that he speaks the angry language of satire. Whatever his motives, they apparently are quite different from his father's. To his enemies, this proved that he was exactly what the sterotype of the deformed said he was, a man with a twisted heart lashing out from the malignancy of his monstrosity. In order to free himself from this stereotype, I believe, Pope does in *Arbuthnot* what Hay does in *Deformity:* he admits to his monstrosity, but he does so in order to redefine the significance of his deformity and its relationship to his character.[52]

Pope discarded the pun on "heir'd" in the subsequent rewritings of *Arbuthnot,* but he poses exactly the same questions about his monstrosity in another, extraordinarily dense couplet:

> Why did I write? what sin to me unknown
> Dipt me in Ink, my Parents', or my own?
> (125–26)

This couplet pictures Pope's entry into poetry by conflating three allusions. The first allusion is to Achilles, who was dipped by his mother in the Styx to protect him in battle. And, indeed, like Achilles in *The Iliad,* in *Arbuthnot* Pope alternates between withdrawing from the battle and throwing himself headlong into it. But it is unclear whether this stance is heroic or whether, like Achilles, Pope is barbarous, cruel, and brutal, driven by an irresponsible, egocentric sensitivity. The second allusion, of course, is to baptism, and it is equally ambiguous. Since

Pope is not baptised by water but is "Dipt . . . in Ink," it is unclear whether he enters his career as a purified soul dedicated to some holy purpose or whether he has dirtied himself, pursuing a life-long career of error and sin. The third allusion, as has been noted often, is to John 9:1–3: "And as Jesus passed by, he saw a man which was blind from his birth. And his disciples asked him, saying, Master, who did sin, this man, or his parents, that he was born blind? Jesus answered, Neither hath this man sinned, nor his parents: but that the works of God should be manifested in him." This passage was referred to again and again in the arguments about the causes of monstrosity and the degree of conformity there was between bodily and spiritual disfigurement.[53] Pope alludes to it here to raise those questions in this poem, and he makes the questions even more pointed by conflating this allusion with the allusion to Achilles. For, according to Pope, Achilles' character was "compounded of Courage and Anger," and his anger makes his character very similar to that of a monster. Achilles, like a monster, obsessively meditates on his injuries ("My Wrongs, my Wrongs, my Constant Thought engage") and lives in "One constant state / Of lashing Rancour and eternal Hate": thinking himself scorned, he is consumed by an "inexorable Resentment [that] will not let him hearken to any Terms of Accomodation." In "Sullenness for an Injury that is done him," he "flies out into Extravagance," becomes "abusive," "savage and bloody," and finally sinks into utter "Inhumanity," "uttering an universal Malevolence to Mankind."[54]

The couplet, then, is completely ambiguous. It can be read to mean that Pope's monstrosity has nothing to do with his character (no "sin," either his parents' or his own, is manifested in his deformity); that his career is a heroic one, a courageous battle against evil; that his motives are pure. On the other hand, the couplet can be read to mean just the opposite: that Pope is a monster and that his monstrosity has affected his character in the way his enemies have always charged (like Achilles, he is driven by an anger and malice that spring from an almost pathological sensitivity about being slighted) and that, consequently, in his poetic career, he has become as deeply stained and polluted as the enemies he attacks. At this point in the poem, the issue is left unresolved, and this couplet, then, asks the questions that the cancelled pun on "heir'd" asked, the questions that I think it is the purpose of the poem to answer, questions about the relationships among Pope's poetic career, his character, his motivation as a writer, and his physical deformity.

By the conclusion of *Arbuthnot,* Pope resolves these questions by setting his motives and behavior against those of his enemies, constructing his identity, as has often been observed, by drawing out the similarities and differences between him and those who have attacked him—enemies whom he appears superficially to resemble but, in the end, whom he differs from profoundly. What has not been observed is the fact that Pope portrays his enemies by using the conventional images and sterotypes of monstrosity. In this way, he asserts his identity in contrast to the identities of his enemies and simultaneously defines himself outside of the imputations of monstrosity.[55]

For instance, it is not Pope who is the spider, but Codrus who spins "the slight, self-pleasing thread" of his "cobweb" (89–90). It is Sporus, not Pope, who is the dog ("So well-bred Spaniels civilly delight / In mumbling of the Game they dare not bite" [313–14]). And although Pope's enemies pictured him as a "hunch-back'd Toad" that "Spits his Venom thro' the Town," the *real* toad, of course, is Sporus again, who "Half Froth, half Venom, spits himself abroad" (320).

It is Pope's enemies, not Pope, whom the character of the deformed truly seems to fit. They are the ones willing to play the "Flatt'rer" (328) and to present an "obliging" (208) front, though behind these appearances, as was thought typical of the deformed, they betrayed their friends in underhanded ways, spreading "slander" and "Libel," "Tales, or Lyes, / Or Spite" (289–90, 321–22). It is Atticus, not Pope, who knows how to indulge his malice behind a carefully crafted mask,

> Damn with faint praise, assent with civil leer,
> And without sneering, teach the rest to sneer.
>
> (201–2)

Pope, on the other hand, scorns both flattery and underhandedness:

> ... Flatt'ry, ev'n to Kings, he held a shame,
> And thought a Lye in Verse or Prose the same.
>
> (338–39)

And though Pope himself can be devious, even devious enough, like Atticus, to "Just hint a fault," his motives are nothing like those of his enemies—nothing like those motives which were supposed to drive the deformed:

> Seiz'd and ty'd down to judge, how wretched I!
> Who can't be silent, and who will not lye;
> To laugh, were want of Goodness and of Grace,
> And to be grave, exceeds all Pow'r of Face.
> I sit with sad Civility, I read
> With honest anguish, and an aking head;
> And drop at last, but in unwilling ears,
> This saving counsel, "Keep your Piece nine years."
>
> (33–40)

Pope's enemies behave like the deformed because they are consumed by the need to "rise," and they will not rest until they have a
crown. Each *will* be "Thron'd in the Centre of his thin designs" (93).
Atticus taps that same well of imaginative energy he had used earlier to
design his play to create a new drama with himself at center stage, all so
that he can "Like *Cato,* give his little Senate laws, / And sit attentive to
his own applause" (209–10). Bufo simply buys his position, spreading
about patronage so that he can rule "the whole *Castalian* State" (230).

Bufo is surrounded by an "undistinguish'd race" and "flattered
ev'ry day" (237, 240). So, too, is Pope, but not by his own design. Nor is
Pope like Atticus, so possessed by a neurotic need to be admired that,
"Dreading ev'n fools," he allows himself to be "by Flatterers besieg'd"
(207). Pope shuts his door against his flatterers. And though he is something like a king, he is not the kind of king that Bufo and Atticus strive
to be, both needing to be the center of attention:

> I sought no homage from the Race that write;
> I kept, like *Asian* Monarchs, from their sight: . . .
> (219–20)

The only realm Pope wants to rule is the "little kingdom" of his estate
at Twickenham,[56] where he has withdrawn in reaction to the corruption of the literary kingdom represented by Bufo and Atticus—and, of
course, he wishes to be king of the kingdom for which Twickenham is
an emblem, the kingdom of the virtuous and self-possessed mind, that
kingdom his father ruled and which he himself yearns to rule ("Oh
grant me thus to live, and thus to die! / Who sprung from Kings shall
know less joy than I" [404–5]).

Possessed with their need for "advancement," Pope's enemies
behave exactly like the stereotype says the deformed will behave: they
strike out at anyone of worth or merit who might threaten their status.
Atticus will "Bear, like the *Turk,* no brother near the throne" (198).
Like the deformed, he sees everyone as a competitor, "View[s] him
with scornful, yet with jealous eyes, / And hate[s] for Arts that caus'd
himself to rise" (199–200). Bufo, too, loathes the worthy because they
cannot be made to praise him, and so (metaphorically, at least) he dis-
poses of them:

> *Dryden* alone (what wonder?) came not nigh,
> *Dryden* alone escap'd this judging eye:
> But still the Great have kindness in reserve,
> He help'd to bury whom he help'd to starve.
> (245–48)

Pope, too, can be the rejecting patron. He turns off Pitholeon, for instance—though not because Pitholeon has worth or merit or because he is perceived as a threat by him. Pitholeon is a worthless place-seeker. True merit and worth—such as possessed by Gay—are nourished and celebrated by Pope.

Driven by their need to "rise," envious of all who threaten their positions, striking out at all maliciously and underhandedly, Pope's enemies conform to the stereotype of the monstrous. But what about Pope? As a satirist, is he not, like Atticus, "Willing to wound," and does not his satire show that he, like Sporus, is consumed with "Spite"? After all, he wields a "Lash" and is "Glad of a quarrel" (303, 67). His enemies had pictured him as a spider eager to crush the butterfly out of pure maliciousness, and even Arbuthnot, taken aback by what appears to be a moment of sadistic violence, asks of Pope, "Who breaks a Butterfly upon a Wheel?" (308).

But when Pope strikes out, he is not motivated by envy or malice. Pope pictures his enemies as monsters so he can establish his identity against theirs and in this way hive off from himself suspicions that he has the typical character of the deformed. He is not, as the stereotype claimed, driven by malicious revenge ("Yet then did *Gildon* draw his venal quill; / I wish'd the man a dinner, and sate still" [151–52]). Nor does he feel that he cannot rest until he is superior ("Did some more sober Critic come abroad? / If wrong, I smil'd; if right, I kiss'd the rod" [157–58]). Nor is he governed by a maliciousness that desires blindly to destroy all:

> Curst be the Verse, how well soe'er it flow,
> That tends to make one worthy Man my foe,
> Give Virtue scandal, Innocence a fear,
> Or from the soft-ey'd Virgin steal a tear!
> (283–86)

Pope's attacks, we discover, come out of long-suffering exasperation, out of the press of circumstance that allows him little choice but to speak out, and always out of a sense of virtue wronged.

This is why Pope's concentration on the body and on disease is crucial. Pope's father was "Healthy" and his "Life, tho' long, to sickness past unknown" (401–2). Pope's own life is a "long Disease," a disease which, according to his maligners, affected his character, and which was, in fact, the cause of his malignancy, his hatred, his need for revenge. What the poem shows is something quite different: the plight of the poet beset by his own physical deformity and disease, to be sure, but driven to write not by those but by the fact that he is surrounded by a society deeply ill and, in its capacity "To spread about the Itch of

Verse and Praise" (224), dangerously infectious.[57] When he asks John to tell his visitors that "I'm sick, I'm dead" (2), underneath the comic exaggeration is the reminder that he *is* sick, "sick of Fops, and Poetry, and Prate" (229), sick of the debasement of values that has spread like a contagion throughout his society, sick of the madness of the times caused by the poisonous "Slaver" and "Venom" (106, 320) of the morally deranged, driven to the point of the death of the soul ("either way I'm sped, / If Foes, they write, if Friends, they read me dead" [31–32]). "What *Drop* or *Nostrum,*" he pleads to Dr. Arbuthnot, "can this Plague remove?" (29). It is *this* disease, and not the literal disease that has twisted his body, that has driven him to write satire.[58]

Thus having shown that his "crazy Shell" has not twisted his character, that his motives for satire have not grown out of envy and malice, in spite of what the stereotype of the deformed claimed, Pope can show that he has preserved the line of his parents. To the extent that he has "erred" from their model of simple virtue and humanity, his deviation can be explained by circumstances and pressures that surround him, from the fact that, unlike his parents, he is a prominent figure who has become an object of envy and malice. But the ways in which he has "erred" the most—being at the center of continual strife, failing to walk innoxious through his age, calling fools fools, in short, being a satirist—spring precisely from the same commitment to virtue, integrity, and decency which characterized his parents. In other words, the fact that he has "erred" from his parents' example proves that he has "heir'd" from them his "Christian Kernel," for it is precisely because he has remained true to their principles and values that Pope has been compelled to act so differently from his parents. (This also resolves the ambiguity about Pope's monstrosity and his baptism into his vocation. Jesus had said that one became a monster not because of his sins or the sins of his parents, but so that "the works of God should be manifest in him." Speaking from his "Christian Kernal," Pope, too, manifests the works of God, and so his baptism into the dirty profession is a true baptism. Pope's point, I assume, is not so much that he is pure as that his commitment to virtue has purified his satire of whatever baseness may derive from him. As he wrote later, "Truth guards the Poet, sanctifies the line, / And makes Immortal, Verse as mean as mine.")[59]

Being the true heir of his father, Pope is true to his father's greatest virtue: like him, he knows "No Language, but the Language of the Heart" (399). He is "soft by Nature, more a Dupe than Wit" (368), while his enemies, like all monsters, are void of natural affection (defined in the poem as the lack of friends).[60] Atticus is the "suspicious friend" (206); as for Bufo, "*Horace* and he went hand in hand" (234) only because Horace is bought and paid for; and Sporus "Wit ne'er tastes, and Beauty ne'er enjoys" (312) because he is immune to anything outside himself. In fact, all three have enthroned themselves at the center of their intense egocentricity. Early in the poem, Pope had toyed with the possibility that he was another Achilles, that his poetry was a product of a monstrously egocentric wrath. By the end of the poem, in contrast to his enemies, it turns out that he *is* like Achilles, but like Achilles in the "softer Parts of his Character": "Generous in his Temper, despising Gain and Booty, . . . and easy to his Friend." Pope's summary of this aspect of Achilles' character—"the truest Friend, the most tender Son, and the most generous Hero"—could easily be a précis of the image he presents of himself in *Arbuthnot*.[61] Thus, at the end of the poem, he turns from his angry attacks on his society to speak of his love for his parents, and throughout he celebrates his friendship with Swift, Gay, and, of course, Arbuthnot. Poetry itself is an appendage of friendship ("The Muse but serv'd to ease some Friend" [131]).

But by "the Language of the Heart," Pope means much more than this capacity to feel as a son and a friend. He means what Hay meant by "heart," and he claims the "Language of the Heart" for the same reason Hay exposed his heart, to assert his identity as a virtuous and benevolent man against the imputation of monstrosity. For the charge Pope is answering in *Arbuthnot* is that he is an envious and malicious monster and that his satire springs from a being devoid of all natural affections and lacking a heart. Hay countered this accusation by exposing a heart of impartial feelings, of "universal Benevolence," a heart so purged of egocentric self-involvement that it responded to the abstract universalities of Virtue and Vice. This is the posture in which Pope portrays himself, not only in *Arbuthnot* but in all of his poems of the 1730s: a man who writes satire not because he is interested in his own advancement ("Know, all the distant Din that World can keep / Rolls o'er my *Grotto,* and but sooths my Sleep"), not because he is another Thersites ("Cursed be the Verse, how well soe'er it flow, / That tends to make one worthy Man my foe"), and surely not out of a festering and self-tormenting malignancy that scorns all human kind—all the motives of a monster. Pope portrays himself as deeply in love with an impersonal Virtue ("TO VIRTUE ONLY and HER FRIENDS, A FRIEND"), not simply disapproving of Vice but offended by it, fully committed to the good because he has widened his natural affections to embrace all of humanity. In short, Pope is a man driven by that which a monster lacks, a heart, and hence he is willing to "perish in the gen'rous Cause" of Virtue:

> Ask you what Provocation I have had?
> The strong Antipathy of Good to Bad.
> When Truth or Virtue an Affront endures,
> Th' Affront is mine, my Friend, and should be yours.
> . . . .
> Mine, as a Friend to ev'ry worthy mind;
> And mine as Man, who feel for all mankind.[62]

Pope's outbursts of satiric anger occur not because he is devoid of natural affections. To the contrary, his lashing of Sporus proceeds from the very heart that turns in tenderness to his friend Arbuthnot and cares for his dying mother.

Pope's self-anatomy of his heart had some success. Many of his readers saw in his self-portrait the man that he had hoped they would see: "Such a noble generosity and amiable tenderness of sentiment," Owen Ruffhead remarked, "seems to have flowed warm from the heart." And another of his earliest biographers found in Pope that quality everyone thought monsters were incapable of having, precisely that quality Hay anatomized his own heart to prove he possessed, "universal benevolence."[63]

V

Of course, what some saw as universal benevolence and love of virtue, others saw as something quite different. What Cibber saw was a "Talent of Self-Commendation." And Joseph Warton thought Pope's writings "tinctured and blemished with a great share of vanity, and self-importance, and with too many commendations of his own integrity . . . and virtue."[64]

Such negative reactions were inevitable. In point of fact, the stereotype trapped monsters in a vicious double bind. Charged with being devoid of natural affection, they were compelled to publish the heart to prove the charge wrong. But by publishing the heart, they ran the danger of verifying the very stereotype they sought to disprove, for every time they insisted on the purity of their hearts, every time they pointed to their love of virtue, they merely confirmed what the stereotype said about them: obsessed with the need to "free themselves from scorn," monsters were driven by an obsessive self-regard.

Because the deformed were put in the impossible contradiction of having to tout without a hint of egocentricity their own humanity and love of virtue, in *Deformity* Hay exposed his "personal Imperfections . . . naked to the World" and in *Arbuthnot* Pope acknowledged how much his behavior seemed that of a monster and admitted (as he does in much of his poetry of the 1730s) to many faults:

> In me what Spots (for Spots I have) appear,
> Will prove at least the Medium must be clear.
> In this impartial Glass, my Muse intends
> Fair to expose myself, . . .
> (*Satire II.i.,* ll. 55–58)[65]

Hay and Pope could prove their hearts "sound and untainted" only after they first established their candor by being impartial—and self-critical—witnesses against themselves, admitting to their deformity and, by doing so, redefining their monstrosity against the grain of the stereotype.

Of course, this response itself easily could be reinterpreted (and in Pope's case it routinely was) as simply a more subtle and duplicitous way which the deformed had found to preen themselves in their ego-centricity, for the stereotype claimed that the monstrous were devious and habitually hid their inner deformity under a plausible mask of vir-tuousness. Thus, the double bind of the stereotype caught the deformed in a nightmare of infinite regression: every gesture they made to free themselves from the stereotype was self-defeating, and every gesture they made to free themselves from their self-defeat sim-ply reconfirmed the truth of the stereotype. A deformed person was compelled to reveal his inner self to prove that he was not like the stereotype claimed he was, but he had been defined as so egocentric and mendacious that his very act of self-revelation was taken as evi-dence of his egocentricity and mendacity. In short, a monster was a "Medium" that could never be clear.[66]

It is obvious, then, why Pope came to put so much stock in his *Let-ters,* which he considered one of the most important projects of the last half of his career. Here was that clear medium in which he would appear in his "natural undress" (to use the language which he used in the letters themselves to prompt his readers to view them as unpremeditated outpourings), a medium in which the reader would find no trace of deformity but only the "marks of a plain mind & unde-signing heart." In the *Letters,* there would be no doubt about what were his "real Sentiments," for they "flow'd warm from his heart," spontaneous and "free from all disguises." All Pope had to do was to dissociate himself from their publication and to give the impression that they were "scribbled with all the carelessness and inattention imaginable." By doing so, he hoped, his letters would be seen as "the most impartial Representations of a free heart."[67]

The stereotype of the deformed, however, was too viciously efficient in trapping its victims in its double binds to be fully circumvented even by this expedient. For every eighteenth-century reader who found in the *Letters* "a Spirit of *universal Benevolence* and *Beneficence*" or who was moved by the writer's "humanity and goodness of heart," there was another who thought they were "studied and artificial," written "always with his reputation in his head," or who saw "all those eloquent expressions of benevolence and affection as too much parade."[68]

Even as early as 1716, Pope seems to have intuited the limitations of letters. In a letter to Mary Wortley Montagu, speaking as he often does of his spontaneity and openness, he is so anxious to convince her that he is uncalculating that he presses his usual metaphor of exposing his heart to a grotesquely literalistic conclusion:

> The freedome I shall use in this manner of Thinking aloud (as somebody calls it) or Talking upon paper, may indeed prove me a fool, but it will prove me one of the best sort of fools, the honest ones. And since what Folly we have will infallibly Buoy up at one time or other, in spite of all our art to keep it down; tis almost foolish to take any pains to conceal it at all, and almost knavish to do it from those that are our friends. If Momus his project had taken of having Windows in our breasts, I should be for carrying it further and making those windows Casements: that while a Man showd his Heart to all the world, he might do something more for his friends, e'en take it out, and trust it to their handling. I think I love you as well as King Herod could Herodias, (tho I never had so much as one Dance with you) and would as freely give you my heart in a Dish, as he did another's head.[69]

One can feel here Pope's sense that he has come up against limits—the limits created by the stereotype of the deformed, which will not allow him to be a credible witness for himself because it has denied him the trust accorded to those who are not monsters; the limits, too, of letters, and probably of language, which cannot body forth the self either convincingly or reliably, the medium being too distant from the thing itself to be compelling and too easily manipulated to be trusted; and surely the limits of human reality, which does not accommodate the pure communion of naked hearts, except in such bizarre fantasies as this self-anatomy.

Hay's *Deformity* ends in a turn that is not only equally bizarre, but one which uncannily echoes Pope's vision of an altruistic autopsy. Hay began his essay, it will be remembered, promising to "expose" his personal imperfections "naked to the World": "When I have thus anatomized my self, I hope my Heart will be found sound and untainted, and my Intentions honest and sincere." And, through the remainder of the essay, he "lay[s] open [his] own Heart to the Reader." In the last paragraph of his essay proper, he returns to the image of the anatomy.

> Mr. *Addison* admires the Humanity of *Cyrus* (or rather of *Xenophon*) in ordering his Body to be buried in the Earth, that it might be useful in manuring it. My Flesh will afford but little Manure: but in another Respect my Carcass may be of eminent Service to Mankind: and therefore if I should die intestate, or not mention it in my Will; let the World take this as my dying Request. As I have for some Years been afflicted with the Stone, and owe the Preservation and Ease of Life since to the continual taking of great Quantities of Soap, I desire my Body may be opened and examined by eminent Surgeons; that Mankind may be informed of its Effect. And if a Stone should be found in my Bladder (as I imagine there will) I desire it may be preserved among Sir *Hans Sloane*'s Collection.—Until that Time comes, I hope to employ the little Remainder of Life in Pursuits not unbecoming a rational Creature.[70]

What is one to make of this extraordinary moment? The sheer extravagance of the gesture is surely a sign of how desperate Hay is to prove his humanity and how much he feels the ways he has tried to free himself from the opprobrium of the stereotype thus far have failed. But it is also his most successful maneuver to assert his human heart, his most subtle variation on acquiescing to the stereotype of the monster in order to subvert it.

Hay admits his deformity in this passage but completely transforms it. For when he delivers his body to that eminent collector of curiosities and monsters, Sloane, he does not hand it over to him to be kept in a cabinet like a freak's. To the contrary, the "monstrosity" of Hay is the abnormality of an everyday disease, "the Stone." His is a common case, a normal abnormality, as it were—and hence a sign of his quotidian humanity. Hay transforms his idiosyncratic monstrosity into the kind of monstrosity all of us share, for it is our common case to be imbruted and suffer incorporation in some form. What is abnormal is what Hay does with his body. By bequeathing his body to Sloane for the betterment of all mankind, he is making a gesture which demonstrates his nobility of spirit, a gesture from his heart, uncommon in its benevolence. He proves his "Humanity" by offering up his "Carcass" on the altar of altruistic Virtue as "an eminent Service to Mankind." Hay does all this in words, to be sure, but his impulse, like Pope's, is to make the window in the bosom a casement so we can touch the thing itself. Language is being pressed to *enact itself* in the real world, to demonstrate as much as language can that it is a reliable witness to what it claims. For what we are reading is a will to which we have been made the executors: "if I should die intestate, or not mention it in my Will; let the

World take this as my dying Request." Should Hay's noble gesture go unfulfilled, it is our failure as executors, not his. (By the way, when Hay died in 1755, his body was delivered up for an autopsy and the results put on deposit in the British Museum.)[71]

Like Hay, Pope found he could not free himself fully from the double bind of the stereotype by merely showing his heart. And so, like Hay, he turned to a kind of self-enactment in language as a way to prove that he was not a monster, that he had a heart that was "sound and untainted" and intentions "honest and sincere." I want to concentrate on *Epistle I.i.* (*To Bolingbroke*), but the strategies Pope uses in this poem, I think, are typical of the strategies he used to construct his self-identity in much of his poetry of the 1730s. *Epistle I.i.* begins this way:

> ST JOHN, whose love indulg'd my labours past
> Matures my present, and shall bound my last!
> Why will you break the Sabbath of my days?
> Now sick alike of Envy and of Praise.
> Publick too long, ah let me hide my Age!
> See modest Cibber now has left the Stage:
> Our Gen'rals now, retir'd to their Estates,
> Hang their old Trophies o'er the Garden gates,
> In Life's cool evening satiate of applause,
> Nor fond of bleeding, ev'n in BRUNSWICK's cause.
>   A Voice there is, that whispers in my ear,
> ('Tis Reason's voice, which sometimes one can hear)
> "Friend Pope! be prudent, let your Muse take breath,
> "And never gallop Pegasus to death;
> "Lest stiff, and stately, void of fire, or force,
> "You limp, like Blackmore, on a Lord Mayor's horse."
>   Farewell then Verse, and Love, and ev'ry Toy,
> The rhymes and rattles of the Man or Boy:
> What right, what true, what fit, we justly call,
> Let this be all my care—for this is All:
> To lay this harvest up, and hoard with haste
> What ev'ry day will want, and most, the last.
>
> (1–22)

The poem opens with Pope expressing his desire to retire from writing poetry. He has earned this "Sabbath" after a long period of creativity, and he wants now to cease from his labor. Since it is Bolingbroke who is urging him to write and since, when the poem was published in March 1738, Bolingbroke was on the brink of returning to England from his "retirement" in France to reinvigorate the Opposition, it is specifically the poetry of ethical and political engagement that Pope wants to retire from, the kind of poetry he had abandoned "Fancy's Maze" for and has dedicated himself to almost exclusively for the past decade, the very kind of poetry he had publicly thanked Bolingbroke in *An Essay on Man* for inspiring him to write. He dismisses this poetry as a mere "Toy," for he is "Now sick alike of Envy and of Praise." Like Cibber, he has played a "Publick" role and has gained a good deal of celebrity for it. But now, he is "satiate of applause," and the way this phrase plays against "Sabbath" suggests that Pope's rejection of his poetry is really symptomatic of a deeper crisis. For "Sabbath" reminds us that this poem is written at his climacteric, and by the end of the third verse paragraph it is clear that he wants to turn his mind to a meditation of last things. His poetry, he feels, partakes too much of worldly desire, and what he now longs for in his "Sabbath" is something more spiritual. (This dichotomy is muted at this point in the poem, but increasingly the corruption of the world is spoken of in the language of appetite and bodily drives, virtue in the language of spiritual longing.) The dichotomy is pointed at again in the couplet that ends the third verse paragraph, where Pope exposes his desire to "harvest up" goods for his final days: the image, developed from the barest hint in Horace, is the traditional biblical image for spiritual, as opposed to worldly, goods.[72]

In spite of these overt statements that he wishes to leave off poetry entirely, Pope betrays, even in these opening lines, a much more mixed and complex attitude. It is true, he thinks of himself as a kind of Cibber, but he almost immediately backs away from this comparison as too sardonic, too untrue, and compares himself to retired generals. To the degree that Pope feels that he, like Cibber, has used his talent in the service of "Publick" entertainment, we can understand why, in this autumnal mood, he is tempted to dismiss it as a "Toy." But in his comparison of himself to the generals, we can hear Pope expressing a different sense of his poetry. For part of Pope's "Publick" role has been to battle the forces of corruption and evil (once he had redirected his career in the 1730s, he often pictured himself as "arm'd for *Virtue*," with satire as his "Weapon" in his war with vice [*Satire II.i.,* 105, 69]). He has labored arduously in the service of his country. Given this context, his comment that retired generals are not "fond of bleeding, ev'n in BRUNSWICK's cause" expresses his desire to turn away from poetry, to be sure, but the emotional color of the dismissal here is entirely different from his dismissal of it as a "Toy." For, by suggesting that Britain's cause has been transmuted mysteriously to "BRUNSWICK's cause," Pope suggests that the cause of this world has become a foreign cause, that the world he has battled for has somehow slipped into the possession of the enemy, and it is no longer in his interest to fight for it. There is a real sense of defeat in the opening verse paragraphs. The reference to Cibber recalls Pope's previous attack on him in *Arbuthnot:*

> Whom have I hurt? has Poet yet, or Peer,
> Lost the arch'd eye-brow, or *Parnassian* sneer?
> And has not *Colly* still his Lord, and Whore?
>   (95–97)

Although Cibber at last had retired from the stage four years earlier, Pope had not driven him from it, and anyway, the joke here is that Cibber kept returning to the stage in spite of his official retirement. Further, the sarcastic "modest" reminds us that Pope in fact has performed no moral transformation either: Cibber is as possessed with pride now as he was when Pope first attacked him. But the cause was just, and in spite of the word "Toy," it is clear that Pope also sees poetry, for all of its inefficacy, as an honorable, even important vocation that he is turning from with some degree of wistfulness.

And yet, for this very reason and in spite of his sense that his battles have all petered out in small ironies, Pope is unable here to reject with complete conviction the "Publick" realm and to devote himself to the private and the spiritual ("What right, what true, what fit, we justly call, / Let this be all my care—for this is All"). If only poetry were merely a "Toy" and not also a noble battle against Vice, perhaps he could turn from this world completely and make a clean break with it. But when he says, "A Voice there is, that whispers in my ear / ('Tis Reason's voice, which sometimes one can hear") and then adds with just a touch of overdone formality, "Farewell then . . . ," we can hear his dry amusement and comic exasperation at this being an old, interminable argument that he has had with himself. Indeed, it was an old argument. "My poetical affairs drawing toward a fair period, I hope the day will shortly come when I may honestly say[,] Nunc versus et cætera ludicra pono . . . ," and Pope goes on quoting these lines, the very lines he is imitating here in *Epistle I.i.* Pope wrote this letter in 1718.[73] And that is why his comparison of himself to Cibber is so ironically apt: for he *is* like Cibber, continually "retiring," but always coming back on the stage. (He had just "retired" a year earlier in *Epistle II.ii.*—in fact, he even used the metaphor of his leaving the stage at the end of the poem.)[74]

By pointing to these ambiguities, in one sense all I am doing is specifying the intellectual and emotional content of the formal paradox on which the poem is constructed: this is an argument against poetry written in poetry. But the way in which the qualifications and contrary points of view surface and then fall away and then surface again as

Pope begins to think about rejecting the world, skeptically at first, then with more warmth, is too fluid, too moody, and seems to be too driven by pre- and half-conscious musing for the poem to be thought of as a static expression of paradox. What is being embodied in the voice of this poem is not simply a complex person in conflict with himself, but a complex person in a dynamic state of flux, exploring, committing himself, then becoming dissatisfied, re-thinking and re-thinking again, and always darting into and out of a hundred evanescent modulations of tone and mood. Later in the poem, Pope will describe the texture of his life this way: "I plant, root up, I build, and then confound, / Turn round to square, and square again to round." This is a poem that enacts a self in motion.

We can see this clearly in the next lines of the poem:

> But ask not, to what Doctors I apply?
> Sworn to no Master, of no Sect am I:
> As drives the storm, at any door I knock,
> And house with Montagne now, or now with Lock.
> Sometimes a Patriot, active in debate,
> Mix with the World, and battle for the State,
> Free as young Lyttelton, her cause pursue,
> Still true to Virtue, and as warm as true:
> Sometimes, with Aristippus, or St. Paul,
> Indulge my Candor, and grow all to all;
> Back to my native Moderation slide,
> And win my way by yielding to the tyde.
>   Long, as to him who works for debt, the Day;
> Long as the Night to her whose love's away;
> Long as the Year's dull circle seems to run,
> When the brisk Minor pants for twenty-one;
> So slow th' unprofitable Moments roll,
> That lock up all the Functions of my soul;
> That keep me from Myself; and still delay
> Life's instant business to a future day:
> That task, which as we follow, or despise,
> The eldest is a fool, the youngest wise;
> Which done, the poorest can no wants endure,
> And which not done, the richest must be poor.
>   Late as it is, I put my self to school,
> And feel some comfort, not to be a fool.
> Weak tho' I am of limb, and short of sight,
> Far from a Lynx, and not a Giant quite,
> I'll do what MEAD and CHESELDEN advise,
> To keep these limbs, and to preserve these eyes.
> Not to go back, is somewhat to advance,
> And men must walk at least before they dance.
>   (23–54)

The complexities and undertones of the beginning of the poem seem to have been forgotten as Pope embraces in his imagination the real possibility of his abandoning his "Publick" role and committing himself to "Life's instant business." His optimism about how easy it is to unshackle himself from stale, unproductive ways of acting and feeling and to find new ways that answer to his soul's varied needs is beautifully captured in the enthusiastic vigor of his vision ("As drives the storm, at any door I knock") and the excited sweep of the verse. And yet, the passage is too optimistic, too simplistic. It is shot through with odd imbalances and confusions. Take, for instance, the matter of how we get here in the first place. The abrupt transition into the passage—"But ask not, to what Doctors I apply? / Sworn to no Master, of no Sect am I"—is quite unprepared for and a bit too knowing. It is as if Pope is speaking from out of his old impulse of craving for Bolingbroke's approval, an impulse so strong that it is liable to break out at any time, no matter how irrelevantly, and this accounts for the school-boyish eagerness with which Pope self-consciously displays, for his greatly admired teacher, how cleverly he has solved a very difficult problem. The hero-worship implied here, of course, contrasts with the explicit statement of these lines—"Sworn to no Master"—but that phrase is suspect anyway because in *An Essay on Man* Pope had addressed Bolingbroke in quite the opposite way: "Come then, my Friend, my Genius, come along, / Oh master of the poet, and the song!" (4.373–74).

Further, the rhetorical confusion of this passage suggests that Pope is being much too facile. He begins orderly enough, insisting that he can move easily between opposites: "As drives the storm, at any door I knock, / And house with Montagne now, or now with Lock." He then moves on to a second, more fully developed opposition: "Sometimes a Patriot, active in debate, / Mix with the World, and battle for the State, / Free as young Lyttelton . . . / Sometimes, with Aristippus, or St. Paul, / Indulge my Candor, and grow all to all." In Horace, the opposition is very clear; Horace states how sometimes he devotes himself to public life and fights for virtue, and how at other times he indulges himself in private pleasures, following Aristippus's advice to savor momentary pleasures; he finishes by neatly, almost epigrammatically, summing up the opposition: "Et mihi res, non me rebus, submittere conor." But in Pope, all of this is much more messy. The same general opposition seems to be at work, for in a footnote he refers to Horace's description of Aristippus as one to whom "every condition and state and circumstance was fitting," and so presumably he means to contrast Aristippus to Lyttelton, who is "active in debate" precisely because he finds present circumstances so unfitting. But the verb phrases that set out this contrast—"Mix with the world" and "Indulge my Candor"—are just unparallel enough to blur the opposition, an opposition that is thrown further off balance by the fact that one exemplar, Lyttelton, has been set against two, Aristippus and St. Paul.

And what *is* St. Paul doing here? His presence more deeply confuses this passage. He and Aristippus are similar, presumably, in that both seem to submit themselves to the things of the world, "grow all to all," and in that way they both contrast to Lyttelton. But St. Paul grew all to all for the purpose of all men's salvation,[75] Aristippus out of hedonistic self-indulgence. And so St. Paul seems to generate a new opposition (to Aristippus) rather than to complete the opposition (to Lyttelton) that the rhetorical structure requires. And further, when Pope says that he, like Aristippus and St. Paul, indulges his candor "and grow[s] all to all," he uses a phrase that he has used earlier in *To Cobham*, a phrase which hardly points to the kind of open-heartedness and innocence that Pope claims he himself achieves. For Pope had used this exact phrase to explain how Wharton brought about the complete dissolution of his character by assuming one self-contradictory role after another: "Grown all to all, from no one vice exempt, / And most contemptible, to shun contempt" (194–95). It is difficult to think of another single phrase in all of his poetry more inappropriate for Pope to use to vindicate his own sliding from role to role.

These confusions do not immediately undercut Pope's statement that he can project himself effortlessly into opposite extremes: his voice is so exuberant that his conviction carries us almost all the way through the passage without our being deeply troubled. But the gradual accretion of these confusions increasingly makes us aware that Pope's formulations are too simplistic, that he is over-optimistic in his claims that such goals are easily achieved.

More to the point, it is Pope who is becoming more aware of his overconfidence. I do not know how otherwise to explain the remarkable shifts in the next verse paragraph—the sudden dampening of his exuberance, the examination of the puzzle of self-identity not only more somberly but also from a point of view opposite from the one he has just expressed. Pope must have heard his own facileness, for suddenly gone are the sense of the effortless assumption of one role after another, the impression of a quick achievement of self-fulfillment, and that almost smug certainty of self-knowledge. Now the tone emphasizes longing and unfulfillment ("Long, as to him who works for debt, the Day"), and now self-possession is perceived as a "task" that requires effort, not something easily won by yielding to the tide.

Most importantly, Pope seems to react against the very substance of how he claimed he could achieve self-possession. Earlier he had assumed that the self could be fulfilled by acting out its needs and impulses through a variety of roles; now, when he speaks of split identity and the pain that comes with that split ("That keep me from Myself"), it is as if he has heard the echo of Wharton in "grow all to all" and realizes that the proliferation of roles atomizes as well as articulates the self, and that in all of his sliding from role to role, his self may be undergoing a kind of dispersion. In fact, he uses this locution of the split self again in the very next verse paragraph, which begins, "Late as it is, I put myself to school, / And feel some comfort, not to be a fool." The contrast with his optimism less than fifteen lines earlier could not be greater. Whereas there he exuded confidence in the possibility of shaping his identity, here he becomes increasingly sober, dwelling not on possibilities but on limitations, especially the unalterable limitations of a diseased and dying body. Whereas earlier he was energized into activity by his number of choices and the prospect of fulfillment, being able to "house" with this and that person, then "Mix," "battle," "pursue," "slide" and finally "win [his] way," now he finds cold comfort in making the bare maintenance of the status quo seem not to be a defeat. And whereas earlier he so confidently believed in the prospects of achieving self-identity that he could actually name this and that role, this and that possibility, now he can define selfhood only by a negative, "not to be a fool."

And then the poem once again turns with astonishing disjointedness from what was just said:

> Say, does thy blood rebel, thy bosom move
> With wretched Av'rice, or as wretched Love?
> Know, there are Words, and Spells, which can controll
> (Between the Fits) this Fever of the soul:
> Know, there are Rhymes, which (fresh and fresh apply'd)
> Will cure the arrant'st Puppy of his Pride.
> Be furious, envious, slothful, mad or drunk,
> Slave to a Wife or Vassal to a Punk,
> A Switz, a High-dutch, or a Low-dutch Bear—
> All that we ask is but a patient Ear.
>   'Tis the first Virtue, Vices to abhor;
> And the first Wisdom, to be a Fool no more.
> But to the world, no bugbear is so great,
> As want of figure, and a small Estate,
> To either India see the Merchant fly,
> Scar'd at the spectre of pale Poverty!
> See him, with pains of body, pangs of soul,
> Burn through the Tropic, freeze beneath the Pole!
>
> (55–72)

The abrupt shifting of his attention from himself to his society, the surprising resurfacing of the topic of poetry, an issue which seemed to have been disposed of many lines ago, the sudden modulation in tone from "philosophic" soberness to dyspeptic irony and then increasingly abrasive satire—the abruptness of all these turns suggests a self mulling over on some fairly submerged level a host of issues that had not until this moment entirely surfaced to consciousness. The only obvious connnection between this section and the preceding one is the diseased body. Pope has just spoken of his own bodily infirmities ("Weak tho' I am of limb, and short of sight"), and then he immediately attacks the moral infirmities of his society, but moral infirmities described pointedly as if they were diseased physiological processes ("Say, does thy blood rebel, thy bosom move / With wretched Av'rice, or as wretched Love?"). And it is precisely thoughts of the diseased body which, I think, create the transition here, throwing Pope forward to a new point of view where he gathers up old, unresolved thoughts and feelings. Pope began the poem complaining about how ineffective and limiting his satirtic poetry was. He turned away from it to cultivate self-possession, but he came to recognize that in this, too, he was just as ineffective. He progressively understands that all of his options are limited because he progressively sees himself as more and more limited—if, by nothing else, by a body that he must continually work at just to keep from getting worse and whose dissolution is pressing him more and more urgently to achieve an internal equanimity that those very limitations are preventing him from achieving. And now he suddenly strikes out satirically. What appears to have happened is this: Pope, after conscientiously criticizing his own inadequacies, failures, and limitations, seeing the contrast between his life and the lives of those less conscientious than himself, abruptly, aggressively, and quite angrily asserts that, as inadequate as his life is, "not to be a fool" *is* better than nothing at all. His diseased body, and his recognition of the limitations it signals, is much to be preferred to the moral disease (a few lines later called "this Fever of the soul") that afflicts most members of society, and to their inability even to perceive that they are sick. (Pope repeats here the central rhetorical gesture of *Arbuthnot,* using his body to contrast himself to a morally diseased and monstrous enemy and thus vindicate himself.)

The issue of poetry reenters the poem, even though Pope had bade it farewell many stanzas earlier, because his thoughts have now turned to the vices of his times and he had always conceived of his poetry as a weapon in his battle against vice, no matter how inefficacious he finally concluded it was. He continues to think of poetry as inefficacious, for he is being sarcastic when he says that it can cure evils. As a lenitive, poetry works only between the fits it is supposed to cure, and it works only if the hearer allows it to work. "All we ask is but a patient Ear." But anyone who has an ear patient enough to listen to criticism of himself obviously has enough self-mastery to control those passions which the poetry is supposed to cure.

Still, the bitterness of the sarcasm is telling. Pope is bitter because he wishes he *did* have something with which to do battle against his evil times, something which would make a difference. And the sheer intensity of this feeling gives away the deep contradictions Pope has uncovered in himself. He began this poem rejecting satiric poetry and turning away from "Publick" concerns in order to settle the needs of his soul and to cultivate personal equanimity. Now, he has turned, willy nilly, back to the "Publick" sphere and is writing satiric poetry— in the teeth of his knowledge that it is ineffective.

Pope's satiric attack on the sins of the age is shaped around one of his most persistent satiric motifs, *ad exemplum regis*. In *Epistle I.i.,* as in much of his political poetry, Pope traces the widespread corruption of the country to the top, the king and his court and his minister. "The People," says Pope,

> are a many-headed Beast:
> Can they direct what measures to pursue,
> Who know themselves so little what to do?
> (119–21)

They do not know what to do because none of the country's leaders has provided an example of what to do. The privileged classes that should act as the head of the body politic have abrogated their responsibility by refusing to master even themselves and their own impulses. The King is "Slave to a Wife[,] . . . Vassal to a Punk"; "From low St. James's up to high St. Paul," the religious and political leaders counsel giving up virtue and pursuing money, that "Harness for a slave" (62, 82, 87). And the court?

> Adieu to Virtue if you're once a Slave:
> Send her to Court, you send her to her Grave.
> (118–19)

Having made themselves slaves to their own impulses, they become as shapeless, as monstrous, as the endless transmutations of those desires ("Did ever Proteus, Merlin, any Witch, / Tranform themselves so strangely as the Rich?" [152–53]), losing all capacity "To act consistent with [themselves] an hour" (137). In their monstrosity, they act as examples only in the most ironic sense, monstrous exemplars of inconsistency that the poor—the "many-headed Beast"—model their own monstrosity on.[76]

Yet in his satiric attack, Pope continues to exhibit those contradictions in his character that had surfaced earlier, and he begins to expose new ones.

At the heart of Pope's indictment of his times is his version of England's having so morally degenerated that it is now the object of two simple, competing voices, the "new Court jargon, or the good old song" (98).

> Here, Wisdom calls: "See Virtue first! be bold!
> "As Gold to Silver, Virtue is to Gold."
> There, London's voice: "Get Mony, Mony still!
> "And then let Virtue follow, if she will."
> (77–80)

Moral conduct thus has come down to making the simple choice between which voice to be guided by:

> Who counsels best? who whispers, "Be but Great,"
> . . . .
> Or he, who bids thee face with steddy view
> Proud Fortune, and look shallow Greatness thro':
> And, while he bids thee, sets th' Example too?
> (101, 107–9)

In a society reduced to such egregious corruption and immorality, Pope simply *must* take a side and speak out against vice one more time. And though we may both understand and admire his gesture, we cannot be blind to the fact that his return to satire contradicts everything he has said earlier about how ineffective it is. Pope certainly is not blind to the contradiction, though at the moment he seems unwilling to move out of the stalemate it has caused, for when he speaks of the voice of Wisdom again ("Yet every child another song will sing, / 'Virtue, brave boys! 'tis Virtue makes a King'" [91–92]), his conceiving of it as the voice of a child betrays the fact that he thinks his singing *his* song is an act of innocence—and naiveté.

There is another contradiction. Pope attacks his society for its inability to hear the voice of good counsel. When Pope writes, "Who counsels best? who whispers, 'Be but Great'," the line recalls the earlier moment, "A Voice there is, that whispers in my ear, / ('Tis Reason's voice, which sometimes one can hear)." The voice was the voice of Wisdom telling Pope to turn away from writing satire, and since Pope is now in the middle of galloping Pegasus to death, he himself has not listened to his own good counsel, a fact made doubly ironic since he praises the voice of Wisdom for its willingness to "set th' Example too!"

And then, in the extraordinary conclusion of the poem, Pope drops this attack on society just as abruptly as he began it and turns his attention to his own case:

> You laugh, half Beau half Sloven if I stand,
> My Wig all powder, and all snuff my Band;
> You laugh, if Coat and Breeches strangely vary,
> White Gloves, and Linnen worthy Lady Mary!
> But when no Prelate's Lawn with Hair-shirt lin'd,
> Is half so incoherent as my Mind,
> When (each Opinion with the next at strife,
> One ebb and flow of follies all my Life)
> I plant, root up, I build, and then confound,
> Turn round to square, and square again to round;
> You never change one muscle of your face,
> You think this Madness but a common case,
> Nor once to Chanc'ry, nor to Hales apply;
> Yet hang your lip, to see a Seam awry!
> Careless how ill I with myself agree;
> Kind to my dress, my figure, not to Me.
> Is this my Guide, Philosopher, and Friend?
> This, He who loves me, and who ought to mend?
> Who ought to make me (what he can, or none,)
> That Man divine whom Wisdom calls her own,
> Great without Title, without Fortune bless'd,
> Rich ev'n when plunder'd, honour'd while oppress'd,
> Lov'd without youth, and followed without power,
> At home tho' exil'd, free, tho' in the Tower.
> In short, that reas'ning, high, immortal Thing,
> Just less than Jove, and much above a King,
> Nay half in Heav'n—except (what's mighty odd)
> A Fit of Vapours clouds this Demi-god.
>   (161–88)

Pope abruptly changes focus because he feels that he cannot maintain his integrity continuing this attack on a world where no single person can "act consistent with himself": for he has become increasingly conscious of "how ill I with myself agree," and since he himself cannot provide an example for the world, he cannot go on to attack society for its failure to live up to the principle of *ad exemplum regis*. Nor can he blame others for not listening to the voice of Wisdom when he himself has not. Nor can he go on claiming that satire is ineffectual and yet continue writing it. Nor can he pretend that he has achieved, and achieved with great ease, equanimity of mind when his heart is driven to anguish at the sight of his country's corruption—and at the sight of his own lack of equanimity. And so on. He has met the enemy, and it is he himself ("White Gloves, and Linnen worthy Lady Mary"). He can maintain his integrity only by admitting his incoherence, the same incoherence he hates in those he satirizes:

> I plant, root up, I build, and then confound,
> Turn round to square, and square again to round.

This couplet echoes Jeremiah 1:10, where God gives the prophet his calling to purify the nation: "See, I have this day set thee over the nations and over the kingdoms, to root out, and to pull down, and to destroy, and to throw down, to build, and to plant." Pope, too, has tried to purify England, but he fails because of his incoherence. But the language of this couplet points to that other drive of Pope, that drive toward spiritual self-possession, which was spoken of in these same images of planting and harvest earlier in the poem: "To lay this harvest up, and hoard with haste / What ev'ry day will want, and most, the last." In this task, too, Pope has failed. Indeed, these two drives, as the structural "incoherence" of the poem continually enacts, subvert each other, the longing for a Sabbath of the soul drawing Pope away from his "Publick" task, his sense of his "Publick" duties drawing him away from the private needs of his soul. And there appears to be no way to resolve these disparate needs of the self, as is suggested by the image of the squaring the circle ("Turn round to square, and square again to round"), a mathematical problem impossible to solve but so enticing that it is equally impossible not to try.

Most often, though, the poem traces the source of incoherence to the body and its passions. The vices corrupting England are imaged as a physiological process, a "Fever of the soul." Love in this society has been reduced to a mechanistic agitation in the "bosom," avarice a rebellion in the "blood," a kind of "Lust" (124). And behind all the vices in this society seem to be working the blind bodily needs of sex and hunger:

> . . . some farm the Poor-box, some the Pews;
> Some keep Assemblies, and wou'd keep the Stews;
> Some with fat Bucks on childless Dotards fawn;
> Some win rich Widows by their Chine and Brawn; . . .
> (128–31)

In the first half of his attack on the corruption of his time, Pope focuses on avarice; in the second half, he abruptly (remarkably so, even in a poem governed by seemingly incoherent transitions) redirects his focus to attack those who fail "To act consistent with [themselves] an hour."

But this is less a shift of focus than it initially appears. Pope's point of view here is that which we have seen throughout this study: when people allow themselves to become slaves to their passions, to use the image the poem constantly returns to, their identities become as incoherent as those passions. This is why Pope figures incoherence as a physiological process. Regardless of the particular passion the English have delivered themselves to, they have abrogated self-mastery by making themselves slaves to the ebb and flow of the passions, whose source is the body. The lineaments of their selves become amorphous. They "Transform themselves" like "Proteus," they become monsters, a "many-headed Beast," because they have abandoned to the body their prerogative of mastery, and the body transmogrifies the self into its own incoherent energies.

Hence, the poem concludes with Pope's admission that his own monstrous amorphousness ("how ill I with myself agree") is rooted in the body, too. He is inconsistent (Pope is obviously speaking of Bolingbroke in these concluding lines, but the language is so brilliantly equivocal that he is speaking simultaneously about Bolingbroke and himself both, deflating his own unrealistic view of the perfection of his mentor while mocking the unrealistic vision of what he wishes he himself could be). The poem is occasioned, it should be remembered, by the crisis of the body, the climacteric. Pope is "half in Heav'n," but he is half in the body, too, and because he is in the body, he is as easily mastered by a "Fit of Vapours" as those whose incoherence he has attacked throughout the poem.

And yet, this admission of his shapelessness is tossed off as a high-spirited joke, in spite of the fact that throughout the poem he has been angered by others' incoherence and anguished by his own. It becomes a joke because of one final revelation of Pope has about own incoherence. As soon as he admits his incoherence, he turns to Bolingbroke to upbraid his mentor for not taking him to task:

> You never change one muscle of your face,
> You think this Madness but a common case, . . .

But, of course, it *is* the common case, and almost as soon as he has said it, Pope realizes that it is, and that is why he turns on himself, contradicting himself one last time, and concludes the poem by making fun of himself for thinking that he somehow is immune from the inconsistency common to humankind.

This last gesture resembles the way that Hay offered himself up for an autopsy in order to free himself from the double bind of the stereotype of the deformed. Like Hay, Pope acknowledges his own monstrosity, and he admits that his incoherence springs from his body and his passions. His poem, in fact, has been a self-anatomy which ends in his laying bare his full deformity. But, by acknowledging his deformity, he displaces it from the singular one of his own twisted body to the normal abnormality of the human estate. He is a monster, but that is the "common case." And further, just as Hay offered up his monstrosity to an autopsy to prove that his heart was "sound and untainted," and did so in language that validated its own claims, so Pope uses this very act of anatomizing his monstrousness to *enact* impulses of a heart that the stereotype denied that the deformed had. For though the "incoherence" of the poem has been caused by Pope's passions, these passions have had their origins in qualities, values, and feelings which the stereotype specifically denied monsters had—in such natural affections as love of country, for instance, and love of virtue, feelings and values which have undermined Pope's consistency because they are at odds with his desire for spiritual fulfillment—another desire, of course, which monsters were not supposed to have. Indeed, Pope's initial anguish in admitting that his is a "common case" springs from a longing for moral perfection that supposedly was beyond the reach of the deformed, just as his final good-humored acceptance of his incoherence demonstrates a humility and a capacity for self-criticism that creatures driven by an egocentric fear of scorn simply are not supposed to possess.

And when, in these last lines, Pope turns this longing for moral perfection and coherence into a joke and embraces the commonness of his case, he exhibits an integrity and identity that belie the monstrousness he just admitted to. To understand the full complexity of this last moment of laughter, it might do well to contrast it to the last moment of that other monster, Gulliver, at the end of *Gulliver's Travels*. Gulliver, of course, does not end with a joke. In fact, he ends bitterly dejected, though this dejection covers over the smug certainty that his is not a "common case" at all, that he is really quite different from the common run of humanity. This incapacity to be truly mortified causes the dispersion of Gulliver's character and identity, his final dissolution to a "Lump of Deformity." Because he has ceased to be flexible enough to get enough distance from himself to know himself, because he is neither truly self-aware nor truly self-critical, he allows his "I" to be swamped by the energies of his lower strata, the energies of his egocentric appetites.

Pope in *Epistle I.i.* ends just the opposite. Unlike Gulliver, Pope catches himself in the arrogance of his rejecting the infirmity he has in common with all humanity, and he catches, too, the absurdity of his tenaciously holding to an unfulfillable ideal, both of which he makes fun of, first by screwing up his rhetoric to ludicrous hyperbole, and then—puncturing all pretentions—by simply acknowledging that he is a creature of the body.

This acceptance of one's monstrosity, I have argued, is central to the Scriblerians' sense of self. As Indamira-Lindamora show, we are monsters. We are not one: the self is heterogeneous, an "&c." of passions and drives. In "the Passions' wild rotation tost," we end a "troubled heap," a "Chaos of Thought and Passion, all confus'd," having no identity but our fluidity, the "Quick whirls, and shifting eddies" that constitute our selves.[77]

But the Scriblerians believed that we also are one. A human being has the capacity, probably a psychological need, and certainly a moral imperative to move toward a singleness of character, an identity. And since personal identity has no existence independent of its moment-by-moment creation out of the lower strata of our heterogeneous energies, we must seize hold of them and fashion them into a self. In his laughter, Pope embraces both these versions of the self. He is, he admits, a monster; the dissatisfaction with which he initially admits that he is incoherent, though, is a commitment to be something other than a monster; and the laughter with which he responds to his own dissatisfaction is an acknowledgment that his limitations will require him to be always fashioning a self, for it will never be fashioned perfectly.

To the Scriblerians, it is crucial to hold fast to both these contradictory notions of the self simultaneously. To deliver oneself over to one's chaotic energies is to become a monstrous Yahoo. To think that one has extricated oneself from them and has established an immutable identity is to become as monstrous as Gulliver. The trick is to admit to monstrosity but not submit to it, to assert an identity but not assert that one has achieved it—or ever will, fully.

Seeing his own monstrosity, knowing what he should make of himself out of this monstrosity, and knowing the limits of what he can make of himself: this is the point of balance that Pope reaches at the end of the poem when that he realizes that his is the "common case" and dissolves his anguish in laughter. Pope would probably describe these high spirits as "good humor"—the attitude Clarissa recommends for Belinda and the quality of mind Pope praises in Martha Blount at the end of *To a Lady,* the quality of mind that makes her "Mistress of herself" (268). Good humor is precisely the quality that is needed to create an identity, for good humor is that capacity of self-division and that flexibility of mind that gives us just enough distance from ourselves to keep the process of mastering our identities from coming to a

dead halt in the smug certainty that we have or ever can master ourselves fully. Good humor keeps alive the dialogue of the self that, as
Shaftesbury said, constitutes the construction of identity, and it is a dialogue that must never come to an end if identity is to be achieved, for as
I understand what the Scriblerians mean by this concept, most of one's
identity resides in the always constructing of it.

I have chosen a poem, of course, in which Pope articulates his monstrous inconsistencies and his struggle to fashion a consistent character
as central themes. But other than this explicitness, I do not believe that
Epistle I.i. is greatly different from his other major poems of the 1730s,
poems he wrote after he abandoned "Fancy's Maze." As is being
increasingly appreciated, in these poems Pope is writing less the "poetry of statement" than he is writing poems about the transitions
between statements, poems in which he is in perpetual dialogue with
himself, trying to construct a coherent vision of things and to fashion a
coherent identity.[78] The articulation of this effort, I think, is what Pope
meant by the "Language of the Heart," and this was the language he
used in the last half of his career to reclaim the humanity that many
claimed he did not have because he was a monster.

VI

The manifold connections among the notions of monstrosity, the
imagination, and personal identity that I have attempted to illuminate
in this study are all rooted in the way many people in the eighteenth
century conceived of the relationship between the mind and the body
and particularly in the way that that relationship was so perplexing
and uncertain that it became a source of anxiety.

By the spring of 1744, it had been almost twenty years since Cheselden
had been called by Dr. Douglas to Mr. Lacy's bagnio to see what he
could make of Mary Toft's claims. Since then, Cheselden had pros-
pered, and he counted a number of prestigious people as his acquain-
tances, among them Pope, to whom he had become both a physician
and a friend. It was more as a friend than as a physician that he came to
Twickenham in mid-May to watch over the last, irreversible decline of
the poet. "His mind [was] like a fine ring of bells," Cheselden observed,
"jangled out of tune."

In this state of confusion, Pope became increasingly subject to hallu-
cinations—"visions," he called them. A few days before his death, at
four o'clock in the morning, an attendant found the poet in his study,

busily writing. He persuaded Pope to return to bed and took away the paper. "It was on the *Immortality of the Soul:* on a theory of his own just then excogitated; in which he speaks of those material things which tend to strengthen and support the soul's immortality, and those which weaken and destroy it." On this scrap of paper, Pope had reasoned that "Generous wines help [the soul's immortality], whereas spiritous liquors destroy it."

Here is a scene straight out of *Hudibras, A Tale of a Tub,* or the *Dunciad,* and if this were not Pope, the last great artist of anti-Enthusiastic satire, a genre whose main business was to laugh at this sort of confusion of body and soul, the scene would be merely pitiful. But, although it is tempting to attribute this muddle to a declining mind on the threshold of death, it seems to me to be just as likely that it is a muddle that had always been at the borders of the consciousness of a man who (like many others of his age) was deeply vexed, even in his most lucid moments, by the interpenetration of mind and body, a muddle of the kind that could give birth to monstrous visions as well as to works of art about monsters.[79]

NOTES

CHAPTER ONE
A New Whim Wham from Guildford

1. Lord Hervey to Henry Fox, 3 December 1726, Hervey MS. 941/47/4, pp. 29–32, Suffolk Record Office, Bury St. Edmunds.

2. *The London Journal,* 24 December 1726; *The Daily Post,* 8 December 1726; *The Weekly Journal,* 17 December 1726.

3. James Ralph, *The Touchstone: Or, Historical, Critical, Political, Moral, Philosophical and Theological Essays Upon the Reigning Diversions of the Town* (London, 1728), 236.

4. Nathanael St. André, *A Short Narrative of an Extraordinary Delivery of Rabbits, Perform'd by Mr. John Howard Surgeon at Guilford* (London, 1727), 23. The best modern account of Mary Toft is S. A. Seligman, "Mary Toft—The Rabbit Breeder," *Medical History* 5 (1961): 349–60. Less complete and accurate, but still important because of its use of different sources, is K. Bryn Thomas, *James Douglas of the Pouch and His Pupil William Hunter* (London: Pitman Medical Publishing Company, 1964), 60–68.

5. Mary Toft's maiden name can be ascertained because Dr. James Douglas noted her brother's name, John Denyer, when he wrote down her confession of 7 December (Mary Toft's three confessions of 7, 8, and 12 December are in the Douglas Papers, D324, D327, and D328). The Godalming parish registers list the christening of Mary, daughter of John and Jane Denyer, for 21 February 1703, and that of her brother John for 28 October 1696. (The Godalming parish registers from 1592 to 1688 have been published as vol. 2 of *The Publications of the Surrey Register Society* [London, 1904]. Those after 1688 are still in the care of the incumbent, with copies at the Guildford Muniment Room, Guildford, Surrey.)

St. André's statement that there was a third child seems to be confirmed by a contradiction in the records of the death of one of the Toft children. Lawrence Lee, a resident of Godalming who recorded the deaths there during the smallpox epidemics of 1701, 1710–11, and 1723, lists for 17 July 1723 "at 3 in the morning Joshua Toft Junior's Childe named Mary" (Lee's lists are reproduced in Hilary Jenkinson, "A Late Surrey Chronicler," *Surrey Archaeological Collections* 27 [1914]: 19). But the Godalming parish registers list for 18 July 1723 the burial of "Ann D of Joshua Toft." Lee may have been misinformed about the true name of the Toft's dead daughter; but, more than likely, he mistook one daughter for another, and therefore Mary would appear to be the name of the Toft's first child.

6. As they became prosperous, many Tofts became respectable citizens of Godalming. In 1659, a John Toft was elected Warden (that is, mayor) and another, George, was chosen in 1673 to replace the previous Warden, who refused to take the oath required by the Test Act. Abraham Toft was Warden twice, once in 1675 and again in 1684; he signed himself "gentleman." Other Tofts held positions in the town and the church. For a list of Wardens, see Ralph Nevill, "The Corporation of Godalming," *Surrey Archeological Collections* 19 (1906): 136–38. A note on the cover of the third volume of the Godalming parish registers records an Abraham Toft as Churchwarden in 1672, and one in the fourth volume indicates that a John Toft held the same position. Lee recounts a childhood incident in which he remembers a John Toft as a bailiff in the 1670s (Jenkinson, "Surrey Chronicler," 7; see also Nevill, "Corporation of Godalming," 113).

As early as the 1650s, apprenticeship records in the Godalming Corporation Book (reprinted in Nevill, "Corporation of Godalming," 140) show three Tofts as masters and "clothiers," the latter term indicating considerable status and success in the trade. Although the records are incomplete and hence my conclusions necessarily impressionistic, the evidence from their wills and the appearance in the burial records of "Mr" or "Mrs" or of a burial, at great expense, within the church, all suggest that many Tofts did very well until the turn of the century. "Mrs. Elizabeth Toft" died in 1671. Joshua Toft and his son Samuel, both of whom died in 1677/8, appear to have been buried in the church. "Mr. George Toft" was buried "in the Church" in 1681; his will (Greater London Record Office, ref. DW/PC/7/1 f.337) describes both him and his deceased son, Joshua, as clothiers. Anne Toft was buried "in the Church" in 1682; her will (GLRO, DW/PA/5/1682) reveals that she was quite well-off. A Jane Toft was buried "in the Church" in 1682. "Mr. Abraham Toft, Senior," who died in 1688/9, described himself as a clothier in his will (GLRO, DW/PA/5/1689). "Mrs. Ann Toft" died in 1694. The parish register lists the death of John Toft, Jr., for 1703, with no indication of his status, but his will (Public Record Office, PROB. 11/471 f.148) shows him to have been comfortably well-off; he describes himself as a clothier.

7. On the replacement of the old cloth trade in this region with framework-knitting, see Martin O'Connell, *Historic Towns in Surrey,* Research Volume of the Surrey Archeological Society no. 5 (Aldershot, Hants: The Arrow Press, 1977), 25; *The Victoria History of the County of Surrey,* ed. H. E. Malden, 5 vols. (Westminster, 1902–14), 2:351–52; and especially Gravenor Henson, *History of the Framework Knitters* (1831; rpt., Newton Abbot: David & Charles Reprints, 1970), a work which draws much of its information from interviews with eighteenth-century Godalming stocking-makers. Henson estimates that there were only "a few" frames in Godalming in 1664; pauperization of the trade was so great that by the 1750s, he remarks, Godalming framework-knitters "could not maintain themselves by their industry, but were compelled to receive parochial relief" (60, 216).

According to the Society of Genealogists' summary of apprenticeship ledgers in the Public Record Office, between 1710–1762, there were five Tofts who were "foreign brothers" of the Framework Knitters' Company. Given the Company's loss of control over the trade and the wholesale flouting of their regulations outside of London, this seems like a surprisingly high number. Other stocking-makers appear in the Godalming parish registers, and the editors of *VHC Surrey* have found still more (2:352).

The Godalming parish registers show the following Tofts to have died in the Workhouse: Abraham (1729); Thomas (1739); John (1740); Henry, alias Duke (1751); a child of Mary (1753); Thomas (1744); Abraham (1757).

8. Mary Toft identifies her husband as a cloth-worker in a sworn deposition of 15 November 1726, printed in St. André, *Short Narrative,* 36. Joshua is also identified as a cloth-worker in the depositions of Edward Costen, Richard Stedman, John Sweetapple, Mary Peytoe, and Mary Costen, all inhabitants of Godalming or Guildford who knew him. (The depositions are printed in *The Several Depositions of Edward Costen, Richard Stedman, John Sweetapple, Mary Peytoe, Elizabeth Mason, and Mary Costen; Relating to the Affair of Mary Toft, of Godalming in the County of Surrey, being deliver'd of Several Rabbits* [London, 1727].) St. André's poor grasp of English was remarked upon by a number of his contemporaries; and as a foreign-born surgeon, there is no reason why he should be expected to understand the structure of the English woolen industry. For the distinction between clothier and cloth-worker, see Ephraim Lipson, *The History of the Woolen and Worsted Industries* (London: A. & C. Black, 1921), 41–56, 67.

9. Daniel Defoe, *A Tour Through the Whole Island of Great Britain,* 2 vols. (London: Dent, 1962), 1:145. For the Surrey wool trade, see O'Connell, *Historic Towns in Surrey,* 25; *VHC Surrey,* 1:401, 2:342–51; Peter J. Bowden, *The Wool Trade in Tudor and Stuart England* (London: Macmillan & Co., 1962), 50–55.

10. Defoe, *Tour,* 1:145. The course of the cloth industry was never steady in the eighteenth century, but in 1718 it went into a sharp decline which progressively worsened through 1721. Although improving somewhat between 1721 and 1725, by the second half of 1726 conditions had worsened again, and there was less and less demand for labor. See T. S. Ashton, *Economic Fluctuations in England, 1700–1800* (Oxford: Clarendon Press, 1959), 143–44. "P. S.," in a letter printed in the *The Political State of Great Britain* 32 (September 1726): 283–90, complains of the "present low price of Wool" caused by the decay of overseas trade, "which makes so many of our Looms stand still, and has reduc'd so many of our Manufacturers to the Necessity of being supported by their respective Parishes." The letter is dated 25 August 1726, about a month before the Mary Toft hoax was being plotted.

11. William Shakespeare, *The Tempest,* ed. Frank Kermode (London: Methuen and Co., 1954), 2.2.28–34; *The Citizen of the World,* in *The Collected Works of Oliver Goldsmith,* ed. Arthur Friedman, 5 vols. (Oxford: Clarendon Press, 1966), 2:190–93; Swift to Thomas Tickell, 16 April 1726, *The Correspondence of Jonathan Swift,* ed. Harold Williams, 5 vols. (Oxford: Clarendon Press, 1963–65), 3:128.

For excellent overviews of monster exhibitions, see Richard F. Altick, *The Shows of London* (Cambridge: Harvard University Press, 1978), 34–49; and Aline Mackenzie Taylor, "Sights and Monsters and Gulliver's *Voyage to Brobdingnag,*" *Tulane Studies in English* 7 (1957): 29–82.

The belief that the exhibitors of monsters made great amounts of money was widespread. Fielding's Wisemore in *Love in Several Masques* remarks that monsters "enrich the possessor" (*The Complete Works of Henry Fielding, Esq.,* 16 vols. [New York: Barnes and Noble, 1967], 8:21), and, on seeing a man in the street with an enormous nose, Ned Ward concludes that "if he would . . . show himself in *Bartholomew-Fair,* . . . he might make his Nose worth two or three Hundred Pounds a Year to him" (*The London-Spy Compleat,* ed. Ralph Straus [London: The Casanova Society, 1924], 96).

Montaigne saw a monstrous child exhibited by its parents ("Of a Monstrous Child," in *Essays,* trans. John Florio, 3 vols. [London: Dent, 1965], 2:439–40). Paré reports "two girls joined together at the kidneys, from the shoulders clear to the buttock[es]; and because their parents were poor, they were carted around to several cities in Italy, in order to collect money from the people, who were burning to see this new spectacle of Nature" (Ambroise Paré, *On Monsters and Marvels,* trans. Janis L. Pallister [Chicago: The University of Chicago Press, 1982], 9). In 1682, Mauriceau saw at the Saint Laurent Fair a "petrified child," exhibited by its parents; he judged it "un pure imposteur, . . . gagner, ou plutôst pour dérober de l'argent" (François Mauriceau, *Observations sur la grossesse et l'accouchement des femmes, et sur leur maladies & celles dans enfins nouveau-nez* [Amsterdam, 1693], 185).

Warnings that beggars disfigured themselves and their children to appear like monsters are fairly common: see, for instance, Paré, *On Monsters,* 78; Fortunius Licetus, *De Monstrorum Caussis, Natura, et Differentiis* (Passau, 1634), 126; Edward Fenton, *Certaine Secrete Wonders of Nature* (London, 1569), 16.

12. Others may have been involved. On 6 December 1726, "Elizabeth the Wife of John Williams" was put under a £100 bond to appear at the Quarter Sessions of Westminster "to give Evidence against Mary Toft for a Cheat and Imposture" (Westminster Sessions Roll for January 5, 13 Geo. I., GLRO, ref. WJ/ SR.2475). This appears to be another older sister of Joshua's (the parish registers record the marriage of Elizabeth Toft and John Williams, 10 October 1725). Whether she simply witnessed something or played an under-role in the plot is impossible to know.

13. For my account of the early stage of the affair, I have had to rely on Mary Toft's three confessions, virtually the only extant documents that give information about the first two months of the hoax. The confessions, of course, are not reliable, shot through as they are with gross fabrications and with versions of the events skewed by Mary Toft to protect her and her family. Still, much of what Mary Toft said in her confessions is probably fairly accurate. About many matters she could not lie because her statements could easily be checked against the testimony of witnesses, and about many facts she need not lie since they had no bearing on the question of her guilt or innocence. Many of the details of Mary Toft's account are confirmed by the anonymous *The Wonder of Wonders: or, A True and Perfect Narrative of a Woman near Guildford in Surrey, Who was Delivered lately of Seventeen Rabbets and Three Legs of a Tabby Cat, &c.* (Ipswich, 1726), written by "A Gentleman at *Guildford.*" The writer clearly had intimate, first-hand knowledge of the case as it unfolded in Godalming and Guildford: many of the facts he rehearses simply could not have been know by someone who was not on the scene.

14. I have assumed throughout that Howard did not connive with the Tofts. At the time, he was almost universally judged guilty, and most people thought that he was the author or at least prime mover of the plot. However, it seems to me that he was innocent. Mary Toft hinted at his complicity in her second confession, but by then she was eager to shift the blame to anyone, and in her third confession, she cleared him of any collusion. Those who judged him guilty had little or no first-hand knowledge of the case and seem to have based their opinions on the testimony of one person, Cyriacus Ahlers, whose accusations, as we shall see, are open to considerable doubt. The two doctors of unquestioned probity who were most intimately involved in the affair, Sir Richard Manningham and James Douglas, were careful not to accuse Howard. Finally, as I shall explain in chapter 3, there were psychological forces at work in the affair that pressed for a scapegoat, and Howard was the likeliest victim.

15. St. André, *Short Narrative,* 24.

16. Ibid., 27, 28.

17. Ibid., 7.

18. John Howard to Henry Davenant, 9 November 1726, in St. André, *Short Narrative,* 5–6 [mispaginated as p. 9].

19. John Nichols, *Biographical Anecdotes of William Hogarth* (1785; rpt., London: Cornmarket Press, 1971), 470. Little about St. André would be known had not Nichols, in the first edition of *Biographical Anecdotes of Hogarth* (1781), made a few derogatory comments about him when discussing Hogarth's *Cunicularii.* These prompted a lengthy rebuttal and vindication by "one who knew him intimately ... for the last twenty years of his life." This defense (signed "Impartial," but probably by Thomas Tyers) was first published in *The Public Advertiser,* reprinted in *The Gentleman's Magazine,* and reprinted once again in the third edition of *Biographical Anecdotes of Hogarth* (1785) in an appendix, along with Nichols' detailed reply. All my quotations from both St. André's apologist and Nichols are taken from this text. I am using "Nichols," of course, as shorthand for him, George Steevens, and Isaac Reed.

20. "St. A-D-E's Miscarriage, A Full and True Account of the Rabbit Woman" (London, 1727); Nichols, *Biographical Anecdotes of Hogarth,* 23.

21. Besides *Short Narrative* and his translation of Garengeot, I have been able to find only one other work by St. André, "An Account of an extraordinary Effect of the *Cholick:* communicated to the *Royal Society,* by that curious Anatomist Mr. *St. Andre,* and read *March 21. 1717,*" *Philosophical Transactions* 351 (1717): 580–83 [mispaginated as p. 393]. His apologist says that he wrote "a bantering pamphlet on Dr. *Mead*" (465), but I have been unable to locate it. Nichols is skeptical about all of St. André's writings: "That he wrote any thing, unless by proxy, or with much assistance, may reasonably be doubted; for the pamphlets that pass under his name are divested of those foreign idioms that marked his conversation" (480). Nichols' suspicions, I am ashamed to admit, are infectious. The title page of his Englishing of Garengeot's *A Treatise of Chirurgical Operations* (London, 1723) has an equivocal layout that might indicate he was trying to take credit for a translation he did not do: "Translated from the FRENCH of *Mons.* Renatus James Croissant Garengeot // Revis'd and Corrected by Mr. St. André."

22. Nichols, *Biographical Anecdotes of Hogarth,* 463–64, 474–75, 486. Nichols' main informant about St. André's professional capabilities was William Hunter, and there was scarcely anyone alive at that time who would give a less objective assessment. When Hunter came to London in 1740, he was befriended by Dr. James Douglas, who helped him to enter St. George's Hospital. In 1741, he moved into Douglas's home and became his student and close friend. After Douglas's death, Hunter continued to live in the household and was tutor to his mentor's son. As we shall see, Douglas was deeply (and, in the end, embarrassingly) involved in the Mary Toft incident. Although he did not believe her story and helped expose the hoax, he himself became an object of public ridicule—for which he could thank St. André. Given his enormous personal, professional, and intellectual debts to Douglas, Hunter had a strong motive for vindicating his friend and benefactor by derogating the man who had damaged his reputation.

Even if he had not used this biased source, Nichols probably would have delivered a harsh judgment on St. André, for after the Mary Toft incident, St. André was pretty much fair game and could be attacked with impunity. Independent evidence, however, suggests that almost all of Nichols' judgments are overdrawn.

St. André's library, in fact, was made up of part of the fine collections of the scientists William and Samuel Molyneux. On St. André's death, the library passed to George Pitt, who, in 1818, sold many of the medical works to the Royal College of Surgeons and, in 1831, presented the rest to the city of Southampton (see City of Southampton Libraries Committee, *A Catalogue of the Pitt Collection* [Southampton, 1964]). Nichols himself concedes in a footnote that St. André's was "a valuable library in the classes of Natural History and Medicine," although he allows to remain in the text above his mean-spirited comment that St. André's "boasted library" perhaps "existed only in his description" (486).

Nichols' appraisal of St. André's collections, including his anatomical preparations, is also questionable. He apparently based his opinion about their "frivolity" on the result of a Christie's auction (486), but St. André's will (PRO, ref. PROB. 11/1019 f.8135) indicates that what was sold at Christie's was merely "the small remains" of a much larger collection destroyed in a fire years earlier. Before the Mary Toft incident, William Stukeley had high praise for St. André's anatomical collection: "Dr. Mead & I visited Mr. St. André to see his fine preparations in Anatomy which are beyond comparison" (*The Family Memoirs of the Rev. William Stukeley, M. D.,* ed. W. C. Lukis, 3 vols. [London: The Publications of the Surtees Society, 1880–83], 1:61).

About his capabilities as a surgeon, it is much more difficult to make an assessment, not only because there is little factual evidence but also because it is difficult to know what kinds of standards to use to measure the competency of surgeons in the eighteenth century. All negative comments on his medical qualifications I have found were published after the Mary Toft incident and are, therefore, suspect. Nichols continually degrades St. André's professional competency, but he is simply incorrect about one event which he used to show that St. André had no repute as a surgeon. In September 1726, just two months before the Mary Toft incident, Pope cut his hand in a coach accident. He was treated by St. André. Nichols insists that St. André was called in "because he happened to be the surgeon nearest at hand" and that, after he bandaged Pope, he "was not admitted a second time into the Poet's company" (491–92). Nichols is wrong on both counts. The letters of Gay to Swift, 16 September 1726, and Bolingbroke to Swift, 22 September 1726 (*Corr.*, 2:399–400, 402–3), make it clear that Pope sent to London for St. André in particular. See also George Sherburn, "An Accident in 1726," *The Harvard Library Bulletin* 2 (1948): 121–23.

23. D'Arcy Power, "St. André, Nathanael" *Dictionary of National Biography* (1917).

24. Nichols, *Biographical Anecdotes of Hogarth,* 471, 490. St. André published accounts of his poisoning in *The London Gazette,* 23 February 1724/5 and *The Daily Post,* 4 March 1724/5. At the height of the furor over Mary Toft, these were published again under the title *À Propos. Mr. St. Andre's Case and Depositions* (London, [1726]).

25. Madden's accusations were published in *A Letter From the Reverend Mr. M–D–N to the Hon. Lady M–n–x, on Occasion of the Death of the Rt. Hon. S—l M–n–x, Esq; who was attended by M. St. A-D-E, a Fr–ch S–g–n* (Dublin, 1730). The charges of defamation St. André brought against Madden made the incident all the more noteworthy. John Byrom reports of the conversation among him and his friends: "We talked much about St. André, and they seemed to say that there was a great ground for suspicion" (*The Private Journals and Literary Remains of John Byrom,* ed. Richard Parkinson, 2 vols. [Manchester: The Chetham Society Publications, 1854–57], vol. 1, pt. 2, 386).

26. Nichols, *Biographical Anecdotes of Hogarth,* 469, 466. Such, too, was the explanation offered by Abel Boyer, one of the few writers who refrained from savaging his character after the exposure of the Mary Toft hoax: "It cannot, indeed, be denied, that Mr. *St. André* was both too precipitate, too busie, and too sanguine, in this whole Affair; . . . But then some Grains of Allowance must be given, both for the Frailties of

human Nature, and the Desire, incident to all Men, especially the Professors of any Science or Art, to inlarge their Reputation" (*The Political State of Great Britain* 32 [December 1726]: 601).

27. St. André may have had a very practical incentive. Just a few days earlier, he published, as he had every winter since 1719, the following advertisement in the London newspapers: "A Course of *Human* and *Comparative* Anatomy; with a Course of Chirurgical Operations, Bandages, and Pathology: By Mr. St. Andre, Surgeon and Anatomist to His Majesty. To begin Monday the 21st Instant, in Northumberland-Court, Charing-Cross" (*The Daily Courant,* 11 November 1726). There is no way of recovering his motives, but it is true that the Mary Toft story could not have surfaced at a more felicitous time and that it offered a real opportunity to swell the crowd at a course of comparative anatomy. And it is also true that St. André exploited his connection with the affair in one other way. On 26 November 1726, a few days after his visit to Guildford had been widely reported in the London newspapers, he advertised in *The British Journal* the republication of his translation of *A Treatise of Chirurgical Operations*.

28. I have given here what strikes me as the most plausible conclusions to be drawn from what is sometimes contradictory evidence. Although St. André himself says that he was invited by Molyneux and although reports in many newspapers state that it was the prince who sent Molyneux, Howard was under the impression that St. André was sent by George I (*Whitehall Evening Post,* 26 November 1724), and another writer even claimed that it was St. André who invited Molyneux (Thomas Brathwaite, *Remarks on A Short Narrative of an Extraordinary Delivery of Rabbets, perform'd by Mr. John Howard, Surgeon at Guilford* [London, 1726], 13). To complicate matters, the following report appeared in the *Whitehall Evening Post,* 12 November 1726, three days *before* St. André claimed was the first time he went to Guildford: "A woman near Guildford in Surrey, having been delivered of seven creatures said to resemble Rabbits, Mr. St. Andre, the King's Surgeon and Anatomist, is gone thither to view them, they being preserved in Spirits." It is possible that St. André, who a year and a half earlier during his "poisoning" had learned the value of newspapers in calling attention to himself, planted this story, either because he was planning to go to Guildford or because he wanted to give the impression he was. The advertisement of his course in comparative anatomy was published just one day before this report appeared.

Members of the royal family played an early and an active role in investigating the matter. Throughout almost the entire month of November, nearly everyone connected with the affair was part of the German entourage surrounding the royal family, a member of the court, or someone specifically appointed by George I to search out the truth of the rumors. Evidence to be introduced later suggests that George I believed the hoax; he certainly took Mary Toft's story seriously enough to have it thoroughly investigated. (The king seems to have been interested in monstrosities and curiosities of all sorts: see Maximillian E. Novak, "The Wild Man Come to Tea," in *The Wild Man Within: An Image in Western Thought from the Renaissance to Romanticism* [Pittsburgh: University of Pittsburgh Press, 1972], 183-221; César de Saussure, *A Foreign View of England in the Reigns of George I and George II,* trans. Madame Van Muyden [New York: E. P. Dutton and Company, 1902], 147-50; and "Extract of several Letters and Certificates sent to his Majesty the King of *Great Britain,* concerning a very particular *Nævus Maternus,* or *Mole.* Communicated by Dr. Steigertahl, Physician to his Majesty, F.R.S.," *Philosophical Transactions* 33 [July/August 1725]: 347-49).

Nichols claims that Caroline had the affair investigated after she found that "the plausibility of [St. André] had imposed on the King, and that some of the pregnant ladies about her own person began to express their fears of bringing into the world an unnatural progeny" (*Biographical Anecdotes of Hogarth,* 478). It should be noted, however, that it was Caroline who was pregnant at the time (*The Weekly Journal,* 26 November 1726).

29. St. André, *Short Narrative,* 8.

30. Ibid., 9; Brathwaite, *Remarks on A Short Narrative,* 16–17.

31. St. André, *Short Narrative,* 11.

32. Ibid., 12–13. "Touch," as used here by St. André and by other doctors involved in the Mary Toft incident, is a term of art. "I would have it rightly understood, that nothing else is meant here by the *Performance* of the TOUCH, than (upon having first pared the *Nails* short, equal, and smooth), *passing the two Fore-fingers of either hand,* (previously *well anointed with Fat or Butter, when proper Oils are not to be had*), *through the* VULVA *into the* VAGINA, *in order to reach the Orifice of the* WOMB, and to discern its FORM, by feeling it on each Side" (John Maubray, *The Female Physician, Containing all the Diseases Incident to that Sex* [London, 1724], 107). For a more detailed, but substantially similar, definition, see William Smellie's chapter "Of Touching" in his *Treatise on the Theory and Practice of Midwifery,* ed. Alfred H. McClintock, 3 vols. (London: The New Sydenham Society, 1876–78), 1:184.

33. St. André, *Short Narrative,* 19–20, 21. "Præternatural" seems to be used by St. André in the sense typical of eighteenth-century obstetrics, which defined such conceptions and births as those "which tho' not according to the *ordinary Institution* of NATURE, are yet however not repugnant to NATURE" (Maubray, *Female Physician,* 353–54). How Mary Toft's birth could possibly be perceived as "not repugnant to NATURE" will be discussed in chapter 2.

34. *The Doctor's in Labour; or a New Whim Wham from Guildford* (London, 1726), plate 9.

35. Cyriacus Ahlers, *Some Observations Concerning the Woman of Godlyman* (London, 1726), sig. a2ᵛ.

36. Ibid., 6.

37. Ibid., sig. a5ᵛ.

38. Ibid., 8–11.

39. Ibid., 12–13. In a deposition of 24 November 1726, Howard gave his version of these events: "This Deponent carried the said Mr. *Ahlers* over to [Mary Toft] with him, and having touched her in his Presence, desired him to examine her, for that he found all things ready for a Delivery. That Mr. *Ahlers* did accordingly examine; but this Deponent finding that he did not hasten her Delivery, nor that he proceeded as one who understands Midwifery should do, this Deponent directed him how to proceed in the Extraction, which after some time Mr. *Ahlers* effected, . . . That some time after Mr. *Ahlers* desired to touch the Woman again; but as at the time before he had put her to a great deal of unnecessary Pain, this Deponent desired him to forbear" (St. André, *Short Narrative,* 33–36).

40. Deposition of John Howard, 25 November 1726, in St. André, *Short Narrative,* 34; Ahlers, *Some Observations,* 13.

41. Ahlers, *Some Observations,* sig. a3ᵛ.

42. *St. James Evening Packet* and *Whitehall Evening Post,* 26 November 1726.

43. *St. James Evening Packet* and *Whitehall Evening Post,* 26 November 1726.

44. Like St. André and Ahlers, D'Anteney was one of those men involved in this stage of the Mary Toft affair who congregated around or were members of the "Ger-

man Court." Born and educated on the continent, he was a virtuoso, interested in geometry, mechanics, and cryptography; he was often part of the informal gatherings of those Royal Society members who went to the Sun in St. Paul's Churchyard after the Society's meetings. A story that Byrom recounts about a squabble that arose at a meeting of the Royal Society in May 1727 is very suggestive about how close D'Anteney (and, by the way, Ahlers) was to the king (*Journals and Remains,* vol. 1, pt. 1, 258–59).

Other minor actors in the affair at this stage came from the same milieu. Brand, who accompanied Ahlers to Guildford, was "a relation of Mr. *Jager,* the King's Apothecary" (Ahlers, *Some Observations,* 2). Ernst August Jäger, who had accompanied George I to England in September 1714 as Court Apothecary, himself took some interest in Mary Toft at this time. He sent his servant, a Mr. Ziegler, to Guildford, presumably to keep abreast of any important developments. It was Ziegler who carried to Ahlers Howard's letter requesting the return of the sixteenth rabbit. Dr. Tessier, who was appointed Physician to the Household in March 1715/16, and Dr. Steighertahl, Physician in Ordinary to George I, attended with the king the comparative anatomy St. André gave 26 November.

45. Deposition of Mary Toft and Mary Coston, 25 November 1726, in St. André, *Short Narrative,* 36.

46. Deposition of Thomas Howard, 27 November 1726, in St. André, *Short Narrative,* 39–40.

47. Ahlers, *Some Observations,* sig. a1ᵛ.

48. St. André, *Short Narrative,* 31–32. Howard, too, must have begun working on a pamphlet of his own about this time, for St. André mentions that "Mr. *Howard* himself intends shortly to publish the whole account, and prove every Circumstance of it, by such Evidences as will put this Matter out of all possibility of Doubt,..." (*Short Narrative,* 3–4).

There is also a possibility that Howard may have written, initiated, or encouraged *The Wonder of Wonders.* The pamphlet reprints his letter of 22 November, and it must have come out shortly after that date, certainly, internal evidence suggests, before 29 November, when Mary Toft was taken to London. This was the period when Howard and St. André were most active in consolidating their public case for the truth of Mary Toft's claims. *The Wonder of Wonders* was written by someone who had detailed knowledge of how the affair progressed in Guildford, it confirmed everything Howard and St. André had been saying, and it gave unusual prominence to the account of the affair by Howard "to be communicated to the World in due time." This is mere speculation on my part, but if Howard did not have a hand in the pamphlet, he and St. André could not have asked for a better—and more timely—vindication.

49. Sir Richard Manningham, *An Exact Diary of what was observ'd during a Close Attendance Upon Mary Toft, The pretended Rabbet-Breeder of Godalming in Surrey* (London, 1726), 8–9.

50. Ibid., 10–11.

51. Ibid., 13–15.

52. Ibid., 17.

53. Ibid., 18–19.

54. One satirist complained that St. André "toss'd our *Mary* up in a fine Coach, and took such fine Lodgings for her near the Prince's Palace" (*A Letter from a Male Physician in the Country, to the Author of the Female Physician in London* [London, 1726], 42). It is difficult to know whether this is a jibe at St. André or a reference to the Prince of

Wales' interest in the affair. The attacks on the royal family for their role in the incident tend to be very oblique. For the possibility of attacks in the visual satires, see F. G.
Stephens, *Catalogue of Prints and Drawings in the British Museum. Division I. Political
and Personal,* vol. 2 (London, 1873), 638 [item 1778].

55. Nathanael St. André to James Douglas, 29 November 1726, Douglas Papers,
D322.

56. James Douglas, *An Advertisement Occasion'd by Some Passages in Sir R. Manningham's Diary Lately Publish'd* (London, 1727), 6; Lord Hervey to Henry Fox, 3
December 1726.

57. Douglas, *Advertisement,* 16.

58. For the reputation and skill of Douglas, see Thomas, *James Douglas of the Pouch*
(cf. n. 6); C. H. Brock, "The Rediscovery of James Douglas," *Bibliotheck* 8 (1977):
168–76; and Sir Norman Moore, "Douglas, James," *Dictionary of National Biography*
(1917).

59. Douglas, *Advertisement,* 4.

60. Manningham, *Exact Diary,* 20; Douglas, *Advertisement,* 7.

61. Douglas, *Advertisement,* 4–5.

62. Ibid., 25, 29.

63. Ibid., 10–11, 15, 12.

64. *The London Journal,* 3 December 1726; *The Weekly Journal,* 3 December 1726;
Manningham, *Exact Diary,* 25; Lord Hervey to Henry Fox, 3 December 1726.

65. *The Daily Journal,* 24 January 1727.

66. Manningham, *Exact Diary,* 20–21; Douglas, *Advertisement,* 11.

67. Brathwaite, *Remarks on A Short Narrative,* 21–23, 32 (cf. n. 7).

68. Douglas, *Advertisement,* 13, 15.

69. Depositions of Mrs. Mason, Edward Costen, and Richard Stedman, 3 and 4
December 1726, in *Several Depositions,* 15–16, 5, 7 (cf. n. 8).

70. Douglas, *Advertisement,* 17.

71. Manningham, *Exact Diary,* 24; Douglas, *Advertisement,* 18, 19.

72. Manningham, *Exact Diary,* 29–30.

73. Ibid., 32.

74. St. André, *Short Narrative,* 21, sig. a1^r. Although it was advertised in *The Daily
Post* and *The Daily Journal* as "This day is publish'd" on 1 December 1726, *A Short Narrative* almost certainly did not come out until 3 December. Douglas, in *An Advertisement,* reports that on 1 December he was shown proof sheets by St. André, and Lord
Hervey, who was anxious to get a copy, states in his letter to Fox, 3 December, that he
expects it to be published on that day. *The Daily Post* and *The Daily Journal* announce
it again as "This Day is Published" on 3 December 1726.

75. *The Daily Journal,* 9 December 1726; *The Daily Post,* 10 December 1726.

76. *The Political State of Great Britain* 32 (December 1726): 587–88.

77. *The Daily Journal,* 9 December 1726; *Mist's Weekly Journal,* 17 December 1726;
"A Song on the Rabbit Breeder" (London, 1727).
The public's sense of the ludicrousness of the medical men was heightened when
several doctors who had negligible roles at all in the affair reacted in panic to clear
themselves of charges that had never been made against them. Dr. Steigertahl asked
Ahlers to insert in his *Observations* this notice: "Monsieur *St. André* having asserted in
his Narrative . . . that all the Facts, as by him there related, were verified before His
Majesty on *Saturday, Nov.* 26. Dr. *Steigertahl* and Dr. *Teissier* being present, I was desired

by Dr. *Steigertahl,* to inform the Publick in his Name, that he all along suspected this whole Affair to be a Fraud and Imposture, and was far from thinking the comparative Anatomy, which is there mention'd by Mr. *St. André,* any ways satisfactory to verifie his Assertions" (Ahlers, *Some Observations,* sig. a5ʳ). Dr. Hampe, whom St. André had briefly mentioned in his *Narrative* as merely having been present at one of his examinations of Mary Toft, published a disclaimer: "Whereas Mr. St. Andre in his Narrative lately publish'd of an extraordinary Delivery of Rabbits, has made use of my Name: I do hereby declare, that this has been done without my Knowledge and Consent, which I never should have given in a Matter, the Truth of which I did not believe" (*The Daily Post,* 13 December 1726).

78. Howard's promise to put out an account of the affair was published, among other places, in *The Daily Post,* 19 December 1726. Nichols says that, after Douglas put out his *Advertisement,* "Sir Richard [Manningham] printed a Reply, in 24 pages, 8vo; but did not think proper to publish it" (John Nichols, *Literary Anecdotes of the Eighteenth Century,* 9 vols. [London, 1812–16], 1:346n). In a rough draft to his *Advertisement,* Douglas said that he was "now preparing" a consideration "on the structure of the parts of generation in a woman compar'd w[i]t[h] those of the rabbits said to be brought forth" (Douglas Papers, D329); in the printed *Advertisement,* he promised that the study would be published (37–38).

Douglas's apprehension about public reaction probably explains the long delay between Manningham's *Exact Diary,* which came out 12 December 1726, and his reply to it, which was not published until early January. Douglas created an ingenious device for protecting himself without opening himself to charges of self-interested vindication. He considered planting anonymously this self-promoting piece in the newspapers: "We hear that Mr. St. André contrary to the expectation of his friends is like to be made a party in the affaire of the Woman of Godliman. He was indeed very much blamed for his Credulity & Ignorance, but the prudent and charitable behavior of Dr. D. to whom the [una]nimous voice of the publick had referrd the examination of this unheard of appearance, had for sometime screen[ed] him in a great measure, and thereby gave him an opportunity of inventing some excuse for his Conduct when the Imposture should be discovered which that Ingenious Physician was always fully convinced could not have remaine[d] a Secret and spared no time nor pains to bring the whole affaire to a certain Issue." This paragraph is written at the bottom of one of his early drafts of his *Advertisement* (Douglas Papers, D330). As far as I can ascertain, it was never published, and Douglas decided to run the risk of a more open self-vindication.

79. Byrom, *Journals and Remains,* vol. 1, pt. 1, 235 (cf. n. 25).

80. *The Post Man* for 6 December 1726 reported, "We hear the Guildford Man-Midwife is bound over, some discoveries being made, which, as is supposed, will set that affair in a true light." On 15 December, Howard swore an affidavit, which concluded, "I shall be always ready to take both my oath and the Sacrament, that I am entirely clear of having any Hand in the Imposture, but did really believe the truth of the Production of the Rabbits, till lately such Discoveries have been made to me of several particular Circumstances, as convince me that it is a Fraud" (printed in *The Political State of Great Britain* 32 [December 1726]: 600). *Mist's Weekly Journal,* 24 December 1726, reported that Howard's apprentice and a woman who had nursed Mary Toft in Guildford (presumably Mary Costen) were brought to London for questioning. The report of Howard's being bound over a second time, quoted above, first appeared in *The Daily Journal,* 11 January 1726/7. He was placed on £800 recognizance "On Condition [he]

Appear at the next Quarter Sessions of the Peace to be held for the City & Liberty of Westm' there to answer what shall be objected against him on Suspition of Conspiring with one Mary Toft . . ." (Westminster Sessions Roll for January 5, 13 Geo. I. [GLRO; ref. WJ/SR. 2475]). The charges against him were dropped. A note added to the Sessions Roll reads, "Johannes Howard tr' ulterius ad comparend' in Banco Regis Io exon'," and *The Daily Journal,* 18 May 1727, reported, "Monday being the last Day of Term, Mr. John Howard of Guildford, Surgeon, moved by his Counsel to be discharged from his Recognizance, and (having given the usual Notice) he was accordingly discharged without any Prosecution."

81. Nichols reports that "the Surgeon of Guildford, and Mary Toft, were continued for two Terms upon their recognisance in the King's Bench, and then discharged" (John Nichols and George Steevens, *The Genuine Works of William Hogarth,* 3 vols. [London, 1810], 2:55). A note against the name of Thomas Howard, James Lacy's servant who was put under a £100 bond to give evidence against Mary Toft, reads "Exon' quia noll' prosec' ex parte Regis," showing that the Crown did not choose to prosecute (Westminster Sessions Roll for January 5, 13 Geo. I. [GLRO; ref. WJ/SR. 2475]). For the use of recognizances and summary committals to Houses of Correction as alternative methods of punishment, see Robert B. Shoemaker, *Prosecution and Punishment: Petty Crime and the Law in London and Rural Middlesex, c. 1660–1725* (Cambridge: Cambridge University Press, 1991).

82. Colonel Pelham to the Duke of Richmond, 14 September 1735, in Charles Henry Gordon-Lennox, Earl of March, *A Duke and His Friends: The Life and Letters of the Second Duke of Richmond,* 2 vols. (London: Hutchinson and Co., 1911), 2:313.

In the Quarter Sessions records at the Surrey Record Office, in a bundle for the Easter 1740 Sessions headed "The Calendar of the House of Correction in Guildford in Surrey April 15th 1740," it is stated that Mary Toft was committed, having been charged with "receiving fowles att several times knowing them to be stole." Another document in the same bundle, headed "Tresspasses to be tryed," states that "Mary Toft pleaded not guilty & acquitted by the jury." The Quarter Sessions Order Books at the Surrey Record Office (ref. Q.S. 2/1/15) for 15 April 1740 show also that she was "acquitted upon trial of an Indictment found against her for a Misdemeanour."

CHAPTER TWO
Doctors in Labor

1. In *The Devil to Pay at St. James,* the Mary Toft affair was characterized as a mindless diversion that appealed to a society addicted to "Amusements" (*The Miscellaneous Works of the Late Dr. Arbuthnot,* 2 vols. [Glasgow, 1751], 1:213–23). Edward Young mocked women who went to view Mary Toft's rabbits because they desired to be "in the public eye" (*Love of Fame, The Universal Passion,* in *The Complete Works, Poetry and Prose,* 2 vols. [1854; rpt., Hildesheim: Georg Olms, 1968], 1:376).

"The public horror was so great, that the rent of rabbit-warrens sunk to nothing; and nobody, till the delusion was over, presumed to eat a rabbit" (Nichols, *Biographical Anecdotes of Hogarth,* 464–65 [cf. ch. 1, n. 19]). Allusions to the collapse of the market occur frequently in the Mary Toft satires. For instance, one author commented that "the Warreners and Poulterers . . . complain that the consumption of Rabbits, within this Metropolis, is become, by two thirds, less that it was formerly" ("Lemuel Gulliver," *The Anatomist Dissected: or the Man-Midwife finely brought to Bed* [Westminster, 1727], 33).

2. James Bramston, *The Art of Politics* (1729; rpt., Los Angeles: Augustan Reprint Society, 1976), 34; *Memoirs of the Life and Writings of Mr. William Whiston, Part III* (London, 1750), 110.

3. *Anatomist Dissected,* 5; *Letter from a Male Physician,* 7 (cf. ch. 1, n. 54); Lord Onslow to Sir Hans Sloane [?4 December 1726], BL Sloane. 4054.76.f.273; Thomas Hearne, *Remarks and Collections,* ed. Charles Edward Doble, David Watson, and H. E. Salter, 11 vols. (Oxford: Clarendon Press, 1885–1914), 9:229; Lord Hervey to Henry Fox, 3 December 1726.

4. *The Daily Post,* 6 December 1726.

5. Many did deplore the indecency the episode gave rise to. "The Rabbit affair is as great a monster in its kind as any, even this age, has produced. . . . It has given, I hear, an occasion to the ladies of our age to show their modesty, in talking modestly upon it such things as their mothers would have thought an affront to them to have had any spoke in their presence" (William Stratford to Edward Harley, 20 December 1726, *Historical Manuscripts Commission. Report on the Manuscripts of His Grace the Duke of Portland, K. G.,* 10 vols. [London: Mackie & Co., 1901], 7:446). Another complained of the "obscene and indecent Images, which for more than these nine Days last past, beyond all Example, have fill'd the Minds, and furnish'd out the conversation of People of all Ranks, Ages and Conditions. And whether Ideas of this Nature are fit to be put into the Heads of rude Boys, Boarding-school Girls, and Old Maids, I leave every discreet and prudent Matron to judge" (*Anatomist Dissected,* 33–34).

6. *Whitehall Evening Post,* 29 December 1726; Lord Hervey to Henry Fox, 3 December 1726; *The Political State of Great Britain* 32 (November 1726): 514.

7. St. André, *Short Narrative,* 32 (cf. ch. 1, n. 4); Whiston, *Memoirs, Part III,* 111, 119; Lord Hervey to Henry Fox, 3 December 1726. Howard, too, thought that Molyneux believed Mary Toft. After remarking that Ahlers and St. André "were both satisfied in the Truth of the wonderous Delivery," he added, "As was Mr. Molineux, Secretary to the Prince, who was also here" (*St. James Evening Packet* and *Whitehall Evening Post,* 26 November 1726).

8. In his account of his and Molyneux's visit to Guildford on 15 November, St. André is quite clear about the fact that he and he alone had delivered Mary Toft (*Short Narrative,* 13–14). Douglas obviously was bothered by the contradiction between St. André's and Molyneux's stories, for when he extracted the three confessions from Mary Toft, he repeatedly asked her about what Molyneux had done so he could clear up the confusion. According to Mary Toft, Molyneux only "touched" her. Molyneux's implying that he delivered the head of the rabbit later became an acute embarrassment to him. As we shall see, it was the central joke of the satiric attack on him in Pope and Pulteney's popular "The Discovery."

9. Lord Hervey to Henry Fox, 3 December 1726. Portions of this letter, from which I have quoted often, have been printed by the Earl of Ilchester, *Lord Hervey and His Friends* (London: John Murray, 1950), 82. He incorrectly gives its date as 2 December. The letter itself is clearly dated 3 December. Lord Hervey's conversation with Dr. Arbuthnot "last night," therefore, occurred on 2 December.

10. Douglas Papers, D330. It is clear that Douglas is referring principally to Arbuthnot since he added "& others" as a superscript.

11. Dr. Deacon to John Byrom, 6 December 1726, in Byrom, *Journals and Remains,* vol. 1, pt. 1, 233 (cf. ch. 1, n. 25).

12. Pope to Caryll, 5 December 1726, *Corr.,* 2:418.

13. Douglas, *Advertisement,* 20–21 (cf. ch. 1, n. 56).

14. Douglas Papers, D330.

15. Whiston, *Memoirs, Part III,* 110–22. Others continued to believe Mary Toft even after she confessed. *Mist's Weekly Journal,* 24 December 1726, reported: "*Guildford.* Dec. 19. Several people who have enter'd into an Opinion of the miraculous Delivery of the Woman of this Place, seem unwilling to give into the Belief of its being a Fraud. . . ."

16. The history of this literature in the fifteenth and sixteenth centuries has been traced by Rudolf Wittkower, "Marvels of the East: A Study in the History of Monsters," *Journal of the Warburg and Courtauld Institutes* 5 (1942): 159–97; Jean Céard, *La nature et les prodiges: L'insolite au XVIe siècle, en France* (Geneva: Librairie Droz, 1977); and Katharine Park and Lorraine J. Daston, "Unnatural Conceptions: The Study of Monsters in Sixteenth- and Seventeenth-Century France and England," *Past and Present* 92 (August 1981): 20–54. For an excellent account of the fascination with "wonders" during this period, see J. Paul Hunter, *Before Novels: The Cultural Contexts of Eighteenth-Century English Fiction* (New York: W. W. Norton & Company, 1990), 195–224. Douglas's notes on Riolanus, Cardanus, Licetus, and Paré are in Douglas Papers, D334.

17. Walter Harris, *Pharmacologia Anti-Empirica: or A Rational Discourse of Remedies Both Chymical and Galenical* (London, 1683), 312.

18. [Peter Cole?], *Culpepper's Directory for Midwives . . . The Second Part* (London, 1662), 146.

19. *Callipaediae: or, An Art How to Have Handsome Children: Written in Latin by the Abbot Claude Quillet. Done into English Verse By Several Hands* (1708-10; rpt., Philadelphia: American Antiquarian Publishing Company, 1872), 59, 53–54. Quillet's work was very popular in England in the early years of the eighteenth century, four separate versions being published from 1708 to 1712.

20. Maubray, *Female Physician,* 62–63 (cf. ch. 1, n. 32).

21. Thomas Fienus, *De Viribus Imaginationis Tractus* (London, 1657), 191. For broad historical surveys of this doctrine of the imagination, see J. W. Ballantyne, *Teratogenesis: An Inquiry into the Causes of Monstrosities* (Edinburgh, 1897); and Joseph Needham, *A History of Embryology,* 2d ed., rev. (New York: Abelard-Schuman, 1959).

22. James Blondel, *The Power of the Mother's Imagination Over the Foetus Examin'd* (London, 1729), 12.

23. Smellie, *Treatise of Midwifery,* 2:146–47, 3:215–17 (cf. ch. 1, n. 32). I do not want to multiply examples needlessly, but one more account may be cited to show the mechanics of the process:

> One *Elizabeth Dooly* of the County of *Kilkenny* was aged 13 Years in *January* last: Her Mother being with Child of her was frighted by a Cow as she milked it, thrown down and hit on her Temple, within an eighth of an Inch of her Eye, by the Cows Teat. This Child has exactly in that place, a piece of Flesh resembling a Cows Teat, about 3 Inches and half in length; 'Tis very red, has a bone in the midst about half the length of it; tis perforated and she Weeps through it; when She Laughs it wrincles up and contracts to two thirds of its length, and it grows in proportion to the rest of her Body. She is as sensible there as in any other part. This is lookt upon to be as strange an instance of the strength of Imagination can be produced.

(Edward Smith, "A Relation of an extraordinary effect of the power of Imagination," *Philosophical Transactions* 16 [July/August 1687]: 334.)

24. *Culpepper's Directory for Midwives,* 146.

25. Ward, *London-Spy,* 324 (cf. ch. 1, n. 11); Paré, *On Monsters,* 8–9 (cf. ch. 1, n. 11).

26. Daniel Turner, *De Morbis Cutaneis* (London, 1726), 175–77. Needless to say, this case was greatly disputed.

27. Blondel, *Power of the Mother's Imagination,* 143, i; *The Blatant-Beast* (1742; rpt., Los Angeles: Augustan Reprint Society, 1965), 5; Daniel Turner, *A Defence of the XIIth Chapter of . . . De Morbis Cutaneis* (London, 1729), 69. Ballantyne concludes that, by the seventeenth century, the doctrine of the imagination "reigned supreme" and was not seriously challenged in England until the 1740s (*Teratogenesis,* 30–39). Excellent discussions about belief in the power of the imagination during this period can be found in Lester King, *The Philosophy of Medicine: The Early Eighteenth Century* (Cambridge: Harvard University Press, 1978), 152–81; G. S. Rousseau, "Pineapples, Pregnancy, Pica, and *Peregrine Pickle,*" in *Tobias Smollett: Bicentennial Essays Presented to Lewis M. Knapp,* ed. G. S. Rousseau and P.-G. Boucé (New York: Oxford University Press, 1971), 79–109; Paul-Gabriel Boucé, "Imagination, Pregnant Women, and Monsters, in Eighteenth-Century England and France," in *Sexual Underworlds of the the Enlightenment,* ed. G. S. Rousseau and Roy Porter (Manchester: Manchester University Press, 1987), 86–100; Marie Hélène Huet, *Monstrous Imagination* (Cambridge: Harvard University Press, 1993), esp. 36–78; and Jacques Roger, *Les sciences de la vie dans la pensée française de XVIIIe siècle* (Paris: Armand Colin, 1963).

In pointing to the hegemony of the doctrine of the prenatal influence of the imagination, I am speaking about historical trends, not absolutes. Some doctors and medical writers continued to accept other explanations for monstrosities well into the eighteenth century (see, for instance, *Aristotle's Compleat Master-Piece,* 19th ed. [London, 1733], 94–97). Still, even in these cases, the tendency was to give precedence to the imagination. Jane Sharp, for example, after briefly discussing other causes of monstrosity, concludes, "But *Imagination holds the first place*" (*The Compleat Midwife's Companion* [London, 1725], 76–77). Maubray, too, lists a number of possible causes for monsters, but he likewise concludes, "I take the Imagination to have the most prevalent *Power*" (*Female Physician,* 368).

When it first came under serious attack at the end of the 1720s, some doctors began to reject the theory, but others held to it. Among those who were not doctors, the doctrine appears to have retained a firm hold. Nothing illustrates this more than the example cited above concerning the child born with the top of his skull missing. The case was recorded by Smellie, who was thoroughly skeptical of the power of the imagination: "I have delivered many women who were prepossessed with things of this kind before delivery, which I have never yet found to happen as they imagine" (*Treatise on Midwifery,* 2:148). However, the case was sent to Smellie by a "Mr. Pierce, of St. Thomas's Hospital, Apothecary," and he seems to have believed it—as did, of course, the mother, who explained the circumstances in the first place.

Finally, even among "the vulgar" the doctrine did not totally usurp other explanations, and it had to compete with the older belief in the power of God or the devil to create monstrosities. Turner reports a case in which a woman resisted his suggestion that he cut away a raspberry birthmark from her forehead, "Superstitiously fancying it both sinful and fruitless to attempt removing a Mark of God Almighty" (*De Morbis Cutaneis,* 186).

28. St. André, *Short Narrative,* 23–24. In a letter probably written in early November 1726, well before St. André entered the case, William Pountney, a surgeon from

Farnham, near Guildford, wrote to his father to pass on the story of Mary Toft that he just had heard: "She says that being with child she went with another woman in ye fields to weeding, & they put up a Rabbit, she ran after itt, & in running put up another; & ran after both, till quite tyr'd[.] ye next morning she went again and clap'd her hatt upon ye little turf where one of ye rabbits satt before in hopes of finding him, but he was not there & has not forbore thinking of Rabbitts ever since" (William Pountney to his father, undated letter, Douglas Papers, D321).

The repeated allusions during the affair to the power of the imagination make it clear that this was the commonly accepted explanation for her rabbits: see, for instance, *St. James Evening Packet*, 15 November 1726; *Doctor's in Labour; A Philosophical Enquiry into the Wonderful CONEY-WARREN, lately discovered at Godalmin near Guilford in Surrey* (London, 1726); *Mist's Weekly Journal*, 7 January 1727; and *The Wonder of Wonders*, 7–9.

Except for the one paragraph in *A Short Narrative*, St. André left no other evidence to suggest how he explained the "præternatural phenomemon." Still, this one paragraph, it seems to me, would be sufficient evidence that he believed that Mary Toft's monstrous births were caused by her imagination were it not for the fact that Boyer claimed that St. André attributed the rabbits to spontaneous generation (*Political State of Great Britain* 32 [December, 1726]: 587-88) and that Voltaire said the same (*Singularités de la nature*, in *Oeuvres*, 70 vols. [Paris, 1785], 31:428). It is difficult to take the claims of either of these men seriously. Spontaneous generation had been so thoroughly discredited by this time that anyone who made this argument would have been subject to vociferous ridicule, and yet St. André was never accused of believing it by anyone close to the case. Voltaire's recounting of the Mary Toft incident is shot through with egregious factual errors. It occurs in the midst of a longer argument ridiculing theories of spontaneous generation and other intellectual systems that deny the birth of all living things from seeds or eggs, and it is probable that he embroidered, twisted, and misshaped the event to suit his own rhetorical ends—much as he did throughout the book.

29. Douglas's ultimate rejection of Mary Toft's claim should not be taken as evidence that he doubted the doctrine of the influence of the imagination. He chooses his words with great care: "I begin by declaring it to have been always my firm Opinion, that this Report was false; in the First Place, because I could never conceive the Generation of a perfect Rabbit in the *Uterus* of a Woman to be possible, it being contradictory to all that is hitherto known, both from Reason and Experience, concerning the ordinary, as well as extraordinary Procedure of Nature, in the Formation of a *Fœtus*" (*Advertisement*, 3). The important word here is "perfect," and Douglas's point is that a human cannot give birth to "an intirely different Species" (38). The notes and outlines he made for his projected treatise on the incident, which include copious comments on the physiology of real rabbits and the anatomy of Mary Toft's, make it clear that one of his major lines of argument would have been that Mary Toft's were "true Rabbit[s]" and therefore could not be "real Monsters" (Douglas Papers, D334).

30. Montaigne, "Of the Force of the Imagination," in *Essays*, 1:101 (cf. ch. 1, n. 11).

31. Thomas Willis, *Two Discourses Concerning the Souls of Brutes*, trans. Samuel Pordage, ed. Solomon Diamond (1683; rpt., Gainesville, Florida: Scholars' Facsimiles and Reprints, 1971), 41.

32. Turner, *De Morbis Cutaneis*, 162; Maubray, *Female Physician*, 60; Daniel Sennert, *De Consensu et Dissensu Galenicorum et Peripateticorum cum Chymicis*, in *Opera*

Omnia, 3 vols. (Lyons, 1650), 3:787. ["Verus hoc statim in principio monendum, effectus illos proxime ab imaginatione non pendere, nec animam tales effectus per imaginationem edere, atque imaginationem per se, directe & propria virtute illos effectus, quae ab ipsa proficisci dicuntur, non producere, nec in alia corpora agere."]

33. The concepts of the imagination and of the psycho-physiological system of which it is a part were formulated within the Aristotelian and Galenic traditions and flourished through the Renaissance. I am merely sketching out its central and most commonly accepted features. My discussion of the imagination, in this and in later chapters, is deeply indebted to E. Ruth Harvey, *The Inward Wits: Psychological Theory in the Middle Ages and the Renaissance* (London: The Warburg Institute/ University of London, 1975); Ruth Leila Anderson, *Elizabethan Psychology and Shakespeare's Plays* (1927; reprint, New York: Russell & Russell, 1966); William Rossky, "Imagination in the English Renaissance: Psychology and Poetic," *Studies in the Renaissance,* ed. M. A. Shaaber, 5 (1958): 49–73; Donald F. Bond, "The Neo-Classical Psychology of the Imagination," *ELH* 4 (December 1937): 245–64; Murray Wright Bundy, *The Theory of Imagination in Classical and Mediaeval Thought,* University of Illinois Studies in Language and Literature, vol. 12, nos. 20–23 (Urbana: University of Illinois Press, 1927); and J. M. Cocking, *Imagination: A Study in the History of Ideas* (London: Routledge, 1991).

34. John Milton, *Paradise Lost,* 5.479–87, in *Complete Poems and Major Prose,* ed. Merritt Y. Hughes (New York: Odyssey Press, 1957).

35. I have taken this useful phrase from Lester King, *Philosophy of Medicine* (cf. ch. 2, n. 27). King's work is enormously helpful in detailing the variety of ways in which specific medical theories performed variations of this maneuver. Also helpful is L. J. Rather, *Mind and Body in Eighteenth Century Medicine* (Berkeley: University of California Press, 1965).

36. "For as the body works on the mind, by his bad humours, troubling the spirits, sending gross fumes into the brain, and so disturbing the soul, and all the faculties of it; . . . so, on the other side, the mind most effectively works upon the body, producing by his passions and perturbations miraculous alterations, as melancholy, despair, cruel disease, and sometimes death itself" (Robert Burton, *Anatomy of Melancholy,* ed. Floyd Dell and Paul Jordan-Smith [New York: Tudor Publishing, 1927], 217–18).

37. Thomas Willis, *The Anatomy of the Brain and the Description and Uses of the Nerves,* trans. Samuel Pordage, ed. William Feindel, 2 vols. (1681; rpt., Montreal: McGill University Press, 1965), 2:87; Henry Power, *Experimental Philosophy* (1664; rpt., New York: Johnson Reprint Corporation, 1966), 72; John Donne, "The Extasie," in *The Poems of John Donne,* ed. Herbert J. C. Grierson, 2 vols. (London: Oxford University Press, 1951), 1:53.

38. Willis, *Two Discourses,* 24–25; Timothy Bright, *A Treatise on Melancholie* (1586; rpt., New York: Columbia University Press, 1940), 35. Compare Burton's slightly different notion: "the body, being material, worketh upon the immaterial soul, by mediation of humours & spirits which participate of both" (*Anatomy of Melancholy,* 318).

39. Bright, *Treatise on Melancholie,* 38, 35.

40. *Two Dissertations Concerning Sense and Imagination* (London, 1728), 69–70; Thomas Wright, *The Passions of the Minde in Generall* (1630; rpt., Urbana: University of Illinois Press, 1971), 51.

41. Daniel Sennert, *The Institutions or Fundamental of the Whole Art, both of Physic and Chirurgery* (London, 1656), 29.

42. Sir John Davies, *Nosce Teipsum,* in *The Poems of Sir John Davies,* ed. Robert Krueger, 2 vols. (Oxford: Clarendon Press, 1975), 1:23.

43. Pierre de Primaudaye, *The French Academie* (London, 1618), 611, as quoted in Anderson, *Elizabethan Psychology and Shakespeare's Plays,* 24.

44. Francis Bacon, *De Augmentis,* in *The Works of Francis Bacon,* ed. James Spedding, Robert Leslie Ellis, and Douglas Denon Heath, 14 vols. (1857–74; rpt., Stuttgart-Bad Cansatt: F. Frommann Verlag, 1961–63), 4:315; *Advancement of Learning,* in *Works of Bacon,* 3:343.

45. *De Anima,* trans. W. S. Hett (Cambridge: Harvard University Press, 1935), 181.

46. Edward Stillingfleet, *Origines Sacræ: or A Rational Account of the Grounds of Natural and Revealed Religion* (Cambridge, 1702), 251; Joseph Glanvill, *The Vanity of Dogmatizing* (1661; rpt., Hove, Sussex: Harvester Press, 1970), 67; Ralph Cudworth, *A Treatise Concerning Eternal and Immutable Morality* (London, 1731), 140–41.

47. *Paradise Lost,* 5.105; *The Faerie Queene,* 2.9.50, in *The Poetical Works of Edmund Spenser,* ed. J. C. Smith and E. de Selincourt (London: Oxford University Press, 1963); *Callipædia, Book the Fourth,* in *The Complete Works of William Diaper,* ed. Dorothy Broughton (London: Routledge and Kegan Paul, 1952), 114. For a survey of some of the ways thinkers in the seventeenth century grappled with this problem, see Emily Michael and Fred S. Michael, "Corporeal Ideas in Seventeenth-Century Psychology," *Journal of the History of Ideas* 50 (January-March 1989): 31–48.

48. *De Augmentis,* in *Works of Bacon,* 4:405–6.

49. Joseph Addison, *Spectator* 421, in *The Spectator,* ed. Donald F. Bond, 5 vols. (Oxford: Clarendon Press, 1965), 3:577; Ralph Cudworth, *Treatise Concerning Morality,* 144–45.

50. See, for instance, this rather complex route of intermediaries: "As the motions of our Passions are hid from our eyes, so they are hard to be perceived: yet for the speculation of this matter, I think it most necessary, to declare the way and maner of them; . . . First then, to our imagination commeth, by sense or memorie, some object to be knowne, convenient or disconvenient to Nature, the which being knowne . . . in the imagination which resideth in the former parte of the braine, . . . when we imagine any thing, presently the purer spirits, flocke from the brayne, by certaine secret channels to the heart, where they pitch at the dore, signifying what an object was presented, convenient or disconvenient for it. The heart immediately bendeth, either to prosecute it, or to eschew it: and the better to effect that affection, draweth other humours to help him, and so in pleasure concurre great store of pure spirites; in paine and sadnesse, much melancholy blood; in ire, blood and choller; and not only (as I sayd) the heart draweth, but also the same soule that informeth the heart residing in other partes, sendeth the humours unto the heart, to performe their service in such a woorthie place: . . ." (Wright, *Passions of the Minde,* 45).

51. Sennert, *De Consensu,* in *Opera,* 3:788 (cf. ch. 2, n. 32). Sennert's argument is a commonplace. His example of the mirror goes back to Aristotle, and Aquinus confirms the belief, using it as an instance of the power of the imagination to change and influence material things.

52. Turner, *De Morbis Cutaneis,* 160–62, 180.

53. For a survey of some of these systems, see King, *Philosohy of Medicine,* 152–81.

54. "Thus, the parents' fancy, by means of a mediating image of things they either desire very ardently or gaze at very attentively, creates a similar image in the substance of the spirits that is adjacent to them. . . . Next, we say that such spirits, by means of a

deeply fixed, mediating image, produce a new [image] similar to that one on the portion of the spirits adjacent to themselves; and so on, successively, until the image has reached the spiritous substance of the semen and the embryo."

["Ita ergo parentum phantasia mediante imagine rerum aut concupitarum ardentius, aut intuitarum attentius consimilem imaginem procreat in spirituum substantia sibi propinqua. . . . Deinde vero dicimus huiusmodi spiritus mediante imagine sibi alte defixa novam illi consimilem in parte spirituum sibi propinqua producere; atque ita deinceps hanc partem in alia, quousque peruentum sit ad spirituosam seminis substantiam, atque ad embryonem"] (Fortunius Licetus, *De Perfecta Constitutione Hominis in Utero* [Passau, 1616], 98).

55. "Phantasia, mediantibus animi passionibus, & humorum & spirituum motu; potest aliquas circa foetum facere mutationes" (Fienus, *De Viribus Imaginationis,* 224 [cf. ch. 2, n. 21]).

56. Fienus, *De Viribus Imaginationis,* 208–77. Fienus summarizes his argument this way: "Therefore, I say that the species irradiate into remote parts of the body by means of the action of the appetite and the passions, which are engaged by the fancy. When the marks are produced by the imagination at the moment of coition, the species irradiate right through the nerves to the [female] testes and are imprinted immediately on the seed; and this seed, when it is received into the uterus, bears those species with it and retains them for some time, so that when the shaping [faculty] begins to shape the seed, it shapes it to the likeness of the species. However, when the marks are caused by the imagination after conception has taken place, the species are communicated to the heart through the nerves by a mediating act of the appetite, and there they are imprinted on the blood and vital spirits, and, unchanged, thence through the arteries of the mother, and finally through the umbilical cord, they are communicated to the fetus."

["Quapropter dico, propter actum appetitus & animi passiones, quae phantasiae conjunguntur, species in remotas partes irradiare. Quando signatura sit propter imaginationem habitam in hora coitus, species irradiant recta per nervos in testes, & semini immediate imprimuntur; quod semen cum in uterum recipitur, secum deserit species illas, & aliquanto tempore retinet, & cum formatrix incipit illud efformare, format ad similitudinem earum: Quando autem sit signatura propter imaginationem habitam post conceptum, tum per nervos mediante actu appetitus species communicantur cordi, ibique sanguini & spiritibus vitalibus imprimuntur, & illis tanquam subjectis, dela[t]ae, inde per arterias matris, & tandem umbilicantes, foetui communicantur"] (272–73).

57. Laz[arus] Riverius, *The Universal Body of Physick,* trans. William Carr (London, 1657), 69.

58. "Hoc certum est, imaginationem per se, immediate atque per simplicem imaginationis actum foetus non immutare; cum . . . sit potentia cognoscens atque immanens: . . . Vero magis consentaneum est, foetum immutari ab imaginatione vel mediantibus animi affectibus per humorum & spiritum motum, vel dirigendo facultatem conformatricem" (Sennert, *De Consensu,* in *Opera,* 3:789).

59. Sir Kenelm Digby, *Of the Sympathetic Powder* (London, 1669), 79–84. Earlier, he had accepted the more conventional explanation of the Galenic tradition: "By which it is manifest, that aboundance of animall spirits do then part from the head, and descend into those parts which are the instruments of generation. Wherefore, if there be aboundance of specieses of any one kind of object then strong in the imagination, it must of necessity be carryd down together with the Spirits to the seed" (*Two Treatises:*

In the one of which, the Nature of Mans Soule is Looked Into: In way of Discovery of the Immortality of Reasonable Soules [London, 1645], 406).

60. Henry More, *The Immortality of the Soul,* in *A Collection of Several Philosophical Writings of Dr. Henry More* (Cambridge, 1662), 169–96.

61. *Malebranch's Search after Truth,* trans. Richard Sault (London, 1694), 119–20; 142; 145–46.

CHAPTER THREE
Enthusiasm Delineated

1. "A Song on the Rabbit Breeder" (London, 1727).

2. The intensity of Clarges's anger can be detected even in the understated account of Manningham:

> On *Monday* the 5*th,* I gave my Opinion to Sir *Thomas,* concerning *Mary Toft;* and lest he should commit her to Prison, I spoke to several Persons of Distinction, and the next Day wrote to the Honourable Mr. *Molyneux* to assist me in that Affair, . . .
>
> After some Difficulty, I prevailed with Sir *Thomas Clarges* to let her remain in the Custody of the *High Constable* of *Westminster,* at Mr. *Lacy*'s Bagnio, till the Cheat should be found out, . . .
>
> On Tuesday the 6*th,* Sir Thomas threaten'd her severely, and began to appear the most proper Physician in her Case, and his Remedies took Place, and seem'd to promise a perfect Cure; . . .
>
> (*Exact Diary,* 26–31 [cf. ch. 1, n. 49])

3. *Much Ado About Nothing: Or, a Plain Refutation of All that has been Written or Said Concerning the Rabbit-Woman of Godalming* (London, 1727), 20–21.

4. John Nichols, *Biographical Anecdotes of Hogarth,* 465 (cf. ch. 1, n. 19).

5. George Vertue, *The Surrey-Wonder[:] an Anatomical-Farce as it was Dissected at the Theatre-Royal Lincolns-Inn-Fields* ([London, 1726]).

6. Manningham, *Exact Diary,* 27; Douglas, *Advertisement,* 24, 4 (cf. ch. 1, n. 56); *The London Journal,* 17 December 1726; *Anatomist Dissected,* 33 (cf. ch. 2, n. 1); *The Daily Journal,* 10 December, 1726; Lord Thomas Onslow to Sir Hans Sloane, 4 December 1726, BL Sloane. 4048. fol. 227; *Anatomist Dissected,* 24–25; *The London Journal,* 17 December 1726; *Anatomist Dissected,* 25, 33.

7. *The Post Man,* 10 December 1726; *Philosophical Enquiry into the Wonderful CONEY-WARREN,* 2 (cf. ch. 2, n. 28); "Mr. P— to Dr. A———t, December 19, 1726," in *TE,* 6:444–46. Pliny's story of the town in Spain undermined by rabbits occurs in *The Natural History of Pliny,* trans. John Bostock and H. T. Riley, 6 vols. (London, 1855–57), 2:295.

One of the most interesting associations between Mary Toft and a national crisis brought about by deceit was made by Lord Hervey several years after the event. Hearing how the Duchess of Parma was using the claim of her pregnancy to retain the throne against the machinations of Don Carlos and Elisabeth Farnese, Hervey wrote: "There came an express yesterday from Parma, but (as the King related the contents of the letters) with very inconsistent accounts. He says they write him word that the incredulity as to the Duchess's being pregnant increases every day, though her belly does so too. The whole puts me continually in mind of the Rabbit woman, but old Dorothea watches her too close for any juggle (if they intend one) to succeed" (Lord

Hervey to Stephen Fox, 27 August 1731, in *Lord Hervey and His Friends,* 81–82 [cf. ch. 2, n. 9]).

8. "Mr. P— to Dr. A————t"; *Much Ado About Nothing,* 22; *Pudding and Dumpling Burnt to Pot, Or, A Complete Key to the Dissertation on Dumpling* (1727; rpt., Los Angeles: Augustan Reprint Society, 1970), 14–15.

9. The Earl of Peterborough to Swift, 29 November 1726, *Correspondence of Swift,* 3:191.

10. *Much Ado About Nothing,* 8–9.

11. *The Surrey-Wonder; "St. A-D-E's Miscarriage."*

12. *Doctor's in Labour,* plate 1 (cf. ch. 1, n. 34).

The strength and persistence of this feeling is suggested by two satires that came out four years later, both of which dwelt on the same themes we have seen here. In 1730, the surgeon Cheseldon, speculating that a person could hear if his eardrum were removed, was granted permission to try his experiment on the prisoner Charles Ray, whose sentence of death was remitted on the condition that he submit to the operation. The incident occasioned two satiric rebuses, presumably by the same anonymous author, "The Rabbit-woman's Epistle to Charles Ray, now a Prisoner in Newgate" and "The Answer to the Rabbit-woman's Epistle." There would seem to be little connection between the Mary Toft affair and the experiment on Ray, but the author remembered the Toft incident because he saw in both cases criminals who were innocent next to the sadistic, conniving doctors ("these jugling, butchering . . . Sons of violence") who were exploiting them.

13. "The Rev^d Mr. Pettener Curate of Worplesdon near Guildford assur'd me 1731 that this very Woman going over ye Warren afterw'ds, slipt into a Burrow & broke her Thigh" (Anonymous Commonplace Book, Guildford Muniment Room, 52/7/5).

For some interesting observations about the anger at Mary Toft, fear of her power, and gender, see Susan Bruce, "The Flying Island and Female Anatomy: Gynaecology and Power in *Gulliver's Travels,*" *Genders* 2 (July 1988): 60–76; and Lisa Cody, "'The Doctor's in Labour, or a New Whim Wham from Guildford,'" *Gender and History* 4 (Summer 1992): 175–96. I regret that Cody's article came out after I had completed the manuscript for this study, but I am pleased that we have reached many of the same conclusions independently.

14. For dating, editions, and a complete text of this poem, see *TE,* 6:259–64.

15. For an overview of the Molyneux family, see Sir Capel Molyneux, *An Account of the Family and Descendants of Sir Thomas Molyneux* (Evesham, 1820). A detailed account of their scientific activities can be found in K. Theodore Hoppen, *The Common Scientist in the Seventeenth Century: A Study of the Dublin Philosophical Society, 1683–1708* (Charlottesville: University Press of Virginia, 1970).

16. John Locke, *An Essay Concerning Human Understanding,* ed. John W. Yolton, 2 vols. (London: J. M. Dent & Son, 1971), 1:114.

17. Locke, *Essay Concerning Human Understanding,* 1:113. For discussions of how thoroughly this and related problems worked their way into literary discourse, see Kenneth MacLean, *John Locke and English Literature of the Eighteenth Century* (New Haven: Yale University Press, 1936), 106–8; and Marjorie Hope Nicolson, *Newton Demands the Muse* (Princeton: Princeton University Press, 1946), 81–85.

18. Samuel Molyneux to the Duke of Marlborough, 29 May and 7 June 1714, in William Coxe, *Memoirs of the Duke of Marlborough, with his Original Correspondence,* new rev. ed. by John Wade, 3 vols. (New York, 1889–93), 3:358–360.

19. For Molyneux's career in Parliament, see Romney Sedgwick, *The History of Parliament: The House of Commons, 1715–1754* (Oxford: Oxford University Press, 1970), 263–64.

20. *Historical Manuscripts Commission. Manuscripts of the Earl of Egmont. Diary of Viscount Perceval Afterwards First Earl of Egmont,* 3 vols. (London: His Majesty's Stationery Office, 1920), 1:375; *The Diary of Mary, Countess Cowper,* ed. Spencer Cowper (London, 1865), 115; Pope to Lady Mary Wortley Montagu, [1718], *Corr.*, 1:470.

21. Years before he wrote "The Discovery," Pope seems to have been attracted to Molyneux precisely because he was the typical courtier. Pope mentions him only twice in his letters (*Corr.* 1:308–9 and 470), but both times he uses Molyneux as a kind of genuine article to lend authenticity to the role of courtier he himself was trying to adopt at the time, as if mentioning his friendship with Molyneux confirmed that he, too, was a court gallant and close to power. But even as early as 1716, Pope was beginning to see him as a typical courtier in a more negative sense. When Molyneux tried his hand at translating parts of Ovid's *Metamorpohoses,* Pope poked fun at him in "Sandy's Ghost" (*TE,* 6:170–76) for being a "Wit and Courtly Squire," one who had come to poetry not out of a sense of vocation, but who was driven to it by a courtly servility—a "Puppy tame" who was willing to truckle to the requirement that, in addition to other roles, a courtier must play the role of wit, too, no matter how unsuited to it.

22. Earlier in the century, Henry Davenant had been among the Whig wits who surrounded Addison. Later, he held a series of appointments from the court: Envoy Extraordinary to the Dukes of Parma and Modena, to the Grand Duke of Tuscany, and to the Republic of Genoa. Macky, in his *Characters of the Court of Britain,* dismissed him as "a very giddy-headed Young fellow" but added that he had "some art" (quoted in *PW,* 5:261). What episode involving his "art" Pope and Pulteney were alluding to when they labeled him a "*Machiavel*" is impossible to know, but there was one incident that William Pulteney certainly knew about from his brother, Daniel. In 1722, false rumors had reached London that John Molesworth, who had been on a diplomatic mission to the Court of Sardinia at Turin since 1715, had died. Daniel Pulteney wrote to Molesworth: "Davenant would, no doubt, have been desirous to be your successor and perhaps might flatter himself that he should." The rumors of Molesworth's death persisted, and there began to grow a suspicion of a more "Machiavelian" plot afoot: "The reports, which, you say, are still kept up of your being dead or in great danger are not, I believe, encouraged by any of Mr. Finch's friends, how far they may be promoted by Mr. Davenant's I can't tell, and I think you need not much care; whatever were to happen, he would not succeed" (Daniel Pulteney to John Molesworth, 19 August 1722 and 31 January 1723, *Historical Manuscripts Commission. Reports on Manuscripts in Various Collections. The Manuscripts of M. L. S. Clements, Esq.,* 8 vols. [London: HMSO, 1913], 8:346, 354).

23. I take this quotation from Douglas's copy of an affadavit that was sworn by an anonymous witness to the events in the bagnio on 4 December (Douglas Papers, D331): "That Dr D——s on Sunday morning ye 4th Instant after Examining Mary Tofts told ye D of Mont: &c. That he was Astonishd at ye Bulk he felt betwixt ye Umbilicus & Os pubis, that he had circumscribd it wt his hands, That he cd scarce believe his own Senses, that He wisht others of ye profession wd satisfie 'emselves of it &c. That in ye Afternoon at 5 ye same day, He, wt Many others; atccouteirs, after touching & narrowly strickly Examining her, came into ye foreroom & publickly said she had all ye Symptoms of an Approaching delivery, and all wou'd be over in half An hour."

24. *Exact Diary,* 9, 24.

25. I can find no biographical information showing that Manningham began his career as an apothecary, but another satire, "A Song on the Rabbit Breeder," also claims that "He was an Apothecary."

26. *Philosophical Enquiry into the Wonderful CONEY-WARREN,* 3. The author of *Much Ado About Nothing* says that he made Mary Toft confess "without the low Artifice of wheedling, or the high Hand of Threatening; but by touching *her in her Tenderest part,* viz. her conscience; . . . " (7). *The Doctor's in Labour* comments,

> Now to the Bagnio flock the Town & Court
> T' improve their Iudgment some and some for sport,
> They're wellcome all to Mary—all that will
> May in her Warren for a Rabbit feel.
> But Moll take care they don't ye Trick discover,
> For then thy Merry days will all be over.

But the single gesture that revealed most unambiguously the feelings many people had about her sexuality was the apparently casual decision to lodge her in Mr. Lacy's bagnio in Leicester Fields. For why should Mary Toft be put in a house that served as a front for a brothel unless it was felt that she too was a whore? For other ways in which Mary Toft was portrayed as a whore, see Cody, "'Doctor's in Labour,'" esp. 184–85 (cf. ch. 3, n. 13).

27. "The Rabbit-Man-Midwife," in *A New Miscellany* (London, 1730), 33. I have argued for the attribution of this poem to Arbuthnot in "New Evidence for Dr. Arbuthnot's Authorship of 'The Rabbit-Man-Midwife,'" *Studies in Bibliography* 41 (December 1987): 247–67.

28. *Much Ado About Nothing,* 12–15.

29. "The Scene opens and discovers a little Town in one of the turnings of which is a mean looking House, and over one door hangs a sign of the Cradle; Enter the Husband and Knocks, at which an Old Matron looks out of the window and beckons him to stay, soon after she comes down with a Candle & Lanthorn, during which time, he fetches an Horse with a Sadle and Pillion on the back of it, but being in a surprize, he puts her a stride on the Sadle, and himself sideways on the Pillon, and so rides away she holding the Bridle and he the Lanthorn" (*Harlequin turn'd Imposture; or, The Guilford Comedy* [London, n.d.], 4–5).

Many years later, Mary Toft was associated with gender inversion again in *The Southwark Wonder: or, The Whole Town in an Uproar* ([London, 1766]), which recounts the case of Edmund Mitchell, a rake who, after unsuccessfully trying to seduce an innocent woman, himself became pregnant.

30. "St. A-D-E's Miscarriage"; *Anatomist Dissected,* title page; *Whitehall Evening Journal,* 29 December 1726; "Mr. P— to Dr. A————t"; *Anatomist Dissected,* 20–22.

31. Though there has been some confusion about his identity, "C" is almost certainly Maubray. Because of his outrageous assertion that he had actually delivered a sooterkin, Maubray's new involvement with Mary Toft's small, monstrous creatures made him a main butt of satire. Thomas Brathwaite said that he was tempted to dedicate his work to Maubray—"The Sooterkin Doctor," Brathwaite calls him, which is precisely how figure "C" in *Cunucularii* is labeled (Brathwaite, *Remarks on A Short Narrative,* sig. B2ʳ [cf. ch. 1, n. 7]). Maubray was attacked in George Vertue's *The Surrey-Wonder* (cf. ch. 3, n. 5); he is shown entering the bagnio holding a bottle containing a

preserved sooterkin. The most lengthy and virulent attack on Maubray was *A Letter from a Male Physician* (cf. ch. 1, n. 54), which I will examine below. Finally, Hogarth's "C" is identified as Maubray in *Much Ado About Nothing*.

I have made more detailed arguments for the identification of Maubray and of all the other characters in the print in "Three Characters in Hogarth's *Cunicularii*—and Some Implications," *Eighteenth-Century Studies* 16 (Fall 1982): 24–46.

32. Manningham, *Exact Diary,* 24.

33. Ibid., 23–25.

34. Samuel Butler, *Hudibras,* ed. John Wilders (Oxford: Clarendon Press, 1967), 3.1.358–94.

35. Maubray, *Female Physician,* 375 (cf. ch. 1, n. 32). It would be supererogatory, I suppose, to point out that Maubray is lying, but it may be of interest to know that he cribbed his description of his sooterkin, almost word for word, from a much earlier description of a monstrous serpent delivered by a woman, an incident first recorded by Levinus Lemnius, *De Miraculis Occultis Naturae* (Antwerp, 1559). The story was quoted by other writers on monstrous birth—most notably Paré (*On Monsters,* 58 [cf. ch. 1, n. 11])—so it is difficult to know where Maubray copied from. But compare Maubray's version with Licetus's rendition of Lemnius: "post modum ab utero serpens est rostro adunco, longo, teretique collo, oculis vibrantibus, cauda acuminata, eximiaque pedum agilitate; qui ortus fremitu, sibilisque totum cubiculum implevit in omnem se partem proripiens, ut latebram nancisceretur" (*De Monstrorum Caussis,* 64 [cf. ch. 1, n. 12]).

36. *Letter From a Male Physician in the Country,* 37–38 (cf. ch. 1, n. 54).

37. *Much Ado About Nothing,* 14. John Byrom, "A Horrid and Barbarous Robbery," in *Selections from the Journal and Papers of John Byrom,* ed. Henri Talon (London: Rockliff Publishing, 1950), 290.

38. Butler, *Hudibras,* 1.1.531, 3.2.638.

39. With the waning of the Puritan threat, the astronomer gradually had replaced the religious fanatic as the exemplar of Enthusiasm. Besides Sidrophel in *Hudibras,* the most complex treatments of this figure are the scientists in Butler's "The Elephant in the Moon," the Laputans in *Gulliver's Travels,* and the mad astronomer in *Rasselas.* Hogarth himself, of course, ranked the astronomer alongside the other traditional examples of Enthusiastic madness in the final plate of *The Rake's Progress.* I have examined the relationship between the religious Enthusiast and the astronomer in "'Pygmalion's Frenzy': Language, Solipsism, and Madness in Pope's *Dunciad*" (Ph.D. diss., Emory University, 1974).

I am not the first to identify figure "B" as Molyneux. Dr. Samuel Merriman, in his collection of Toft material now in the possession of the Royal Society of Medicine, after noting the usual identification of "B" as Manningham, remarked: "*B. the Occult Philosopher searching into the Depth of Things* does not at all apply to Sir Richard Manningham but very well to Mr. Molyneux whose Telescope is laughed at in the 'Much ado about nothing.'" He passed this information on to John Nichols—the man more than anyone else responsible for the tradition of identifying "B" as Manningham— whose reply dated 7 July 1841 is also in this collection: "If you will oblige me with a letter on the Print of Cunicularii, I think it would be worth while to throw out the correction in A Gentleman's Magazine, as Sir Rd Manningham has been generally considered the Physician laughed at" ("Collection of tracts relative to Mary Toft, the pretended rabbit-breeder," The Royal Society of Medicine, L. 7. C. 24/19582). Merriman subsequently published a short article identifying "B" as Molyneux in *The Gentleman's Magazine* (1842): 266–68.

40. Sir William Temple, *Of Poetry,* in Joel Elias Spingarn, *Critical Essays of the Seventeenth Century,* 3 vols. (Oxford: Clarendon Press, 1908–9), 3:76. Hogarth himself came to *Cunicularii* having just finished his illustrations for *Hudibras,* a series of prints explicitly in the tradition of anti-Enthusiastic satire, and in these he overlays the venality and hypocrisy of the characters with a sense of their delusion and their desire to exist in a world of heroic fantasy. As a result, his Enthusiasts appear as innocent as they are guilty: see Ronald Paulson, *Hogarth: His Life, Art, and Times,* 2 vols. (New Haven: Yale University Press, 1971), 1:149–55.

41. Although Whiston did not publish his opinions in print until 1750 in his *Memoirs,* by his own account he was airing his views freely while Mary Toft was still in Mr. Lacy's bagnio. He is laughed at for his opinions in *Philosophical Enquiry into the Wonderful CONEY-WARREN,* 2, and in "The Rabbit-Man-Midwife." The only other work I have been able to find that links the incident with religious fanaticism in any literal way is a two-paragraph piece in *Political State* 32 (December 1726): 601–2, and even here the author's point is to show "what a wonderful Use PRIEST-CRAFT might have made of this Imposture in a POPISH IGNORANT COUNTRY."

42. Swift, *Tale of a Tub,* in *PW,* 1:108; Henry More, *Enthusiasmus Triumphatus,* ed. M. V. Deporte (1662; rpt., Los Angeles: Augustan Reprint Society, 1966), 4.

43. Glanvill, *Vanity of Dogmatizing,* 200, 67, 97, 93 (cf. ch. 2, n. 46).

44. Thomas Hobbes, *Leviathan* (Oxford: Clarendon Press, 1965), 13; John Locke, journal entry for 22 January 1678, as quoted in Kenneth Dewhurst, *John Locke: Physician and Philosopher* (London: Wellcome Historical Medical Library, 1963), 101.

45. More, *Enthusiasmus Triumphatus,* 3.

46. Thomas Tryon, *A Discourse of the Causes, Natures and Cures of Phrensie, Madness or Distraction* (1689; rpt., Los Angeles: Augustan Reprint Society, 1973), 253.

47. More, *Enthusiasmus Triumphatus,* 4.

48. More, *Enthusiasmus Triumphatus,* 38, 3–4; Swift, *Tale of a Tub,* in *PW,* 1:100. Meric Casaubon explained Enthusiasm in similar terms: "Certain it is, that upon some distempers of the brain, a man shall think, even awaking, that he seeth those things which he doth not see; things which are not, nor perchance can be . . . . But whatever the cause, the effect is certain; confirmed by the learned Fracastorius in these words: . . . *Whether the* species *comes to the eyes from without or from within, is not materiall at all, in point of apparition: for they believe they see, and are astonished, and grow besides themselves"* (Meric Casaubon, *A Treatise Concerning Enthusiasme* [1655; rpt., Gainesville, Florida: Scholar's Facsimiles and Reprints, 1970], 146).

49. *Hudibras,* 1.1.139–50.

50. René Descartes, *Discourse on the Method,* in *The Philosophic Writings of Descartes,* ed. John Cottingham, Robert Stoothoff, and Dugald Murdoch, 3 vols. (Cambridge: Cambridge University Press, 1984–91), 1:129; Descartes, *Meditations on First Philosophy,* in *Philosophic Writings of Descartes,* 2.19.

51. *Tale of a Tub,* in *PW,* 1:36.

52. Swift, *A Discourse Concerning the Mechanical Operation of the Spirit,* in *PW,* 1:174.

53. John Trenchard, *Natural History of Superstition* (London, 1709), 12; Burton, *Anatomy of Melancholy,* 224. After describing the bizarre behavior of Enthusiasts, Trenchard concludes: "As these and many other surprising Appearances, are only the co-operations and united force of different, and sometimes contrary Passions, so our Pas-

sions are the Mechanical and Necessary Effects of the Complexion, Constitution, and Distempers of our Bodies" (*Natural History of Superstition,* 36).

54. Swift's indebtedness to the physiological explanation of Enthusiasm, and especially to Burton, Casaubon, and More, has been fully documented. See, for instance, Phillip Harth, *Swift and Anglican Rationalism: The Religious Background of "A Tale of a Tub"* (Chicago: University of Chicago Press, 1961), esp. 58–75, 101–24; and Thomas L. Canavan, "Robert Burton, Jonathan Swift, and the Tradition of Anti-Puritan Invective," *Journal of the History of Ideas* 34 (April-June 1973): 227–42. Still relevant are the three important articles by Clarence M. Webster: "Swift's *Tale of a Tub* Compared with Earlier Satires of the Puritans," *PMLA* 47 (1932): 171–78; "Swift and Some Earlier Satirists of Puritan Enthusiasm," *PMLA* 48 (1933): 1141–53; and "The Satiric Background of the Attack on the Puritans in Swift's *Tale of a Tub,*" *PMLA* 50 (1935): 210–23. In chapter 4, I will argue that Swift is subverting this explanation even while he is using it.

55. More, *Enthusiasmus Triumphatus,* 2.

56. *Anatomist Dissected,* 11.

57. *Tale of a Tub,* in *PW,* 1:99.

58. George Lavington, *The Enthusiasm of Methodists and Papists Compared* (London, 1748), pt. 1, 49.

59. Trenchard, *Natural History of Superstition,* 43, 26, 50. For the Renaissance attribution of religious Melancholy to physiological causes, see Lawrence Babb, *The Elizabethan Malady: A Study of Melancholia in English from 1580 to 1642* (East Lansing: Michigan State College Press, 1951), esp. 47–54. For surveys of the medical explanation of Enthusiasm, see John F. Sena, "Melancholic Madness and the Puritans," *Harvard Theological Review* 66 (July, 1973): 293–309; and George Rosen, "Enthusiasm," *Bulletin of the History of Medicine* 42 (September-October, 1968): 393–421. Michael Heyd explores how Melancholy and Enthusiasm were linked in the medical tradition in "Robert Burton's Sources on Enthusiasm and Melancholy: From a Medical Tradition to Religious Controversy," *History of European Ideas* 5 (1984): 17–44.

Finally, note how Lavington's explanation of Enthusiasm from the mid-eighteenth century is even less determinate than Trenchard's, though it continues to preserve the basic notion that it is a psychosomatic disease of the imagination: "Nor is it to be doubted, but the greatest Part of these *strange Feelings* and *Sufferings, Dejections of Mind* and *dreadful Apprehensions,* &c. proceed from *Disease,* caused perhaps by a *Flatulency* from much *Fasting,* or the Fumes of *Indigestion,* or Want of *Exercise,* deep Intention of *Thought,* and various *Affections* and *Passions*; which *Physicians* can much better account for than myself. And we may easily conceive that the Effects of such *Disease* must of Course be *stronger,* when the *indisposed Body* wears a *melancholic* and enthusiastic *Head*; Strength of *Imagination* and *Distemper* concurring" (*Enthusiasm of Methodists,* pt. 2, 54).

60. *Mechanical Operation,* in *PW,* 1:188; *Tale of a Tub,* in *PW,* 1:105.

61. Trenchard, *Natural History of Superstition,* 11–14, 23; More, *Enthusiasmus Triumphatus,* 11–12.

62. Casaubon, *Treatise Concerning Enthusiasme,* 22; More, *Enthusiasmus Triumphatus,* 12–13, 14, 17. The thought was commonplace. See, for instance, Lavington's explanation of why both Methodists and Catholics depict holy love in terms of carnal love: "For these excesses of the *spiritual and carnal* affections are nearer *allied* than is generally thought; arising from the same irregular emotions of the blood and animal Spirits. And the *Patient* is hurried on either way according to the *nature of the Object.* And I am much mistaken, and so is History too, if some of the warmest and *most Enthusiastic Pre-*

tenders to the *Love of God* have not entertained the same *violence* and *Passion* (not quite so *spiritual*) for *some* of their *neighbours*" (*Enthusiasm of Methodists*, pt. 1, 59).

Hogarth portrays Mary Toft again in *Credulity, Superstition and Fanaticism* (figure 3), printed in 1762. The occasion of this print was the Cock Lane Ghost—a hoax in which the ghost of Miss Fanny Lynes regularly communicated by knockings to the eleven-year-old daughter of William Kent. The seances attracted the curious and the gullible, who pressed into the bedchamber of the young girl in huge crowds reminiscent of those which had pressed into Mary Toft's rooms forty years earlier. Because the Cock Lane Ghost was a fraud and because it was commonly linked to Enthusiasm (the incident was exploited, or was thought to be exploited, by the Methodists), it is not surprising that Hogarth associated this new hoax with Mary Toft's older one, or that, once again, he returned to the central themes of *Cunicularii*.

Credulity depicts the interior of a Methodist meeting house, and Hogarth fills it with figures of famous hoaxers. The figure beneath the clerk's desk is the Boy of Bilston, who vomited rags, pins, and nails and was believed to have been bewitched; the two figures on the pulpit are George Villiers's and Mrs. Veal's ghosts; the figure on top of the Spiritual Thermometer is the ghost of the Tedworth Drummer; the woman writhing on the floor, of course, is Mary Toft; and the images held by the congregation are icons of the latest example of Enthusiastic credulity, the Cock Lane Ghost. (For the identification of many of the details in the print, I am indebted to Ronald Paulson, *Hogarth's Graphic Works*, 2 vols. [New Haven: Yale University Press, 1965], 1:244–49.)

As in *Cunicularii*, Hogarth sees the social history of Enthusiasm as an affair of fools and knaves, but in this print, his psychology is considerably more simple. Perhaps because *Credulity* was reworked from an earlier print, *Enthusiasm Delineated*, or perhaps because Hogarth wanted to speak to what he considered an unsophisticated audience, *Credulity*, unlike *Cunicularii*, does not play with the proposition that a single person can be both a fool and a knave, nor does it explore the psychological condition of a mind "fooling itself." Here, there is no figure who knavishly plays on his own foolishness. Enthusiasts are fools, and knaves take advantage of their credulity. As the puppets imply, fools and knaves are separate individuals, one of whom plays on the other.

Although he has simplified the relationship between fools and knaves, Hogarth still focuses on precisely that other aspect of Enthusiasm which he dwelt on in *Cunicularii*, the transformation of spirit into body. Hence he equates Catholicism and Enthusiasm (the preacher's wig flies off his head, revealing a monk's tonsure), for in Catholicism matters of the spirit are reduced to idolatry, just as in Enthusiasm the spirit is rooted in the physical image. Hogarth makes the same point in other ways. The lines on the clerks' desk from Whitefield's hymn—"Only Love to us be giv'n, / Lord we ask no other Heav'n"—are acted out carnally by the man and woman in front of it. Hell is given a physical topography on the chandelier. And the congregation, in a literalistic enactment of transubstantiation, are eating images of the Cock Lane Ghost. All these perversions are epitomized in the Jew who stands before a Bible open to a picture of a sacrificial altar and a knife inscribed with the word "Bloody." He is crushing a louse between his nails. The implication is that the New Covenant's transformation of blood sacrifice to spiritual salvation through Christ has been transfigured downward to its literalistic beginnings, that the spiritual antitype has been reduced to its physical type.

This is the theme Hogarth still presses, as he pressed it in *Cunicularii*, though now he has simplified his statement to a single visual pun, repeated over and over again. Hogarth's numerous references in the print to ghosts—Caesar, George Villiers, Mrs. Veal,

Figure 3. William Hogarth, *Credulity, Superstition, and Fanaticism* (copyright British Museum)

the Tedworth Drummer, the Cock Lane Ghost—suggests that his point about Enthusiasm is that the literalizing imagination transforms things of the spirit into mere "spirits," ghosts.

Because he continues to view the essence of Enthusiasm in this way, Hogarth uses Mary Toft as he used her in *Cunicularii,* as a woman who has the power of reducing the spiritual to the physical. Placed at the far left border, she acts as the "introduction" to our "reading" of the print, adumbrating the quintessential fact about Enthusiasm which the rest of the print details. In short, in *Credulity* and well as in *Cunicularii*, she symbolizes the very *process* of Enthusiasm: the imagination's wholesale replacement of the spirit by a monstrous conversion downward to a corporeal parody.

63. Malebranche, *Search after Truth*, 152 (cf. ch. 2, n. 61).

64. Thomas Nashe, *The Terrors of the Night*, in *The Works of Thomas Nashe*, ed. Ronald B. McKerrow, 5 vols. (London: Sidgwick & Jackson, Ltd., 1904–10), 1:354.

65. Burton, *Anatomy of Melancholy*, 140; George Puttenham, *The Arte of English Poesie*, ed. Gladys Dodge Willcock and Alice Walker (Cambridge: Cambridge University Press, 1936), 18–19. "In all points our brains are like the firmament, and exhale in everie respect the like grose mistempred vapors and meteors; of the more fœculent combustible ayrie matter whereof, afrighting formes and monstrous images innumerable are created. . . . And as the firmament is still mooving and working, so uncessant is the wheeling and rolling on of our braines; which everie hower are tempring some newe peece of prodigie or other, and turmoyling, mixing, and changing the course of our thoughts" (*Terrors*, in *Works of Nashe*, 1:377–78). For numerous examples of teratological language used to describe Melancholy and Enthusiasm, see Rossky, "Imagination in the English Renaissance."

Edward Reynolds speaks about the imagination's shaping of the fetus and its Enthusiastic delusions as the same, or nearly the same, processes:

> Hence those gastly Apparitions, dreadful Sounds, blacke Thoughts, Tremblings, and Horrors, which the strong workings of the Imagination doth present unto, or produce in men; disquieted either with the uglinesse of their Sinnes, or heavinesse of their Natures, making them to feare, where no feare is: which, whether it be done by affecting onely the Fancie, or by the impression of such formes and shapes upon the Spirits, which go unto the outward senses, as may thereby affect them with the same Images (not by reception from without, but by impressions and transfusion from within) it is manifest, not onely by various relations, but by continuall experience, what strong and strange effects those distempers have produced.
>
> Neither are wee to conceive this impossible, when we see as admirable effects in another kind wrought by the same faculty, and, as is probable, by the same means; I mean, the impression of likeliness of an Infant in the Wombe, unto the Parents, or some other, who shall worke a stronger conceit in the Fancie: Or if this be not ascribed unto the working of this power, but rather to a secret reall vertue intrinsecall unto the Seed of the Parents (as many doe affirme) yet that other effect of stamping on the Body the Images and Colours of some things, which had made any strong and violent immutation on the Fancie, must needs be hereunto ascribed.

(*A Treatise of the Passions and Faculties of the Soule of Man* [1640; rpt., Gainesville, Florida: Scholars' Facsimiles and Reprints, 1971], 25–26.)

66. Malebranche, *Search After Truth*, 157–58. Marie Hélène Huet, in an excellent analysis of Malebranche and the notions of the maternal imagination, concludes: "The maternal imagination is thought faithfully to reproduce what it sees and feels. *It is truthful and literal*, almost impersonal to the extent that the images' impressions left on the monstrous brain of the fetus show no sign of critical intervention, that is, of interpretation or judgment. Yet, for the same reason, the maternal imagination is a source of

errors, because appearances are deceiving, and the imagination of women is concerned only with 'the surface of things'" (*Monstrous Imagination,* 55 [cf. ch. 2, n. 27]).

Malebranche, of course, used the theory of the power of the mother's imagination to explain Original Sin, which he conceived of specifically as a Fall into corporeality:

> But what I chiefly desire should be observed, is, there is all possible probabilities, that Men retain in their Brain to this day the traces and impressions of our first Parents. . . . Our first Parents, after their Sin, received such great impressions, and profound traces of sensible things in their Brain, as they might very well communicate to their Children; so that this great propensity we have from the Womb to all sensible things, and the great distance from God we are in, by our present state, may in some manner be explained by what has been said. . . .
>
> Thus it is impossible but that we should be born with Concupisence, and Original Sin. We must be born with Concupiscence, if Concupiscence is only the Natural effort that the traces of the Brain make upon the Mind to engage it to sensible things; and we must be born in Original sin, if Original Sin is nothing else but the Dominion of Concupiscence, and that these efforts become Victorious and Masters over the Mind and Heart of the Child. Now it is very probable, that the dominion or the victory of Concupiscence, is what we call Original Sin in Children, and actual in Men. (*Search After Truth,* 153–54)

The notion that the maternal imagination initiates a kind of Fall into corporeality is endemic to the thinking of this time, though usually not so literalistically conceived as in Malebranche. More typical is this passage from Maubray, who (echoing scores of midwifery texts before him) cautions that a pregnant woman "ought discreetly to suppress all *Anger, Passion,* and other *Perturbations* of Mind, and avoid entertaining too *serious* or *Melancholick* Thoughts: since all such tend to impress a *Depravity* of Nature upon the Infant's *Mind,* and *Deformity* on its Body" (*Female Physician,* 75–76).

Many years after the Mary Toft incident, Smollett wrote in *Peregrine Pickle* about how the pregnant Mrs. Pickel was taken with "a pernicious appetite" for peaches and how her sister-in-law, Mrs. Grizzle, fearing "the child might be affected with some disagreeable mark," did all she could to keep them from her. Mrs. Pickle next longs for pineapples:

> The name of this fatal fruit was no sooner pronounced than Mrs. Grizzle, who incessantly watched her sister's looks, took the alarm, because she thought they gave certain indications of curiosity and desire; and, after having observed that she herself could never eat pineapples, which were altogether unnatural productions, extorted by the force of artificial fire out of filthy manure, asked with a faltering voice, if Mrs. Pickle was not her way of thinking? This young lady, who wanted neither slyness nor penetration, at once divined her meaning, and replied with seeming unconcern, that, for her own part, she should never repine, if there was not a pineapple in the universe, provided she could indulge herself with the fruits of her own country.

(Tobias Smollett, *Peregrine Pickle,* 2 vols. [New York: E. P. Dutton, 1962], 1:21–22.)

Smollett's brilliant combination of motifs shows how thoroughly the power of the theory of the mother's imagination was steeped in the myth of the Fall. The eating of the "fatal fruit" takes place in the garden; the mother is a second Eve, driven by her "pernicious appetite"; the child bears the mother's perverse desire, marked with the sign of her wantonness as surely as the children of Adam and Eve were marked with their parents' Original Sin. Indeed, the pineapple is a symbol of this process of mutation. Pineapples are "unnatural productions, extorted by the force of artificial fire out of filthy manure." So, too, the mother's passion is a "fire" that perverts the laws of nature and produces an unnatural, monstrous child. The child, the "fruit" of this passion, is tainted by Original Sin, by perversity, and by sheer physicality, the "filthy manure" from which he sprang.

Smollett did not believe in the doctrine of the prenatal influence of the imagination; here, he explodes what he takes to be its ludicrous conflation of religion and physiology. And the passage is valuable precisely because it is the judgment of someone close to but just enough outside of the doctrine to have an accurate sense of the source of its power and the direction of its implications for a slightly earlier age.

CHAPTER FOUR
We Beg Leave to Assure You That We Are, &c.

1. James Blondel, *Power of the Mother's Imagination,* i (cf. ch. 2, n. 22).

2. For discussions of the historical importance of the Turner-Blondel controversy, see Ballantyne, *Teratogenesis,* 34–37 (cf. ch. 2, n. 21); King, *Philosophy of Medicine,* 152–81 (cf. ch. 2, n. 27); Rousseau, "Pineapples, Pregnancy, Pica, and *Peregrine Pickle*" (cf. ch. 2, n. 27); Roger, *Les sciences de la vie,* 213–14 (cf. ch. 2, n. 27); Glennda Leslie, "Cheat and Impostor: Debate Following the Case of the Rabbit Breeder," *The Eighteenth Century: Theory and Interpretation* 27 (Fall 1986): 269–86; and Philip K. Wilson, "'Out of Sight, Out of Mind?': The Daniel Turner-James Blondel Dispute Over the Power of the Maternal Imagination," *Annals of Science* 49 (1992): 63–85.

3. Malebranche, *Search after Truth,* 142 (cf. ch. 2, n. 61).

4. James Blondel, *The Strength of Imagination in Pregnant Women Examin'd* (London, 1727), 58.

5. Blondel, *Power of the Mother's Imagination,* 116, 118, 120.

6. Blondel, *Strength of Imagination,* 57, 74.

7. Daniel Turner, *The Force of the Mother's Imagination upon her Fœtus in Utero, Still farther Considered* (London, 1730), 140, 16.

8. For this brief history of embryology in the eighteenth century, I have drawn from F. J. Cole, *Early Theories of Sexual Generation* (Oxford: Clarendon Press, 1930); Joseph Needham, *A History of Embryology* (cf. ch. 2, n. 21); Howard B. Adelman, *Marcello Malpighi and the Evolution of Embryology,* 5 vols. (Ithaca, New York: Cornell University Press, 1966); and Elizabeth B. Gasking, *Investigations in Generation, 1651–1828* (Baltimore: The Johns Hopkins University Press, 1967).

9. John Cook, *An Anatomical and Mechanical Essay on the Whole Animal Oeconomy,* 2 vols. (London, 1730), 1:12.

10. Henry Baker, *The Microscope Made Easy* (London, 1742), 148–49.

11. Cook, *Anatomical and Mechanical Essay,* 1:7; John Harris, *Lexicon Technicum: Or, An Universal English Dictionary of Arts and Sciences* (1710; rpt., Johnson Reprint Corporation, 1966), s.v. "Generation."

12. Henry Baker, *The Universe. A Poem* (London, [1734?]), 23.

13. Ephraim Chambers, *Cyclopaedia: Or, An Universal Dictionary of Arts and Sciences* (London, 1741), s.v. "Generation."

14. Cook, *An Anatomical and Mechanical Essay,* 2:256; Blondel, *Power of the Mother's Imagination,* 141.

15. George Cheyne, *Philosophical Principles of Religion,* 2 vols. (London, 1736), 1:129. See, too, John Cook: "But [God], in a literal Sense, *made us and not we ourselves; much less our Parents*" (*The New Theory of Generation, According to the Best and Latest Discoveries in Anatomy* [London, 1762], 4).

16. William Wollaston, *The Religion of Nature Delineated* (London, 1738), 91.

17. Blondel, *Power of the Mother's Imagination,* 141, 110–11.

18. Turner, *Force of the Mother's Imagination,* 70; Blondel, *Power of the Mother's Imagination,* x.

19. See Peter J. Bowler, "Preformation and Pre-existence in the Seventeenth Century: A Brief Analysis," *Journal of the History of Biology* 4 (1971): 221–44; and Roger, *Les sciences de la vie,* 163–384 (cf. ch. 2, n. 27).

20. Baker, *Microscope Made Easy,* 152.

21. John Denne, *The Wisdom of God in the Vegetable Creation* (London, 1730), 5–6.

22. Blondel, *Power of the Mother's Imagination,* 130, 134, 141.

23. Turner, *De Morbis Cutaneis,* 156–57 (cf. ch. 2, n. 26).

24. Turner, *Force of the Mother's Imagination,* 138.

25. Turner, *Defence of the XIIth Chapter,* 97–98 (cf. ch. 2, n. 27).

26. By using "Plastic Power" to explain monstrosities, Turner is invoking the argument of James Drake (see Wilson, "'Out of Sight, Out of Mind?'," 78). Drake himself acknowledged that the "Plastic Power" was an "old and exploded . . . Opinion," and he turned to it, he confessed, in a kind of desperation ("I must however embrace it, even tho' I know not exactly wherein it lies"), unable to find any other hypothesis that could explain the processes of generation (*Anthropologia Nova: or, A New System of Anatomy,* 2 vols. [London, 1707], 2:336 [mispaginated as 352]).

Drake (and others before him) derived this power from the "Plastic Nature" of the Cambridge Platonists, and all of them conceived of it as a quasi-immaterial force that could bridge the gap between mind and matter and thus mitigate a thoroughgoing mechanism. For a particularly clear discussion of these "Plastic" forces, including how and why they were used to explain the origin of monstrosities, see William B. Hunter, Jr., "The Seventeenth Century Doctrine of Plastic Nature," *Harvard Theological Review* 43 (July 1950): 197–213.

27. *Defence of the XIIth Chapter,* 113; *Force of the Mother's Imagination,* 19; *Defence of the XIIth Chapter,* 71, 76. Theodore M. Brown, in "From Mechanism to Vitalism in Eighteenth-Century English Physiology," *Journal of the History of Biology* 7 (Fall 1974): 179–216, documents how, at this time, a number of English physiologists rejected, just as Turner did, their own earlier, uncritical acceptance of mechanism. What I find striking about Brown's survey is that it reveals that few of these physiologists were able to articulate a substantive alternative to the mechanism they were growing increasingly skeptical of. As Brown says, they moved toward a "non-theoretical empiricism."

28. Blondel, *Strength of Imagination,* sig. a2ᵛ; Turner, *Defence of the XIIth Chapter,* 72, 76, 97–98.

29. Turner, *De Morbis Cutaneis,* 159; Turner, *Force of the Mother's Imagination,* 143. "If you ask me how Nature works from this Exemplar in the Imagination, I willingly

confess my Ignorance; when you resolve me how I move my Fingers, either one or t'other, by simply willing, I may perhaps acquaint you; which nevertheless I know not how the same is done, I want no Arguments to convince me, that *so it is*" (*Force of the Mother's Imagination,* 25–26).

30. Maubray, *Female Physician,* 57–59 (cf. ch. 1, n. 32).

31. "Sed quomodo ad foetus immutationem faciat imaginatio, ita obscurum est, ut omnes doctissimi viri in caussa reddenda hic haereant" (Sennert, *De Consensu,* in *Opera,* 3:789 [cf. ch. 2, n. 32]).

32. Daniel de Superville, "Some Reflections on *Generation,* and on *Monsters,* with a Description of some particular Monsters," *Philosophical Transactions* 41 (part 1), no. 456 (May/June 1740): 306–7.

33. John Mauclerc, *Dr. Blondel Confuted: or, the Ladies Vindicated, With Regard to the Power of the Imagination in Pregnant Women* (London, 1745), 42.

34. The rise in this period of the importance of the animal spirits, which in many ways replaced the earlier, more intricate systems of mediation, is instructive. Mandeville noted that "we may justly conclude, that we consist of a Soul and a Body," but he had to admit that "How they reciprocally work upon and affect one another, 'tis true, we cannot tell." Obviously, there had to be some "intermediate Officers between the Soul and the grosser parts of the Body," and they were conventionally called the animal spirits. But Mandeville is unwilling to state outright that the animal spirits actually existed; "whether there really are, or are not Animal Spirits, such as are generally allowed, I make use of the Name to express the Instruments of Motion and Sense; or whether the Nerves perform this by any Motion undiscoverable by us, or by any Juice or Steam, or Spirit of *Aether,* or whatever it be" (Bernard Mandeville, *A Treatise of the Hyponchondri-ack and Hysterick Diseases* [1730; rpt., Delmar, New York: Scholars' Facsimiles and Reprints, 1976], 155–56, 163). George Cheyne was equally as troubled. He, too, admitted that there must be "Intermediaries between *pure, immaterial Spirit,* and *gross matter.*" He assumed that "this intermediate material Substance" was the animal spirits, but he confessed he did not understand how they functioned (George Cheyne, *The English Malady* [1733; rpt., Delmar, New York: Scholars' Facsimiles and Reprints, 1976], 60).

It is clear that the animal spirits answered to the intuition of the interdependency of body and mind, but the tentativeness and skepticism expressed by both men suggests that they were aware of how untenable their position was. Matter, however ethereal, is no more capable of crossing over into mind than the grossest of solids. For both men, the animal spirits appear to have become an expedient, a name for saving the appearances, perhaps a desperate metaphor. There seems to be in many of the discussions of animal spirits an almost willful delusion, and I agree with John Yolton that the theory seems to have been driven by a desire to make mechanism less objectionable (*Thinking Matter: Materialism in Eighteenth-Century Britain* [Minneapolis: University of Minnesota Press, 1983], 203).

35. Descartes to Princess Elizabeth of Bohemia, 28 June 1643, in *Philosophic Writings of Descartes,* 3:226–29.

36. Jonathan Swift, "On the Trinity," in *PW,* 9:164; John Locke, *An Examination of P. Malebranche's Opinion of Seeing All Things in God,* in *Works* (London, 1823), 9:217, as quoted in John Yolton, *Perceptual Acquaintance From Descartes to Reid* (Minneapolis: University of Minnesota Press, 1984), 127.

Henry Lee, too, found that "the Communication of Motion by *Thought* or an Act of the Will" was "inexplicable" but went on to argue, "That our Minds can and do communicate Motion to some Parts or their whole Bodies at some times, meerly by *Volition,* is as certain as that one Body moves another by *Contact;* but the Mode of both is equally unintelligible" (Henry Lee, *Anti-Skepticism, Or, Notes upon each Chapter of Mr. Lock's Essay Concerning Human Understanding* [1702; rpt., Hildesheim: Georg Olms Verlag, 1973], 144–45). Isaac Watts, also, was stymied: "We cannot conceive how any corporeal motions or figures impressed or traced in the brain, should have an efficacious power in and of themselves, to give any notices to the soul, or to raise perceptions or ideas in a mind or spirit" ("Essay III" of *Philosophical Essays on Various Subjects,* in *The Works of the Reverend and Learned Isaac Watts, D.D.,* 6 vols. [1810; rpt., New York: AMS Press, 1971], 5:535).

Such examples could be greatly multiplied, but I would like to give only one more, this from an eighteenth-century medical work, which illustrates how the ghost of Galenic hierarchical structure remained, though gutted of any explanatory power:

> Now although Thinking, by its own Power of Reflection, may begin of itself, yet, . . . it evidently appears to terminate in the Fibre; and the Perception of Pleasure and Pain, and all their several Degrees, may begin in the Fibre, and end in the Imagination, which more or less affects the Body, as the Parts where they happen are more or less nervose, as the Matter, with which those Sensations are struck, is more or less agreeable or displeasing.
>
> In this Scale of Motions, both ways ascending and descending, we perceive a Connexion of Cause and Effect, which begins in gross, palpable Matter, and terminates in the Understanding, the highest Faculty of the Soul, and *vice versa.*
>
> So that I may safely venture to lay it down as a *Postulatum,* that *Thought can move Matter, so predispos'd by the Divine Power, as to be influenc'd by the Director of the Will;* but what kind of Mechanism or Arangement of Particles, is necessary to make up a System of Matter to be directed by Thought, or the Influence of the Will, is a Question, I must confess, that again puzzles my Philosophy, and can only be resolv'd by the Supreme Author of nature, who has thus fearfully and wonderfully made us.

(Nicholas Robinson, *A New Theory of Physick and Diseases, Founded on the Principles of the Newtonian Philosophy* [London, 1725], 12–13.)

After a close survey of the period, John Yolton reaches the (wonderfully understated) conclusion that "no one was very clear about how intentions and volitions do fit into or help cause actions" and that orthodox thinkers "could go no further than to say we are able to interfere with our physiology" (*Thinking Matter,* 194–95, 203).

As Robert L. Armstrong has shown, the mainstream of British philosophy was baffled by the problem. Unable to establish a convincing explanation of the link between immaterial and material substances, between external causes in the physical world and perceptions in the mind, or between volitions in the mind and movements in the body, they abandoned the question and turned to matters, such as the "way of ideas," that they thought could be handled with more certainty, thus creating an "epistemology without ontology." See *Metaphysics and British Empiricism* (Lincoln: University of Nebraska Press, 1970).

37. *Treatise on Man,* in *Philosophical Writings of Descartes,* 2:108. Much of the anxiety about the replacement of psychological by physiological processes crystalized around his doctrine of the beast-machine. For detailed accounts of the opposition, see

Leonora Cohen Rosenfield, *From Beast-Machine to Man-Machine* (New York: Octagon Books, 1968); Aram Vartanian, *La Mettrie's L'Homme Machine: A Study in the Origins of an Idea* (Princeton: Princeton University Press, 1960); and Wallace Shugg, "The Cartesian Beast-Machine in English Literature," *Journal of the History of Ideas* 29 (April-June 1968): 279–92.

38. Samuel Clarke, *A Collection of Papers, Which passed between the Late Learned Mr. Leibnitz, and Dr. Clarke* (London, 1717), 325; Bolingbroke, *Essay the First of Letters or Essays Addressed to Alexander Pope,* in *The Works of the Late Right Honorable Henry St. John, Lord Viscount Bolingbroke,* 5 vols. (Dublin, 1793), 3:552.

39. Ralph Cudworth, *The True Intellectual System of the Universe* (1678; rpt., Stuttgart-Bad Cannstatt: Friedrich Frommann Verlag, 1964), 761. For an account of the contemporary responses to Hobbes' materialism, see Samuel I. Mintz, *The Hunting of Leviathan: Seventeenth-Century Reactions to the Materialism and Moral Philosophy of Thomas Hobbes* (Cambridge: Cambridge University Press, 1962).

40. Locke, *Essay Concerning Human Understanding,* 2:147.

41. Lee, *Anti-Skepticism,* 246, 124.

42. Edward Stillingfleet, *A Discourse in Vindication of the Trinity* (London, 1697), 234.

43. Lee, *Anti-Skepticism,* 246. For an overview of iatromechanism and mechanistic physiology, see King, *Philosophy of Medicine,* 95–124 (cf. ch. 2, n. 27); for a discussion of the resistence to it, see Brown, "From Mechanism to Vitalism."

44. Humphrey Ditton, *The New Law of Fluids* (London, 1714), 9, 23–24, as quoted in Yolton, *Thinking Matter,* 43.

45. Typical is Richard Bentley. After proving by reason that there must be in man an immaterial substance and showing the folly of conceiving of man as merely a corporeal automaton, he finally turns, after three sermons, to the question of the interrelation of the mind and the body and, like Turner, quickly admits his own ignorance and retreats into mystery: "It remains therefore, that [sense and perception] must necessarily proceed from some Incorporeal Substance within us. And though we cannot conceive the manner of the Soul's Action and Passion; nor what Hold it can lay on the body, when it voluntarily moves it: yet we are as certain, that it doth so, as of any Mathematical Truth whatsoever; . . . I discern some excellent Final Causes of such a vital Conjunction of body and soul; but the Instrumental I know not, nor what invisible Bands and fetters unite them together. I resolve all that into the sole Pleasure and *Fiat* of our omnipotent Creator" (Richard Bentley, *Matter and Motion cannot think: . . . A Sermon Preached . . . April 4. 1692* [London, 1692], 31–32; in *Eight Boyle Lectures on Atheism* [1692–93; rpt., New York: Garland Publishing, 1976]).

For a broader discussion of mechanism in England, see Robert E. Scholfield, *Mechanism and Materialism: British Natural Philosophy in An Age of Reason* (Princeton: Princeton University Press, 1970); and for a general overview of the orthodox reaction to the threat of mechanism, see John Redwood, *Reason, Ridicule and Religion: The Age of Enlightenment in England, 1660–1750* (Cambridge: Harvard University Press, 1976).

46. *Memoirs of the Extraordinary Life, Works and Discoveries of Martinus Scriblerus,* ed. Charles Kerby-Miller (New Haven: Yale University Press, 1950; rpt., Oxford: Oxford University Press, 1988), 140.

In the following discussion of the relationship between immaterial substance and personal identity, I am greatly indebted to two studies: Lazare Mijuskovic, *The Achilles of Rationalist Arguments: The Simplicity, Unity, and Identity of Thought and Soul From the Cambridge Platonists to Kant* (The Hague: Martinus Nijhoff, 1974) and John Yolton, *Thinking Matter.* Mijuskovic shows how the arguments about immaterial substance and the grounding of personal identity in it developed independently in England prior to Descartes as a reaction to the perceived threat of the rise of Epicureanism and the newer forms of materialism. Yolton details the intense sensitivity of orthodox thinkers to the threat materialists posed to immaterial substance and documents their defenses against the threat.

When I speak about contemporary reactions to Locke and about the Clarke-Collins debate, I tend to elide issues that, in a more extended treatment, should be sifted more carefully. Specifically, I talk about Locke's and Collins's assertion that personal identity resides in consciousness as if it were necessarily implicated in the separate proposition that consciousness inheres in the mechanical properties of matter. In Locke, "thinking matter" and identity-as-consciousness are two quite independent propositions, and at any rate the first is merely a speculation that Locke later rejects as improbable. But those who argued against Locke often took the position that he believed both, and it is these moments in the debate that I have dwelt on. Collins probably *was* arguing that personal identity resided in consciousness *and* that consciousness was the product of systems of matter; this was certainly how he was interpreted.

47. Samuel Clarke, *A Third Defence of an Argument Made Use of in a Letter to Mr. Dodwell,* in *The Works of Samuel Clarke, D.D.,* 4 vols. (London, 1738), 3:851. The entirety of the Clarke-Collins debate is printed here, and all reference are to this edition. For a discussion of Clarke's position, see Howard M. Ducharme, "Personal Identity in Samuel Clarke," *Journal of the History of Philosophy* 24 (1986): 359–83.

48. Cudworth, *True Intellectual System,* 826.

49. *Works of Clarke,* 3:751, 787, 844.

50. Joseph Butler, *Personal Identity,* in *The Analogy of Religion to the Constitution and Course of Nature,* ed. Howard Malcom (Philadelphia, 1857), 320. Butler is referring to, and in part quoting from, Collins.

51. *Works of Clarke,* 3:730.

52. *Works of Clarke,* 3:761, 784. Cudworth, too, argued that to assume "an Antecedent Life and Understanding in . . . Matter" meant that "every Atom of Matter must needs be a Distinct Percipient, Animal, and Intelligent Person by it self," and consequently man would be "a Heap of Innumerable Animals and Percipients" (*True Intellectual System,* 72). This was a fairly common argument: see, for instance, Bentley, *Matter and Motion cannot Think,* 14–15; and Lee, *Anti-Skepticism,* 125.

53. The uses of the Clarke-Collins debate are documented in detail by Christopher Fox, *Locke and the Scriblerians: Identity and Consciousness in Early Eighteenth-Century Britain* (Berkeley: University of California Press, 1988); and Kerby-Miller in his notes to the *Memoirs of Martinus Scriblerus,* esp. 280–93.

54. *Memoirs of Martinus Scriblerus,* 138–42. The joke on "are" has been noted by Fox, *Locke and the Scriblerians,* 109.

55. Butler, *Personal Identity,* in *Analogy of Religion,* 319. Butler concludes that such a person would not only have no identity, but would be a person only "in a fictitious sense" (320–21). Clarke, too, saw that this was the consequence of Collins's argument: "You make *individual Personality* to be a mere *external imaginary Denomination,* and nothing at all in reality" (*Works of Clarke,* 3:844).

56. Isaac Watts, "Essay IX" of *Philosophical Essays,* in *Works of Watts,* 5:581n.

57. [Thomas Burnet], *Third Remarks upon An Essay Concerning Humane Understanding* (London, 1697), 22, in *Remarks Upon an Essay Concerning Humane Understanding: Five Tracts,* ed. Peter A. Schouls (New York: Garland Publishing, 1984).

58. "Know Yourself," in *The Life and Works of John Arbuthnot,* ed. George A. Aitken (Oxford: The Clarendon Press, 1892), 436–39.

59. Jerome Gaub, *Sermo Academicus de Regimine Mentis* (1747), in L. J. Rather, *Mind and Body in Eighteenth Century Medicine,* 34.

Even Descartes, for all the rigor of his dualism, had to admit this: "I am not merely present in my body as a sailor is present in a ship, but . . . I am very closely joined and, as it were, intermingled with it, so that I and the body form a unit" (*Meditiations,* in *Philosophical Writings of Descartes,* 2:56). Although the orthodox thinkers I have been examining argue for the immaterial substance as the necessary ground for the coherence and persistence of identity, they admitted that the full identity of an individual person was constituted by both material and immaterial substance, that "the Identity of Man depends neither upon the Notion of Place for his Body, nor upon the Soul consider'd by it self, but upon both these, as actually united and making one Person" (Stillingfleet, *The Bishop of Worcester's Answer to Mr. Locke's Second Letter* [London, 1698], 172–73).

60. Quoted in John Ashton, *Social Life in the Reign of Queen Anne* (London, 1883), 210.

61. "Observationiones Anatomico-Medicae, de Monstro bicorporeo Virgineo A. 1701," *Philosophical Transactions* 50 (1757): 311.

62. Swift to Dean Stearne, [10] June 1708, *Correspondence of Swift,* 1:90.

63. *The British Apollo* 36 (June 11–16, 1708); 37 (June 16–18, 1708); 38 (June 18–23, 1708); 39 (June 23–25, 1708); and 42 (July 2–7, 1708).

64. *Memoirs of Martinus Scriblerus,* 146. In this section, all references to the *Memoirs* are put in parentheses in the text.

65. Three works have been very helpful for my understanding of the *Memoirs.* Fox, in his *Locke and the Scriblerians,* lucidly summarizes the intellectual background to the discussion of identity in the *Memoirs* and shows the importance of the presence of Locke throughout the work. Robert A. Erickson, "Situations of Identity in the *Memoirs of Martinus Scriblerus,*" *Modern Language Quarterly* 26 (1965): 388–400, analyzes the puzzles of identity the Scriblerians have created. And Roger D. Lund, "Martinus Scriblerus and the Search for the Soul," *Papers in Language and Literature* 25 (Spring 1989): 135–50, investigates the pervasive attacks on materialism in the work.

66. *Works of Clarke,* 3:838.

67. *Personal Identity,* in *Analogy of Religion,* 320.

68. James Arbuckle, *A Collection of Letters and Essays on Several Subjects,* 2 vols. (1729; rpt., New York: Garland Publishing, 1970), 2:185–87. For discussions of the effects that this collapse of a solid boundary between mind and body had on the conception of the imagination, especially after Pope and Swift, see the two studies of G. S. Rousseau, "Science and the Discovery of the Imagination in Enlightenment England," *Eighteenth-Century Studies* 3 (Fall 1969): 108–35; and "Nerves, Spirits, and Fibres: Towards Defining the Origins of Sensibility," in *Studies in the Eighteenth Century,* ed. R. F. Brissenden and J. C. Eade (Toronto: University of Toronto Press, 1976), 3:135–57.

69. Richard Steele, *The Christian Hero,* ed. Rae Blanchard (1932; rpt., New York: Octagon Press, 1977), 35–36.

70. The phrase is Thomas Parnell's, in his invitation to the Earl of Oxford to join the Scriblerians: reprinted in the *Memoirs of Martinus Scriblerus,* 353.

71. *Mechanical Operation,* in *PW,* 1:189; *Tale of a Tub,* in *PW,* 1:99.

72. It should be obvious by now how deeply the Mary Toft incident is implicated in the antifeminist thinking and misogynistic rhetoric of the eighteenth century. One way to see this is to recall the way Mary Toft was spoken of in the satires: She was perceived as possessing some terrifying, subversive power, a power of destruction that sprang, paradoxically, from her fecundity and power of generation; a power, moreover, that seemed to be directed against men specifically, attracting them only to humiliate them (she possesses a "tempting place" that "Makes the Wisest Man an Ass"), a power of sexuality which, because of her *"large Capassite"* and "depe *Kuntrivansis,"* swallowed men up, making them impotent, feminizing them, and finally assimilating them; and for this, she was to be punished, perhaps by imprisonment, but certainly by these very satires. And here are the findings of Felicity Nussbaum (*The Brink of All We Hate: English Satires on Women, 1660–1750* [Lexington: University Press of Kentucky, 1984], 75) about the way male satirists typically respond to women in the period:

> [They] assume woman's lust, inconstancy, and vanity; they curse her fecundity, her sexual appetite, and her ability to disrupt men's expectations and illusions, while a simultaneous impulse describes her sexual autonomy and power. The satires deplore women's attractiveness and their ability to feminize men even as they lament men's self-hatred and emasculation. At the same time that the satirist narrator wallows in the satiric myth of impotence as a lover, however, the force of his words creates a potent weapon.

The anxiety provoked by Mary Toft, to the degree that it can be named, I believe to be the fear of boundary dissolution and the consequent dispersion of identity as the self is swallowed up in the body. It is a fear, in short, of becoming those alien energies from below, a fear of becoming an Other. All of those who responded to the Mary Toft episode whom I have been able to identify have been males, and they appear to have dealt with this fear of becoming the Other with the language typically used to express fear of the Other, the language of misogyny. This makes Mary Toft, and the imagination, one of those "female monsters" that Susan Gubar has identified, a figure that "allows the satirist to exorcise his fear of mortality and physicality by projecting it into the Other" ("The Female Monster in Augustan Satire," *Signs* 3 [Winter 1977]: 380–94). In the case of Mary Toft, as in the case of the female monster, "Birth becomes a grotesque testimonial to the filthy materiality of life.... She illustrates Simone de Beauvoir's thesis that the female has been made to represent man's ambivalent feelings about his inability to control his own existence, his own birth and death. As the Other, the woman is associated with contingency, with life made to be destroyed: 'It is the horror of his own carnal contingence, which he projects on her.' By projecting it as a detested attribute which defines the monstrous female, the satirist can escape recognition of his own immanence" (391–92).

CHAPTER FIVE
A Lump of Deformity

1. *Gulliver's Travels,* in *PW,* 11:13. In this chapter, subsequent references to *Gulliver's Travels* are cited parenthetically in the text.

2. Quoted in Ashton, *Social Life in the Reign of Queen Anne,* 219–20 (cf. ch. 4, n. 60). Models were very popular sights: in his brief visit to London in 1710, von Uffenbach

saw four (Zacharias Conrad von Uffenbach, *London in 1710,* trans. and ed. W. H. Quarrel and Margaret Mare [London: Faber and Faber, 1934], 34, 41, 78–79, 102).

3. It is by means of peepshows that Martin Scriblerus "was brought acquainted with all the Princes of Europe" (*Memoirs of Martinus Scriblerus,* 170 [cf. ch. 4, n. 46]). For a discussion of peepshows, see Altick, *Shows of London,* 56–57 (cf. ch. 1, n. 11).

4. *The Diary of Ralph Thoresby, F.R.S.,* ed. Joseph Hunter, 2 vols. (London, 1830), 2:41 (11 February 1709). For a technical discussion of moving pictures as well as photographs of some of those still extant, see Alfred Chapuis and Edmond Droz, *Les automates: Figures artificielles d'hommes et d'animaux* (Neuchatel: Editions du Griffon, [1949]), 147–62).

5. For an indication of the variety and complexity of early eighteenth-century clockworks, see Chapuis and Droz, *Les automates.* Pepys describes the clockworks he saw at the fairs in *The Diary of Samuel Pepys,* ed. Robert Latham and William Matthews, 11 vols. (Berkeley: University of California Press, 1970–83), 4:298, 8:423.

6. The phrase "Pygmy Actors" is Ned Ward's, in *Hudibras Redivivus: Or, a Burlesque Poem of the Times* (London, 1705), pt. 4, vol. 2, p. 3. My information on early eighteenth-century puppet theatre is drawn from George Speaight, *The History of the English Puppet Theatre* (London: George G. Harrap, 1955); Sybil Rosenfeld, *The Theatre of the London Fairs in the Eighteenth Century* (Cambridge: Cambridge University Press, 1960); and Powell's advertisements in *The Spectator.* On the importance and pervasiveness of the puppet in Swift's satiric rhetoric, see John M. Bullitt, *Jonathan Swift and the Anatomy of Satire* (Cambridge: Harvard University Press, 1953), 170–81.

7. Notices of many eighteenth-century diversions and exhibitions can be found in two scrapbooks in the British Library, BL C70.h.6(2)and BL 551.d.18. Some material from both, as well as additional material from other collections, has been reprinted in Ashton, *Social Life in the Reign of Queen Anne;* Henry Morley, *Memoirs of Bartholomew Fair* (London, 1859); and Thomas Frost, *The Old Showmen and the Old London Fairs* (London, 1881). In addition, I have drawn from the invaluable manuscript of James Paris (Du Plessis), *A Short History of Human Prodigies & Monstrous Births* (BL Sloane MS. 5246), a compilation of monsters exhibited in the late seventeenth and early eighteenth centuries, many of which Paris himself had seen. All quotations in this chapter which are not footnoted are from items in these collections.

I have tried to pay particular attention to the diversions and exhibitions that were in London the years Swift was, but I have not restricted myself to these years, and this for several reasons. First, much of this material is impossible to date with any precision. Secondly, my argument is not that Swift refers to specific diversions, spectacles, and monsters but rather to the general kinds of sights and shows that could have been seen on the streets and in the fairs in any year. Finally, the Fair, the site of many of these diversions and shows, was a remarkably conservative institution. To read Ned Ward's description of the 1699 Bartholomew Fair in *The London-Spy* next to Wordsworth's description of his 1802 visit recorded in *The Prelude* or, better yet, William Hone's exhaustive survey of the 1824 Fair published in *The Every-Day Book* is a revelation: the Fair remained largely unchanged throughout this period.

8. Nehemiah Grew, *Musæum Regalis Societatis; Or, a Catalogue Description of the Natural and Artificial Rarities Belonging to the Royal Society* (London, 1681), 373, 154–55, 174, 351–58.

9. Jacob Hall probably stands behind the incident of the rope-dancers in Lilliput,

specifically the near-disaster of Flimnap: "I was assured, that a Year or two before my Arrival, *Flimnap* would have infallibly broke his neck, if one of the *King's Cushions,* that accidentally lay on the Ground, had not weakened the Force of his Fall" (23). When Hall became the lover of Lady Castlemaine, mistress of Charles II, he constructed an illegal performance booth at Charing Cross. Ordered to demolish it, he refused and was committed to prison. Lady Castlemaine obtained his release and had him granted permission to re-erect the booth and perform there. This incident was a well-known scandal at the time (see [Anthony Hamilton], *Memoirs of the English Court, During the Reigns of K. Charles II and K. James II* [London, 1719], 110) and retained enough of a life into the eighteenth century for Pope to mention it in *Sober Advice from Horace,* 86 (*TE,* 4:83).

I am not arguing that the "cushion" is Lady Castlemaine and that Flimnap is Jacob Hall. Whether interpreted as a specific allusion (usually thought to refer to Walpole and the Duchess of Kendal) or, what is more probable, a general comment on court politics, the incident clearly refers to ministerial relations to the crown. I am only pointing to how thoroughly the particulars of popular entertainments are implicated in the surface texture of *Gulliver Travels.*

10. Sir William Davenant, "The Long Vacation in London," in *The Shorter Poems, and Songs from the Plays and Masques,* ed. A. M. Gibbs (Oxford: Clarendon Press, 1972), 129. For Swift's use of the contemporary "sights" of rope-dancers, contortionists, and acrobats in these scenes, see Pat Rogers, *Literature and Popular Culture in Eighteenth-Century England* (Totowa, New Jersey: Barnes and Noble, 1985), 71–86. Throughout his study, Rogers reveals how deeply fascinated all the Scriblerians were with popular entertainments and how often they satirized them in their works.

11. The public display of the very old appears to have been rare. More usually, they were visited in their own homes, where the curious viewer, like Gulliver in Luggnagg, gave them a modest gratuity. On the basis of the number of accounts of the very old in the early eighteenth century and the records of visits in Paris's collection, I gather that the viewing of the old was a fairly common diversion.

12. See Altick, *Shows of London,* 50–54; Ward, *London-Spy,* 256–57 (cf. ch. 1, n. 11); and von Uffenbach, *London in 1710,* 84–85. In addition, Swift may have had in mind the special effects of the drolls at the fairs. Tom Brown had already complained that the traditional "humble stories" of the drolls were being driven off the stage by newfangled "operas" which traded heavily in machinery and spectacle: "it traffics in heroes; it raises ghosts and apparitions" (*Amusements Serious and Comical,* ed. Arthur L. Hayward [London: George Routledge & Sons, 1927], 143). Further, the way the ghosts disappear (the Governor of Glubbdubdrib "dismissed all his Attendants with a Turn of his Finger, at which to my great Astonishment they vanished in an Instant, like Visions in a Dream, when we awake on a sudden" [178]) is reminiscent of the instantaneous appearances, disappearances, and transformations, usually achieved at the wave of a finger or wand, that were de rigueur for these spectacles.

13. Compare Gulliver's description ("The Noise was so great, that I could hardly distinguish the Tunes. I am confident, that all the Drums and Trumpets of a Royal Army, beating and sounding together just at your Ears, could not equal it" [110]) to Ward's description of a "*Musick Booth*" at Bartholomew Fair: "The *Kettle-Drums* and *Trumpets* began to express their willingness to oblige us, which was perform'd with that Harmonious Excellence, that no *Sow-Gelder* with his *Horn,* and Cooper with his *Adds* and *Driver,* could have gratified our Ears with more Delightful Musick" (*London-Spy,* 259–60).

14. Viewing bones was a common tourist pastime. See Thoresby, *Diary,* 2:235; Pepys, *Diary,* 1:150; Saussure, *Foreign View of England,* 41 (cf. ch. 1, n. 28); and *British Curiosities in Nature and Art* (London, 1713), 42. A single whale's rib was shown at St. James Palace; according to Ward, *London-Spy,* 177–78, it was thought by the ignorant to be from a human giant.

15. John Stow, *A Survey of the Cities of London and Westminster . . . Corrected, Improved, and very much Enlarged By John Strype,* 2 vols. (London, 1720), 1:43.

16. [John Macky], *A Journey through England* (London, 1714), 193. That Swift had the London Bridge Waterworks in mind seems likely because it is a happy confluence of so many of the satiric targets he aims at in Balnibarbi. The original waterworks were owned by the Morris family, who had operated them from 1582. But when their profitability was destroyed by the opening of the New River, the family negotiated with the City to build additional engines. They then sold the existing works and the rights for £38,000 to Richard Soams who, in 1703, formed a stock company and sold three hundred shares at £500 each (Stow, *Survey of London,* 1:27). In short, the waterworks was "unnatural" not only in the sense that it reversed the flow of water but also in the sense that it answered no real need: the new engines were added solely to compete economically with the New River. Here, then, are those targets—economic projectors, joint stock companies, and engineering innovations—that Pat Rogers argues for as an important thread of the satiric fabric of the book ("Gulliver and the Engineers," *Modern Language Review* 70 [April 1975]: 260–70).

17. "The turret has plate-glass windows, through which one can observe the works, which are not cased in wood but left quite free; . . . One hears with amazement how accurately all the springs fit into each other" (von Uffenbach, *London in 1710,* 330.) Like von Uffenbach, Swift visited the top of St. Paul's in 1710: see Jonathan Swift, *Journal to Stella,* ed. Harold Williams, 2 vols. (Oxford: Clarendon Press, 1963), 1:53 (13 October 1710).

18. "In a pretty high Place, which lies very open, they have surrounded a Circumference of two or three hundred Paces Diameter with a sorry Kind of Ballustrade, or rather with Poles plac'd upon Stakes, but three Foot from the Ground; and the Coaches drive round and round this" (*M. Misson's Memoirs and Observations in his Travels over England,* trans. [John] Ozell [London, 1719], 126).

19. *London-Spy,* 186–87. Swift visited "the tombs at Westminster" on 25 November 1710 (*Journal to Stella,* 1:104).

Another tourist sight, the Tower, may have served Swift as the inspiration for one of the most famous scenes in Lilliput: "About the middle of the *Wharf* was a Stone Arch over the Passage to *Traytors-Gate,* where stood a Sentinel, who, I observed, was very careful no Body should lean upon it, or touch it, lest their Elbows or their Fingers should wear away Her Majesties Free-Stone; and to Piss against it was a Crime that deserved Capping at least, except for every such Offence you would forfeit Six-pence; so that I found it was held much better by the Guards, that a good Subject bursts himself, then they lose the Advantage of a Ridiculous and *Shameful Custom,* which oftentimes frights *Fools* out of their Money, and serves *Wisemen* to Blush at" (Ward, *London-Spy,* 323).

20. Taylor, "Sights and Monsters," 29–82 (cf. ch. 1, n. 11). Although Taylor's article discusses the historical background of monster-showings in only the first two chapters of book 2, I cannot emphasize enough how seminal her article has been to my thinking about the whole of *Gulliver's Travels.*

21. Stow, *Survey of London,* 1:285.

22. Walking under the arm of a giant was a typical way of taking a purchase on his height. See Pepys' comment: "calling by the way at Charing-Cross and there saw the great Dutchman that is come over, under whose arm I went with my hat on" (*Diary,* 5:242–43; see also 9:406–7).

23. Examples are legion. James Paris, in his *Short History* (cf. ch. 5, n. 7), remarks that the giant he saw in 1716 "was seen by George I, the Queen, the prince of Wales, the rest of the Royal Family and the Court, at Windsor." "The Living Colossus ... has had the honour to show himself to most princes in Europe, particularly to his late majesty the King of France, who presented him with a noble scymiter, and a silver mace." (One recalls that the Emperor of Blefuscu presented Gulliver "with fifty Purses of two hundred *Sprugs* a-piece, together with his Picture at full length" [62].)

By the way, Joyce, like Gulliver, was accused of drawing the eye of a great lady, who became "all the talk of the town" for having written a letter to him in which she said she was grieved "to see so noble a talent misemployed, and that strength thrown away upon undeserving horses that cannot reward your labour, which might much better divert the requiting woman" (Brown, *Amusements,* 147–48 [cf. ch. 5, n. 12]).

24. Swift certainly knew of the "Little Family" (which included the "little Horse"), probably first-hand, and certainly through Arbuthnot, for the Black Prince plays a prominent role in "Double-Mistress" episode of the *Memoirs of Martinus Scriblerus;* see Taylor, "Sights and Monsters," 63–69.

25. *The Diary of John Evelyn,* ed. E. S. de Beer, 6 vols. (Oxford: The Clarendon Press, 1955), 3:359.

26. Pepys, *Diary,* 9:297; see also 9:301.

27. A few minor motifs in *Gulliver's Travels* seem to be drawn from the exhibitions of monsters. Take, for instance, the repeated attention Gulliver pays to sewing and the making of clothes throughout his travels and especially the "trick" he makes the Houyhnhnm perform: "I have seen a white mare of our Family thread a Needle (which I lent her on Purpose)" (258). Threading needles, sewing, and making clothes were typical ways in which deformed monsters demonstrated their dexterity. The armless John Valerius "threads a very fine small needle and sews very prettily." The "Wonder of the World," a young English girl born without fingers or toes, demonstrated her dexterity in the same way: "The girl is ingenious and can work at her needle and several other things worth observation." Another woman without fingers or toes advertised that she could "knit [and] soe." The "EIGHTH WONDER OF THE WORLD," a young man born without arms, touted in his advertisements that "he can thread a needle, embroider, and play upon several sorts of musick." This last skill was another common way in which deformed monsters displayed their abilities and recalls Gulliver's attempt to flaunt his talents before the Brobdingnagian king by playing the piano. Matthew Buchinger, a dwarf who lacked hands and feet, "threads a fine needle very quick" and "plays upon the dulcimer as well as any musician."

Even Gulliver's facility with languages has its analogue in monster exhibitions, for such a facility was a common assertion in the handbills. Helena and Judith, twins joined at the hip, "Talk three different Languages"; John Valerius wrote "in five different languages"; and the legless boy from Vienna "speaks divers different languages as High Dutch, Low Dutch, Sclavonian, French and English." The "Wonderful Strong and Surprizing Persian Dwarf" spoke (or so proclaimed his handbill) eighteen languages.

28. Swift to John Barber, 10 August 1732, *Correspondence of Swift,* 4:57. See Swift's

other comment on visiting the tourist sights in London: "Lady Kerry, Mrs. Pratt, Mrs. Cadogan, and I, in one coach; Lady Kerry's son and his governor, and two gentlemen in another; maids and misses, and little master (lord Shelburn's children) in a third, all hackneys, set out at ten o'clock this morning from lord Shelburn's house in Piccadilly to the Tower, and saw all the sights, lions, &c. then to Bedlam, then dined at the Chophouse behind the Exchange; then to Gresham College (but the keeper was not at home) and concluded the night at the Puppet-Shew, whence we came home safe at eight, and I left them" (*Journal to Stella* 1:121–23 [13 December 1710]). Swift's pointedly calling attention to the children's accompanying them is significant. Typically, the sophisticated understood these tourist jaunts as activities fit only for children. In the *Tatler,* Isaac Bickerstaff wrote of taking "Three Lads who are under my Guardianship a rambling in an hackney-coach, to show 'em the Town, as the Lions, the Tombs, *Bedlam,* and the other Places which are Entertainments to raw Minds, because they strike forcibly on the Fancy" (*Tatler* 30; in *The Tatler,* ed. Donald F. Bond, 3 vols. [Oxford: Clarendon Press, 1987], 1:224).

29. *London-Spy,* 256; untitled poem, c. 1760, in BL C70.n.6(2); *London-Spy,* 241, 172, 173; "Part of the Seventh Epistle of the First Book of Horace," in *The Poems of Jonathan Swift,* ed. Harold Williams, 2d ed., 3 vols. (Oxford: Clarendon Press, 1958), 1:172.

30. Brown, *Amusements,* 146; *Spectator* 141, in *The Spectator,* 2:56; *The Weekly Oracle* (London, 1737), 216; *Tatler* 1, in *The Tatler,* 1:39.

31. *Bickerstaff Papers,* in *PW,* 2:148; "In pity to the empty'ng Town," in *Poems of Swift,* 1:135.

32. "The Virtues of Sir Hamet the Magician's Rod," in *Poems of Swift,* 1:135.

33. *PW,* 9:285. In an earlier attack, "The Wonderful Wonder of Wonders" (*PW,* 9:281–84), Swift toyed with this same strategy by casting the satire in the form of a handbill for a monster.

34. *The Examiner* 39, in *PW,* 3:147.

35. There is the same association of ideas in his letter about the monstrous Helena and Judith. Swift slides with no transition from spectacles to public executions and implies that both are equally mindless diversions: "Here is a sight of two girls joined together at the back, which, in the news-monger's phrase, causes a great many speculations; and raises abundance of questions in divinity, law, and physic. The boys of our town are mightily happy for we are about to have a beheading next week, unless the Queen will interpose her mercy" (Swift to Dean Stearne, [10] June 1708, *Correspondence of Swift,* 1:82).

36. *Journal to Stella,* 2:647 (21 March 1712/13). Cf. "To-day I was all about St. Paul's, and up at the top, like a fool" (*Journal to Stella,* 1:53 [13 October 1710]).

37. Entry for the week of 20–27 August 1709 in *The Account Books of Jonathan Swift,* ed. Paul V. Thompson and Dorothy Jay Thompson (Newark: University of Delaware Press, 1984), 77.

38. "Part of the Seventh Epistle of the First Book of Horace," *Poems of Swift,* 1:172. See also "A Character, Panegyric, and Description of the Legion Club," *Poems of Swift,* 3:839, where Swift addresses Hogarth: "Were but you and I acquainted, / Every Monster should be painted."

39. *Poems of Swift,* 3:776–77.

40. *Tale of a Tub,* in *PW,* 1:81.

41. *The Diary of Robert Hooke, 1672–1680,* ed. Henry W. Robinson and Walter Adams (London: Taylor and Francis, 1935), 208.

42. Thoresby, *Diary,* 2:259.

43. Pepys, *Diary,* 9:398.

44. *The New Organon,* in *Works of Bacon,* 4:169.

45. Thoresby, *Diary,* 2:77.

46. Monstrous breasts, as it happens, were displayed at Bartholomew Fair: "Next door to the *Golden Hart* in *West-Smithfield,* between *Hospital-Gate* and *Pye-Corner,* during the time of *Bartholomew Fair,* is to be seen the Admirable Work of Nature, a Woman having Three Breasts; and each of them affording milk at one time, or differently, according as they are made use of. . . . And there never hath been any extant of such sort, which is Wonderful to all that ever did, or shall behold them."

47. My sense of the experience of the monstrous has been greatly influenced by Jean Céard, *La nature et les prodiges,* esp. 45–51 (cf. ch. 2, n. 16); and Leslie Fiedler, *Freaks: Myths and Images of the Secret Self* (New York: Simon and Schuster, 1978).

48. Evelyn, *Diary,* 3:198. James Granger identifies her as Barbara Vanbeck, born in Augsburg in 1651. "Vanbeck married this frightful creature, on purpose to carry her about for a show" (*A Biographical History of England,* 4 vols. [London, 1769], 3:107).

49. Pepys, *Diary,* 5:243; Evelyn, *Diary,* 3:132. Given this context, it is difficult not to recall Gulliver's lengthy defense of the Brobdingnagians as "a comely Race of people" who "appeared very well proportioned" and not "actually deformed" (76).

50. *Daily Courant,* 6 September 1718, as quoted in Rosenfeld, *Theatre of the London Fairs,* 79 (cf. ch. 5, n. 6).

51. *London-Spy,* 173. I have simplified this coupling of the normal and the abnormal in the exhibition of monsters. Additional factors were at work. First, by calling attention to some normal accomplishment (like playing the harpsichord or delivering theological disquisitions), the exhibitors were meeting the age's demand for "rational amusement": see Altick, *Shows of London,* esp. 3–4; and Robert W. Malcolmson, *Popular Recreations in English Society, 1700–1850* (Cambridge: Cambridge University Press, 1973), 89–157. Perhaps just as important were the demands of some of those who were exhibited. Although there is almost no evidence about what the "monsters" themselves felt, what little does exist is very suggestive, especially the case of "Count" Joseph Boruwlaski. Eight inches at his birth in 1739, by thirty he had reached his full growth of only three feet, three inches. Early in his life, he was patronized by the wealthy and by several royal families. But he fell on bad times and had to scramble for ways of providing for himself and his normal-sized wife and child. In the last third of his autobiography he records, with increasing despair, his attempts to avoid showing himself for money, which he felt was "beneath my birth, education, and sentiments" (*Memoires du Célèbre Nain, Joseph Boruwlaski,* trans. [Jean Thomas Hérisant] Des Carrieres [London, 1788], 203). The expedient he finally settled on was to offer guitar concerts. As far as I can tell, this shift to preserve his self-respect was successful, for he states with apparent sincerity that people came to see him because of his "talents" (167), not because he was a dwarf.

But even assuming that some of those who were exhibited maintained their self-respect by performing a "normal" activity, that accounts for their motives, not the audience's in coming to see them. The fact is that the coupling of the normal and the freakish can be found in *all* exhibitions of monsters, including those of monsters which could make no demands at all—such as animals.

52. Th[omas] B[edford], *A True and Certaine Relation Of a Strange-Birth . . . Together with the Notes of a Sermon, preached Octob. 23, 1635* (London, 1635), 18.

53. This dismissal of monsters is paralleled by the general trend of teratological the-

ories in the seventeenth and eighteenth centuries. Earlier, monsters were seen as manifestations of non-quotidian orders of reality disrupting the everyday: they were divine
omens or portents, evidence of the wrath of God or the power of demons, or products
of exotic lands and climates. Even when subsumed into a larger, overarching regular-
ity, monsters retained their power to unsettle. Thus, St. Augustine's famous argument
(*City of God,* trans. Marcus Dods [New York: Random House, 1950], 531) that monsters were "diversities which . . . contribute to the beauty of the whole" of creation
emphasized their power to disquiet us: their apparent anomalousness called attention
to a variety whose order is incomprehensible to us, and they reproached us with the fact
of our utter ignorance of God's wisdom as manifested in that variety.

By the seventeenth century, this sense of the monstrous was radically revised. Monsters were no longer seen as disruptive, for they were understood to be the products of
the *known* laws of an orderly universe. "Nature proceeds *as regularly* (or the laws of
nature have as regular an effect), when a *monster* is produced, as when the *usual* issue
in common cases" (Wollaston, *Religion of Nature Delineated,* 84–85 [cf. ch. 4, n. 16]). A
little over six months after *Gulliver's Travels* was published, Blondel put out the first of
his works on the origins of monstrosities. He argued that the causes of monsters were
"easily deduced from the Laws of Motion, which God has established amongst Bodies." "There's nothing," he concluded, "but what is according to the Course of Nature"
(*Power of the Mother's Imagination,* x [cf. ch. 2, n. 22]; *Strength of the Imagination,* 100 [cf.
ch. 4, n. 4]).

Malebranche had the same sentiments:

> Order demands that the laws of nature by which God produces this infinite
> variety found in the world be very simple and small in number, as they in fact
> are, for this conduct bears the mark of infinite wisdom. Now, the simplicity of
> these general laws produces in certain particular cases, due to the disposition of
> the subject, irregular kinds of motion, or rather, monstrous arrangements of
> them, and consequently, it is because God wills order that there are monsters.
> Thus, God does not will positively or directly that there should be monsters, but
> He wills positively certain laws of the communication of motion, of which mon-
> sters are necessary consequences. And He wills these laws because, being very
> simple, they are always capable of producing that variety of forms which we can-
> not admire too much.

(*Elucidations,* in *The Search After Truth,* trans. Thomas M. Lennon and Paul J. Olscamp
[Columbus: Ohio State University Press, 1980], 589.)

Malebranche's echo of Augustine's argument that monsters are part of the variety
of God's creation is quite deceptive. For Malebranche, monsters do not evince an infinite variety that bespeaks the unknowable order of God, nor consequently do they
reproach us with our inability to grasp the order of the universe. To the contrary, monsters tell us what we already know. For, by "variety of forms" Malebranche really means
mere variation on the few simple, uniform laws of a universe that has been completely
solved. Products of the known laws of the universe, monsters have ceased to say anything unsettling. And so when Malebranche says that "we cannot admire [monsters]
too much," his "admire" has come very close to the mindless "wonder" produced at the
monster-booths at Bartholomew Fair. By the eighteenth century, monsters, in essence,
had disappeared: "Nature well known," Pope remarked, "no prodigies remain" (*To
Cobham,* 208, in *TE,* 3.2.31).

54. William Congreve, *Letters and Documents,* ed. John C. Hodges (New York: Harcourt, Brace, 1964), 178.

55. Wonder, of course, is the most common reaction not only to monsters but also to the alien worlds explored by European voyagers and recorded in their travel accounts— those accounts which are the most obvious objects of parody in *Gulliver's Travels.* As Stephen Greenblatt has shown (*Marvellous Possessions: The Wonder of the New World* [Chicago: The University of Chicago Press, 1991]), what I have called mindless wonder often was used as a psychological and rhetorical mechanism to dismiss the humanity of the alien, to take possession of the land, and to deny one's own moral culpability for doing so. One of the effects of Swift's mapping of monster exhibitions onto travel accounts, I think, is to expose the barbarity of this kind of mindless wonder and, more ambitiously, to bring home the point that, to the eye of the ego, all others are aliens and monsters and, as such, need not be accorded the common decencies of humanity.

56. Although none of the creatures fully listens to Gulliver, they do fall into a rough "scale of curiosity." Generally speaking, the less admirable and wise the creatures, the less curious they are about Gulliver. The king of Laputa "discovered not the least Curiosity to enquire into the Laws, Government, History, Religion, or Manners of the Countries where I had been" (150). The Struldbruggs "had not the least curiosity to ask me a question" (197). The Lilliputians are often filled with "wonder" and "admiration" for Gulliver, but this is curiosity at its most superficial because they never show any interest in his life, country, or ideas. Munodi, on the other hand, "Desired to be informed in the Affairs of *Europe,* the Laws and Customs, the Manners and Learning of the several Countries where I had traveled. He listened to me with great Attention, and made very wise Observations on all I spoke" (157–58). The Brobdingnagian king, initially contemptuous of Gulliver, later becomes "curious and inquisitive upon every Particular" (117) of Gulliver's country, and he questions him closely, hoping "that the Knowledge of our Conduct might be useful" (114–15), and was "glad to hear of anything that might deserve Imitation" (111). The Houyhnhnms are positively eager to learn about Gulliver: "The Curiosity and Impatience of my Master were so great, that he spent many Hours in his Leisure to instruct me"; "He was extremely curious to know from what Part of the country I came, and how I was taught to imitate a rational Creature" (218, 219). For a much more sophisticated analysis of curiosity in *Gulliver's Travels,* see Patrick Reilly, *Jonathan Swift: The Brave Desponder* (Carbondale: Southern Illinois University Press, 1982), 152–73.

57. This episode should be compared to the broadside of William Joyce. Joyce's "frequent and repeated (tho' unparalleled) performances in and about the City of *London* and parts adjacent, gained so much fame and applause in most parts of *England,* that his Majesty *King William* had a desire to see him perform something Extraordinary, and accordingly on *Wednesday* last, he was introduced before his Majesty at *Kensington.*" After performing several feats "to the admiration of His Majesty and His Nobles, . . . His Majesty was mightily well Pleas'd (and it is said) has ordered him a considerable Gratuity."

58. I have merely enumerated several of Gulliver's defenses. For a particularly good detailing of these and others, see Frederick M. Keener, *The Chain of Becoming: The Philosophical Tale, the Novel, and a Neglected Realism of the Enlightenment* (New York: Columbia University Press, 1983), 89–126.

59. C. J. Rawson, *Gulliver and the Gentle Reader* (London: Routledge & Kegan Paul, 1973), 17, 129; Frederik N. Smith, "Vexing Voices: The Telling of Gulliver's Story,"

Papers in Language and Literature 21 (Fall 1985): 288–89; Robert M. Ryley, "Gulliver, Flimnap's Wife, and the Critics," *Studies in the Literary Imagination* 5 (October 1972): 56–57; Denis Donoghue, *Jonathan Swift: A Critical Introduction* (Cambridge: Cambridge University Press, 1969), 162; Robert C. Elliott, *The Power of Satire: Magic, Ritual, Art* (Princeton: Princeton University Press, 1960), 200.

60. The first two roles are those named by Swift (Swift to Mrs. Howard, 27 November 1726, *Correspondence of Swift,* 3:187). The third is suggested by his famous comment to Pope, 29 September 1725, *Correspondence of Swift,* 3:103; the character of Timon is Lucian's. For the other roles I listed and additional ones I have not, see W. B. Carnochan, "Some Roles of Lemuel Gulliver," *Texas Studies in Literature and Language* 5 (Winter 1964): 520–29; Elliott, *Power of Satire,* 184–222; and Jon S. Lawry, "Dr. Lemuel Gulliver and 'The Thing Which Was Not,'" *Journal of English and German Philology* 67 (April 1968): 212–34.

61. See Everett Zimmerman, *Swift's Narrative Satires: Author and Authority* (Ithaca: Cornell University Press, 1983), 119–20.

62. *Tale of a Tub,* in *PW,* 1:77.

63. John R. Clark, *Form and Frenzy in Swift's "Tale of a Tub"* (Ithaca: Cornell University Press, 1970), 125.

64. More, *Enthusiamus Triumphatus,* 2 (cf. ch. 3, n. 42). Christopher Fox has argued that Gulliver "cannot differentiate an idea grounded in sense from one that finds its existence solely in the imagination," and hence his "discursive universe . . . needs to be connected more closely to the mad and private worlds of other Swiftian projectors in *A Modest Proposal* and *A Tale of a Tub*" ("Of Logic and Lycanthropy: Gulliver and the Faculties of the Mind," in *Literature and Medicine During the Eighteenth Century,* ed. Marie Mulvey Roberts and Roy Porter [London: Routledge, 1993], 101–17).

65. "Thoughts on Various Subjects," in *PW,* 1:244.

66. Anthony Ashley Cooper, Earl of Shaftesbury, *Characteristics of Men, Manners, Opinions, Times,* ed. John M. Robertson, 2 vols. in 1 (Indianapolis: Bobbs-Merrill, 1964), 1:138, 112, 105–106, 113, 184, 122–23.

67. *Essay on Man,* 2.1–18, in *TE,* 3.1:53–56.

CHAPTER SIX
The Mighty Mother, and Her Son

1. Dr. James Douglas makes a brief appearance in 4.393–94 in a context which recalls the Mary Toft incident. I will discuss this appearance below. For a good summary of what is known about the dates of the early composition of the *Dunciad,* see David L. Vander Meulen, *Pope's Dunciad of 1728: A History and Facsimile* (Charlottesville: University Press of Virginia, 1991), 3–16.

All quotations from the *Dunciad* are from *TE,* 5, and are identified by book and line numbers, which in this chapter are put in parentheses in the text. Quotations are from the 1743 *Dunciad,* unless designated "A," in which case they are from the 1729 *Dunciad Variorum.* Passages from the prose apparatus are identified by the page numbers in this text.

Quotations from all other Pope poems are from the *Twickenham Edition,* and in this and the next chapter are identified by line or by book and line numbers alone except in those cases where reference to the *TE* volume is helpful or necessary for clarity.

2. Dulness has been linked to the imagination before, in David Fairer, *Pope's Imagination* (Manchester: Manchester University Press, 1984), 113–52. Although there is

inevitably some overlap between his discussion and mine, I have tried to avoid going over the territory his argument covers.

3. "Preface," in *TE,* 7:5, 7, 12, 3, 4, 9, 10, 11.

4. "Preface," in *TE,* 7:4.

5. "Preface," in *TE,* 7:9.

6. "Preface," in *TE,* 7:5.

7. *Iliad,* 5.1054n.

8. Pope to John Caryll, Jr., 5 December 1712, *Corr.,* 1:163.

9. *Spectator* 316 (3 March 1712), in *The Prose Works of Alexander Pope,* 2 vols., vol. 1, *The Early Works, 1711–1720,* ed. Norman Ault (1936; rpt., New York: Barnes and Noble, 1968), 32–36. Pope thought idleness one of his own great failings and lamented it often in his letters. In his copy of Montaigne's *Essays,* in the margin beside Montaigne's comment that "[My manners] had no other vice but Sloth and want of Mettal. There was no fear that I would do ill, but that I would do nothing," Pope wrote, "Alter Ego." (Maynard Mack, "A Finding List of Books Surviving from Pope's Library with a Few That May Not Have Survived," *Collected in Himself: Essays Critical, Biographical, and Bibliographical on Pope and Some of His Contemporaries* [Newark: University of Delaware Press, 1982], 427).

10. Pope to Cromwell, 12 November 1711, *Corr.,* 1:135; *Epistle to Dr. Arbuthnot,* 340.

11. In his poetry, Pope almost always associates the word "giddy" with profound confusion and loss of direction (*Iliad,* 1.760–64; *Odyssey,* 9.75–80, 14.334–40), often with the additional meaning of an abstraction from reality (*Rape of the Lock,* 1.91–94), and occasionally with the total abstraction and confusion of madness (*Dunciad,* 4.647–48). In *An Essay on Man,* 2.23–28, he uses both "giddy" and "mazy" to describe solipsistic withdrawal ending in confusion:

> Go, soar with Plato to th' empyreal sphere,
> To the first good, first perfect, and first fair;
> Or tread the mazy round his follow'rs trod,
> And quitting sense call imitating God;
> As Eastern priests in giddy circles run,
> And turn their heads to imitate the Sun.

For a similar description of the confusion often attendant on imaginative activity, see Pope's letter to a friend: "Those Aeriall Ladies [the muses] just discover to me enough of their Beauties to urge my Pursuit, and draw me [on] in a wandring Maze of Thought, still in hopes (& only in hopes) of attaining those favors from 'em, which they confer on their more happy admirers elsewhere. We grasp some more beautifull Idea in our Brain, that our Endeavors to express it can set to the view of others; & still do but labour to fall short of our first Imagination. The gay Colouring which Fancy gave to our Design at the first transient glance we had of it, goes off in the Execution; like those various Figures in the gilded Clouds, which while we gaze long upon, to seperate the Parts of each imaginary Image, the whole faints before the Eye, & decays into Confusion" (Pope to Cromwell, 12 November 1711, *Corr.,* 1:135).

I have ignored some of the complexities of tone in the 1712 letter to Caryll, Jr., in order to bring out the contrasts Pope is making. Pope, in fact, does not present Caryll's activity as an unalloyed ideal, emphasizing as he does its hectic, almost mock-heroic energy, nor does he paint his own retreat into the imagination in quite the humorless terms I have. Still, and in spite of the fact that this letter is something of a set piece in which he is performing himself and getting a good deal of pleasure in doing so, Pope is expressing an anxiety that he often expresses elsewhere. He was at work on *Windsor-Forest* at the time. One of the major contrasts in *Windsor-Forest* is that between the hunter and the poet, the one representing the active, the other the contemplative life. The ideal is the mean between the two, embodied in the man who

> Attends the Duties of the Wise and Good,
> T'observe a Mean, be to himself a Friend,
> To follow Nature, and regard his End.
>
> (250–52)

By his complete withdrawal into his fancy, in which he neither regards his end nor attends his duties and has even lost a "perfect Sense" of himself, Pope obviously has fallen quite short of his ideal.

Perhaps closer to the drift of the letter to Caryll is Pope's contribution to the *Spectator* earlier the same year. Here, too, he contrasts the indolence of the dreamer to the riotous activity of the hunter. Neither one is to be admired, neither the dreamer, whose idleness "undermines the Foundation of every Virtue," nor the hunter, the purpose of whose activity is only "to teaze a poor Animal" and "run away from [his] own Thoughts" (*Spectator* 316, in *Prose Works of Pope*, 1:33–34).

12. Just how traditional Pope's conception was can be seen by comparing it to the following passage from Johnson, which also sounds the themes prominent in Pope: idleness, enclosure, the loss of touch with reality, the destruction of the sense of social duties: "There is nothing more fatal to a man whose business it is to think, than to have learned the art of regaling his mind with those airy gratifications. Other vices or follies are restrained by fear, reformed by admonition, or rejected by the conviction which the comparison of our conduct with that of others, may in time produce. But this invisible riot of the mind, this secret prodigality of being, is secure from detection, and fearless of reproach. The dreamer retires to his apartments, shuts out the cares and interruptions of mankind, and abandons himself to his fancy; new worlds rise up before him, one image is followed by another, and a long sucession of delights dances round him. He is at last called back to life by nature, or by custom, and enters peevish into society, because he cannot model it to his own will. He returns from his idle excursions with the asperity, tho' not with the knowledge, of a student, and hastens again to the same with the eagerness of a man bent upon the advancement of some favourite science. The infatuation strengthens by degrees, and, like the poison of opiates, weaken his powers, without any external symptom of malignity" (*The Rambler* 389, in *The Yale Edition of the Works of Samuel Johnson*, 16 vols., vol. 4, *The Rambler*, ed. W. J. Bate and Albrecht B. Strauss [New Haven: Yale University Press, 1969], 106).

13. Pope to Caryll, [13] July [1714], *Corr.,* 1:236; Pope to Jervas, 16 August 1714, *Corr.,* 1:243; Pope to Trumbull, 16 December 1715, *Corr.,* 1:324; "The Preface" to *The Works* (1717), in *Prose Works of Pope*, 1:290, 294.

14. Pope to Broome, 16 June [1715], *Corr.,* 1:297.

15. *Epistle to Dr. Arbuthnot*, 129; "The Preface" to *The Works* (1717), in *Prose Works of Pope*, 1:294, 292; Pope to Caryll, 13 July 1714, *Corr.,* 1:236; Pope to Broome, 4 December 1724, *Corr.,* 2:274.

Particularly in the 1710s and 1720s, Pope's anxiety about being perceived as having abandoned the larger good for the self-indulgent pleasures of poetry and the imagination is palpable, and he is always careful to show that he has the correct priorities: "Tho' I live here . . . in a glut of company, yet I can keep some thinking hours to myself, which I ought to employ (since they are not many) in thoughts of more serious importance than versifying deserves. I hope they'll turn to that which one may justly call, one's best advantage, and I know your own way of thinking so well, that I'm sure you'll approve of this method of employing my time, much more, than if it were spent in poetry" (Pope to Caryll, [?May 1722], *Corr.,* 2:117). And: "As to your question, what am I doing? I answer, just what I have been doing some years, my duty; secondly relieving my self with necessary amusements, or exercises, which shall serve me instead of physic as long as they can; thirdly, reading till I am tired; and lastly, writing when I have no other thing in the world to do, or no friend to entertain in company" (Pope to Fenton, 5 May [1720], *Corr.,* 2:45–46).

16. Pope to Bolingbroke, 9 April 1724, *Corr.,* 2:226–27.

17. In the last two works in particular, Pope obviously tries to work out the antagonistic possibilities of the imagination and reconcile the imagination to his sense of his obligations to the real world. In *Rape of the Lock,* the reconciliation appears to be be successful because he attributes to Belinda all those dangerous tendencies of the solipsistic imagination—its temptation to idleness and egocentric withdrawal, its ability to cause giddiness and confusion—and reserves for poetry (such as the kind he is writing) the insight and moral vision available to the Homeric imagination. Thus Pope contrasts Belinda's real but superficial and transient artistry at her toilet, an artistry which in the end cannot preserve her lock, to the artistry of his own poem, which can see beneath surfaces, perceive truths, and preserve things of value.

But this exquisite balance is achieved in only this one poem. In a work of only a few years later, *Eloisa to Abelard,* Pope seems to view the imagination with much less certainty. Eloisa, like Belinda, is a creature of the fancy, a "visionary maid" (162). She is caught in her endless cycle, moving from virtue to passion, from flesh to spirit, and back again, precisely because she is so thoroughly possessed by her imagination, which (typically) precipitates her into a confusion of the spiritual and physical, so that the "lov'd Idea" of Abelard becomes "mix'd with God's" (12). In *Rape,* Pope offers the poetic imagination as a viable alternative to the solipsistic fancy of Belinda. In *Eloisa,* as I understand it, he can offer no alternative at all. Indeed, at the end of the poem, he identifies the plight of the poet with hers. In doing so, he implies that the human condition is to be in the body, and a token of that fact is the tyranny of the imagination itself, which can conceive of disembodied states of the spirit but can conceive of them only in the quasi-physical terms of images, binding the mind to the body in the very act of the mind's reaching for transcendence. For an excellent account of the role of imagination in both of these poems, see Fairer, *Pope's Imagination,* 25–81 (cf. ch. 6, n. 2).

It is significant that in both *Rape* and *Eloisa* Pope displaces his fear and suspicion of the imagination to women; he displaces them to a woman one more time, I am arguing, when he creates the Goddess Dulness.

18. Pope to Caryll, 6 December 1730, *Corr.,* 3:155; *Essay on Man,* 1.3–14.

19. *Epistle to Dr. Arbuthnot,* 28, 340; Pope to Cromwell, 12 November 1711, *Corr.,* 1:135.

20. *Essay on Man,* 4.391–92.

21. On the pervasiveness in the poem of the paradoxes of sleep and wakefulness and of inertia and energy, see Tony Tanner, "Reason and the Grotesque: Pope's *Dunciad,*"

in *Essential Articles for the Study of Alexander Pope,* ed. Maynard Mack, rev. ed. (Hamden, Conn.: Archon Books, 1968), 825–44.

22. On the various genres in the *Dunciad,* see George Sherburn, "The *Dunciad,* Book IV," *University of Texas Studies in English* 24 (1944): 174–90; and Aubrey Williams, "Literary Backgrounds to Book Four of the *Dunciad,*" *PMLA* 68 (September 1953): 806–13.

Many critics have commented on the downright strangeness of the *Dunciad,* seeing it as an attempt to replicate the confused perceptions of the Dunces, "to present and explore . . . the world as a dunce would see it and as a dunce would transform it" (H. H. Erskine-Hill, "The 'New World' of Pope's *Dunciad,*" in *Essential Articles,* 803–24). For a brilliant analysis of this "giddiness," see Fredric V. Bogel, "Dulness Unbound: Rhetoric and Pope's *Dunciad,*" *PMLA* 97 (October 1982): 844–55. One of the best descriptions of "the strange in-between world" of the *Dunciad* is still chapter 3 of Aubrey Williams, *Pope's "Dunciad": A Study of its Meaning* (1955; rpt., [Hamden, Conn.]: Archon Books, 1968), 60–86. Williams argues that, in its "tension between the real and the unreal," the poem maneuvers the reader into an "ambiguous perplexity," "a momentary state of indecision" as he attempts to distinguish the real and the unreal: "The result . . . is a curiously ambiguous realm of half-truth in which the reader wanders, never quite sure as to the validity of what he reads, never certain what is fact, what is make believe."

23. "New World" was a catch-phrase for the product of imaginative creation. See, for instance, Cowley's apostrophe to the muse: "Thou speak'st, great *Queen* in the same *Stile* as [God], / And a *new World* leaps forth when *thou* say'st, *Let it be*" ("The Muse," in Abraham Cowley, *Poems,* ed. A. R. Waller [Cambridge: Cambridge University Press, 1905], 185). Oldham described Ben Jonson as one who erected "a beauteous new-made world of Poetry" ("Upon the Works of Ben. Johnson," in *The Poems of John Oldham,* ed. Harold F. Brooks [Oxford: Clarendon Press, 1987], 195). Pope himself had used the phrase in *Essay on Criticism,* 484–87:

> So when the faithful *Pencil* has design'd
> Some *bright Idea* of the Master's Mind,
> Where a *new World* leaps out at his command,
> And ready Nature waits upon his Hand; . . .

24. The metaphor, as I have said, was commonplace, but these particular phrases are taken from Thomas Carew, "An Eligie Upon the Death of the Deane of Pauls, Dr. John Donne"; Matthew Prior, "To the Countess of Exeter, Playing on the Lute"; Abraham Cowley, "On the Death of Mr. Crashaw"; Alexander Pope to Martha Blount, 3 June [1715]; Sir John Denham, "On Mr. Abraham Cowley"; Alexander Pope to Judith Cowper, 9 November [1723]; Ben Jonson, "Dedicatory Epistle of Volpone"; Matthew Prior, "Prologue for Delia's Play"; Edmund Waller, "To Mr. Creech, On His Translation of 'Lucretius'"; Henry Fielding, *Tom Jones;* Sir Philip Sidney, "Sonnet 1," *Astrophel and Stella;* Sir John Suckling, "A Sessions of Poets"; Ben Jonson, *Timber, or Discoveries;* Matthew Prior, "Satyr on the Poets"; John Dryden, "Prologue to *Troilus and Cressida*"; Sir William Temple, "Of Poetry"; Sir Robert Howard, "Preface to Four New Plays."

For the use of normal and monstrous childbirth as metaphors for the creative imagination, see Jay L. Halio, "The Metaphor of Conception and Elizabethan Theories of the Imagination," *Neophilologus* 50 (October 1966): 454–56; and Terry J. Castle, "Lab'ring Bards: Birth *Topoi* and English Poetics," *Journal of English and Germanic Philology* 78 (April 1979): 193–208.

25. Fulke Greville, *A Treatise of Humane Learning,* in *The Poems and Dramas of Fulke Greville, First Lord Brooke,* ed. Geoffrey Bullough, 2 vols. (London: Oliver and Boyd, 1939), 1:156; Puttenham, *Arte of Poesie,* 19 (cf. ch. 3, n. 65).

26. Sir William Davenant, "Preface to Gondibert"; John Sheffield, Earl of Mulgrave, "An Essay Upon Poetry"; William Congreve, *Concerning Humour in Comedy;* and George Granville, Lord Lansdowne, "An Essay Upon Unnatural Flights in Poetry," in Spingarn, *Critical Essays,* 2:3, 293; 3:244, 292 (cf. ch. 3, n. 40).

27. Abraham Cowley, "A Proposition for the Advancement of Learning," in *The Essays and Other Prose Writing,* ed. Alfred B. Gough (Oxford: Clarendon Press, 1915), 27; Swift, *The Battle of the Books,* in *PW,* 1:154; Henry Reynolds, *Mythomystes,* in Spingarn, *Critical Essays,* 1:148.

Montaigne also claimed that mental withdrawal produced monsters, which, like Pope, he saw as the offspring of idleness:

> It is not long since I retired my selfe unto mine owne house, with full purpose, as much as lay in me, not to trouble my selfe with any businesse, but solitarily and quietly to weare out the remainder of my well-nigh-spent life; where me thought I could doe my spirit no greater favour, than to give him the full scope of idleness, and entertaine him as he best pleased, and withall, to settle him-selfe as best he liked: which I hoped he might now, being by time become more setled and ripe, accomplish very easily: but I find,

> *Varium semper dant otia mentem*—LUCAN, IV. 704
>> Evermore, idlenesse,
>> Doth wavering mindes addresse.

> That contrariwise playing the skittish and loose-broken jade, he takes a hundred times more cariere and libertie unto himself, than hee did for others; and begets in me so many extravagant *Chimeraes,* and fantasticall monsters, so orderlesse, and without any reason, one hudling upon another, that at leasure to view the foolishnesse and monstrous strangenesse of them, I have begun to keepe a register of them, hoping, if I live, one day to make him ashamed, and blush at himselfe.

("Of Idleness," in *Essays,* 1:43–44 [cf. ch. 1, n. 11])

28. *Peri Bathous,* in *The Prose Works of Alexander Pope,* Vol. 2, *The Major Works, 1725–1744,* ed. Rosemary Cowler (Hamden, Conn.: Archon Books, 1986), 196, 192, 191. Prior also associated poetic creation for "private Pleasure" with chance (here, the "airy Seeds" of Epicurean creation) and monstrosity:

> Atoms You cut; and Forms You measure,
> To gratifie your private Pleasure;
> 'Till airy Seeds of casual Wit
> Do some fantastic Birth beget: . . .

(Matthew Prior, *Alma,* 3.29–32, in *The Literary Works of Matthew Prior,* ed. H. Bunker Wright and Monroe K. Spears, 2d ed., 2 vols. [Oxford: Clarendon Press, 1971], 1:500).

29. Aristotle, *Generation of Animals,* trans. A. L. Peck (Cambridge: Harvard University Press, 1963), 109.

30. William Shakespeare, *Troilus and Cressida,* ed. Kenneth Palmer (London: Methuen, 1982), 1.3.311–12.

31. Christopher Pitt, "Psalm CXXXIX. Paraphrased in Miltonic Verse," in *The Works of the English Poets,* ed. Alexander Chalmers, 21 vols. (London, 1810), 12:385.

32. Montaigne, "Of the Institution and Education of Children," in *Essays,* 1:179–80. In the *Dunciad,* 1.101–102, Pope uses the metaphor of the bear licking her cub into shape in much the same way Montaigne uses it here.

33. John Oldham, "A Letter from the Country to a Friend in Town, giving an Account of the Authors Inclinations to POETRY," in *Poems of Oldham,* 153; "Prologue" to *The Modern Husband,* in *Works of Fielding,* 9:9 (cf. ch. 1, n. 11).

34. John Dryden, "To Roger, Earl of Orrery," in *Of Dramatic Poesy and Other Critical Essays,* ed. George Watson, 2 vols. (London: Dent, 1962), 1:2.

35. Aristotle, *Generation of Animals,* 425.

36. *Mac Flecknoe,* in *The Poems and Fables of John Dryden,* ed. James Kinsley (London: Oxford University Press, 1962), 238–43.

37. Maynard Mack, *The Last and Greatest Art: Some Unpublished Poetical Manuscripts of Alexander Pope* (Newark: University of Delaware Press, 1984), 103.

38. "To Mr. Addison, Occasioned by his Dialogues on Medals," 39–48, in *TE,* 6:202–207.

39. Joseph Addison, *Dialogues Upon Medals,* in *The Works of the Right Honourable Joseph Addison,* 6 vols. (London, 1854–56), 1:263, 340, 345–46.

40. "To Mr. Addison," 25, 31–32, and 54–55.

41. See, for instance:

> The Coyn must sure for *currant Sterling* pass,
> Stamp'd with old *Chaucer's Venerable Face.*
> But *Johnson* found it of a gross *Alloy,*
> Melted it down, and flung the Dross away[.]
> He dug pure silver from a *Roman Mine*
> And prest his Sacred Image on the Coyn.
> We all rejoyc'd to see the pillag'd Oar,
> Our Tongue inrich'd, which was so poor before.
> Fear not, Learn'd Poet, our impartial blame,
> Such Thefts as these add Lustre to thy name.

(Samuel Cobb, *Of Poetry* [1707; rpt., Los Angeles: The Augustan Reprint Society, 1946], 189.) The *Dunciad* itself makes use of the image again, turning the Dunces, like Annius, into counterfeiters: "Whereas certain *Haberdashers of Points and Particles,* being instigated by the spirit of *Pride,* and assuming to themselves the name of *Critics* and *Restorers,* have taken upon them to adulterate the common and current sense of our *Glorious Ancestors,* Poets of this Realm, by clipping, coining, defacing the images, mixing their own base allay, or otherwise falsifying the same; which they publish, utter, and bend as genuine: . . ." ("By the Author, A Declaration," p. 237).

42. This meaning of "refund" is not listed in the OED, but see Pope's statement to Spence about how Bolingbroke "will sit down to the same subject and refund it (that was his word for new-cast it) all in his mind, after which it should have all the same weight and metal in it, only it would appear under some new form" (Joseph Spence, *Observations, Anecdotes, and Characters of Books and Men,* ed. James M. Osborn, 2 vols. [Oxford: Clarendon Press, 1966], 1:120).

43. *Faerie Queene,* 3.10.13, 3.3.22.

44. *Spectator* 316, in *Prose Works of Pope,* 1:32–34.

45. The details of this parody are worked out exhaustively by Jessie Rhodes Chambers, "The Episode of Annius and Mummius: *Dunciad* IV, 347–96," *Philological Quarterly* 43 (April 1964): 185–92. As Richard Nash has shown, there is even another layer of significance to this episode, an attack on Duncical translating and editing, and Pope's point here, too, is how the Dunces extirpate the spirit and leave the worthless body of the text. See Richard Nash, "Translation, Editing, and Poetic Invention in Pope's *Dunciad*," *Studies in Philology* 89 (Fall 1992): 470–84.

46. See Terry J. Castle, "Lab'ring Bards" (cf. ch. 6, n. 24).

47. Even on a literal level, monstrous birth was seen as a yielding, out of weakness or perversity, to the fancy. There is a persistent admonitory and moralistic strain in midwifery and medical texts which assumes that monstrous birth results from moral depravity or a willful refusal to restrain the imagination and that it can be prevented by the exercise of control on the part of the mother-to-be or by the firm, guiding hand of reason on the part of the husband. These strictures against the indulgence of the imagination should be seen as part of the broader tendency of these texts to deal with the "female" diseases by emphasizing standards of conduct. For this wider view, see Delores Peters, "The Pregnant Pamela: Characterization and Popular Medical Attitudes in the Eighteenth Century," *Eighteenth-Century Studies* 14 (Summer 1981): 432–51.

48. Thomas Rhymer, "The Tragedies of the Last Age Consider'd and Examin'd by the Practice of the Ancients and by the Common Sense of All Ages," in Spingarn, *Critical Essays,* 2:192.

49. Pope to Caryll, 14 August 1713, *Corr.,* 1:185–86.

50. The notion expressed in this passage that the son resembled his father through the agency of the mother's imagination was, in fact, the way in which exponents of the power of the mother's imagination typically explained paternal resemblance: the mother, because her imagination dwelt on the features of the father, impressed his features on her children.

Pope's use of images, metaphors, and symbols of birth and creation is so extensive and the implications he draws from them so manifold, no single discussion can hope to do them justice. For a very suggestive survey, see Philip Brockbank, "The Book of Genesis and the Genesis of Books: The Creation of Pope's *Dunciad,*" in his *The Creativity of Perception: Essays in the Genesis of Literature and Art* (Oxford: Basil Blackwell, 1991), 85–104.

CHAPTER SEVEN
What the Body Says

1. Plato, *The Symposium,* trans. W. Hamilton (Harmondsworth: Penguin Books, 1951), 86–91; Sir John Denham, "On Mr. Abraham Cowley his Death and Burial amongst the Ancient Poets," in *The Poetical Works of Sir John Denham,* ed. Theodore Howard Banks, Jr. (New Haven: Yale University Press, 1928), 152. In this chapter, whenever it is possible to do so without confusion, I have put references to Pope's poetry in parentheses in the text, identifying them by title and line number or, if the context makes the title obvious, by line number alone.

2. Matthew Green, *The Spleen,* in *The Spleen and Other Poems by Matthew Green,* ed. Richard King Wood (Kensington: The Cayme Press, 1925), 21; Ben Jonson, "To the Memory of My Beloved, the Author, Mr. William Shakespeare, And What He Hath Left Us," in *Ben Jonson,* ed. Ian Donaldson (Oxford: Oxford University Press, 1985), 455.

3. Marie Hélène Huet, in *Monstrous Imagination* (cf. ch. 2, n. 27), demonstrates how

the fear of the erasure of the name, title, lineage, and identity stood behind many of the medical discussions of the power of the mother's imagination and how this fear infiltrated some important nineteenth-century literature.

4. Pope to Swift, 15 October 1725, *Corr.*, 2:332; Swift to Pope, 26 November 1725, *Corr.*, 2:342–43.

5. Pope to Swift, 14 December 1725, *Corr.*, 2:349–50.

6. Even a week later Pope seems to have held fast to his decision to give up the poem, for he uses again the metaphor he used in his reply to Swift when he tells Caryll that he has decided not to respond to "the railing papers about the *Odyssey*," that by simply publishing his own good work, he will destroy the Dunces: "If I take any notice of such fellows, it must be a wretched work of supererogation. If [the translation of *The Odyssey*] has merit . . . it will extinguish all such sh—— scandal, as the sun puts an end to stinks, by *shining out*" (Pope to Caryll, 25 December 1725, *Corr.*, 2:352).

7. Pope would have felt particularly vulnerable about these contradictions because he had portrayed himself as a man who was above responding to the dull and who had the good sense to avoid petty literary squabbles: "'Tis best sometimes your Censure to restrain, / And *charitably* let the Dull be *vain*" (*Essay on Criticism*, 596–97). In the "Preface" to the 1717 *Works*, he had argued that dull writers should not be made "object[s] of ridicule" but treated with "humanity," and he went on to assert, "I was never so concern'd about my works as to vindicate them in print, believing if any thing was good it would defend itself. . . . I insulted no adversary with ill language, or when I could not attack a Rival's works, encourag'd reports against his Morals" (*Prose Works of Pope*, 1:290, 295–96). Pope's critics were quite eager to point out these contradictions after he published the *Dunciad*. See J. V. Guerinot, *Pamphlet Attacks on Alexander Pope, 1711–1744* (New York: New York University Press, 1969).

8. Pope to Swift, 23 March 1727/28, *Corr.*, 2:480–81; Pope to Swift, 12 October 1728, *Corr.*, 2:522; Pope to Hill, 14 March 1730/31, *Corr.*, 3:182.

9. Pope to the Earl of Burlington, 2 November 1729, *Corr.*, 3.67. Pope's "Resentments" were strong, and there is a substratum of real cruelty in the *Dunciad* that he might well be concerned about exposing: "I won't publish the fourth *Dunciad* as 'tis new-set till Michaelmas, that we may have time to play Cibber all the while. . . . He will be stuck, like the man in the almanac, not deep, but all over. He won't know which way to turn himself to. Exhausted at the first stroke, and reduced to passion and calling names, so that he won't be able to write more, and won't be able to bear living without writing" (Pope to Lord Marchmont, 21–25 February 1743, in Spence, *Observations*, 1:148–49 [cf. ch. 6, n. 42]).

10. Pope to Dr. Sheridan, 12 October 1728, *Corr.*, 2:523. See also Pope to Caryll, 8 April 1729, *Corr.*, 3:31; and Pope to Swift, 12 [October] 1728, *Corr.*, 2:522.

11. Pope to Swift, 6 January 1733/4, *Corr.*, 3:401–402; Pope to Caryll, 30 May 1729, *Corr.*, 3:36.

12. Pope to the Earl of Burlington, [1728/9], *Corr.*, 3:4.

13. Pope to Teresa and Martha Blount, [September 1717], *Corr.*, 1:430; Pope to Swift, 16 February 1732/3, *Corr.*, 3:347. Pope's language is conventional. Sprat said of Cowley, "I know well that he has given the world the best image of the own mind in those immortal Monuments of his Wit" (Thomas Sprat, *An Account of the Life and Writings of Mr. Abraham Cowley*, in Spingarn, *Critical Essays*, 2:120 [cf. ch. 3, n. 40]).

14. "On Dedications," *Guardian* 4, in *Prose Works of Pope*, 1:77; Pope to Swift, 20 April 1733, *Corr.*, 3:366.

15. Pope to Teresa and Martha Blount, 13 September 1717, *Corr.,* 1:428; Pope to Fortescue, 27 March [1739], *Corr.,* 4:169; Pope to Caryll, 5 December 1712, *Corr.,* 1:160–61.

Although Pope often spoke of poetry's promise of a *"second* life" (*Essay on Criticism,* 480), he also expressed the anxiety that his identity, like the Dunces', might be obliterated by his own works. "In this office of collecting my pieces," he said in the "Preface" to the 1717 *Works,* "I am altogether uncertain, whether to look upon my self as a man building a monument, or burying the dead." He admitted that being published felt like "being executed in the face of the World" and that his collecting his works was like performing a "solemn funeral of my Remains" (*Prose Works of Pope,* 1:295; Pope to Cromwell, 1 November 1708, *Corr.,* 1:51).

16. Pope to Mallet, 1 November [1729], *Corr.,* 3:66. Cf. the same mixture of humor and discomfort in a slightly earlier comment: "I have the punishment of the Dunciad & all my other sins, in my Head this day, the offending part suffers, but pray believe my Heart is free" (Pope to the Earl of Oxford, [13 June 1728], *Corr.,* 2:498.

17. Pope to Cromwell, 11 July 1709, *Corr.,* 1:67; Pope to Caryll, 25 January 1710/1, *Corr.,* 1:114; Pope to Cromwell, 24 June 1710, *Corr.,* 1:89; Pope and Bolingbroke to Swift [9 April 1730], *Corr.,* 3:101.

18. *The Blatant-Beast* (1740; rpt., Los Angeles: Augustan Reprint Society, 1965), [3]; [John Dennis], *A True Character of Mr. Pope, and His Writings* (1716; rpt., New York: Garland Publishing, 1975), 10; Lady Mary Wortley Montagu and John Lord Hervey, *Verses Address'd to the Imitator of the First Satire of the Second Book of Horace,* in Lady Mary Wortley Montagu, *Essays and Poems and "Simplicity, A Comedy,"* ed. Robert Halsband and Isobel Grundy (Oxford: Clarendon Press, 1977), 268.

19. [John Lord Hervey and Colley Cibber], *The Difference Between Verbal and Practical Virtue* (1742; rpt., Los Angeles: Augustan Reprint Society, 1967), 5–6.

20. [Edward Ward], *Apollo's Maggot in his Cups* (1729; rpt., New York: Garland Publishing, 1975), 48. In the play *Mr. Taste, The Poetical Fop,* Lady Airy, after hearing a character sketch of Alexander Taste, a deformed poet whose main talent is personal abuse, says, "This verifes the common saying, *as crooked in Mind as in Body:* and I have observed several Instances of it within my own knowledge; for which reason I never could endure to have a deformed Person in my House" (*Mr. Taste, The Poetical Fop* [1732; rpt., New York: Garland Publishing, 1975], 64). Similarly, in fictional dialogue between Pope and Charles Coffey, the Irish dramatist whose physical deformities were much like the poet's, Coffey says to Pope, "Nature has form'd us very much alike to outward Appearance; and it is not unreasonable to suppose our Virtues, Vices, Passions much alike" ("A Dialogue Between Mr. P—e and Mr. C—fe, Poets," in *The History of Martin* [1742; rpt., New York: Garland Publishing, 1975], 13).

21. William Shakespeare, *King Richard III,* ed. Antony Hammond (London: Methuen, 1981), 1.2.57. Johnson commented, "Shakespeare very diligently inculcates, that the wickedness of Richard proceeded from his deformity" ("Notes to *Richard III,"* in *Works of Samuel Johnson,* 8:613 [cf. ch. 6, n. 12]).

Bacon's "character" had a vigorous life in the eighteenth century. William Hay, who set out to explode the damaging stereotype of the deformed in *Deformity: An Essay* (London, 1754), spent nearly one half of his lengthy essay in a point-for-point refutation of Bacon. He also debunked the notion that Thersites and Shakespeare's Richard III accurately represented the typical personality structure of the deformed.

22. "Of Deformity," in *Works of Bacon*, 4:480–81; William Shakespeare, *The Third Part of King Henry VI*, ed. Andrew S. Cairncross (London: Methuen, 1964), 5.6.68.

23. "Notes to *Richard III*," in *Works of Samuel Johnson*, 8:613.

24. *Richard III*, 1.3.242, 246, 290–91. For other instances of these metaphors, see, for example, 1.2.151; 4.4.46–50, 81, 146; and 5.5.15.

25. The translation is Pope's: *Iliad*, 2.263–70. In his note on this passage, Pope argued that what we see in Thersites is not the character of a deformed person but "the Picture of a pernicious Creature of Wit."

26. *3 Henry VI*, 5.6.91; *Richard III*, 4.4.51; *3 Henry VI*, 3.2.165–71.

27. *Richard III*, 1.3.289–91.

28. *Richard III*, 1.1.37; 2.2.27; 1.1.32–33; 1.3.325–26, 336–38; *3 Henry VI*, 3.2.182–85.

29. *Richard III*, 1.2.78; *3 Henry VI*, 5.6.78–83, 2.2.136–38.

30. Dennis, *True Character of Pope*, 10; Montagu and Hervey, *Verses to the Imitator*, in Montagu, *Essays and Poems*, 269–70. "A vertuous Man has strongly implanted in him a Philanthropy or innate Humanity, which restrains him from reflecting too severely on the Frailties of his Fellow Creatures, as remembering, that they are all of them of one Species. But [Pope,] distinguished indeed, in a most remarkable Manner, by Nature, from the rest of Mankind; has no Tenderness or Regard for them, but looks upon himself as one of a quite different Race of Beings. . . . Whatsoever is the Definition [of Man], He still appears excluded from the Human Species, which may in some Measure account for, as well as excuse his universal ill Will to our Race" (*Pope Alexander's Supremacy and Infallibility Examin'd* [1729; rpt., New York: Garland Publishing, 1975], 17–18).

31. [Montagu and Hervey], *Verses to the Imitator*, in *Essays and Poems*, 268; [Leonard Welsted], *Of Dulness and Scandal* (London, 1732), as quoted in *Pope: The Critical Heritage*, ed. John Barnard (London: Routledge & Kegan Paul, 1973), 266; *Daily Journal*, 30 March 1733, as quoted in James A. Winn, *A Window in the Bosom: The Letters of Alexander Pope* (Hamden, Conn.: Archon Books, 1977), 31; Edmund Curll, *The Curliad* (1729; rpt., New York: Garland Publishing, 1975), 32–34.

32. *Durgen* (1729; rpt., New York: Garland Publishing, 1975), 54; *Pope Alexander's Supremacy*, 14; *Sawney and Colley, A Poetical Dialogue* (1742; rpt., Los Angeles: Augustan Reprint Society, 1960), 7; *Blatant-Beast*, 11; *An Essay on the Dunciad* (1728; rpt., New York: Garland Publishing, 1975), 7; *Characters of the Times* (1728; rpt., New York: Garland, 1975), 20; [Atex. Burnet], *Achilles Dissected* (1733; rpt., New York: Garland Publishing, 1975), 22; [James Ralph], *Sawney. An Heroic Poem* (1728; rpt., New York: Garland Publishing, 1975), iv; John Dennis, *Remarks Upon Several Passages in the Preliminaries to the Dunciad* (1729; rpt., New York: Garland Publishing, 1975), 3–4.

33. [Charles Gildon], *A New Rehearsal, or Bays the Younger* (1714; rpt., New York: Garland Publishing, 1975), 39; [Ralph], *Sawney*, 7; *Pope Alexander's Supremacy*, 16; [Welsted], *Of Dulness and Scandal*, as quoted in *Pope: Critical Heritage*, 267; [Giles Jacobs], *The Mirrour: or, Letters Satyrical, Panegyrical, Serious and Humorous, On the Present Times* (1733; rpt., New York: Garland Publishing, 1975), 77; Dennis, *Remarks upon the Dunciad*, sig. [A1ᵛ]; *A Compleat Collection of all the Verses, Essays, Letters and Advertisements, Which Have been occasioned by the Publication of Three Volumes of Miscellanies, by Pope and Company* (1728; rpt., New York: Garland Publishing, 1975), 50–51.

34. Dennis, *Remarks upon the Dunciad*, 46; *Pope Alexander's Supremacy*, 6; [Leonard Welsted and James Moore Smythe], *One Epistle to Mr. A. Pope* (1730; rpt., Los Angeles:

Augustan Reprint Society, 1965), 18; *Durgen,* 32; *Essay on the Dunciad,* 26; *Sawney and Colley,* 7; *Blatant-Beast,* 5; [John Breval], *The Confederates* (1717; rpt., New York: Garland Publishing, 1975), [1]–2; John Dennis, *Remarks Upon Mr. Pope's Translation of Homer* (1717; rpt., New York: Garland Publishing, 1975), 19; [Burnet], *Achilles Dissected,* 21; [Montagu and Hervey], *Verses to the Imitator,* in *Essays and Poems,* 267; Colley Cibber, *A Letter From Mr. Cibber to Mr. Pope* (1742; rpt., Los Angeles: Augustan Reprint Society, 1973), 61; John Dennis, *Remarks on Mr. Pope's Rape of the Lock* (1728; rpt., New York: Garland Publishing, 1975), x–xi; *Compleat Collection of Verses,* 51–52; Edmund Curll, *A Compleat Key to the Dunciad* (1728; rpt., New York: Garland Publishing, 1975), 20.

35. [Hervey and Cibber], *The Difference Between Verbal and Practical Virtue,* 6; Dennis, *True Character of Pope,* 10, 15; [Curll], *Compleat Key to the Dunciad,* [iii]-iv; Dennis, *True Character of Pope,* 6; *Codrus: or, The Dunciad Dissected* (1728; rpt., New York: Garland Publishing, 1975), 6.

36. John Dennis, *Reflections Critical and Satyrical, Upon a Late Rapsody, Call'd, An Essay Upon Criticism* (1711; rpt., New York: Garland Publishing, 1975), sig. A3^r; *Durgen,* sig. A2^r; *Achilles Dissected,* 28; Dennis, *Remarks on Rape of the Lock,* ix; Dennis, *Remarks Upon Pope's Homer,* 92; [Ralph], *Sawney,* 34; *Blatant-Beast,* 6; [Hervey and Cibber], *Difference Between Verbal and Practical Virtue,* 5; Dennis, *Remarks Upon Pope's Homer,* 92; *Blatant-Beast,* 9; *Sawney,* 36; [Welsted and Smythe], *One Epistle to Pope,* 13; [Welsted], *Of False Fame,* 20–21; "Verses Presented to the Countess of Warwick," in *The Progress of Dulness* (1728; rpt., New York: Garland, 1975), 31; *Durgen,* 41.

37. *Blatant-Beast,* 7; Dennis, *Reflections Critical and Satyrical,* 26; [Curll and Thomas], *Codrus,* 18; *An Epistle to the Little Satyrist* (London, 1733), as quoted in *Pope: Critical Heritage,* 276; "The Butterfly and Spider" in [J. H.], *Remarks on Squire Ayre's Memoirs of the Life and Writings of Mr. Pope* (1745; rpt., New York: Garland Publishing, 1975), 36.

An excellent index to what disturbed Pope most about the attacks on him is his *A Master Key to Popery,* where, in the persona of a dull and mean-spirited critic, he reiterates all those moral failings his enemies have charged him with. It is significant that by far what pained Pope most was the representation of him as having a "Bad heart" entirely governed by "Spite & Malice" (in a pamphlet of just a few pages, Pope "attacks" himself at least fourteen times for his maliciousness!). The rest of the persona's attack follows exactly the contours I have sketched for the "character" of a monster: driven by an irrational and ungovernable envy, Pope strikes out wantonly, attacking everyone who is above him (in social status and merit) and betraying his friends out of jealousy; his methods are the underhand ones of lies and slander. See *Prose Works of Pope,* 2:410–21.

38. Pope to Caryll, 6 December 1730, *Corr.,* 3:155.

39. Pope to Swift, 19 December 1734, *Corr.,* 3:445.

40. Hay, *Deformity,* 4. Hay was born in 1695 and died in 1755. He sat in the House of Commons for Seaford, a Whig and, generally, a supporter of Walpole. He dabbled in poetry and translation. The entry in the *DNB* should be supplemented by the preface to his *Works,* published in 1794.

41. Hay, *Deformity,* 2–3.

42. Ibid., 41–46.

43. Pope to Hill, 9 June 1738, *Corr.,* 4:102; "Advertisement" to *Epistle to Dr. Arbuthnot;* Pope to Hugh Bethel, 17 June 1728, *Corr.,* 2:501; Pope to Arbuthnot, 3 September [1734], *Corr.,* 3:431.

"Though it would be wrong to attribute Pope's interest in imitating Horace to any single cause, Horace's satires and epistles supply a powerful opportunity for favorable self-presentations that Pope seized and magnified, and it may well be that one reason he did so was to satisfy a psychic as well as poetic need to establish against all that his enemies had said of him, or against the responses that he knew others might feel to his person (and that possibly he had internalized), an amiable identity" (Maynard Mack, "'The Least Thing Like a Man in England': Some Effects of Pope's Physical Disability on His Life and Literary Career," in his *Collected in Himself*, 372–92 [cf. ch. 6, n. 9]). In this essay and throughout his biography, *Alexander Pope: A Life* (New Haven: Yale University Press, 1985), Mack takes quite a different tack in analyzing the effects of Pope's deformity on his career, one that yields extraordinary insights. The fact that our analyses overlap very little testifies to how central Pope's deformity was in his life and how manifold its effects were.

44. Increasingly, critics have recognized that one of the major impulses behind the poems of the 1730s was autobiographical and that the poems were, in Frederick Keener's phrase, "exercises in self-representation" (*An Essay on Pope* [New York: Columbia University Press, 1974], 141). No one, of course, views these poems as naively self-expressive, and it is part of my purpose in the remainder of this chapter to explore in what ways these poems are "self-representational" and what Pope would understand to be the "self" he was representing. My starting point is the succinct formulation of Dustin H. Griffin (*Alexander Pope: The Poet in the Poems* [Princeton: Princeton University Press, 1978], 12): "Self-revelation in his poems and letters is almost always a carefully calculated performance, acted out in a public arena and designed to persuade an audience. . . . Pope, though always personal, is never private. He writes apology: 'this proves my integrity'."

45. *Epistle to Dr. Arbuthnot*, 353, "Advertisement."

46. Mack, *Last and Greatest Art*, 435–37 (cf. ch. 6, n. 37). I am following the order of the manuscript as reconstructed by John Butt in his "Pope's Poetical Manuscripts," in *Essential Articles*, 545–65 (cf. ch. 6, n. 21).

47. Mack, "'The Last and Greatest Art': Pope's Poetical Manuscripts," in *Collected in Himself*, 332–33; and Marjorie Hope Nicolson and G. S. Rousseau, *"This Long Disease, My Life": Alexander Pope and the Sciences* (Princeton: Princeton University Press, 1968), 12–13.

48. See, too, the next two couplets, where Pope states, "My Mother judgd no wedded Wife a *Whore*," and then immediately says, "And cou'dst thou think my Father was unknown / Meerly because thou dost not knowe thy own?"

49. For Pope's relationship with Walpole in the early 1730s, see Maynard Mack, *Pope: A Life*, 501–504.

50. *Satire II.i.*, 69, 101, 113. While it is literally true that Pope, like his father, "ne'er knew Law Suit," in fact Gilliver acted as his agent in the 1729 suit against the pirates of the *Dunciad Variorum*: see David Foxon, *Pope and the Early Eighteenth-Century Book Trade*, rev. and ed. James McLaverty (Oxford: Clarendon Press, 1991), 110–14, 242.

51. Pope to Dr. Arbuthnot, 25 August 1734, *Corr.*, 3:428.

52. For a different analysis of many of these same themes in the poem, see Ripley Hotch, "The Dilemma of an Obedient Son: Pope's *Epistle to Dr. Arbuthnot*," in *Pope: Recent Essays by Several Hands*, ed. Maynard Mack and James A. Winn (Hamden, Conn.: Archon Books, 1980), 428–43.

53. See, for example, Ulisses Aldrovandus, *Monstrorum Historia* (Bologna, 1642), 393; and Paré, *On Monsters*, 4 (cf. ch. 1, n. 11).

54. *Iliad,* 1.155n, 16.72, 22.339–40, 1.155n, 1.213n, 9.406n, 1.298n, 18.379n, 22.496n, 16.122n.

55. For two very fine explorations of how Pope uses his enemies in *Arbuthnot* to articulate his own identity, see J. Paul Hunter, "Satiric Apology as Satiric Instance: Pope's *Arbuthnot,*" in *Pope: Recent Essays,* 444–68; and Howard D. Weinbrot, *Alexander Pope and the Traditions of Formal Verse Satire* (Princeton: Princeton University Press, 1982), 240–75.

56. Pope describes Twickenham as "my little kingdom" in a letter to Atterbury, 19 March 1722, *Corr.,* 2:109.

57. As Weinbrot has pointed out in reference to this line, Johnson defines "Itch" as "A Cutaneous disease extremely contagious, which overspreads the body with small pustules filled with a thin serum, and raised, as microscopes have discovered, by a small animal. It is cured by sulphur" (*Pope and the Tradition of Satire,* 253).

58. I have merely sketched in how Pope dramatizes the fact that it is the disease of his society, not the disease of his own body, that is causing him to write satire. The pattern has been fully analyzed by Elias F. Mengel, Jr., "Patterns of Imagery in Pope's *Arbuthnot,*" in *Essential Articles,* 566–76.

59. *Epilogue to the Satires: Dialogue II,* 246–47. For a similar view, see Rebecca Ferguson, *The Unbalanced Mind: Pope and the Rule of Passion* (Philadelphia: University of Pennsylvania Press, 1986), 150–51.

60. On the centrality of friendship in *Arbuthnot,* see Lawrence Lee Davidow, "Pope's Verse Epistles: Friendship and the Private Sphere of Life," *Huntington Library Quarterly* 40 (February 1977): 151–70.

61. *Iliad,* 16.8n, 18.99n.

62. *Satire II.i.,* 123–24; *Epistle to Dr. Arbuthnot,* 283–84; *Satire II.i.,* 121, 117; *Epilogue to the Satires: Dialogue II,* 197–204. The image of the satirist Pope had in mind in his self-portraits was that most famously articulated by Steele when he proposed "that Good-Nature [is] an essential Quality in a Satyrist" (*Tatler* 242, in *The Tatler,* 3:241–42): "The ordinary Subjects for Satyr are such as incite the greatest Indignation in the best Tempers, and consequently Men of such a Make are the best qualified for speaking of the Offences in Humane Life. These Men can behold Vice and Folly when they injure Persons to whom they are wholly unacquainted, with the same Severity as others resent the Ills they do themselves. A good-natured Man cannot see an over-bearing Fellow put a bashful Man of Merit out of Contenance, or outstrip him in the Pursuit of any Advantage; but he is on Fire to succour the Oppressed, to produce the Merit of the one, and confront the Impudence of the other." Cf. Pope's own statement: "I've often thought, Good nature, properly felt, would make a rigorous Judge, & give a sort of Joy in passing the Sentence, both as it is *Justice,* and as it is *Example*" (Pope to Fortescue, 16 August 1736, *Corr.,* 4:27).

63. Owen Ruffhead, *The Life of Alexander Pope, Esq.,* 2 vols. (1769; rpt., New York: Garland Publishing, 1974), 2:37; W. H. Dilworth, *The Life of Alexander Pope, Esq.* (1759; rpt., New York: Garland Publishing, 1974), 134.

64. Colley Cibber, *A Letter from Mr. Cibber to Mr. Pope,* 39; Joseph Warton, *An Essay on the Genius and Writings of Pope,* 2 vols. (London, 1806), 2:401.

65. For an analysis of other ways in which Pope habitually used his physical monstrosity to silence his attackers and portray himself as a satiric hero, see Helen Deutsch, "The 'Truest Copies' and the 'Mean Original': Pope, Deformity, and the Poetics of Self-Exposure," *Eighteenth-Century Studies* 27 (Fall 1993): 1–26; and David B. Morris,

Alexander Pope: The Genius of Sense (Cambridge: Harvard University Press, 1984), 259–69.

66. Even a reader so sympathetic to Pope as Maynard Mack can be critical of the poet's egregious self-praise: "He has a way at times—and the habit grew upon him as he aged—of pretending to the fashionable virtues of magnanimity and serene self-possession, so immoderately, so ludicrously, that one could be forgiven for wondering whether his intent is not to parody the conventional values of his day by exaggerating them to the point of farce. Alas, it is not so: he appears to be deadly serious. . . . How can so intelligent a man have known himself so little? Alternatively, how can so astute an observer of others have imagined that these sentiments would deceive?" ("'These Shadows of Me': Pope's Letters," in *Collected in Himself,* 367–68).

I simply want to suggest that the double bind created by the stereotype may be an important source of many of those instances of self-fashioning which we find so repugnant.

67. Pope to Caryll, 19 November 1712, *Corr.,* 1:155; Pope to Hugh Bethel, 2 November 1736, *Corr.,* 4:39; "Preface" to the *Letters* (1737), *Corr.,* 1:xxxvii; Pope to Hugh Bethel, undated fragment, *Corr.,* 3:519; Pope to Lady Mary Wortley Montagu, 18 August [1716], *Corr.,* 1:352–53.

The notion that one spontaneously exposed one's heart in a letter was entirely conventional during Pope's life, which is what made the publication of his letters such an attractive prospect for him, for the conventions of the genre would help him overcome suspicions of manipulation and hypocrisy. On the conventions of correspondence and the ways Pope worked within them, see Wendy L. Jones, *Talking on Paper: Alexander Pope's Letters* (Victoria, B.C.: English Literary Studies, University of Victoria, 1990), 7–24; Rosemary Cowler, "Shadow and Substance: A Discussion of Pope's Correspondence," in *The Familiar Letter in the Eighteenth Century,* ed. Howard Anderson, Philip B. Daghlian, and Irvin Ehrenpreis (Lawrence: University of Kansas Press, 1966), 34–48; and especially Winn, *Window in the Bosom* (cf. ch. 7, n. 31). The degree to which Pope's publication of his letters was a specific response to the attacks on him is very suggestively explored by Jones, *Talking on Paper,* 36–52.

68. *The Life of Alexander Pope, Esq.: With Remarks on His Works* (1744; rpt. New York: Garland Publishing, 1974), 69; Thomas Gray to Horace Walpole, 3 February 1746, as quoted in *Pope: Critical Heritage,* 358; Samuel Johnson, "Life of Pope," in *Works of the English Poets,* 12:83; Catherine Talbot to Elizabeth Carter, 16 August 1751, as quoted in *Pope: Critical Heritage,* 366.

69. Pope to Lady Mary Wortley Montagu, 18 August [1716], *Corr.,* 1:353.

70. Hay, *Deformity,* 74–75.

71. "Preface" to *The Works of William Hay,* 2 vols. (London, 1794), 1:xvii-xviii.

Hay's use of the anatomy is very similar to the way Thomas W. Laqueur has argued the autopsy was used as a "humanitarian narrative" in the eighteenth and nineteenth centuries, which "relies on the personal body, not only as the locus of pain but also as the common bond between those who suffer and those who would help" and which describes "the pains and deaths of ordinary people in such a way as to make apparent the causal chains that might connect the actions of its readers with the suffering of its subjects" ("Bodies, Details, and the Humanitarian Narrative," in *The New Cultural History,* ed. Lynn Hunt [Berkeley: University of California Press, 1989], 176–204).

72. See Thomas Maresca, *Pope's Horatian Poems* (Columbus: Ohio University Press, 1966), 176. This and the following discussions of *Epistle I.i.* have aided me enormously

in my understanding of the poem: Jacob Fuchs, *Reading Pope's Imitations of Horace* (Lewisburg: Bucknell University Press, 1989), 128–42; Brean S. Hammond, *Pope and Bolingbroke: A Study of Friendship and Influence* (Columbia: University of Missouri Press, 1984); Fredric V. Bogel, *Acts of Knowledge: Pope's Later Poems* (Lewisburg: Bucknell University Press, 1981), 141–60; and Frank Stack, *Pope and Horace: Studies in Imitation* (Cambridge: Cambridge University Press, 1985), 245–74.

73. Pope to Caryll, 4 February [1717/18], *Corr.*, 1:464.

74. The contradiction between his longing for retirement to cultivate his soul, on the one hand, and his sense of his duty to be actively engaged in his society, on the other, is the dramatic tension at the heart of almost all of the poems he wrote in the 1730s: see Maynard Mack, *The Garden and the City: Retirement and Politics in the Later Poetry of Pope, 1731–1743* (Toronto: University of Toronto Press, 1969); and Griffin, *Pope: Poet in the Poems*, 55–60.

75. "I am made all things to all men, that I might by all means save some" (I Corinthians 9:22).

76. I do not wish to analyze the politics of this section in any detail; it is foreign to my purpose and it has been done more than adequately by others. See, in addition to the discussions already cited, Barbara Lauren, "Pope's *Epistle to Bolingbroke:* Satire from the Vantage of Retirement," *Studies in English Literature* 15 (Summer 1975): 419–30.

77. *To Cobham*, 41, 45; *Essay on Man*, 2.13; *To Cobham*, 30. "All our Passions are Inconsistencies, & our very Reason is no better. But we are what we were Made to be" (Pope to Fotescue, 7 June 1733, *Corr.*, 3:374).

78. "Useful as it is to distinguish the voices Pope employs, the meat of his art is in the transitions between them" (Keener, *Essay on Pope*, 84). What I sense as the dialectic of Pope's formulation of his identity has been intelligently explored by two students of Pope. S. L. Goldberg has argued that Pope was driven by, on the one hand, an "impulse to 'fix' his true character," and, on the other, an impulse to admit the mobility and contradictions of the self; since his self was comprised of both impulses, "the full integrity of his own life was something Pope could realize only 'dramatically'" ("Integrity and Life in Pope's Poetry," in *Studies in the Eighteenth Century*, ed. R. F. Brissenden and J. C. Eade [Toronto: University of Toronto Press, 1976], 185–207). Similarly, Bogel argues that the poems of the 1730s are "not statements but dramatizations," whose "action is the poet's quest for genuine knowledge and a genuine self," and whose real subjects, therefore, are "the development . . . of a point of view . . . and the labor of achieving it." Bogel concludes that Pope arrives at "a moral rather than a metaphysical 'answer' to the problem [of identity], but it permits Pope to include in his conception of man the possibility of a resignation of the human, and to place the effort to achieve a moral identity and a stable self at the center of that conception" (*Acts of Knowledge*, 36, 21–22, 26).

79. Cheselden's remark is in Spence, *Observations*, 1:264. I have conflated two sources of Pope's hallucination: Warburton's, as recorded in Spence, *Observations*, 1:265 (cf. ch. 6, n. 42); and Ruffhead, *Life of Pope*, 2:171.

For the fate of the theory of the power of the mother's imagination and its effect on the literature of the nineteenth century, see Huet, *Monstrous Imagination* (cf. ch. 2, n. 27).

INDEX

In the following entries, *MT* stands for *Mary Toft*.